Grammatical and Syntactical Approaches in Architecture:

Emerging Research and Opportunities

Ju Hyun Lee
University of New South Wales, Australia

Michael J. Ostwald
University of New South Wales, Australia

A volume in the Advances in
Systems Analysis, Software
Engineering, and High Performance
Computing (ASASEHPC) Book Series

Published in the United States of America by
 IGI Global
 Engineering Science Reference (an imprint of IGI Global)
 701 E. Chocolate Avenue
 Hershey PA, USA 17033
 Tel: 717-533-8845
 Fax: 717-533-8661
 E-mail: cust@igi-global.com
 Web site: http://www.igi-global.com

Library of Congress Cataloging-in-Publication Data

Names: Lee, Ju Hyun, 1973- author. | Ostwald, Michael J., author.
Title: Grammatical and syntactical approaches in architecture : emerging
 research and opportunities / by Ju Hyun Lee and Michael J. Ostwald.
Description: Hershey, PA : Engineering Science Reference, 2020. | Includes
 bibliographical references. | Summary: "This book illustrates
 syntactically derived and grammatically interpolated approaches for
 architectural configuration, analysis, and design generation" Provided
 by publisher.
Identifiers: LCCN 2019032868 (print) | LCCN 2019032869 (ebook) | ISBN
 9781799816980 (h/c) | ISBN 9781799816997 (s/c) | ISBN 9781799817000
 (eISBN)
Subjects: LCSH: Architecture--Philosophy. | Architecture--Methodology.
Classification: LCC NA2500 .L438 2020 (print) | LCC NA2500 (ebook) | DDC
 720.1--dc23
LC record available at https://lccn.loc.gov/2019032868
LC ebook record available at https://lccn.loc.gov/2019032869

This book is published in the IGI Global book series Advances in Systems Analysis, Software
Engineering, and High Performance Computing (ASASEHPC) (ISSN: 2327-3453; eISSN: 2327-
3461)

British Cataloguing in Publication Data
A Cataloguing in Publication record for this book is available from the British Library.

For electronic access to this publication, please contact: eresources@igi-global.com.

Advances in Systems Analysis, Software Engineering, and High Performance Computing (ASASEHPC) Book Series

ISSN:2327-3453
EISSN:2327-3461

Editor-in-Chief: Vijayan Sugumaran, Oakland University, USA

MISSION

The theory and practice of computing applications and distributed systems has emerged as one of the key areas of research driving innovations in business, engineering, and science. The fields of software engineering, systems analysis, and high performance computing offer a wide range of applications and solutions in solving computational problems for any modern organization.

The **Advances in Systems Analysis, Software Engineering, and High Performance Computing (ASASEHPC) Book Series** brings together research in the areas of distributed computing, systems and software engineering, high performance computing, and service science. This collection of publications is useful for academics, researchers, and practitioners seeking the latest practices and knowledge in this field.

COVERAGE

- Computer System Analysis
- Parallel Architectures
- Metadata and Semantic Web
- Engineering Environments
- Software Engineering
- Virtual Data Systems
- Computer Graphics
- Enterprise Information Systems
- Human-Computer Interaction
- Computer Networking

IGI Global is currently accepting manuscripts for publication within this series. To submit a proposal for a volume in this series, please contact our Acquisition Editors at Acquisitions@igi-global.com or visit: http://www.igi-global.com/publish/.

Titles in this Series

For a list of additional titles in this series, please visit:
https://www.igi-global.com/book-series/advances-systems-analysis-software-engineering/73689

For an entire list of titles in this series, please visit:
https://www.igi-global.com/book-series/advances-systems-analysis-software-engineering/73689

701 East Chocolate Avenue, Hershey, PA 17033, USA
Tel: 717-533-8845 x100 • Fax: 717-533-8661
E-Mail: cust@igi-global.com • www.igi-global.com

Table of Contents

Chapter 8

Chapter 9

Foreword

Architecture is amongst the oldest professions and is concerned with the creation of interior and exterior spaces in buildings, spaces that humans respond to. Architecture has largely been both practised and taught on the basis of informal knowledge that is founded more on experience than on formal theory. Generation, one of the most basic activities, has been viewed as an idiosyncratic activity without an articulated formalism to support it. Two millennia ago, Vitruvius, in his *Ten Books of Architecture,* provided some design guidance in the form of rules, but these are case specific and cannot be generalised. The enormous increase in formal representations of concepts in mathematics and logic in the nineteenth and early twentieth centuries did not have a significant effect on architectural theory in the way it did on physics. However, the activities of mathematicians and scientists in World War II demonstrated that research not only produced knowledge but that it could be brought to bear on problems, and that mathematics and science were applicable to real-world problems. This gave mathematics and science a position in the intellectual world they had not previously enjoyed. The launch by the Soviet Union of the *Sputnik* satellite in the mid-1950s came as a surprise to western countries and spurred them to dramatically increase civilian research funding. The success of applying research in World War II and the setting up of government research agencies gave research a higher value and status, particularly in universities and also in fields that had previously not valued research highly. At the same time the expectation was that fields other than science advanced through research.

Mathematics and logic provide representations for concepts and science is a paradigm for a way of finding and testing ideas empirically. It took the advent of the computer to give agency to testing and exploring instantiations of ideas represented in mathematics and logic. Computation is carried out through algorithms but algorithms do not need to have a formal mathematical or logical foundation. They could be based on any sequence of instructions that matches a view of the activity including heuristics. This coupled with computation being about symbols not mathematics or logic opened computing to new areas. One of these new areas was design, and by the mid-1960s a number of architecture schools in the US, UK and Australia had introduced computing into their architecture curriculum.

The confluence of heuristics and symbolic computation laid the foundation for a new kind of architectural research whose focus included synthesis or generation. This book presents advances into two of the areas of research that potentially have profound implications for architecture: Shape Grammars and Space Syntax. Shape Grammars have been used to model and generate architectural floor plans and much more. Space syntax has been used to model and analyze urban spatial configurations. The authors of this book have integrated Shape Grammars and Space Syntax and applied the resulting approach to the analysis and generation of architectural plans. This combined approach is both novel and useful and singles this volume out from other treatments of these two approaches.

The increasing digitalization of aspects of our lives has contributed to reducing the friction in the processes that engage us and overflows into architecture. The formalization of representations of architecture contributes to this digitalization and offers the potential for a similar reduction in friction in the analysis and generation of architectural plans. The synthesis of Shape Grammars with Space Syntax lays the foundation for an increased understanding of architecture by providing a new formalization to analyze. At the same time this new combined approach has the capacity to generate plans and offers the basis of new digital tools for architects.

John S. Gero
University of North Carolina at Charlotte, USA & Krasnow Institute for
Advanced Study, USA

Preface

INTRODUCTION

Language is both essential for the development and transmission of knowledge, and our capacity to understand the past, analyse the present and shape the future (Chomsky, 2005). Bruni Zevi argues that "without a language, we cannot speak" and without a detailed understanding of language, we may "forget how to speak" at all, being left to "utter inarticulate meaningless sounds that carry no message" (Zevi, 1987, p. 3). John Summerson (1964) reiterates the importance of understanding the origins of a language, claiming that a person needs to develop a knowledge of its grammar and syntax before being able to communicate effectively. Charles Jencks (1977) warns that language is constantly evolving, developing new phrases, uses and traditions, and these need to be carefully interpreted to understand their meanings. In all three cases – Zevi, Summerson and Jencks – the languages they are talking about are not those of words and sounds, but of form and space. Summerson's (1964) *The Classical Language of Architecture*, Jencks's (1977) *Language of Post-Modern Architecture* and Zevi's (1987) *The Modern Language of Architecture* are all about the formal and spatial properties of buildings and the way these are shaped by their contexts and reflect the values of their creators.

The idea that architecture is a type of language is a common one, and while it has its limitations, it remains an important way of thinking about the built environment. Most often, sets of buildings that look similar or have similar functions or structures are described as constituting an architectural language. For example, consider the famous seventeenth century Canal Houses of Amsterdam, with their narrow brick facades, raised entries and steep gabled roofs, each surmounted by a pulley. Individually these houses may have different features but collectively they possess a distinct visual character and corresponding interior spatial structure. Furthermore, the expression of the architecture is not accidental. The narrow facades reflect high land values, the raised entries are a response to flooding, and the pulleys are the only way to move furniture between floors. As such, the Canal House is an example of an architectural language that has a distinct visual expression founded on recurring elements that serve functional or practical needs. This first type of architectural language could be thought of as a regional *dialect*.

Sets of works by individual architects are also often referred to as being examples of a distinct architectural language. For example, architect Le Corbusier created a new language of architecture in his series of white, geometric houses. Designed in the early twentieth century for sites in France and Germany, these early Modernist works were often raised above the ground on columns, they had steel balustrades, horizontal expanses of glass and roof gardens. Several of these properties were a direct result of new materials and construction techniques that allowed architects to create large openings and use non-load bearing walls. Furthermore, the interior planning of these designs reflects changing social structures that partially rejected the hierarchical building plans developed in the previous century. In its place, Le Corbusier's planning was more open and exposed, allowing for a newfound social freedom to be reflected in the way space was inhabited and used. Ultimately, Le Corbusier's distinctive architectural language sought to demonstrate the new possibilities of the twentieth century. This second type of architectural language is an example of an *idiolect*, or personal communication style.

In architectural practice, the concept of an architectural language has also been used to understand building types. For example, the office building has a set of well defined, recurring elements including core or service spaces, lobbies or foyers, meeting rooms and enclosed or open offices. While individual office buildings may differ in appearance, or in their responses to particular site conditions or business models, they are part of a distinct architectural language. Similar typological languages have been developed by architects and scholars for libraries, prisons, hotels, hospitals and airports. For practicing architects, understanding these typological languages is an important precursor to the design of any new instances of these building types. Indeed, architects have become reliant on these "common" or "trade" languages of practice as their work becomes increasingly international in its outlook. This third language is an example of architectural *lingua franca*, a language which is adopted by multiple groups as a common reference point.

All of these types of architectural languages are crucial for architects and scholars to support an improved understanding of the past, respond sensitively to the needs of the present, and assist with planning future places and spaces.

Developing methods to support the measurement, analysis and generation of architectural linguistic properties is therefore a significant and timely topic. In response, the present book is concerned with two of the most important linguistic properties of architecture; the *grammar* of architectural form and the *syntax* of architectural space.

CONTEXT

Fisher (2016, np) observes that the connections between architecture and language are largely reliant on the view that architecture exists as a "corpus of design ideas" which are constructed in accordance with "a set of rules" (syntax or grammar) that can convey "meaning (semantics)" and are "subject to contextual sensitivity and internal or relational constraints on deployment and realization (pragmatics)." Significantly, each of these aspects of the linguistic analogy – the *rules*, *relations* and *constraints* – are able to be defined, counted or measured. As such, regardless of whether the design language in question is a regional *dialect*, a personal *idiolect* or a typological *lingua franca*, it is possible to use computational methods to analyse the rules, structures and controls that govern it. This is an important realisation, because over the last four decades, architectural and design practices have become increasingly reliant on computational tools. Where once architecture was viewed as an art form, it is now a discipline that uses and generates "big data", examines multi-factor variables and resolves sub-optimal conditions. Today a design for a major building is never developed without first modelling its environmental performance, structural efficiency or compliance standards. Despite such developments, the concept of an architectural language remains a complex one, and architectural educators and practitioners tend to resort to aesthetic and phenomenological explanations for the importance of architectural form and space. There are, however, several computational methods available for measuring form and space in an architectural language, two of which are the subject of the present book.

A "Shape Grammar" is a computational approach that is used to identify and understand the rules required to produce the formal properties of a design, or model the design process used by an architect. "Space Syntax" is another computational approach which uses mathematics to measure the social, cognitive or experiential properties of a building or city plan. In essence, the former is concerned with the rules which shape a building's visual expression and the latter with the topological relationships which characterise its spatial properties. These two computational methods have been extensively developed and tested over the last forty years, and they remain the subject of a growing number of applications and projects today. Despite this, they are largely unknown in architectural practice and only a relatively small group of academics have a genuine understanding of them. As such, the first half of this book provides a timely introduction and explanation of these two important approaches for investigating an architectural language.

While Shape Grammar and Space Syntax theories and relevant techniques have been developed and applied since the 1970s and 80s, they have, thus far, existed largely in isolation from each other. With a few exceptions, scholars have analysed *either* the spatial, *or* the formal properties of an architectural language. In contrast, the second half of this book proposes a new method which combines aspects of both methods, to investigate the combined grammatical and syntactical properties of an architectural language for the first time.

From this background it should be apparent that this book is intended for architects, designers, scholars and academics who are interested in analysing the spaces and forms of the built environment. It assumes that the reader has a broad awareness of both basic architectural terminology and concepts (plan, elevation, façade, section, roof, wall, etc.) and mathematical terms and processes (sum, mean, median, algebra, formula, etc.). The primary computational methods which are the focus of this book are introduced and demonstrated through detailed case studies, however the present work is not intended to be an exhaustive explanation of the "basics" of computational analysis. For this reason, most chapters include references for readers who may be less familiar with the approaches contained herein and readers are encouraged to access these works for further information. By revisiting Shape Grammar and Space Syntax approaches, and by demonstrating a unique combined application of them, this book presents new techniques for architectural analysis, optimisation and generation.

Just as it is important to define the core content and themes of this book, so too it is worth clarifying what the book will not do. First and foremost, while this book does draw on historic architectural treatises, cases and examples, it is not a book about the history of architecture or languages. Throughout history, the concept of an architectural language has been theorised and debated, and various drawing and modelling systems have been proposed to demonstrate ideal architectural solutions to specific problems or building types. While some of these historic examples have a degree of logic or systematisation to them, that appears to prefigure computational thinking, they are not the same as the grammatical and syntactical systems used in the present book.

Similarly, a wide range of graphical analysis systems are available for the investigation of architectural properties, but these are not computational, in the sense that most do not follow a rigorous, repeatable rule-based process, and it is rare for any of these approaches to produce mathematical data. For example, post-structuralist architect and theorist Peter Eisenman (1987) produced a famous detailed graphical analysis and generative technique for architectural form. Eisenman's (1999) method uses a "diagram language" (later called a "diagram diary") to question the importance of functionality in design. In a different way, postmodern architect and theorist Rob Krier (1988) used diagramming and model-making to create a contemporary architectural evocation of historic urban forms and types. Both Eisenman's and Krier's languages have a similar procedural and analytical sense, but neither can be replicated nor provide any clear mathematical basis for deeper analysis or generation. In contrast, the syntactical and grammatical methods which are the focus of this book are innately computational and repeatable, and this is why they offer great potential for multiple purposes. In particular, as this book demonstrates, they can be applied to the architecture of any era or location.

STRUCTURE AND CONTENT

This book is structured in three sections. Section 1 and Chapter 1 introduce the complete work, its themes, concepts and cases. Section 2 comprises four chapters which describe and demonstrate the two main computational methods used in the book and trace emerging research in the field. Chapters 2 and 3 are focused on Shape Grammar approaches while Chapters 4 and 5 are concerned with Space Syntax approaches. Section 3, which has four chapters, proposes a new computational method for analysing the language of architecture. This new method combines aspects of both Space Syntax and Shape Grammar approaches. Chapter 6 introduces the method and Chapters 7 and 8 apply it to the works of Glenn Murcutt and Frank Lloyd Wright, respectively. Chapter 9 concludes the book with a summary of important trends and developments. Many of these chapters draw on ideas and arguments developed in past journal papers by the authors. In such cases references are provided in the chapter to the original works, although the versions contained herein are all more advanced or expanded. The detailed contents of each chapter are described hereafter.

Chapter 1, "The Language of Architecture", provides a background to the basic linguistic analogies in architectural thinking, tracing their use in a historic architectural treatise. Thereafter, the chapter introduces the two most well-known linguistic concepts, "grammar" and "syntax", and the equivalent computational design approaches, Shape Grammar and Space Syntax. General applications of these two approaches are then summarised along with their basic principles. In addition, throughout this book new grammatical and syntactical approaches are typically demonstrated using famous architectural examples. As such, Chapter 1 also introduces three architects and their works which form the basis for the various cases examined throughout. These architects are Andrea Palladio, Frank Lloyd Wright and Glenn Murcutt. This chapter provides a brief historical background to each architect and to their architectural styles or languages.

Chapter 2, "Shape Grammar Approaches in Architecture", reviews emerging grammatical research, identifying three important themes: (1) design analysis and generation, (2) automated design and generative algorithms, and (3) algebraic Shape Grammar. The review of emerging research encompasses 77 papers sourced from three online databases. The first of the three themes – design analysis and generation – has remained relatively consistent from the early years of Shape Grammar research. In Chapter 2, this theme is discussed from five perspectives: theoretical approaches, two-dimensional architectural design, three-dimensional architectural design, urban design, and art and engineering design. In contrast, the second theme is concerned with emerging research on computer-aided design (CAD) and design automation using generative algorithms. The discussion of this theme in Chapter 2 highlights four perspectives in the recent research: design automation, procedural modelling, genetic algorithms and other types of algorithmic generation and evaluation. Lastly, Chapter 2 reviews the algebraic framework for Shape Grammars as an important new direction in the field, wherein design automation and optimisation are merged into, or used alongside, more standard grammatical approaches.

Chapter 3, "Mathematical Analysis and Generation of Palladian Designs", provides a detailed explanation of the Shape Grammar approach, introducing a simple "Palladian Grammar" as an example. This new Shape Grammar consists of four stages and eleven rule sets, which cover the stages from the initial generation of a planning grid system to terminating the generation process. Chapter 3 also demonstrates a mathematical approach to analysing and generating design instances of an architectural style using the frequencies of applied rule sets. The frequencies not only serve as quantitative design knowledge to identify the level of disparity of each design instance and its style, but also provide convenient guides for design generation within that style. Normalised distance and transition probability are introduced as new measurements for this purpose.

Chapter 4, "Space Syntax Approaches in Architecture", reviews emerging research in the field of Space Syntax and highlights three techniques – axial line analysis, convex space analysis and visibility graph analysis (VGA). The chapter's review of new research encompasses 207 research papers sourced from three online databases. The first technique, axial line analysis, is typically used to understand the spatial configuration of urban environments or public buildings. As an example of this, Chapter 4 presents a case study analysis of four streets and their corresponding urban neighbourhoods in Seoul, South Korea. The second group of papers reviewed uses or develops convex space analysis and the justified plan graph (JPG) to develop mathematical measures of the topological configuration of an architectural plan. The last group of papers is concerned with the concepts of isovists and visibility graphs. The VGA technique is often used to model human spatial perceptions and responses in a specific architectural setting. The chapter includes a detailed demonstration of the use of VGA in a case study of the spatial and social properties of architectural plans for four residential aged care developments, two in Australia and two in South Korea.

Chapter 5, "Syntactical and Mathematical Measures of Spatial Configuration", explains and demonstrates the convex space analysis technique, focusing on the JPG and its mathematical measures. The JPG was the first practical analytical method developed as part of the theory of Space Syntax. It has been adopted to provide both a graphical and a mathematical model for analysing the spatial configuration of buildings. Nonetheless, the JPG method is rarely explained in its totality and there is also a marked lack of consistency in how the results are interpreted. For these reasons, this chapter first demonstrates how a JPG is constructed (using a Palladian villa plan as an example) and how to calculate the syntactical and mathematical measures from it. The chapter then examines some limits of the method before describing an alternative approach: a weighted and directed JPG. This alternative uses centrality measures – degree centrality, centrality closeness and betweenness – to overcome the problems of distance and multiple connections between spaces.

Chapter 6, "A Combined Grammatical and Syntactical Method", presents a new method for investigating the combined spatial and formal properties of architecture. The chapter commences with an overview of its schematic framework, consisting of node, link and shape. This framework encapsulates different types of spatial and formal information and provides a conceptual foundation for understanding the combined grammatical and syntactical method. The new method commences with a JPG grammar and illustrates the grammatical interpretation of the structure of this syntax to identify both grammatical patterns and syntactical properties. It is then followed by a massing grammar, which adds a parallel consideration of architectural form. Chapter 6 presents two generic grammars as configurational grammars that make up the method, the JPG grammar and the massing grammar.

Chapter 7, "The Language of Glenn Murcutt's Domestic Architecture", provides the first full demonstration of the new method, in this case using ten of Murcutt's rural domestic designs as cases. After developing the JPG-grammar, the chapter describes the massing grammar that configures the form of each design, defining block properties, composition and roof types. Mathematical measures of the properties of each house are developed and a dominant design is generated, showing how the new method can be used to not only create designs that look like Murcutt's architecture, but that have the same social structure and spatial hierarchy. The chapter concludes by generating a new "dominant design", being one which best represents the way Murcutt creates functional relationships in space.

Chapter 8, "The Language of Frank Lloyd Wright's Prairie Houses", analyses nineteen of Wright's Prairie style works using the new syntactical and grammatical method. As in the previous chapter, this requires the generation of a specific JPG-grammar and massing grammar. The data derived from the two grammars is used to provide mathematical insights into the topological and formal properties of Wright's Prairie style language. The results are also used to generate a new, socially and formally derived and compliant instance of his style.

Chapter 9, "Conclusion", summarises the major themes uncovered in the emerging research and the new method developed in the book. It also revisits the strengths and limitations of the new method, and some of the findings developed through its application.

CONCLUSION

This book seeks to shape the broader field of architectural computing and design in four ways.

The first is largely pedagogical, as the book explains two major computational methods, providing detailed examples of the applications of each. This is significant because there are relatively few works of this type available for new users. The second purpose is to categorises the approaches and findings of almost 300 recent research studies about Shape Grammars and Space Syntax. The volume of this work is such that it presents a significant obstacle for researchers who are attempting to understand new developments or emerging trends. By critically reviewing recent research, classifying its content, and presenting it thematically, this book provides a window into the next decade of computational design research.

The third goal of this book is the most important. It has been noted in the past that the Shape Grammar and Space Syntax methods are largely incompatible. With only a few exceptions, scholars have developed and applied these methods separately to the analysis of form *or* space without considering the potential of analysing form *and* space. This book presents a new, combined syntactical and grammatical method for analysing space and form in a body of work. Not only does the new method develop data which can provide insights into architecture, but it can be used to generate new designs, which have particular spatial and formal properties. Furthermore, while this book uses historic architectural cases as examples, its use extends far beyond the history of architecture. The methods explained and developed herein are equally applicable to solving contemporary design problems. Similarly, while the majority of the cases examined in this book are domestic scale works, the existing and new methods are applicable to different types and scales of buildings.

Finally, Andrea Palladio, Frank Lloyd Wright and Glenn Murcutt are amongst the most important architects of their generations and their works provide the main cases examined in this book. The preliminary insights developed in this process – into Palladio's, Wright's and Murcutt's planning, design processes and buildings – are just the start of the process. The data presented here can be used to identify typical or atypical designs in their oeuvres, as well as generating new versions of their architecture which comply with the formal and spatial properties of the original works. Furthermore, this book includes new investigations of urban streetscape character and a detailed case study comparing international differences in residential aged care design. Collectively these cases provide a foundation for future computational research into architectural languages, be they regional *dialects*, personal *idiolects* or typological *lingua franca*.

Ju Hyun Lee
The University of New South Wales (UNSW Sydney), Australia

Michael J. Ostwald
The University of New South Wales (UNSW Sydney), Australia

REFERENCES

Chomsky, N. (2005). *Language and Mind* (3rd ed.). Cambridge, UK: Cambridge University Press.

Eisenman, P. (1987). *House of Cards*. New York: Oxford University Press.

Eisenman, P. (1999). *Diagram Diaries*. New York: Universe.

Fisher, S. (2019). Philosophy of Architecture. In E. N. Zalta (Ed.), *The Stanford Encyclopedia of Philosophy* (Winter 2016 ed.). Stanford, CA: Metaphysics Research Lab, Stanford University. Retrieved from https://plato.stanford.edu/archives/win2016/entries/architecture/

Jencks, C. (1977). *The Language of Post-Modern Architecture*. New York, NY: Rizzoli.

Krier, R. (1988). *Architectural Composition*. London: Academy Editions.

Summerson, J. (1964). *The Classical Language of Architecture*. Cambridge, MA: MIT Press.

Zevi, B. (1978). *The Modern Language of Architecture*. Canberra, Australia: ANU Press.

Acknowledgment

This book has evolved out of research undertaken over the last decade by the authors and it has been supported by many people whose contributions we wish to acknowledge. First, special thanks to our close confidant, Professor Ning Gu at University of South Australia, for contributing to our early grammatical and syntactical research. We also wish to express our sincere gratitude to eminent Professor John Gero for writing the foreword to this book and for his advice and support. We would especially like to thank our colleagues and research assistants, Professor Hyunsoo Lee, Maria Roberts, Dr. Rongrong Yu, Dr. Michael J. Dawes and Dr. Peiman Amini Behbahani. The ideas contained in this volume were also shaped by the generous responses of the editors and anonymous referees of *Environment and Planning B: Urban Analytics and City Science*, *Architectural Science Review*, *Nexus Network Journal: Architecture and Mathematics*, *Frontiers of Architectural Research*, *Design Computing and Cognition*, *International Space Syntax Symposium*, *International Conference of the Architectural Science Association* and *International Conference of Computer Aided Architectural Design Research in Asia*. We gratefully acknowledge the support of a UNSW Built Environment Editing Grant. Finally, a special thanks to the Authors' families. Ju Hyun Lee wishes to express appreciation to Ji Suk and DongGeun for their endless support and love. He could never have competed even the first draft of this book without their help and encouragement. Michael Ostwald wishes to thank Toni and Trish for their continuing love and support.

Section 1

Chapter 1
The Language of Architecture

ABSTRACT

This chapter provides a background to the common "linguistic" analogies in architectural thinking, which are concerned with the "grammar" of form and the "syntax" of space. The chapter then links these linguistic properties to the classical Vitruvian architectural values of firmness, commodity, and delight. Thereafter, the chapter introduces the two most well-known computational design approaches, Shape Grammar and Space Syntax, and briefly outlines the general applications of each. In addition, throughout this book, new grammatical and syntactical approaches are typically demonstrated using the domestic architecture of Andrea Palladio, Frank Lloyd Wright, and Glenn Murcutt. Thus, this chapter also introduces these three architects and their architectural languages.

BACKGROUND

A typical definition of the general concept of a "language" has three components. First, it is a set of well-defined verbal or visual elements. Second, these elements must be combined in accordance with an agreed structure and usage to communicate a message. Third, the way these elements are combined within the structure determines the "style" of the language and its expression. As such, language is the combination of formal elements, structural relations and stylistic expressions. Given this definition, it is not surprising that throughout history architecture has been repeatedly described as a language. Architecture relies on the use or adaption of various recurring

DOI: 10.4018/978-1-7998-1698-0.ch001

elements (like walls, columns and beams), which are combined in stable or consistent ways (to create shelter or serve a specific function), with the result having a distinct style (and aesthetic and experiential presence). While architectural linguistic analogies of this type have many practical limitations, they remain a pervasive and useful way of examining and understanding the built environment.

The oldest known example of the linguistic analogy in architecture is found in the work of Vitruvius, a first century (BC) Roman architect and military engineer. Vitruvius described how the architectural orders (the Doric, Ionic and Corinthian architecture of ancient Greece) provide the architect with a set of parts and a proportional system to combine them in, and thereby create an ideal assemblage. As such, the orders use form and structure to create a harmonious outcome. While the Classical Greek orders are no longer used in this way, Vitruvius offered a definition of architecture that is still in use today and is closely associated with linguistic analogies. Vitruvius argued that architecture has three properties – *firmitas*, *utilitas* and *venustas* – which are translated as either soundness, utility and attractiveness or firmness, commodity and delight, respectively (Rowland & Howe, 1999; Smith, 2003). In the late twentieth century, when discussions about the language of architecture were revitalised by computational design researchers, *firmitas*, *utilitas* and *venustas* were reconceptualised as, respectively, the grammar, syntax and style of architecture.

Firmness (*firmitas*) is associated with the tangible presence of architecture, which is more commonly known as the "form" of a building. Form refers to the shape, dimensionality and actual or intended physical properties of a design (Gelernter, 1995). Architectural form is the part of a building that can be seen and touched. As the forms are the recurring elements that make up the corpus of a language, they can also be thought of as the "grammar" of architecture.

Commodity or utility (*utilitas*) is the property of a building that facilitates "faultless, unimpeded use through the disposition of space" (Rowland & Howe, 1999, p. 26). The word "utility" suggests a degree of usefulness or functionality and the adjective "commodious" refers to things that are generous, capacious or accommodating. Both of these readings confirm that the second component of Vitruvius's definition is concerned with spatial rather than formal properties. Architectural space is the void enclosed by the walls of a room, or the area around the form of a building. It is the part of a building that can be walked through, looked into or over and inhabited. As spaces and the connections between them are the functional structure of a building, they can also be thought of as the "syntax" of architecture.

The third component of Vitruvius's definition, delight (*venustas*), can refer to either the aesthetic refinement embodied in a building's form or to the emotional impact it has on an observer. The former is the product of an artful or considered assemblage of forms, whereas the latter is the intellectual, emotional or psychological response people have to it. In a linguistic sense, the combination of the grammar of a building's formal composition and the syntax of its spatial structure determines its style.

The relationship between form, space and aesthetics, or grammar, syntax and style, is an intricate one.

Ching argues that form and space comprise a "unity of opposites" (Ching, 2007, p. 96) that collectively creates "order". He suggests that form in architecture refers to the "configuration or relative disposition of the lines or contours that delimit a figure" (Ching, 2007, p. 34). In contrast, space is that which is either enclosed by, or shaped by, form. Thus, a building delineates both the space it contains (its interior) and, to a lesser extent, the space it is contained within (its site or context). However, despite the fact that space and form cannot be separated from each other, architectural theories have tended to focus largely on form. In part this is because form is, by definition, easier to see, feel or grasp, whereas space is something that must be understood intellectually (by measuring the voids between walls) or emotionally (by feeling the size, scale or directionality of the voids). From Pevsner's (1936) celebration of symbolic architecture to Frampton's (1995) call for a regional tectonic practice, form has become central to the ethical or moral interpretation of design. Similarly, from Jencks's and Baird's (1969) meditations on semiotics to Pallasmaa's (2005) phenomenology of place, architecture is typically read through its formal expression and the way in which the human body experiences or interprets that expression. Certainly, space is often considered alongside form when defining an architectural style, or hypothesising the impact buildings have on peoples' physical and emotional responses (Birkerts, 1994). Space, however, is not only the machine that makes architecture function in a practical sense, it is the medium through which cognitive and emotional responses are developed. Thus, simplistically, the combination of form and space determines the aesthetic properties of a building, and the combination of grammar and syntax determines the style of an architectural language.

Despite the reciprocal relationship between space and form, early computational design researchers developed tools and methods to investigate *either* space *or* form, but not both together. The first of these computational methods was focused on the rules used to describe or generate the compositional properties of a design. This became known as a "Shape Grammar" approach, and it was developed throughout the last three decades of the twentieth century (Cagdas, 1996; Knight, 1994; Koning & Eizenberg, 1981; Stiny & Gips, 1972). Shape grammar research can be used to reveal the logical systems that underlie the two and three-dimensional geometric properties of a design, which are in turn, the tangible expression of its style. Shape Grammar research could be regarded as the study of form *without* consideration of space. The second computational approach was used for analysing spatial topologies and social relations and became known as "Space Syntax". It developed largely over the last two decades of the twentieth century and it focused exclusively on spatial connectivity or structure (Hillier, 1999; Hillier & Hanson, 1984). Space Syntax proponents argue that space may be empty, invisible and amorphous, but it does have two critical qualities, depreciable difference and permeability. The first of these qualities refers to the capacity to differentiate one space from any other, and the second refers to the way in which spaces are physically connected or configured. This way of looking at spatial configuration entails the rejection of two conventional geographic concerns, "the concept of location" and the "notion of distance" (1984, p. xii). Neither of these properties, they argue, are useful for understanding space as it is isolated from form. Instead, various "morphological qualities", including the relationships between spaces and their relative permeability or complexity, can be studied. Thus, Space Syntax could be regarded as the study of space *without* consideration of form.

While Shape Grammar and Space Syntax approaches have been separately very successful, attempts to combine the two are rare. Furthermore, both approaches continue to be developed in isolation, and refined in important ways, but the fundamental disconnection between them remains. Conceptually, the former deals with *typological* and descriptive issues in architecture, while the latter addresses its *topological* and spatial configurations. But what could be gained if space and form could be collectively analysed and generated?

The prospect of combining the analytical and generative strengths of these two computational methods would seem to offer the potential for uncovering new insights into architecture. The generative power of the grammar could be extended to develop rules for evolving the social structure of the design language. Alternatively, the social structure of a building can be used as the basis for understanding its formal expression. The idea of combining form and space in computational design, or grammar and syntax in the language of architecture, is the motivation behind the present book. It commences by introducing the two computational methods in isolation in Section 2, before examining emerging research in both methods. Thereafter in Section 3, a new combined grammatical and syntactical method is presented, selectively capturing aspects of both the formal and spatial properties of architecture.

SHAPE GRAMMAR

The first technologically enabled computational approaches to architecture are conventionally traced to the 1960s and 1970s (Alexander, 1964; March & Steadman, 1971). One of the most famous of these approaches, Shape Grammar, views architecture primarily as a type of formal language, examining the logical relationships between elements in the two or three-dimensional shape of a building. Since Stiny and Gips' seminal article (1972), a variety of shape grammars have been developed in the architecture and design domains and more recently some of these have been expanded to take advantage of parametric software. For example, Shape Grammar researchers have explored the specific architectural styles of famous architects such as Andrea Palladio (Stiny & Mitchell, 1978), Giuseppe Terragni (Flemming, 1981), Frank Lloyd Wright (Koning & Eizenberg, 1981) and Glenn Murcutt (Hanson & Radford, 1986a). Vernacular designs have also been studied using Shape Grammars, including traditional Taiwanese, Turkish and Japanese dwellings and rooms (Chiou & Krishnamurti, 1995; Downing & Flemming, 1981; Knight, 1981). In these examples, a Shape Grammar is used to identify the operations and transformations needed to generate a design. As such, it could be regarded as a production model, or system, that has many variations, including graph, functional, parallel, parametric and set grammars. In architectural research, a typical Shape Grammar approach treats a building's form or plan as a set of shapes, examining the logical relationships between various sub-shapes that collectively make up its properties (Stiny & Gips, 1972). The Shape Grammar is therefore the set of rules delineating how a building is composed from shapes and sub-shapes. Often derived from typological considerations, a particular Shape Grammar can be used not only to describe a design style, but also to generate new designs that conform to the principles of this style (Lee, Ostwald, & Gu, 2015a, 2017, 2018).

In Shape Grammar research, design is assumed to be a rigorous and rational process and it is modelled as such. While we know that every design process is potentially more complex and contingent than this model, the aim is not to replicate the actual process used by an individual architect for a particular project, but rather to develop an idealised, logical and repeatable version of the process (Stiny, 1990). This conceptual understanding of the design process is central to most grammatical studies and this reasoning allows researchers to rigorously capture possible processes for generating a language of design (Economou, 2000; Knight, 1981). The exact processes vary between grammars, with, for example, Stiny and Mitchell (1978) using eight steps to define the rules for several of their projects, while Hanson and Radford (1986a) use twelve steps to generate design instances. The rules, in such cases, start with an initial shape and then proceed iteratively by applying rules or modifiers to that shape until an end-state has been reached (Knight, 1994). By analysing these possible processes, new knowledge is developed, which can then be tested by generating new designs that capture the characteristics of the original architecture (Flemming, 1981; Hanson & Radford, 1986a; Koning & Eizenberg, 1981; Stiny & Mitchell, 1978). Shape Grammars are examined and explained in detail in Chapters 2 and 3 of the present book.

SPACE SYNTAX

Winston Churchill's aphorism, "we shape our buildings and thereafter they shape us", has become famous in spatial psychology, architecture and planning. Multiple theories have been used to try to explain the reciprocal relationship between spatial properties and human responses. For example, Appleton's habitat theory and prospect-refuge theory (1975) are among the most well-known explanations for environmental preference in architecture. Gibson's ground theory (1950, 1979) and Kaplan and Kaplan's information theory (1989) are also used to explain human responses to spatial arrangements. Such theories use psychological and philosophical constructs to analyse environments and their social and behavioural properties, and because of this, their results are not always reproducible (Stamps, 2005).

Quantitative theories and methods have also been developed to understand and model the relationship between space and social patterns. Among the most famous of these methods, in architecture at least, is Space Syntax, a method that uses the mathematics of graph theory to measure various properties of plans.

Space syntax is concerned with spatial topologies and social relations (Hillier & Hanson, 1984). It uses, for example, maps of visually-defined and enclosed spaces (called a "convex map") to analyse programmatic spaces and their connectivity. Environmental and behavioural research identifies that enclosure is an important property of a space, because it limits or shapes movement and perception. Space Syntax also uses maps of spatial connectivity (called an "axial map") made up of the longest lines of sight or movement that pass through and connect all of the habitable spaces of a plan (Hillier & Hanson, 1984). Such maps capture behavioural characteristics, including movement potential and navigational choice. The purpose of Space Syntax is largely analytical, and its conventional application is to question the epistemological properties of a design. Hillier and Hanson argue that "however much we may prefer to discuss architecture in terms of visual styles, its most far-reaching practical effects are not at the level of appearances at all, but at the level of space" (Hillier & Hanson, 1984, p. ix). Space is the fundamental medium through which architects provide shelter, structure society and serve the basic needs of communities; an idea emphatically expressed in Hillier's adage, "space is the machine" (1999), the central maxim of Space Syntax theory. In the present book, Chapters 4 and 5 are focused on Space Syntax techniques and emerging research in this field.

A Syntactical And Grammatical Method

Obvious potential exists for a computational method that can capture both the grammatical and syntactical properties of architecture. It could even be argued that, despite the successes of Shape Grammar and Space Syntax approaches, both have suffered from criticisms of their incapacity to handle, respectively, the role of space in design generation and the role of form in social and cognitive behaviour. Perhaps because of this, a small number of examples are available of attempts to selectively combine aspects of the two (Eloy & Duarte, 2011; Heitor, Duarte, & Pinto, 2004). Such examples commence with the development of a Shape Grammar to generate design variations of a style (a grammatical, form-based process) and then employ graph theory to decide which design options are most significant or suitable for use (a syntactical analysis of productions). Such approaches essentially privilege *form* over *function* (space), as they are largely grammatically derived and only use a small part of the syntactical method to prioritise various formal rules. While these attempts are notable, the famous Modernist aphorism in architecture, *form follows function*, suggests that spatial relations must be resolved and prioritised ahead of formal ones. This is not just a modernist attitude; contemporary pedagogical models argue that broad spatial relationships and connectivity should be refined in a design process before formal properties are considered. As such, any attempt to combine the two computational methods should ideally prioritise spatial and programmatic concerns ahead of aesthetic or formal ones.

The new method proposed in this book was developed throughout a series of stages in response to the desire to commence the analysis or generation of architecture with a consideration of space, and then consider form as an adjunct to space (Lee, Ostwald, & Gu, 2013, 2015a, 2015b, 2017, 2018). The method commences by defining the spatial or syntactical properties of a design using a special type of JPG and then derives a set of rules to generate its corresponding three-dimensional form. This sequence, which mirrors the standard design process, effectively starts with functional issues and then derives forms to contain or house them. In this way, the arrangement of major functional spaces precedes, or at least moderates, decisions about form. Chapter 6 in the present book introduces the new combined syntactical and grammatic method and it is applied in Chapters 7 and 8.

Palladio, Wright and Murcutt

It is difficult to describe and apply a method for analysing the language of architecture, without using examples. As such, this book demonstrates both existing and new computational approaches using the domestic designs of three architects: Andrea Palladio (1508 – 1580), Frank Lloyd Wright (1867 – 1959) and Glenn Murcutt (1936 –). The works of all three have previously been studied using computational approaches because they each, in different ways, developed a consistent, rigorous architectural language. While they come from different eras and traditions, being respectively known for neo-classical, organic modernist and critical regionalist architecture, their works demonstrate a commitment to developing a distinct and enduring architectural language. It is this last point that makes them ideal subjects for computational analysis. Analysing architecture, like surveying people or recording empirical observations, is more effective the more data there is. Although the numbers of designs by each of these architects is still too low to produce a statistically significant result, there are recurring themes and tropes in these architects' works that make them ideal for syntactical and grammatical analysis.

Andrea Palladio was an Italian architect who worked during the sixteenth century in the Vicenza area of the Venetian Republic. Influenced by classical Greek and Roman architecture, Palladio created a distinct, symmetrically planned villa style, which was often raised on a podium and had a strong classical portico on the main façade. His approach to architecture, which was influenced by Vitruvius, was described in his book, *I Quattro Libri dell'Architettura* (*Four Books of Architecture*) (Palladio, 1715). In this work he emphasises the importance of proportional ratios, which he views as responsible for "the beauty of an edifice". He proposes that the "exact proportion of the parts within themselves, and of each part with the whole" is the primary aesthetic concern (Palladio, 1715, p. 1 Book I). As such, many researchers have explored the relationships between his architecture and mathematics, mainly examining proportions (Djordjević, 1990; Fletcher, 2001; Howard & Longair, 1982; March, 1999, 2001; Rowe, 1976; Seebohm & Chan, 2001). Such was the power of his work that he influenced many later designers and a style of architecture, "Palladian", was named after him and applied in major public buildings and monuments. The study of Palladian architecture has attracted significant academic interest in the last century as historians and theorists sought to better understand its properties (Hersey, Freedman, & Palladio, 1992; Williams & Giaconi, 2003).

In Chapter 3 of the present book, ten plans for Palladian villas from *I Quattro Libri dell'Architettura* are examined. These include his famous *Villa Barbaro* (begun c. 1556), *Villa Malcontenta* (begun c. 1558) and *Villa Emo* (begun c. 1560). These villas, from Palladio's later period, are widely considered to be his masterpieces. As Wassell (2008) argues, Palladio "heightened his command of classical Roman architectural theory" and "ancient Greek arithmetic and geometry" in his major domestic designs (Wassell, 2008, p. 217). Colin Rowe compares Palladio's *Villa Malcontenta* to Le Corbusier's *Villa Stein* in his famous essay written in 1947, "The Mathematics of the Ideal Villa" (Rowe, 1976). He reveals that both Palladio's and Le Corbusier's villas have a common proportional framework in their planning. In another example of the connection to geometry, the *Villa Emo* is often explored mathematically in an attempt to understand Palladio's design theory, and especially its "harmonic" (Wittkower, 1988) or "golden" proportions (Fletcher, 2001; March, 2001). In Chapter 3 of the present book the plans of ten Palladian villas are examined using Palladio's dominant grid systems (5×3 and 5×4 grids) to develops a simple grammar based on the proportional spacing

9

(horizontally and vertically) between cells in the underlying tartan grid. The Palladian Grammar is then used to generate schematic plans illustrating four main functional spaces: loggia (including portico), *sala* (the largest room for a formal gathering), *stanze* (mid-sized rooms for sitting rooms) and *camerini* (the smallest rooms for storages, washrooms or staircases). In addition to this formal investigation in Chapter 3, in Chapter 5 three Palladian villas – *Villa Saraceno*, *Villa Sepulveda* and *Villa Poiana* – are used as examples to explain and demonstrate the mathematical measures of a JPG.

Frank Lloyd Wright was an iconoclastic American architect whose career spanned from 1886 to 1959 and resulted in more than 400 completed works. During his career Wright developed three major stylistic oeuvres for his domestic architecture – Prairie style, Textile Block and Usonian architecture – as well as designing stand-alone masterpieces, like *Fallingwater* and the *Hollyhock House*. Chapter 8 in the present book is focused on Wright's Prairie style architecture, which originated in the midwestern United States of America in the early years of the twentieth century. Wright's Prairie style typically features strong horizontal lines, low-pitched roofs with wide, overhanging eaves (Lind, 1994) and cruciform or T-shaped plans. The social spaces are generally on the ground floor with a smaller upper level containing bedrooms and bathrooms (Amini Behbahani, Ostwald, & Gu, 2016; Chan, 1992). The 1896 *Heller House* and the 1899 *Husser House* are often considered the first of Wright's Prairie style works (K. Frampton, 1992; Pinnell, 2005), even though his primary themes are not fully developed in them. Unlike the ornate Queen Anne and Colonial Revival architecture of the era, the *Heller* and *Husser* houses have a sense of a central axis and a slightly more pronounced horizontal formal modelling than was typical of the era. Wright himself identifies the *Winslow House* as the first Prairie-style work, despite its Victorian floor plan and symmetrical front façade (Wright, 1941). Nevertheless, the true formulation of the style occurred in 1901, when Wright published its general principles in an article entitled "a home in a Prairie town".

Chapter 8 of this book provides an in-depth review of the language of Wright's nineteen Prairie houses, using the combined grammatical and syntactical method. Whereas past research (Koning & Eizenberg, 1981) has shown how Wright's architecture might be computationally generated solely on the basis of its formal composition, Chapter 8 examines how its social and functional properties can also be replicated as part of such a process.

Glenn Murcutt is a Pritzker-prize-winning Australian architect who is often associated with the critical regionalist movement. Like Wright's Prairie style, Murcutt's architecture has been described as embodying a distinct, coherent architectural language of space and form. In particular, his rural domestic buildings are typically interpreted as a local variant of a more universal type (Drew, 1985; Fromonot, 1995; Spence, 1986). The close relationship between form and inhabitation of Murcutt's architecture has been extensively discussed in many publications. His early rural domestic designs have been described as exemplars of Arcadian minimalism, a rigorous modern evocation of the form and tectonics of the primitive hut and the Palladian villa (Ostwald, 2011b). Murcutt's early houses, including the *Marie Short House* and *Nicholas House*, are typically characterised by a clear formal type, the so-called "long thin open pavilion" (Spence, 1986). These buildings frequently feature an extensive external covered veranda space and have a modernist, linear pavilion plan. Drew (1985) indicates that Murcutt's rural houses share many external formal similarities, and Pallasmaa (2006) highlights the significance of "order in form" and "order in organising and structuring space".

As observed in these examples, Murcutt's architecture seemingly possesses a high degree of consistency and clarity in the way he approaches form. Hanson and Radford (1986a, 1986b) previously developed a design grammar for a class of Murcutt's rural houses that has a consistent pattern of development in its response to the environment and brief. They developed a set of syntactic and abductive rules to understand the formal properties of Murcutt's architecture as well as to generate a subset of it. Most interestingly, Hanson and Radford (1986a) generated a design using their shape grammar for Murcutt, and then asked him to evaluate the design. Their production was close to Murcutt's style at the time, however their grammar could only consider limited designs and Murcutt's philosophy and design process has evolved since then. Ostwald's (2011a, 2011b) more recent research uses a Justified Plan Graph (JPG) technique to undertake visual, mathematical and theoretical analyses of Murcutt's rural architecture. He found that there could be less differentiation between the integration levels of spaces in Murcutt's houses and therefore that geometry might be more important than topology in shaping his designs. These results suggest that Murcutt's primary considerations could be climate and tectonics, not space and form (Gusheh, Heneghan, Lassen, & Seyama, 2008).

Chapter 7 examines ten of Murcutt's rural houses, which were constructed between 1975 and 2005 on isolated rural sites in Australia. While Hanson and Radford (1986a, 1986b) investigate the formal properties of Murcutt's early houses and generate a variation through their shape grammar for Murcutt, the grammatical and syntactical method in Chapter 7 records and extrapolates design instances from a set including more recent works by Murcutt, taking into account both their formal and spatial properties. The chapter also generates a new dominant design that is reminiscent of Murcutt's *Walsh House*, and which may best represent the way Murcutt creates functional relationships in space.

CONCLUSION

There are two motives for writing the present book. The first is to trace the development of two of the great computational design techniques developed in the last 40 years by examining more than 280 recent publications about their application and refinement. The emerging trends and applications investigated in this way provide a rich context for the book. The second motive is to introduce and demonstrate a new, spatially-driven method for investigating both the syntactical and grammatic properties of architecture, and generating new instances of a particular architectural language. The new computational technique is intended to be used in architectural analysis of historic and contemporary buildings, but it also has other applications in design research. Finally, to fulfil these motives, the book uses the domestic designs of three of the world's great architects as cases.

The works of Palladio, Wright and Murcutt have been repeatedly studied, copied and adapted, presenting historians and mathematicians with valuable subjects for analysis and speculation. They have also all been interpreted through the lens of the Vitruvian triad – firmness commodity and delight – with multiple studies attempting to dissect their properties in these terms. The present book does not undertake a detailed analysis of any of these three, as its purpose is largely methodological and epistemological, but it does begin to illuminate several properties of these architect's works which have not been uncovered in any previous research.

REFERENCES

Alexander, C. (1964). *Notes on the synthesis of form*. Cambridge, UK: Harvard University Press.

Amini Behbahani, P., Ostwald, M. J., & Gu, N. (2016). A syntactical comparative analysis of the spatial properties of Prairie style and Victorian domestic architecture. *The Journal of Architecture*, *21*(3), 348–374. doi:10.1080/13602365.2016.1179661

Appleton, J. (1975). *The experience of landscape*. New York, NY: Wiley.

Birkerts, G. (1994). *Process and expression in architectural form*. Norman, OK: University of Oklahoma Press.

Cagdas, G. (1996). A shape grammar: The language of traditional Turkish houses. *Environment and Planning. B, Planning & Design*, *23*(4), 443–464. doi:10.1068/b230443

Chan, C.-S. (1992). Exploring individual style in design. *Environment and Planning. B, Planning & Design*, *19*(5), 503–523. doi:10.1068/b190503

Ching, F. D. K. (2007). *Architecture: Form, space and, order*. Hoboken, NJ: John Wiley and Sons.

Chiou, S. C., & Krishnamurti, R. (1995). The grammar of Taiwanese traditional vernacular dwellings. *Environment and Planning. B, Planning & Design*, *22*(6), 689–720. doi:10.1068/b220689

Djordjević, I. (1990). Palladio's theory of proportions and the second book of the "Quattro Libri dell'Architettura". *Journal of the Society of Architectural Historians*, *49*(3), 279–292. doi:10.2307/990519

Downing, F., & Flemming, U. (1981). The bungalows of Buffalo. *Environment and Planning. B, Planning & Design*, *8*(3), 269–293. doi:10.1068/b080269

Drew, P. (1985). *Leaves of iron: Glenn Murcutt*. Sydney, NSW: The Law Book Company.

Economou, A. (2000). *Shape grammars in architectural design studio*. Paper presented at the 2000 ACSA Technology Conference, Hong Kong.

Eloy, S., & Duarte, J. (2011). A transformation grammar for housing rehabilitation. *Nexus Network Journal*, *13*(1), 49–71. doi:10.100700004-011-0052-x

Flemming, U. (1981). The secret of the Casa Giuliani Frigerio. *Environment and Planning. B, Planning & Design*, 8(1), 87–96. doi:10.1068/b080087

Fletcher, R. (2001). Palladio's Villa Emo: The golden proportion hypothesis defended. *Nexus Network Journal*, 3(2), 105–112. doi:10.100700004-001-0025-6

Frampton, K. (1992). *Modern architecture, a critical history*. London, UK: Thames and Hudson.

Frampton, K. (1995). *Studies in tectonic culture: The poetics of construction in nineteenth and twentieth century architecture*. Cambridge, MA: MIT Press.

Fromonot, F. (1995). *Glenn Murcutt buildings and projects*. London, UK: Thames and Hudson.

Gelernter, M. (1995). *Sources of architectural form: A critical history of western design theory*. New York, NY: St. Martin's Press.

Gibson, J. J. (1950). *The perception of the visual world*. Cambridge, UK: Riverside Press.

Gibson, J. J. (1979). *The ecological approach to visual perception*. Hillsdale, NJ: Lawrence Erlbaum Associates.

Gusheh, M., Heneghan, T., Lassen, C., & Seyama, S. (2008). *The architecture of Glenn Murcutt*. Tokyo, Japan: TOTO.

Hanson, N. L. R., & Radford, A. D. (1986a). Living on the edge: A grammar for some country houses by Glenn Murcutt. *Architecture Australia*, 75(5), 66–73.

Hanson, N. L. R., & Radford, A. D. (1986b). On modelling the work of the architect Glenn Murcutt. *Design Computing*, 1(3), 189–203.

Heitor, T., Duarte, J., & Pinto, R. (2004). Combing grammars and space syntax: Formulating, generating and evaluating designs. *International Journal of Architectural Computing*, 2(4), 492–515. doi:10.1260/1478077042906221

Hersey, G. L., Freedman, R., & Palladio, A. (1992). *Possible Palladian villas (plus a few instructively impossible ones)*. Cambridge, MA: The MIT Press.

Hillier, B. (1999). *Space is the machine: A configurational theory of architecture*. Cambridge, UK: Cambridge University Press.

Hillier, B., & Hanson, J. (1984). *The social logic of space* (Vol. 1). Cambridge, UK: Cambridge University Press. doi:10.1017/CBO9780511597237

Howard, D., & Longair, M. (1982). Harmonic proportion and Palladio's "Quattro Libri". *Journal of the Society of Architectural Historians*, *41*(2), 116–143. doi:10.2307/989675

Jencks, C., & Baird, G. (Eds.). (1969). *Meaning in architecture*. New York, NY: G. Braziller.

Kaplan, R., & Kaplan, S. (1989). *The experience of nature: A psychological perspective*. Cambridge, UK: Cambridge University Press.

Knight, T. W. (1981). The forty-one steps. *Environment and Planning. B, Planning & Design*, *8*(1), 97–114. doi:10.1068/b080097

Knight, T. W. (1994). *Transformations in design: A formal approach to stylistic change and innovation in the visual arts*. Cambridge, UK: Cambridge University Press.

Koning, H., & Eizenberg, J. (1981). The language of the prairie: Frank Lloyd Wright's prairie houses. *Environment & Planning B*, *8*(3), 295–323. doi:10.1068/b080295

Lee, J. H., Ostwald, M. J., & Gu, N. (2013). Combining Space Syntax and Shape Grammar to investigate architectural style: Considering Glenn Murcutt's domestic designs. In Y. O. Kim, H. T. Park, & K. W. Seo (Eds.), *Proceedings of the Ninth International Space Syntax Symposium* (pp. 005:1-13). Seoul, South Korea: Sejong University.

Lee, J. H., Ostwald, M. J., & Gu, N. (2015a). A syntactical and grammatical approach to architectural configuration, analysis and generation. *Architectural Science Review*, *58*(3), 189–204. doi:10.1080/00038628.2015.1015948

Lee, J. H., Ostwald, M. J., & Gu, N. (2015b). Using a JPG grammar to explore the syntax of a style: An application to the architecture of Glenn Murcutt. In J. S. Gero & S. Hanna (Eds.), *Design computing and cognition '14* (pp. 589–604). Cham, Switzerland: Springer International Publishing. doi:10.1007/978-3-319-14956-1_33

Lee, J. H., Ostwald, M. J., & Gu, N. (2017). A combined plan graph and massing grammar approach to Frank Lloyd Wright's Prairie architecture. *Nexus Network Journal*, *19*(2), 279–299. doi:10.100700004-017-0333-0

Lee, J. H., Ostwald, M. J., & Gu, N. (2018). A Justified Plan Graph (JPG) grammar approach to identifying spatial design patterns in an architectural style. *Environment and Planning B. Urban Analytics and City Science*, *45*(1), 67–89. doi:10.1177/0265813516665618

Lind, C. (1994). *Frank Lloyd Wright's Prairie houses*. Petaluma, CA: Archetype Press.

March, L. (1999). Architectonics of proportion: A shape grammatical depiction of classical theory. *Environment and Planning. B, Planning & Design*, *26*(1), 91–100. doi:10.1068/b260091

March, L. (2001). Palladio's Villa Emo: The golden proportion hypothesis rebutted. *Nexus Network Journal*, *3*(2), 85–104. doi:10.100700004-001-0024-7

March, L., & Steadman, P. (1971). *The geometry of environment*. London, UK: RIBA Publications.

Ostwald, M. J. (2011a). Examining the relationship between topology and geometry: A configurational analysis of the rural houses (1984-2005) of Glenn Murcutt. *Journal of Space Syntax*, *2*(2), 223–246.

Ostwald, M. J. (2011b). A justified plan graph analysis of the early houses (1975-1982) of Glenn Murcutt. *Nexus Network Journal*, *13*(3), 737–762. doi:10.100700004-011-0089-x

Palladio, A. (1715). The architecture of A. Palladio, in four books. London, UK: Printed by John Watts for the author. doi:10.5479il.395807.39088006535397

Pallasmaa, J. (2005). *The eyes of the skin: Architecture and the senses*. Chichester, UK: Wiley-Academy.

Pallasmaa, J. (2006). The poetry of reason. In K. Frampton (Ed.), *Glenn Murcutt, architect* (Vol. 1, pp. 15–20). Sydney, NSW: Editions.

Pevsner, N. (1936). *Pioneers of modern design*. London, UK: Faber and Faber.

Pinnell, P. (2005). Academic tradition and the individual talent. In R. McCarter (Ed.), *On and by Frank Lloyd Wright* (pp. 22–55). New York, NY: Phaidon.

Rowe, C. (1976). *The mathematics of the ideal villa and other essays*. Cambridge, MA: MIT Press.

Rowland, I. D., & Howe, T. N. (Eds.). (1999). *Vitruvius: Ten books on architecture*. Cambridge, UK: Cambridge University Press.

Seebohm, T., & Chan, D. (2001). The design space of schematic Palladian plans for two villa topologies. In *Reinventing the discourse - how digital tools help bridge and transform research, education and practice in architecture: Proceedings of the twenty first annual conference of the Association for Computer-Aided Design in Architecture* (pp. 156-165). Buffalo, NY: SUNY Buffalo.

Smith, T. G. (2003). *Vitruvius on architecture*. New York, NY: Monacelli.

Spence, R. (1986, Feb.). At Bingie Point house, Moruya, New South Wales. *The Architectural Review*, 70-75.

Stamps, A. E. III. (2005). Isovists, enclosure, and permeability theory. *Environment and Planning. B, Planning & Design*, *32*(5), 735–762. doi:10.1068/b31138

Stiny, G. (1990). What is a design? *Environment and Planning. B, Planning & Design*, *17*(1), 97–103. doi:10.1068/b170097

Stiny, G., & Gips, J. (1972). Shape grammars and the generative specification of painting and sculpture. In C. V. Freiman (Ed.), *Information processing 71* (pp. 1460–1465). Amsterdam, The Netherlands: North-Holland.

Stiny, G., & Mitchell, W. J. (1978). The Palladian grammar. *Environment & Planning B*, *5*(1), 5–18. doi:10.1068/b050005

Wassell, S. R. (2008). Andrea Palladio (1508–1580). In S. R. Wassell & K. Williams (Eds.), *Nexus network journal: Canons of form-making in honour of Andrea Palladio 1508–2008* (pp. 213–226). Basel, Switzerland: Birkhäuser Basel.

Williams, K., & Giaconi, G. (2003). *The villas of Palladio*. New York, NY: Princeton Architectural Press.

Wittkower, R. (1988). *Architectural principles in the age of humanism*. New York, NY: St. Martin's Press.

Wright, F. L. (1941). *Frank Lloyd Wright, on architecture: Selected writings, 1894-1940* (F. Gutheim, Ed.). New York, NY: Duell, Sloan, and Pearce.

Wright, F. L. (1943). *An autobiography*. New York, NY: Duell, Sloan and Pearce.

Section 2

Chapter 2
Shape Grammar Approaches in Architecture

ABSTRACT

This chapter reviews emerging Shape Grammar research, categorising it into three themes: design analysis and generation, automated design and generative algorithms, and algebraic Shape Grammars. The first theme consists of theoretical Shape Grammar approaches, two-dimensional architectural design, three-dimensional architectural design, urban design, and design in art and engineering. The second theme addresses four alternative perspectives to grammatical approaches based on design automation, procedural modelling, genetic algorithms, and other algorithmic generation and evaluation methods. The last theme examines research using algebraic shape descriptions and operations. The purpose of this chapter is to provide a critical summary of recent trends in Shape Grammar research and an overview of the relationship between grammatical and generative systems in architecture.

INTRODUCTION

Shape Grammars are amongst the most well-known computational design methods used in architecture, although it is important to realise that the word "computational" does not necessarily refer to the use of a computer. A computational method is one that follows a rigorous formal logic, akin to a mathematical process, to produce an outcome. In the 1970s and 80s, when the first major developments in design computing occurred, the "computation"

DOI: 10.4018/978-1-7998-1698-0.ch002

was typically manual or graphic. That is, written or drawn processes were used as the basis for computational logic, in large part because software and hardware to automate these processes were not available. In more recent years, with rapid advances in computing and visual programming languages, the manual or graphic processes used in Shape Grammars have been increasingly embedded in software. Thus, throughout the present chapter, references to computing are largely about a process, rather than the tools (hardware, software or methods) used to enable it.

Conceptually, a Shape Grammar is a "production system" that consists of two parts: a set of rules about shape transformations and a generation or behaviour engine that determines which rules are applied and when. The transformation rules typically include geometric operations like "rotating", "enlarging" or "mirroring" a shape. The engine determines the orders in which these geometric operations occur, because a grammar is not random. The output of the production system is a shape that conforms to the rules and behaviours of the larger system, or language, it was derived from.

The origins of Shape Grammar research are traditionally traced to the seminal works of Stiny and Gips (1972) and Stiny and Mitchell (1978). The former of these used grammatical means to analyse the shapes used in painting and sculpture, while the latter applied a similar method to the architecture of Andrea Palladio, effectively creating the first architectural Shape Grammar. Since that time, art, design, architecture and engineering languages have been the most common subjects of Shape Grammars. Shape Grammar research in architecture can also be broadly categorised in terms of the three levels of architectural representation the grammars cover: schematic, two-dimensional and three-dimensional. The first of these, the schematic level, addresses the composition of spatial programs using basic modular shapes, much like a "bubble diagram" in the early stages of the architectural design process (J. H. Lee & Gu, 2018; Stiny & Mitchell, 1978). The second level, two-dimensional representation, deals with architectural dimensions and orientations as well as various types of design elements, like walls, doors or windows. The third level, three-dimensional representation, requires a more complex grammatical approach to the configuration of connections between forms (Cui & Tang, 2014; Flemming, 1990; Koning & Eizenberg, 1981). Because three-dimensional architectural forms require larger and more complex rule sets, two-dimensional Shape Grammars, typically floor plans, have been the most common type (Cagdas, 1996; Eloy & Duarte, 2011).

This chapter presents an overview of Shape Grammar research published between 2008 to 2018 and indexed in three online journal databases: Taylor & Francis online, SAGE Journals and ScienceDirect. These databases cover many of the major international journals in the architecture and design domains and could be regarded as capturing any emerging trends in these fields over the last decade. The first two databases allow us to identify articles using "Shape Grammar" or "Shape Grammars" as "author-specified keywords", while the last permits a search only in "title, abstract or author-specified keywords". Nonetheless, most of the collected articles from the last database list "Shape Grammar" or "Shape Grammars" as keywords.

This chapter reviews the general characteristics of the emerging research in the three databases and then provides an in-depth review of three main themes in the research: descriptive analysis, design generation, and generative applications. The first of these three also includes a background to the theme, which introduces many key concepts that are applied in the next chapter (Chapter 3).

EMERGING SHAPE GRAMMAR RESEARCH

The 77 separate research papers identified in the online database search between 2008 and 2018 include nine in Taylor & Francis online, 28 in SAGE Journals and 40 in ScienceDirect. The journals that published these papers are listed in Table 1. Just five of these journals published 55.8% of the collected articles. *Environment and Planning B: Urban Analytics and City Science* – which was previously *Environment and Planning B: Planning and Design* – published the most articles on Shape Grammars (22 papers, 28.6%), following by *Automation in Construction* (7 papers, 9.1%), *Computer-Aided Design* (6 papers, 7.8%), *Computers & Graphics* (4 papers, 5.2%) and *Design Studies* (4 papers, 5.2%). While papers in architecture and design journals dominate the set of 77 works, research in the fields of engineering, structures, art, archaeology and heritage also occasionally employ Shape Grammars . As such, while this chapter is primarily concerned with grammatical approaches in architecture, it also includes references to studies in other domains.

Table 1. Journals publishing Shape Grammar papers between 2008 and 2018

Journal	Number of Papers
Environment and Planning B: Planning and Design	22 (28.6%)
Automation in Construction	7 (9.1%)
Computer-Aided Design	6 (7.8%)
Computers & Graphics	4 (5.2%)
Design Studies	4 (5.2%)
Advanced Engineering Informatics	3 (3.9%)
Graphical Models	2 (2.6%)
International Journal of Architectural Computing	2 (2.6%)
Procedia Technology	2 (2.6%)
Proceedings of the Institution of Mechanical Engineers, Part B: J. Eng Manuf.	2 (2.6%)
Thin-Walled Structures	2 (2.6%)
Applied Soft Computing	1 (1.3%)
Architectural Engineering and Design Management	1 (1.3%)
Architectural Science Review	1 (1.3%)
Computer-Aided Design and Applications	1 (1.3%)
Computers, Environment and Urban Systems	1 (1.3%)
Concurrent Engineering	1 (1.3%)
Energy and Buildings	1 (1.3%)
Entertainment Computing	1 (1.3%)
Geographic Knowledge Infrastructure	1 (1.3%)
International Journal of Architectural Heritage	1 (1.3%)
International Journal of Parallel, Emergent and Distributed Systems	1 (1.3%)
International Journal of Space Structures	1 (1.3%)
Journal of Archaeological Science	1 (1.3%)
Journal of Asian Architecture and Building Engineering	1 (1.3%)
Journal of Cultural Heritage	1 (1.3%)
Journal of Mathematics and the Arts	1 (1.3%)
Journal of Spatial Science	1 (1.3%)
Landscape and Urban Planning	1 (1.3%)
Microelectronic Engineering	1 (1.3%)
Procedia – Social and Behavioral Sciences	1 (1.3%)
Spatial Cognition & Computation	1 (1.3%)
Sum	77 (100.0%)

The number of Shape Grammar papers in these databases reaches a peak between 2012 and 2015 of around 11 per year, with between zero and three each year prior to this, and seven to nine after 2015 (Figure 1). There are several possible reasons for the relatively sudden increase from 2008 to 2012, one of which might be the fact that before 2012 *Environment and Planning B* did not include keywords in the database. However, even using an abstract index search for this journal, only a few additional papers between 2008 and 2012 were uncovered. It is also possible that other major Shape Grammar journals prior to 2012 were simply not indexed in these databases, or that research in this field was largely published in conference proceedings prior to that time, but neither of these would explain the trend in the data. It is more likely that, despite the efforts of the pioneers in the field in the 1980s and early 90s (people like George Stiny, Charles Eastman, Lionel March, Ramesh Krishnamurti and Terry W. Knight), interest in Shape Grammars diminished in the following decade. Indeed, there is a sense that, as the primary examples of grammatical analysis were limited to a consideration of stylistic expression, researchers stopped finding new or important applications for it for more than a decade. A further possible explanation for the rise in interest in 2011, and the partial fall after 2015, may be associated with parametric design. In the early 2000s there was growing interest in automation in Computer Aided Design (CAD) using generative algorithms, which were often conceptually similar to Shape Grammars. There is some evidence that the growth of interest in parametric and algorithmic design triggered a new interest in grammars. However, as practical applications of parametric and generative design grew, its lineage to Shape Grammar research began to be replaced with a range of analogies drawn from bio-morphism or complex systems theory. Nevertheless, the three emerging areas of Shape Grammar research identified in this chapter all have a connection to generative concepts. These three areas, which are the subject of the follow sections, are: design analysis and generation, automated design and generative algorithms, and algebraic Shape Grammars.

DESIGN ANALYSIS AND GENERATION

Since their inception, Shape Grammars have tended to be used for analysis and generation, although various alternative applications exist. The development of a typical Shape Grammar for design analysis and generation involves three steps:

Figure 1. Number of articles by publication year

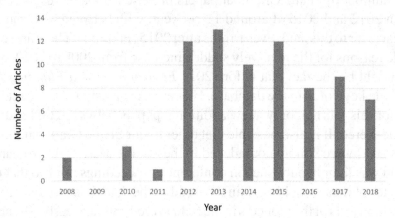

(i)   defining a vocabulary of shapes and a set of spatial relations between them that are common to the design instances of the style.

(ii) defining shape rules that fix the occurrences of the spatial relations.

(iii) providing an initial shape to start the application (Knight, 1994).

Stiny and Gips (1972) define a Shape Grammar (*SG*) as a 4-tuple, or a finite ordered list with four elements:

$$SG = (V_T, V_M, R, I),$$

where V_T is a finite set of shapes, V_M is another finite set of shapes, R is a finite set of ordered pairs (u, v) – u is a shape consisting of an element of V_T * combined with an element of V_M and v is a shape consisting of the element of V_T* contained in u or the element of V_T* contained in u combined with an element of V_M or the element of V_T* contained in u combined with an additional element of V_T* and an element of V_M – and I is a shape consisting of elements of V_T* and V_M.

Eight years later Stiny (1980) offered a simpler definition of a Shape Grammar, also using a 4-tuple set:

$$SG = (S, R, L, I),$$

where the elements are a vocabulary set S (shape), a set of rules R (rule), a set of symbols L (label), and an initial shape I to make up a formal language.

Figure 2. Examples of shape rules

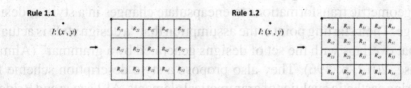

Each of Stiny's (1980) shape rules consists of a left-hand side (LHS) and a right-hand side (RHS) separated by an arrow (LHS → RHS). The LHS consists of a shape and a marker, whereas the RHS depicts how it is transformed through the application of a rule. Figure 2 illustrates examples of two simple shape rules that generate grid systems (5×3 and 5×4) from an initial shape (*I*).

Knight (1999) suggests there are six types of Shape Grammars: (i) basic, (ii) non-deterministic basic, (iii) sequential, (iv) additive, (v) deterministic and (vi) unrestricted grammars. The basic grammar has several limits to the way rules are formatted and ordered. For example, "all rules are addition rules (that is, each rule adds a labelled shape). In terms of rule ordering, rules are linearly ordered and each rule applies under one similarity transformation to the labelled shape added by the previous rule" (Knight, 1999, p. 17). The six different grammar types are based on the relationship between formatting and ordering of rules. In addition to types of grammars, Yue and Krishnamurti (2014) record multiple grammatical classifications, which are based on: definition (structure grammars or set grammars); the field of formal linguistics (finite versus infinite grammars); and properties of shape rules or their rule application (non-parametric versus parametric Shape Grammars; marker-driven versus sub-shape-driven Shape Grammars; context-free versus context-sensitive Shape Grammars). Rather than using any of these technical classifications, for the purposes of the present chapter five sub-themes in Shape Grammar research are reviewed hereafter, each of which is classified by application. The five are: theoretical approaches, two-dimensional architectural design, three-dimensional architectural design, urban design, and art and engineering design.

Theoretical Approaches

The first sub-theme in emerging Shape Grammar research is concerned with theoretical developments. For example, Ahmad and Chase (2012) revisit previous design grammars to formally define the concept of style in the design languages generated using grammatical means. Their research addresses the use of geometric transformations to encapsulate changes in a style or design language. Their starting point is the assumption that "a design style is actually a set that overlaps with the set of designs generated by a grammar" (Ahmad & Chase, 2012, p. 496). They also propose a style description scheme for comparing aesthetic qualities of grammatical elements. Al-kazzaz and Bridges (2012) present a framework for four types of adaptation in Shape Grammars. The first is adaptation techniques, including transformation, substitution and hybridisation. The second is adaptation strategies, which includes where to locate and how to build. The third is adaptation tools, which encompasses rule format, rule order and grammar structure. The last is adaptation output, meaning whether it produces an original grammar or a new adapted grammar. Al-kazzaz and Bridges (2012) argue that transformation is the most dominant adaptation technique and the other techniques typically support transformation. The prevailing strategies use attached adaptation and incremental design approaches to synthesise new adapted designs. The dominant adaptation tools are parametric variation and specifications variation. The adaptation is achieved by implementing a new adapted grammar for new and existing designs. Ibrahim and Chase (2017) suggest that using a Shape Grammar as a design tool, alongside other conventional and creative design techniques, could provide a more comprehensive and viable model for developing students' design competencies. In a related way, Ashton (2010) proposes integrating access graph modelling and Shape Grammars in a mathematics class. She argues that Frank Lloyd Wright's architectural designs, which are partially developed using Froebel block kindergarten toys as models, can be used to illustrate the rules of symmetry.

Liu, Zhang, Kong, Zou and Zeng (2018) review spatial-enabled grammars with a focus on Shape Grammars and spatial graph grammars. Their grammar uses façade images as input and applies rules to divide the input image into semantically meaningful rectangles (windows, walls, floors). The generative part of their grammar is used for "scene reconstruction" for building model generation. For example, the split grammar (Wonka, Wimmer, Sillion, & Ribarsky, 2003) divides a façade hierarchically in a top-down manner, whereas the Computer Generated Architecture (CGA) Shape Grammar (Müller, Wonka, Haegler, Ulmer, & Gool, 2006), which enables automatic rule derivation (so-called "procedural modelling'), generates large urban models. To compare different spatially-enabled grammars, Liu et al. (2018) propose four criteria: (i) parsing and generation, (ii) granularity of spatial specification, (iii) form of spatial specification and (iv) two-dimensional and three-dimensional modelling. The parsing process supports interpretation and validation of the internal structure of an input graph, while the generation process develops an unlimited set of designs that observe the given requirements. Granularity deals with spatial relations defined in terms of discrete values (directions such as north and south) or continuous values (such as coordinates). The third criteria, the form of spatial specification, is concerned with visualising the specification of spatial relations, while the last, "two-dimensional and three-dimensional modelling", considers the extension of the definition of shapes in grammars from two- to three-dimensional Euclidean space.

Two-Dimensional Architectural Design

Shape Grammars for two-dimensional architectural design languages have been a common topic of research since the late 1970s and they continue to be to the present day. In the majority of cases, these are grammars for analysing and generating architectural plans. For example, Benrós, Duarte and Hanna (2012) develop a new Palladian Shape Grammar as an alternative to the Palladian grammar originally presented by Stiny and Mitchell (1978). The alternative grammar employs different parametric shape rules in its methodology. Its initial stage sets the rectangular boundary (originally the "grid definition" stage) and then encompasses subdivision rules (horizontal and vertical division). The fourth stage of the original grammar was "interior-wall realignment", whereas the fourth stage of the new grammar involves "wall thickening", which is converting the basic single line wall into a wall with depth or thickness. In this way, they explore a new corpus of solutions and argue that the new subdivision rules allow for a more economical formulation, compared with the original Palladian grammar. Eilouti and Hamamieh Al Shaar (2012) develop a Shape Grammar of traditional Damascene houses which defines the vocabulary of elements and types for each part of the house plan. Rules in the grammar are associated with numerical parameters based on a mathematical analysis of the building type. In addition to using the grammar as an analytical tool, it can also derive new emergent designs that belong to the same architectural style. In a similar way, Yavuz and Bülüç (2014) analyse the design language of Ankara Yenimahalle residences using a Shape Grammar. Their analysis considers three main parameters: relationship between indoor-and outdoor spaces, plan analysis (functional analysis) and circulation units (shaping stairs).

Eloy and Duarte (2015) develop a descriptive transformation grammar for a specific housing type in Lisbon known as "*rabo-de-bacalhau*". After identifying and encoding the principles and rules embodied in the existing houses, their grammar is used to support the adaptation of existing buildings to serve new functions. Erem and Abbasoğlu Ermiyagil (2015) revisit the architectural language of the planning of Turkish vernacular houses (existing vernacular housing grammar) and generate new designs with adapted shape rules (adapted housing design grammar) to create contemporary equivalents of vernacular architecture. They analyse spatial organisations, dimensional requirements and shape rules in their housing grammar and then create a socially and physically adapted grammar using new vocabulary elements. Ligler and Economou (2016) present a Shape Grammar for American architect John Portman's design language. Their parametric Shape Grammar, which seeks to capture the compositional logic of Portman's *Entelechy I,* consists of four stages: framework, configuration, style and termination. The first rule of the first stage (framework) identifies the initial shape and compositional centre of a design and then develops an initial grid from the centre. The second stage adds spatial variety and generates the basic configuration of a design (for example, private family and public entertaining areas). The third stage defines exterior and interior details to finalise the architectonic style of the design. The final stage of the grammar terminates the production process, removing labels and layers. In this way, the grammar generates the original design as well as its variations.

Lambe and Dongre (2017) develop a Shape Grammar for the planning of a traditional *Pol* house in Ahmedabad, India. Their grammar consists of thirteen different stages of grammar formulation, from "placement of the *chowk* (courtyard)" to "rules for the roof". The grammar is used for analysing the existing architectural style and then generating new designs in this style. In their research, context is explored as part of the grammar of the surrounding built forms because it is the physical context for the new development. That is, the Shape Grammar interprets the context as a socio-cultural experience as well as identifying contemporary demands and needs. Griz, Amorim, Mendes, Holanda and Carvalho (2017) propose a grammar to describe the customisation process required for apartment planning in Recife, Brazil. Their research framework consists of three phases, development of an analytical grammar of original designs (ODs), development of a customisation grammar, and development of a grammar of ODs with high potential for customisation. The customisation grammar highlights four groups of spatial alteration rules,

Figure 3. An example of the generation processes of a three-dimensional Shape Grammar

| Module and block | Composition | Roof type |

which are rules of agglutination (SR_A), of division (SR_D), of scalar change (SR_{SC}) and of label change (R_{LC}).

Three-Dimensional Architectural Design

Despite their inherent complexity, Shape Grammars that encompass three-dimensional properties are being continuously developed in architectural and urban design and they have also recently been applied to engineering design and in virtual environments. One example of a three-dimensional Shape Grammar for analysing an architectural language was developed by Lee, Ostwald, and Gu (2015) to investigate Glenn Murcutt's domestic architecture. This grammar, which is developed in a later chapter of the present book, consists of four shape- or form-related generation processes: module, block, composition and roof configuration. The three-dimensional basis for this is a block system, like the Froebel kindergarten system used by Frank Lloyd Wright (Koning & Eizenberg, 1981). The Murcutt grammar also determines the material types of blocks (open, transparent, semi-transparent and solid) and roof shapes (flat, shed, gable, hipped and butterfly roofs).

Quattrini and Baleani (2015) describe the use of a three-dimensional Palladian grammar for modelling the architect's unbuilt designs. They present a framework for the *Barchessa* model of the *Villa Thiene*, highlighting the use of dimensional and geometric data from a site survey, combined with a three-dimensional model and a geoweb model (using the Google Earth platform). Their framework has a three-part sequential process: knowledge, representation and dissemination data. In their study, the structure of the Shape Grammar uses a pre-established set of tree-shaped formal rules. The modelling of the *Villa Thiene* involves, (i) a semantic model partitioning of the main body, (ii) a hierarchical "parent-child" structure, and (iii) composite order proportioning. A KMZ file (a google earth file), obtained from the Andrea

Palladio three-dimensional-Geodatabase and its adopted Shape Grammar (Apollonio, Corsi, Gaiani, & Baldissini, 2010), allows for dissemination of the three-dimensional model on the web. Apollonio, Gaiani and Benedetti (2012) also present a three-dimensional, reality-based artefact model for the management of archaeological sites. Their method uses a semantic reality-based structure for the digital reconstruction, classification, management and visualisation processes. While their system uses three-dimensional GIS, it can be combined with a Shape Grammar. In contrast, Tumbeva, Wang, Sowar, Dascanio and Thrall (2016) propose a "quilt-inspired engineering" design strategy for generative structural design for temporary military or disaster relief sheltering. Their motivation is to optimise structural forms to incorporate a consideration of both manufacturing and constructability properties. Using a series of quilt-inspired concepts (Alaska homesteads, sawtooth stars and card tricks) they develop a structural topology using Shape Grammar rules. These rules consist of three categories: two-dimensional rules (adding or subtracting lines and surfaces), a functional rule (determining the purpose of a surface) and three-dimensional rules (dictating how the two-dimensional pattern becomes three dimensional). They evaluate the quilt-inspired forms generated using the grammatical rules using measures of global drift, buckling, weight per area and manufacturing efficiency.

Urban Design

One important expansion of the Shape Grammar approach is in the field of urban design. Mandić and Tepavčević (2015) conducted a critical review of grammatical approaches to urban design, identifying two main approaches: grammars based on sets of specific, pre-existing designs and generic or context-independent grammars. The former is suitable for a particular local context with a strong urban design language, whereas the latter can be used for a variety of contexts, being more flexible and adaptable for specific user needs. Two grammars that are included in the latter approach are Computer Generated Architecture (CGA), used in CityEngine software, and Grammars for Designing (GfD) for CityMaker software. Mandić and Tepavčević suggest that CGA is more flexible as it is based on "general rule types which enable free creation of project specific patterns" (2015, p. 685). Such software packages use variations of procedural modelling algorithms (Grêt-Regamey, Celio, Klein, & Wissen Hayek, 2013; Neuenschwander, Wissen Hayek, & Grêt-Regamey, 2014), to generate urban patterns. This approach, which has connections to grammatical thinking, is discussed in more detail in later sections of the present chapter.

In another example of an urban Shape Grammar, Beirão, Duarte, Stouffs and Bekkering (2012) generate design patterns that they call "urban induction patterns". Their system uses GIS-based assessment tools for context analysis and allows for the fast generation of alternative designs. As such, it can be regarded as a design support tool as well as a design decision support tool. Their discursive grammar accommodates the reflective structure found in the typical design process. In contrast, Gong, Li, Liu and Wang (2018) present two bottom-up Shape Grammars; a "context-free grammar" for orthogonal urban landscape and a "context-sensitive grammar" for non-orthogonal urban patterns. The former is used for dense, aggregated built forms, while the latter is used for interactions between streets and plots. They use both grammars to formulate a hypothetical self-build process in two stages: grammar derivation and designer intervention. Laurini (2017) also employs Shape Grammars to analyse urban or territorial structures with a focus on geographic objects and complex structures.

Art and Engineering

The last sub-category of Shape Grammar research in design analysis and generation covers applications in art and engineering design. Like the earliest Shape Grammars (Stiny & Gips, 1972), Lee, Park, Lim and Kim (2013) present a descriptive grammar for a traditional Korean pattern known as "bosangwhamun" (BSWM). They do this by using a hierarchical deconstruction of the pattern into global and local geometry. The global geometry of the pattern is generated using a set of rules over 12 steps, taking into account both the symbolic structure and the construction method of BSWM. The local geometry is a product of the formal relationship between the basic elements defined by the global geometry. This approach supports their investigation of the evolutionary development of this Korean pattern and the generation of its variations. Gürsoy and Özkar (2015) present a Shape Grammar for generating *dukta* patterns (transformations of visual shapes) and material manipulations (transformations of material shapes), which allow for creatively exploring the physical character of the material. Muslimin (2017) develops a design grammar for passura (ornamental engravings) of the Toraja people, an ethnic group indigenous to South Sulawesi, Indonesia. The grammar uses the logic of the imagery in the passura to generate new compositions that are similar to traditional passura designs. Guo, Lin, Xu and Jin (2014) develop a Shape Grammar tailored for the generation of three-dimensional monsters ('creature grammar') for the arts, cinema and gaming. Their goal is to support the creative design of a large collection of various unexpected, but still visually plausible, creatures.

Hyun, Lee, Kim and Cho (2015) develop a hybrid methodology for quantification and analysis of design styles. Their analysis involves the use of a taxonomic evaluation method and a numeric style evaluation method. A mixture of Fourier decomposition, eye tracking and grammatical analysis is used to evaluate similarities, visual significance and combinations of nineteen automotive design elements. The hybrid style quantification methodology highlights the use of a similarity index of design elements, weighting elements (visual significance of car parts) and brand synthesis and analysis. Their method can be used to synthesise alternative designs within a brand's design styles and evaluate design trends. Aqeel (2015) also develops a Shape Grammar for automotive design, focussing on Porsche and its brand hierarchy. In Aqeel's grammar, "Porsche DNA" is defined by extracting key characteristics of previous Porsche designs. The Porsche grammar consists of two sets of rules, feature creation and feature modification. The former can generate all previous Porsche models, while the latter generates similarly shaped features, allowing for variability. Bluntzer, Ostrosi and Sagot (2014) also use a Shape Grammar to analyse automotive styling. After extracting seven characteristic lines, they generate an average line of French cars and compare its properties with those of an average line of German cars.

One emerging area of grammatical research in design is concerned with evaluation and optimisation. Grammars, and parametric processes, can be used to create new instances of a design language, but how do we know which of the new instances are more or less important or useful? Ozdemir and Ozdemir (2017) employ two multi-criteria decision-making (MCDM) techniques – fuzzy analytic hierarchy process (AHP) and fuzzy analytic network process (ANP) – to evaluate planning alternatives generated using a Shape Grammar. Their approach uses a generalised Choquet integral method to consider interactivity between main criteria and sub-criteria in a grammar (Y. Ozdemir & S. Ozdemir, 2017). Furthermore, Shape Grammars may be employed to reduce the number of unconventional designs or non-compliant shapes developed in a parametric or emergent process. In structural engineering, shape annealing is a method that combines Shape Grammars and a stochastic search algorithm to ensure the outcomes satisfy an optimisation criterion (Cagan & Mitchell, 1993; Lee, Mueller, & Fivet, 2016). The following section deals with the topic of optimisation in grammatical processes, focusing on automated design and generative algorithms.

AUTOMATED DESIGN AND GENERATIVE ALGORITHMS

In the field of Computer-Aided Design (CAD) Shape Grammars are often associated with automated design and generative algorithms (Singh & Gu, 2012). For example, recent Shape Grammar studies employ generative algorithms to automatically create design variations as well as to optimise or evaluate them. This section of the chapter reviews Shape Grammar research with a focus on four perspectives: design automation, procedural modelling, genetic algorithms, and other algorithmic generation and evaluation. The first point of view, design automation, presents an overview of automated design research, while the other three perspectives deal with more practical applications and algorithms.

Design Automation

Because a Shape Grammar has both a defined set of rules and a behaviour engine to determine how the rules are applied, its outcomes are necessarily constrained and, within limits, predictable. In contrast, a human designer might need to explore the impact of a new rule on their architectural language before determining if it makes a positive contribution or not. As such, Hou and Stouffs (2018) highlight the need for developing an algorithmic design grammar that maps design logic or knowledge onto the development and organisation of rules. Their assessment of the issue identifies five key issues – fixed (inputs), flexible elements (variables), evolution direction, generation mechanism and control techniques – required to automate the application of a grammar's rules into an algorithmic pattern (sequence, selection and iteration). Alternative design grammars are then demonstrated using different deductive strategies (spread, centrifugal and centrifugal-most-constrained) to show how new rules may be tested, adopted or rejected in a grammatical structure. Sönmez (2018) offers a historical survey of the approaches taken to automating architectural design tasks. This survey starts with the way a traditional Shape Grammar uses a "style" as raw data for a production method. In general, the process of automation using "case-based" and "similarity-based" design elevation and generation is a common one that has developed over several stages. The key stages include, the introduction of the split grammar (Wonka, et al., 2003) and procedural modelling studies, followed by automated Shape Grammar extraction, computer vision and semantic modelling and machine learning for design generation. Sönmez's (2018) review confirms that initial manual or graphic Shape Grammars have now given way to automated systems that are reliant on the capabilities of computer hardware and software. Furthermore, case-based automation processes can evolve through the use of AI techniques and similarity-based evaluation – which compares candidate image textures (or designs) with target images (or designs) to determine which of them are more desired – and can be extended to include similarity-based evolution and similarity-based generation. Machine learning and computer vision are also potential intermediaries for connecting multiple related generative and grammatical approaches.

Sass (2008) presents a "physical" production system (a design grammar) for layered manufacturing machines, considering automated translation from a surface to a series of objects – from an initial shape in CAD to its subdivision into interlocking objects. The physical design grammar starts with a solid model in CAD and sub-divides the initial shape into a grid that can be translated into objects that are produced by layered manufacturing and hand assembly. In this way, the grammar supports the automated generation of higher-level objects within the physical production system. Merrick, Isaacs, Barlow and Gu (2013) present a framework for a procedural content generation (PCG) system and demonstrate it with a Shape Grammar "designer application", generating instances for use in MMORPGs (massively multiplayer online role-playing game). PCG is typically defined as the programmatic generation or adjustment of the content of a computer game environment. It is used to automatically generate new designs that capture the usefulness and value of existing designs, as well as introducing novel or surprising variations. The Shape Grammar designer application consists of six steps: (i) selecting the starting position, end position, non-player character and object shapes; (ii) creating compound-shapes; (iii) defining shape rules; (iv) a completed grammar, ready to generate and "plot" new designs; (v) setting relative shape frequencies and selecting the generation type; and (vi) a generated design. Their application also combines the generative shape grammar formalism with the Wundt curve model, plotting interest against novelty. In this way, the PCG system can "automate the process of analysing and decomposing an existing design, extracting design knowledge and creating new designs" (Merrick, et al., 2013, p. 126).

Procedural Modelling

Procedural modelling, as part of an automatic generative grammar, is widely used for creating three-dimensional geometries using a series of instructions, rules or algorithms (Müller et al., 2006; Wonka et al., 2003). As an example, Tepavčević and Stojaković (2013) present a solution for the automated virtual reproduction of typological and stylistic varieties in architecture. They apply a procedural modelling algorithm, based on a statistical and fuzzy inference approach, to automated simulation of the characteristics of a group of buildings. The statistical and fuzzy inference is demonstrated with the probabilities of each analysed shape attribute of Neo-Gothic chapels. To express the [0, 1]-fuzzy set grade that each building has in a fuzzy set, correction factors are also calculated from the relation of relative frequencies for each building's property. Using the Computer Generated Architecture (CGA) grammatical programming rules within the framework of CityEngine software, they generate three-dimensional mass models that represent the typical appearance of an architectural type and its procedural variations. As another example of the combination of procedural and grammatical approaches, Hohmann, Havemann, Krispel and Fellner (2010) present a Generative Modelling Language (GML) grammar for semantically enriched three-dimensional building models. This language, which is based on a split grammar, highlights a unified view of grammars and imperative modelling (beyond conventional shape grammars, which are typically declarative). CityEngine software focuses more on the random generation of large-scale city models, while Hohmann et al.'s method supports practical reconstruction of a complex facility with interiors. It is demonstrated with a detailed case study of facility surveillance as a practical application. In a related way, Kim and Wilson (2015) present a framework for potential three-dimensional indoor routing applications using existing data sources and tools. They use CityEngine and the CGA Shape Grammar to generate an interior and exterior building models using CAD files and building footprints. The use of CityEngine's output (WebGL) is also demonstrated as a cross-platform, open-source library. Grêt-Regamey, et al. (2013) further suggest an interactive procedural modelling workflow consisting of (i) encoding shape grammars based on design specifications and landscape ecological pattern-process relations for quantifying ecosystem services (ES), (ii) GIS-based three-dimensional procedural modelling, and (iii) pattern evaluation with interactive rulers showing ES provision. They highlight the importance of assessing ES trade-offs in different urban designs for sustainable urban planning. Their approach is demonstrated with a case study in Abu Dhabi, Masdar City. Their interactive visualisation approach is connected to parametric shape grammars for the design of generative urban patterns as well as the reporting of urban ES.

Thaller, Krispel, Zmugg, Havemann and Fellner (2013) develop a new method using split operations on convex polyhedra (not a bounding box) for procedural modelling of architecture. Past generative research could be described as being reliant on a box grammar (a parametric Shape Grammar), where each shape is primarily characterised by its bounding box. In contrast, Thaller et al. suggest using a convex polyhedra-based definition of a non-terminal shape that consists of an arbitrary label L, a convex polyhedron S (called the scope), a rigid transformation C that defines a local coordinate system, arbitrary geometry, G, and a set A of user-defined named attributes (name-value pairs). That is, the A non-terminal shape is a tuple (L, S, C, G, A). Split operations on convex polyhedra enable a volumetric decomposition into convex elements and arbitrary planes. Their research implements a straightforward context-free Shape Grammar interpreter based on the scripting language GML. Edelsbrunner, Havemann, Sourin and Fellner (2017) address round geometries in procedural modelling whose main components are coordinate system, scope, shape, split tree, operator, rule function and alignment element. A multitude of operators allows for the modification of shapes, scopes and coordinate systems. Important operators include sub-divide, repeat, call-rule, bounds-expand, fit-cylindrical-into-cartesian, fit-pointed-arch-into-cartesian and wrap-cartesian-over-cylindrical. While the most common approach to the procedural generation of architecture employs a split grammar and a scripting approach, Edelsbrunner et al's method creates shapes with different coordinate systems automatically and allows users to specify high-level input to arrange procedurally generated elements. Conversely, Krecklau and Kobbelt (2012) also use procedural modelling to create complex and detailed objects and scenes, highlighting both the professional mode (P-Mode) and the high-level mode (HL-Mode). The P-Mode, which is the text-based authoring of procedural models, is used to implement high-level primitives (HL-Primitives) that have a well-defined set of parameters to create a specific class of geometric objects. In contrast, the HL-Mode, which consists of three interaction concepts (replacement, parameter adjustment and local modifications), provides an easily operated program combining any of the existing modules. Krecklau and Kobbelt's approach allows for the intuitive and interactive creation, modification and composition of complex procedural grammars. Neuenschwander, et al. (2014)

use procedural modelling and visualisation for developing alternative urban design patterns (in particular, urban green spaces) where multiple ecosystem services (ES) should be provided. They suggest the integration of ES into procedural three-dimensional modelling and visualisation, enabling a close collaboration between stakeholders. In their system, green spaces are mapped with information on ES and their parameters, and designs of the green space types are described using a form-based code. They claim that the procedural model allows for more rapid interactive visualisation of urban patterns and calculation of simple indicator values about offering ES.

Genetic Algorithm

Genetic algorithms use bio-inspired "operators" including "mutation", "crossover" and "selection" to evolve or generate new states or instances, which are also called "reproductions" (Mitchell, 1996). Mutation occurs when one or more variables in the genetic information (or grammatical rules) are modified to create a new variation of an existing state. Crossover occurs when genetic information from two states or outcomes is combined to create a third. Selection is the process wherein certain genetic states or outcomes are isolated because they possess properties that are useful for mutation of crossover operations.

"Genetic algorithms search for an optimal solution by checking the fitness of a set of individuals and creating a next generation from these" (Granadeiro, Pina, Duarte, Correia, & Leal, 2013, p. 377). Following a Darwinian analogy, those individuals that perform at a higher level have a greater probability of being used to generate the next level of outputs. "This arises from the application of the variation operators, crossover and mutation, to the genotypes of the selected individuals. The crossover operator generates a genotype "child" with genes from two "parents" and the mutation operator modifies the value of each gene of a genotype" (Granadeiro, et al., 2013, p. 377). Gero and Kazakov (2001) highlight the analogues of evolutionary operators to find a population of states in a search space that optimise a fitness function. As such, the genotype space is mapped onto a phenotype search space and "fitness" is a function of a state in the phenotype space. A genotype is the genetic constitution of a design, rather than its physical appearance, while a phenotype is related to the observable properties of a design, being generally its form (Gero & Kazakov, 2001). Lee, Herawan and Noraziah (2012) present an evolutionary grammar-based design framework, combining a Shape Grammar with evolutionary computing. The evolutionary computing (algorithmic based) framework enhances the generative capability of the Shape Grammar. Thus, the genetic algorithm defines a new combination of shape features, which extends the traditional grammar to an interactive context combining generative and evolutionary computing methods. Lee et al. (2012) finally suggest the use of three strategies to support a creative design process: (i) potential use of three-dimensional Shape Grammar and additional grammar; (ii) loose fit rules and organic growth of rules and; (iii) product form exploration and product design strategies.

Granadeiro, Duarte, Correia and Leal (2013) develop a Shape Grammar-based parametric design system as a methodology to assist design decision-making for architectural façades. Interestingly, they apply the methodology to a grammar for Frank Lloyd Wright's prairie houses (Koning & Eizenberg, 1981). Although the Prairie house grammar is a parametric Shape Grammar, they convert it into a parametric design system consisting of a geometric model that comprises the topological relations between various parts of designs and their dimensional variations. The parametric design system generates alternative envelope shape designs, and an integrated energy simulation in the design system calculates the energy demand of each design. Thus, their design system allows both early design generation and automated energy simulation. They also examine the ideal envelope (building shape) for low energy demand, using stochastic optimisation algorithms. For the implementation of the genetic algorithms, they present a general representation that uses standard variation operators (crossover and mutation) and defines both continuous and discrete variables from a single type of gene. Lee, et al., (2016) also develop a grammar-based design methodology as an alternative to the conventional parametric design paradigm. Their method uses an automatic random generation algorithm (not a generic algorithm) and a shape grammar to generate a diverse range of structures, all of which feature equilibrium conditions under graphic statics (a graphical method of computing forces and equilibrium for discrete structures under axial loads).

Kitchley and Srivathsan (2014) present a design tool that uses several generative methods for settlement planning. The generative methods include: (i) allocation of each design element's space and geometry; (ii) defining the rules, constraints and relationships governing the elements of design; (iii) the purposeful search for better alternative solutions, and; (iv) quantitative evaluation of the solution based on spatial, comfort and complexity criterions to ensure the usability of the solutions. Grammatical geometric optimisation and genetic algorithms are integrated in this approach into the generative methods.

The solutions are produced by using genetic algorithms to deduce design solutions in the predefined solution search space. The genetic algorithm's search mechanism is supported by the classic evolutionary operators: crossover and mutation. For example, mutation occurs when a function randomly selects the highest fitness value, a lower fitness value solution and a sub-zone. The fittest solutions are reproduced, and the solutions are weighted in terms of their fitness levels. The solutions with higher fitness are then weighted with a higher probability. In this way, the genetic algorithm produces a series of new design solutions, while the final suitable solution is determined by the user's preferences and objectives. In engineering design, Franco, Duarte, Batista and Landesmann (2014) propose a cold-formed steel (CFS) Shape Grammar to support simplicity of implementation and customisation. For optimisation, they employ a genetic algorithm that can operate over populations (sets) of solutions. Franco and Batista (2017) also present a CFS grammar to analyse and improve buckling behaviour and structural strength of thin-walled stiffened trapezoidal CFS.

Other Algorithmic Generation and Evaluation

Although both procedural modelling algorithms and genetic algorithms have been applied to grammatical applications, several alternative automated systems have also been used to generate, optimise and evaluate design variations. For example, Shea, Ertelt, Gmeiner and Ameri (2010) develop a new approach and framework for design-to-fabrication automation. Their framework for Computer Numerical Controlled (CNC) machining uses Shape Grammars and automated fixture design. An ontological approach to automated material and workpiece selection is a key requirement in autonomous design-to-fabrication. Their material selection algorithm has two steps: classification and ranking. In their Shape Grammar, a finite set of shapes (vocabulary) is used to encode the volume that can be removed within a single operation by the machine tool. Ruiz-Montiel et al. (2013) propose a new approach for complementing the generative power of Shape Grammars using reinforcement learning techniques. Their system is used for the computational design problem of automatic, partially-directed generation of design alternatives. A simple, or "naïve", Shape Grammar system is used to generate a large variety of different designs, and this process is guided using reinforcement learning techniques to ensure the outcomes satisfy given design requirements (being, in this case, a design guide created for a regional government in Andalusia,

Spain). The naïve grammar, which generates planning layouts for single-family housing units, consists of six phases: (i) generation of a contour, (ii) labelling the distribution hall, (iii) placing the kitchen modules, (iv) placing the bathroom modules, (v) labelling non-specialised spaces, and (vi) labelling the entrance. In Ruiz-Montiel et al.'s method, policies are learnt automatically in the algorithmic system through provision of rewards.

Veloso, Celani and Scheeren (2018) develop a generative application, a design customisation system, for the generation of plan layouts as well as for the production of construction documents. The workflow of their system starts with the architect defining the Shape Grammar's rules for generating plans and then a user interface for allowing future home-owners to interactively customise their apartment plans in accordance with the grammatical rules. Finally, the plans are automatically converted into Building Information Models (BIM) models, which allow for the addition of custom finishes, estimating building costs, and generating construction drawings automatically. Their rule-based system supports two classes of rules: division and union, creating a shape-action graph, representing a shape-action graph in CAD, and translating geometry into object-oriented code. Since a Grasshopper definition connects the CAD representation of the shape-action graph with the plan customisation GUI and BIM (i.e., Grasshopper to ArchiCAD), a new GUI and interoperability are carefully considered in their system. Finally, they suggest three recommendations to support the implementation of interactive custom architectural design. First, the use of a generative or grammatical tool that has the capacity to develop and define project-specific rules. Second, the need for a simplified representation of an architectural plan that can be translated into a BIM model. Third, "a customisable and intuitive online user interface that could be used by customers for both the design iteration process and to test different combinations of finishes and dimensions" (Veloso, et al., 2018, p. 235).

A further recent research trend has been the use of sub-shape detection algorithms to explore emergent design variations. Trescak, Esteva and Rodriguez (2012) develop a general Shape Grammar interpreter that is programmed for multiple operating systems. It enables the automatic synthesis of designs (rectilinear forms) and user's active participation in the generation process. Two algorithms, "tree-search based algorithms" and "subshape detection algorithm", are implemented in their interpreter for grammatical design generation. The tree-search algorithms store the state of the generation process in a hierarchical graph-like structure which suggests the next rule to apply. The optimised sub-shape detection algorithm supports real time execution and detection of sub-shapes of existing shapes. Thus, the latter algorithm can produce a wider set of designs and potentially more appealing ones. Trescak et al. also suggest a performance evaluation method for the proposed algorithms.

Jowers, Prats, McKay and Garner (2013) develop a prototype shape exploration system for a two-dimensional vector-based sketch editor using an eye tracking interface. Since human gaze is an implicit indicator of attention and intention, eye tracking could be a viable interface for such a process. The eye tracking interface enables interpretations of generated shapes and sub-shape selection using a shape library with a sub-shape detection algorithm. In a related way, Ruiz-Montiel et al. (2014) develop a ShaDe system, a new computer-aided conceptual design (CACD) tool built for the commercial CAD software SketchUp. ShaDe provides a general editor and interpreter of two-dimensional shape rules, logic predicates (constraints and goals), and layers, automatically offering multiple feasible design alternatives. They suggest a layered sub-shape detection algorithm with procedures for integrating logic design constraints and goals. Their system decomposes the underlying shape grammar into layers to reduce the computational "cost" of algorithms for grammar interpretation. After demonstrating the system with two cases, they claim that their layered approach not only leads to a considerable improvement in time performance but also presents several important advantages for knowledge specification.

Cui and Tang (2013) present a two-level generative Shape Grammar for Zhuang ethnic embroidery. A coarse level in their grammar defines the structure and skeletal framework, while a refined level determines embodiment issues (for instance, petal shapes and colours) for every segment specified at the former level. For its computational implementation, they employ a "detection algorithm" for the sub-shape detection problem, and a "B-spline knot interpolation algorithm" to generate embroidery instances. To find the best solution from the potentially numerous alternatives produced using this system, they use a generative system for aesthetic evaluation based on four dimensions: structure, element, complexity and subjective. Cui and Tang argue that such a generative system could support designers in their creative processes.

An optimisation technique for design generation and evaluation is an essential component in many recent Shape Grammar applications. Youssef, Zhai and Reffat (2018) present an optimisation method and design tool for Building Integrated Photovoltaics design from a given building envelope design with specified design targets or criteria. In their optimisation framework, the first section, "main inputs", considers the initial shape (for example, rectangle, L-shape and U-shape), details and required criteria, and generates a large number of alternatives. It also selects optimal values in terms of building energy consumption using a generic algorithm. Then, energy consumption simulation of the initial shape is conducted using a DOE-2 engine (building energy analysis software). Their method then combines optimisation of building geometry (using the DOE-2 engine) and surfaces to be integrated with photovoltaics using a "system advisor model". Ang, Ng and Pham (2013) combine an optimisation technique (the Bees Algorithm) with a Shape Grammar to develop a computational architecture that generates branded design concepts satisfying a specified functional requirement. The combination of the Bees Algorithm and Shape Grammar not only generates a family of new design concepts that maintain the product brand identity, but also fulfils specified functional requirements of a product. Grzesiak-Kopec and Ogorzalek (2014) present a flexible software architecture framework to support three-dimensional layout design for different engineering design assignments. Their framework is demonstrated using three-dimensional integrated circuit (IC) layout design. An optimisation search algorithm enables an efficient search of large and discontinuous spaces (problem formulation) and both evaluating design alternatives and evolving designs states are used to identify promising solutions.

Nandi, Siddique and Cengiz Altan (2011) present a new approach, based on Shape Grammars, for the design of composite material products. Their grammatical approach generates the shape of a component and selects appropriate composite materials to achieve various property performance goals. Their approach has four phases: functional design, form design, material and loading design, and laminate design. In the material and loading design phase, basic knowledge in mechanics is used to define the rules of the Shape Grammar and determine the possible critical sections of the loaded component. The composite material selection and customisation processes are then conducted using three sub-approaches: weight efficiency, manufacturing efficiency and cost efficiency. Smith and Ceranic (2008) develop a knowledge-based computer design environment (so-called "SGEvac') for generating multiple spatial layout solutions with effective fire evacuation analysis. Their system provides for automatic generation of solutions at the preliminary design level and a method for quantitative assessment of fire evacuation simulations. Its Shape Grammar and functional logic design rules incorporate design knowledge and guidance. Their system consists of three modules, "expert knowledge", "layout" and "testing" modules. The expert knowledge module develops design knowledge – for example, fire strategy design (based on London underground station planning standards and guidelines), feasibility studies, project brief requirements, passenger flow data, infrastructure size calculation and high-level brief development – to facilitate accurate Shape Grammar generations of layout design. With this knowledge supplied, the grammar generations commence in the layout module consisting of three steps, layout composition, production and analysis. Layout composition deals with area and adjacency planning and layout option appraisal, while layout production generates multiple layouts using Shape Grammar rules. Layout analysis conducts layout interrogations and design team judgement. The last testing module uses the fire evaluation simulation Simulex, a building evacuation modelling software package. This system also follows the guided generation-evaluation process using automatic design generation and evaluation guided by design knowledge or algorithms.

These automated design and generative algorithms in Shape Grammar applications are applied using algebraic descriptions of shapes. Thus, the final perspective of this literature survey on recent Shape Grammar approaches is the algebraic grammar.

ALGEBRAIC SHAPE GRAMMARS

As the previous sections have revealed, automated design methods and generative algorithms are typically based on computational frameworks using algebraic shape grammars. This algebraic framework itself is an emerging topic in grammatical research. The present section reviews recent articles which address the algebraic nature of grammatical methods.

Since the first Shape Grammar (Stiny & Gips, 1972) used algebraic descriptions and operations, many grammars have explored the algebraic nature of grammatical computing. For example, Stouffs (2016a) reviews the formal notation of descriptions and description rules in grammars, identifying eighteen schemes. He also revisits selected applications of description grammars and redevelops them using a general notation system, highlighting descriptions as expressions, verbal descriptions as reflections, descriptions as a design brief and descriptions as a generative guide (Stouffs, 2017b).

In a typical algebraic framework for a grammar, an algebra X_{ij} formalises the interaction of i-dimensional elements on a j-dimensional space (Stiny, 1991). That is, a shape algebra U_{ij} represents "a finite set of geometric elements defined in dimension i, $i = 0, 1, 2,$ or 3, and manipulated in dimension j, $j \geq$

i. The elements are: points for $i = 0$; lines with finite, nonzero lengths for $i = 1$; planes with finite, nonzero areas for $i = 2$; or solids with finite, nonzero volumes for $i = 3$" (Krstic, 2001, p. 152). Keles, Özkar and Tari (2012) propose a technical framework that transforms a U_{12} shape into a W_{22} shape (defining the entire canvas as a weighted shape) and detects embedded parts in a Seljuk two-dimensional geometric pattern. Their method consists of two parts, a weight function (locally identifying shapes and their part relations) and a genetic algorithm (efficiently matching parts of shapes). MacLachlan and Jowers (2016) also employ weights in shape computations to explore multi-material surfaces. In their research, w is assigned a value between 1 and 100 ($0 < w \leq 100$), which means that when $w = 100$, the material is black and very soft and flexible, while when $w = 1$, the material is near-white, very hard and rigid. They also suggest that other material properties can be defined in such a way, as W_{ij} algebras.

In a recent study, Stouffs and Krishnamurti (2018) present a uniform characterisation of augmented shapes and review different shape attribute propositions from previous Shape Grammars. Their research is based on an algebraic introduction of shapes and attributes and an exploration of the partial order relations underlying the algebraic representation of shapes. Based on a graph grammar, Grasl and Economou (2013) develop a Shape Grammar library (called "GRAPE') that facilitates grammatical implementations. Their method supports both emergent sub-shapes in the algebras of design U_{1j} – shapes consisting of lines in two-dimensional or three-dimensional space – and parametric rules based on isomorphic sub-graph recognition. Kotsopoulos, Carra, Graybill and Casalegno (2014) develop a dynamic façade pattern grammar consisting of a calculating part (engaging an algebraic framework) and a syntactic–interpretive part. The latter addresses "production rules confining the syntactic (structure) and semantic (meaning) attributes of sets of products, which are conventionally called *languages*" (Kotsopoulos et al., 2014, p. 693). Their approach allows the state of dynamic façade patterns to be configured based on both performance and aesthetic criteria.

Knight and Stiny (2015) present an algebra for the making of objects, or things. "Like Shape Grammars, making grammars have rules of the form A → B. A and B are things, and the arrow → is a formal replacement operation …The replacement operation (→) is a general operation which subsumes all kinds of doings and sensings, whether simultaneous or independent" (Knight & Stiny, 2015, p. 15). They argue that designing is a kind of making and an activity engaging with materials in the world. Importantly, Woodbury (2016) notes that "conventional Shape Grammars are not very appealing in practice" and that "parametric Shape Grammars are difficult to implement" in practice. Furthermore, the majority of Shape Grammar interpreters "work across representations that lack, in some way, the property of emergence in their representations … Consequently, researchers can (and do) devise grammars but cannot readily use those grammars to generate designs, having to write special-purpose, often unvalidated, code to do so" (p. 152). Woodbury (2016) introduces shape schema grammars to generalise parametric Shape Grammars, expressing both rules and the objects using schemata that capture a class of shapes. He concludes that "shape schema grammars provide the first general algorithm for parametric grammatical action over shape-like objects" (Woodbury, 2016, p. 178). Conversely, Yue and Krishnamurti have published research about tractable grammars (Krishnamurti & Yue, 2015; Yue & Krishnamurti, 2013, 2014). They review previous Shape Grammar definitions with a focus on marker-driven and sub-shape-driven grammars. In their studies, parametric sub-shape recognition is non-deterministic polynomial time that is barely tractable. They identify three factors that influence the tractability of a Shape Grammar: (i) computational complexity of the basic operations (e.g., t, $-$, $+$, $\leq$, and R); (ii) number of matching candidates; (iii) indeterminacy – number of possible transformations for each matching candidate (Yue & Krishnamurti, 2013). As for practical grammar interpreters, they suggest three sub-framework exemplars – rectangular, polygonal and graph sub-frameworks – which support practical parametric grammars by sub-dividing grammars into sub-classes of tractable grammars. Each sub-framework consists of an underlying data structure, manipulation algorithms and a metalanguage. Their tractable grammars highlight the rectangular sub-framework, relying on a graph-like data structure. "Graph grammars are most useful", they conclude, "when dealing with those Shape Grammars which are dimensionless and context free" (Yue & Krishnamurti, 2014, p. 117). Importantly, they consider three distinct frameworks, "*rectangular*, for grammars that are primarily directed at generating plans; *polygonal*, for designs essentially determined by subdivision; and *graph*, for shapes specified by topological relationships" (Krishnamurti & Yue, 2015, p. 977). Finally, they develop and encode a new tractable Shape Grammar for the Baltimore vernacular rowhouse using their rectangular framework. The tractable Shape Grammar comprises 26 rules over five phases, while the Baltimore rowhouse grammar is further developed into 52 rules over eight phases (Krishnamurti & Yue, 2015).

CONCLUSION

This chapter has reviewed emerging Shape Grammar research focusing on three themes: design analysis and generation, automated design and generative algorithms, and algebraic Shape Grammars. In each case the chapter has introduced key concepts, and summarised new developments. The first of the three themes could be regarded as the traditional domain of grammatical research in architecture and design, and, as such, it has not developed at the same rate as the other themes. The second theme, which is concerned with automation, procedural modelling and generative algorithms has, not surprisingly, been a major source of growth and innovation. Advances in software and hardware in the last decade have provided scholars with many new tools to transform grammars from largely manual graphical or logical systems into software applications that can be used by designers and their clients. The last theme, algebraic thinking in grammatical research, has also begun to make a significant contribution to design automation and optimisation. The algebraic expressions of graph grammars also provide a fundamental basis for the new methods developed in the present book. Section 3 of this book develops and applies a combined Shape Grammar and Space Syntax approach that builds on recent advances into algebraic grammars (Lee, Ostwald, & Gu, 2015, 2018). But before this new method is introduced, the following chapter, Chapter 3, describes an example of a design grammar (a simple Palladian grammar) and then presents a new approach to visually and mathematically analyse the properties of design instances of this language. Alternative designs within this language are also developed based on distinct rule set properties. The design grammar is an example of a two-dimensional architectural shape grammar discussed in the chapter, and the computational approaches are closely related to a generative algorithm approach to analysis and generation, also introduced in this chapter.

REFERENCES

Ahmad, S., & Chase, S. C. (2012). Style representation in design grammars. *Environment and Planning. B, Planning & Design*, *39*(3), 486–500. doi:10.1068/b37074

Al-kazzaz, D. A., & Bridges, A. H. (2012). A framework for adaptation in Shape Grammars. *Design Studies*, *33*(4), 342–356. doi:10.1016/j.destud.2011.11.001

Ang, M. C., Ng, K. W., & Pham, D. T. (2013). Combining the Bees Algorithm and Shape Grammar to generate branded product concepts. *Proceedings of the Institution of Mechanical Engineers. Part B, Journal of Engineering Manufacture, 227*(12), 1860–1873. doi:10.1177/0954405413494922

Apollonio, F. I., Corsi, C., Gaiani, M., & Baldissini, S. (2010). An integrated 3D geodatabase for Palladio's work. *International Journal of Architectural Computing, 8*(2), 111–133. doi:10.1260/1478-0771.8.2.111

Apollonio, F. I., Gaiani, M., & Benedetti, B. (2012). 3D reality-based artefact models for the management of archaeological sites using 3D Gis: A framework starting from the case study of the Pompeii archaeological area. *Journal of Archaeological Science, 39*(5), 1271–1287. doi:10.1016/j.jas.2011.12.034

Aqeel, A. B. (2015). Development of visual aspect of Porsche brand using CAD technology. *Procedia Technology, 20,* 170–177. doi:10.1016/j.protcy.2015.07.028

Ashton, B. A. (2010). Integrating elements of Frank Lloyd Wright's architectural and decorative designs in a liberal arts mathematics class. *Journal of Mathematics and the Arts, 4*(3), 143–161. doi:10.1080/1751347 2.2010.492029

Beirão, J., Duarte, J., Stouffs, R., & Bekkering, H. (2012). Designing with urban induction patterns: A methodological approach. *Environment and Planning. B, Planning & Design, 39*(4), 665–682. doi:10.1068/b38052

Benrós, D., Duarte, J. P., & Hanna, S. (2012). A new Palladian Shape Grammar: A subdivision grammar as alternative to the Palladian grammar. *International Journal of Architectural Computing, 10*(4), 521–540. doi:10.1260/1478-0771.10.4.521

Bluntzer, J.-B., Ostrosi, E., & Sagot, J.-C. (2014). Styling of cars: Is there a relationship between the style of cars and the culture identity of a specific country? *Proceedings of the Institution of Mechanical Engineers. Part D, Journal of Automobile Engineering, 229*(1), 38–51. doi:10.1177/0954407013517221

Cagan, J., & Mitchell, W. J. (1993). Optimally directed shape generation by shape annealing. *Environment and Planning. B, Planning & Design, 20*(1), 5–12. doi:10.1068/b200005

Cagdas, G. (1996). A Shape Grammar: The language of traditional Turkish houses. *Environment and Planning. B, Planning & Design*, *23*(4), 443–464. doi:10.1068/b230443

Cui, J., & Tang, M.-X. (2013). Integrating Shape Grammars into a generative system for Zhuang ethnic embroidery design exploration. *Computer Aided Design*, *45*(3), 591–604. doi:10.1016/j.cad.2012.08.002

Cui, J., & Tang, M.-X. (2014). Representing 3D Shape Grammars in a generative product design system. In J. S. Gero (Ed.), *Design Computing and Cognition "12* (pp. 377–392). New York: Springer. doi:10.1007/978-94-017-9112-0_21

Edelsbrunner, J., Havemann, S., Sourin, A., & Fellner, D. W. (2017). Procedural modeling of architecture with round geometry. *Computers & Graphics*, *64*, 14–25. doi:10.1016/j.cag.2017.01.004

Eilouti, B. H., & Hamamieh Al Shaar, M. J. (2012). Shape Grammars of traditional Damascene houses. *International Journal of Architectural Heritage*, *6*(4), 415–435. doi:10.1080/15583058.2011.575530

Eloy, S., & Duarte, J. (2011). A transformation grammar for housing rehabilitation. *Nexus Network Journal*, *13*(1), 49–71. doi:10.100700004-011-0052-x

Eloy, S., & Duarte, J. P. (2015). A transformation-grammar-based methodology for the adaptation of existing housetypes: The case of the "rabo-de-bacalhau". *Environment and Planning. B, Planning & Design*, *42*(5), 775–800. doi:10.1068/b120018p

Erem, Ö., & Abbasoğlu Ermiyagil, M. S. (2015). Adapted design generation for Turkish vernacular housing grammar. *Environment and Planning. B, Planning & Design*, *43*(5), 893–919. doi:10.1177/0265813515600442

Flemming, U. (1990). Syntactic structures in architecture: teaching composition with computer assistance. In M. McCullough, W. J. Mitchell, & P. Purcell (Eds.), *The electronic design studio: Architectural knowledge and media in the computer era* (pp. 31–48). Cambridge, MA: MIT Press.

Franco, J. M. S., & Batista, E. M. (2017). Buckling behavior and strength of thin-walled stiffened trapezoidal CFS under flexural bending. *Thin-walled Structures*, *117*, 268–281. doi:10.1016/j.tws.2016.11.027

Franco, J. M. S., Duarte, J. P., Batista, E. M., & Landesmann, A. (2014). Shape Grammar of steel cold-formed sections based on manufacturing rules. *Thin-walled Structures*, *79*, 218–232. doi:10.1016/j.tws.2014.01.005

Gero, J. S., & Kazakov, V. (2001). A genetic engineering approach to genetic algorithms. *Evolutionary Computation*, *9*(1), 71–92. doi:10.1162/10636560151075121 PMID:11290285

Gong, Q., Li, J., Liu, T., & Wang, N. (2018). Generating urban fabric in the orthogonal or non-orthogonal urban landscape. *Environment and Planning B. Urban Analytics and City Science*, *2399808318761667*. doi:10.1177/2399808318761667

Granadeiro, V., Duarte, J. P., Correia, J. R., & Leal, V. M. S. (2013). Building envelope shape design in early stages of the design process: Integrating architectural design systems and energy simulation. *Automation in Construction*, *32*, 196–209. doi:10.1016/j.autcon.2012.12.003

Granadeiro, V., Pina, L., Duarte, J. P., Correia, J. R., & Leal, V. M. S. (2013). A general indirect representation for optimization of generative design systems by genetic algorithms: Application to a Shape Grammar-based design system. *Automation in Construction*, *35*, 374–382. doi:10.1016/j.autcon.2013.05.012

Grasl, T., & Economou, A. (2013). From topologies to Shapes: Parametric Shape Grammars implemented by graphs. *Environment and Planning. B, Planning & Design*, *40*(5), 905–922. doi:10.1068/b38156

Grêt-Regamey, A., Celio, E., Klein, T. M., & Wissen Hayek, U. (2013). Understanding ecosystem services trade-offs with interactive procedural modeling for sustainable urban planning. *Landscape and Urban Planning*, *109*(1), 107–116. doi:10.1016/j.landurbplan.2012.10.011

Griz, C., Amorim, L., Mendes, L., Holanda, M. A., & Carvalho, T. (2017). A Customization Grammar: Describing the customization process of apartment design. *International Journal of Architectural Computing*, *15*(3), 203–214. doi:10.1177/1478077117734671

Grzesiak-Kopec, K., & Ogorzalek, M. J. (2014). Computer-aided 3D ICs layout design. *Computer-Aided Design and Applications*, *11*(3), 318–325. doi:10.1080/16864360.2014.863503

Guo, X., Lin, J., Xu, K., & Jin, X. (2014). Creature grammar for creative modeling of 3D monsters. *Graphical Models*, *76*(5), 376–389. doi:10.1016/j.gmod.2014.03.019

Gürsoy, B., & Özkar, M. (2015). Visualizing making: Shapes, materials, and actions. *Design Studies*, *41*, 29–50. doi:10.1016/j.destud.2015.08.007

Hohmann, B., Havemann, S., Krispel, U., & Fellner, D. (2010). A GML Shape Grammar for semantically enriched 3D building models. *Computers & Graphics*, *34*(4), 322–334. doi:10.1016/j.cag.2010.05.007

Hou, D., & Stouffs, R. (2018). An algorithmic design grammar for problem solving. *Automation in Construction*, *94*, 417–437. doi:10.1016/j.autcon.2018.07.013

Hyun, K. H., Lee, J.-H., Kim, M., & Cho, S. (2015). Style synthesis and analysis of car designs for style quantification based on product appearance similarities. *Advanced Engineering Informatics*, *29*(3), 483–494. doi:10.1016/j.aei.2015.04.001

Ibrahim, M. S., & Chase, S. C. (2017). Digital tools devising pedagogical approaches: Exploring the potential of rule-based design in developing student competencies. *International Journal of Parallel, Emergent and Distributed Systems, 32*(sup1), S89-S100. doi:10.1080/17445760.2017.1390096

Jowers, I., Prats, M., McKay, A., & Garner, S. (2013). Evaluating an eye tracking interface for a two-dimensional sketch editor. *Computer Aided Design*, *45*(5), 923–936. doi:10.1016/j.cad.2013.01.006

Keles, H. Y., Özkar, M., & Tari, S. (2012). Weighted shapes for embedding perceived wholes. *Environment and Planning. B, Planning & Design*, *39*(2), 360–375. doi:10.1068/b37067

Kim, K., & Wilson, J. P. (2015). Planning and visualising 3D routes for indoor and outdoor spaces using CityEngine. *Journal of Spatial Science*, *60*(1), 179–193. doi:10.1080/14498596.2014.911126

Kitchley, J. J. L., & Srivathsan, A. (2014). Generative methods and the design process: A design tool for conceptual settlement planning. *Applied Soft Computing*, *14*, 634–652. doi:10.1016/j.asoc.2013.08.017

Knight, T. W. (1994). *Transformations in design: A formal approach to stylistic change and innovation in the visual arts.* Cambridge, MA: Cambridge University Press.

Knight, T. W. (1999). Shape Grammars: Six types. *Environment and Planning. B, Planning & Design*, *26*(1), 15–31. doi:10.1068/b260015

Knight, T. W., & Stiny, G. (2015). Making grammars: From computing with shapes to computing with things. *Design Studies*, *41*, 8–28. doi:10.1016/j.destud.2015.08.006

Koning, H., & Eizenberg, J. (1981). The language of the prairie: Frank Lloyd Wright's prairie houses. *Environment & Planning B*, *8*(3), 295–323. doi:10.1068/b080295

Kotsopoulos, S. D., Carra, G., Graybill, W., & Casalegno, F. (2014). The dynamic façade pattern grammar. *Environment and Planning. B, Planning & Design*, *41*(4), 690–716. doi:10.1068/b38121

Krecklau, L., & Kobbelt, L. (2012). Interactive modeling by procedural high-level primitives. *Computers & Graphics*, *36*(5), 376–386. doi:10.1016/j.cag.2012.03.028

Krishnamurti, R., & Yue, K. (2015). Developing a tractable Shape Grammar. *Environment and Planning. B, Planning & Design*, *42*(6), 977–1002. doi:10.1177/0265813515610673

Krstic, D. (2001). Algebras and grammars for shapes and their boundaries. *Environment and Planning. B, Planning & Design*, *28*(1), 151–162. doi:10.1068/b2681

Lambe, N. R., & Dongre, A. R. (2017). A Shape Grammar approach to contextual design: A case study of the Pol houses of Ahmedabad, India. *Environment and Planning B. Urban Analytics and City Science*, 2399808317734207. doi:10.1177/2399808317734207

Laurini, R. (2017). Complex geographic objects and structures. In R. Laurini (Ed.), *Geographic knowledge infrastructure* (pp. 139–156). Elsevier. doi:10.1016/B978-1-78548-243-4.50007-4

Lee, H. C., Herawan, T., & Noraziah, A. (2012). Evolutionary grammars based design framework for product innovation. *Procedia Technology*, *1*, 132–136. doi:10.1016/j.protcy.2012.02.026

Lee, J., Mueller, C., & Fivet, C. (2016). Automatic generation of diverse equilibrium structures through Shape Grammars and graphic statics. *International Journal of Space Structures*, *31*(2-4), 147–164. doi:10.1177/0266351116660798

Lee, J. H., & Gu, N. (2018). A design grammar for identifying spatial uniqueness of Murcutt's rural houses. In J.-H. Lee (Ed.), *Computational studies on cultural variation and heredity* (pp. 189–203). Singapore: Springer Singapore. doi:10.1007/978-981-10-8189-7_15

Lee, J. H., Ostwald, M. J., & Gu, N. (2015). A syntactical and grammatical approach to architectural configuration, analysis and generation. *Architectural Science Review*, *58*(3), 189–204. doi:10.1080/00038628.2015.1015948

Lee, J. H., Ostwald, M. J., & Gu, N. (2018). A Justified Plan Graph (JPG) grammar approach to identifying spatial design patterns in an architectural style. *Environment and Planning B. Urban Analytics and City Science*, *45*(1), 67–89. doi:10.1177/0265813516665618

Lee, J.-H., Park, H.-J., Lim, S., & Kim, S.-J. (2013). A formal approach to the study of the evolution and commonality of patterns. *Environment and Planning. B, Planning & Design*, *40*(1), 23–42. doi:10.1068/b38102

Ligler, H., & Economou, A. (2016). Entelechy revisited: On the generative specification of John Portman's architectural language. *Environment and Planning B. Urban Analytics and City Science*, *45*(4), 623–648. doi:10.1177/0265813516676489

Liu, Y., Zhang, K., Kong, J., Zou, Y., & Zeng, X. (2018). Spatial specification and reasoning using grammars: From theory to application. *Spatial Cognition and Computation*, *18*(4), 315–340. doi:10.1080/13875868.2018.1490290

MacLachlan, L., & Jowers, I. (2016). Exploration of multi-material surfaces as weighted shapes. *Graphical Models*, *83*, 28–36. doi:10.1016/j.gmod.2015.07.002

Mandić, M., & Tepavčević, B. (2015). Analysis of Shape Grammar application as a tool for urban design. *Environment and Planning. B, Planning & Design*, *42*(4), 675–687. doi:10.1068/b130084p

Merrick, K. E., Isaacs, A., Barlow, M., & Gu, N. (2013). A Shape Grammar approach to computational creativity and procedural content generation in massively multiplayer online role playing games. *Entertainment Computing*, *4*(2), 115–130. doi:10.1016/j.entcom.2012.09.006

Mitchell, M. (1996). *An introduction to genetic algorithms*. Cambridge, MA: MIT Press.

Müller, P., Wonka, P., Haegler, S., Ulmer, A., & Gool, L. V. (2006). Procedural modeling of buildings. *ACM Transactions on Graphics, 25*(3), 614–623. doi:10.1145/1141911.1141931

Muslimin, R. (2017). Toraja Glyphs: An ethnocomputation study of Passura indigenous icons. *Journal of Asian Architecture and Building Engineering, 16*(1), 39–44. doi:10.3130/jaabe.16.39

Nandi, S., Siddique, Z., & Cengiz Altan, M. (2011). A grammatical approach for customization of laminated composite materials. *Concurrent Engineering, 19*(2), 157–174. doi:10.1177/1063293X11406146

Neuenschwander, N., Wissen Hayek, U., & Grêt-Regamey, A. (2014). Integrating an urban green space typology into procedural 3D visualization for collaborative planning. *Computers, Environment and Urban Systems, 48,* 99–110. doi:10.1016/j.compenvurbsys.2014.07.010

Ozdemir, S., & Ozdemir, Y. (2017). Prioritizing store plan alternatives produced with Shape Grammar using multi-criteria decision-making techniques. *Environment and Planning B. Urban Analytics and City Science, 45*(4), 751–771. doi:10.1177/0265813516686566

Ozdemir, Y., & Ozdemir, S. (2017). Extended prioritizing of store plan alternatives produced with Shape Grammar using the generalized Choquet integral method. *Environment and Planning B. Urban Analytics and City Science, 2399808317739892.* doi:10.1177/2399808317739892

Quattrini, R., & Baleani, E. (2015). Theoretical background and historical analysis for 3D reconstruction model. Villa Thiene at Cicogna. *Journal of Cultural Heritage, 16*(1), 119–125. doi:10.1016/j.culher.2014.01.009

Ruiz-Montiel, M., Belmonte, M.-V., Boned, J., Mandow, L., Millán, E., Badillo, A. R., & Pérez-de-la-Cruz, J.-L. (2014). Layered Shape Grammars. *Computer Aided Design, 56,* 104–119. doi:10.1016/j.cad.2014.06.012

Ruiz-Montiel, M., Boned, J., Gavilanes, J., Jiménez, E., Mandow, L., & Pérez-de-la-Cruz, J.-L. (2013). Design with Shape Grammars and reinforcement learning. *Advanced Engineering Informatics, 27*(2), 230–245. doi:10.1016/j.aei.2012.12.004

Sass, L. (2008). A physical design grammar: A production system for layered manufacturing machines. *Automation in Construction, 17*(6), 691–704. doi:10.1016/j.autcon.2007.12.003

Shea, K., Ertelt, C., Gmeiner, T., & Ameri, F. (2010). Design-to-fabrication automation for the cognitive machine shop. *Advanced Engineering Informatics*, *24*(3), 251–268. doi:10.1016/j.aei.2010.05.017

Singh, V., & Gu, N. (2012). Towards an integrated generative design framework. *Design Studies*, *33*(2), 185–207. doi:10.1016/j.destud.2011.06.001

Smith, G., & Ceranic, B. (2008). Spatial layout planning in sub-surface rail station design for effective fire evacuation. *Architectural Engineering and Design Management*, *4*(2), 99–120. doi:10.3763/aedm.2008.0078

Sönmez, N. O. (2018). A review of the use of examples for automating architectural design tasks. *Computer Aided Design*, *96*, 13–30. doi:10.1016/j. cad.2017.10.005

Stiny, G. (1980). Introduction to shape and Shape Grammars. *Environment and Planning. B, Planning & Design*, *7*(3), 343–351. doi:10.1068/b070343

Stiny, G. (1991). The algebras of design. *Research in Engineering Design*, *2*(3), 171–181. doi:10.1007/BF01578998

Stiny, G., & Gips, J. (1972). Shape Grammars and the generative specification of painting and sculpture. In C. V. Freiman (Ed.), *Information processing 71* (pp. 1460–1465). Amsterdam: North-Holland.

Stiny, G., & Mitchell, W. J. (1978). The Palladian grammar. *Environment & Planning B*, *5*(1), 5–18. doi:10.1068/b050005

Stouffs, R. (2016a). Description grammars: A general notation. *Environment and Planning B. Urban Analytics and City Science*, *45*(1), 106–123. doi:10.1177/0265813516667300

Stouffs, R. (2016b). Description grammars: Precedents revisited. *Environment and Planning B. Urban Analytics and City Science*, *45*(1), 124–144. doi:10.1177/0265813516667301

Stouffs, R., & Krishnamurti, R. (2018). A uniform characterization of augmented shapes. *Computer Aided Design*. doi:10.1016/j.cad.2018.12.004

Tepavčević, B., & Stojaković, V. (2013). Procedural modeling in architecture based on statistical and fuzzy inference. *Automation in Construction*, *35*, 329–337. doi:10.1016/j.autcon.2013.05.015

Thaller, W., Krispel, U., Zmugg, R., Havemann, S., & Fellner, D. W. (2013). Shape grammars on convex polyhedra. *Computers & Graphics*, *37*(6), 707–717. doi:10.1016/j.cag.2013.05.012

Trescak, T., Esteva, M., & Rodriguez, I. (2012). A Shape Grammar interpreter for rectilinear forms. *Computer Aided Design*, *44*(7), 657–670. doi:10.1016/j.cad.2012.02.009

Tumbeva, M. D., Wang, Y., Sowar, M. M., Dascanio, A. J., & Thrall, A. P. (2016). Quilt pattern inspired engineering: Efficient manufacturing of shelter topologies. *Automation in Construction*, *63*, 57–65. doi:10.1016/j.autcon.2015.12.005

Veloso, P., Celani, G., & Scheeren, R. (2018). From the generation of layouts to the production of construction documents: An application in the customization of apartment plans. *Automation in Construction*, *96*, 224–235. doi:10.1016/j.autcon.2018.09.013

Wonka, P., Wimmer, M., Sillion, F., & Ribarsky, W. (2003). Instant architecture. *ACM Transactions on Graphics*, *22*(4), 669–677. doi:10.1145/882262.882324

Woodbury, R. (2016). An introduction to shape schema grammars. *Environment and Planning. B, Planning & Design*, *43*(1), 152–183. doi:10.1177/0265813515610671

Yavuz, A. Ö., & Bülüç, E. (2014). Proposing a model developed by rule based approaches in architectural design education. *Procedia: Social and Behavioral Sciences*, *143*, 334–338. doi:10.1016/j.sbspro.2014.07.415

Youssef, A. M. A., Zhai, Z., & Reffat, R. M. (2018). Generating proper building envelopes for photovoltaics integration with Shape Grammar theory. *Energy and Building*, *158*, 326–341. doi:10.1016/j.enbuild.2017.09.077

Yue, K., & Krishnamurti, R. (2013). Tractable Shape Grammars. *Environment and Planning. B, Planning & Design*, *40*(4), 576–594. doi:10.1068/b38227

Yue, K., & Krishnamurti, R. (2014). A paradigm for interpreting tractable Shape Grammars. *Environment and Planning. B, Planning & Design*, *41*(1), 110–137. doi:10.1068/b39107

Chapter 3
Mathematical Analysis and Generation of Palladian Designs

ABSTRACT

This chapter describes the development of a schematic "Palladian Grammar" for analysing and generating Palladian villa plans. This grammar has four stages using eleven rule sets, which start by generating initial modules and end with the application of a termination rule. Thereafter, the chapter introduces a mathematical approach to measuring and comparing the grammatical properties of selected design instances of Palladian villas. Normalised distance is used to identify the level of disparity implicit in each design instance, relative to the grammatical rule-set. Alternative design instances are generated using rule probabilities to illustrate the transition sequences of the grammar application. The method both generates design instances and measures their grammatical levels of disparity to support the production of more appropriate design instances in the language. The computational techniques provide both a quantitative and qualitative examination of the schematic "Palladian Grammar."

DOI: 10.4018/978-1-7998-1698-0.ch003

INTRODUCTION

This chapter presents a Shape Grammar for analysing and generating Palladian schematic plan layouts. This process involves specifying the set of rules required for this purpose and delineating how these are combined to replicate existing, or create new designs. Conventionally, this process is used to develop insights into a design language and then generate new designs that capture the stylistic characteristics of the original set of works. In the present context, however, the Palladian Grammar is largely used to demonstrate the development of a Shape Grammar for a set of buildings and then provide a new method for improving grammatical applications for design analysis and generation. As such, the grammar's purpose is largely methodological and developmental. The new method is significant because most grammatical analyses are descriptive or focused on the development of definitions of shapes, rules and sequences of the rule application. However, more recent studies have identified the importance of quantitative approaches for design analysis using Shape Grammars (Merrick, Isaacs, Barlow, & Gu 2013). For example, Tepavčević and Stojaković (2013) use mathematical and fuzzy inference measures developed from the frequencies and probabilities of each shape attribute of design instances. They also calculate correction factors based on the relative frequencies for each building's properties. In Eilouti and Hamamieh Al Shaar's research (2012), Shape Grammar rules are associated with numerical parameters developed from a mathematical analysis of a set of domestic designs. More recently, Hyun, Lee, Kim and Cho (2015) present a style analysis method using a similarity index of design elements and weighting elements. Such examples demonstrate the growing importance of quantitative analysis of grammatical data, and the present chapter develops this idea, seeking to enhance the analytical potential of Shape Grammar research as well as providing a more systematic understanding of an entire language.

There is also a further reason for focusing on the mathematical properties of a grammar. Contemporary, generative or procedural grammars can produce a seemingly endless series of compliant instances of a language, even though many are unacceptable or non-viable. Two solutions are typically proposed for this problem. The first defines detailed conditions for each rule during its application (that is, creating conditional rules to limit the generation of non-viable outputs). The second uses a formal guideline for design generation and selection. The former solution, involving detailed conditions, tends to be very complex, because every condition has to be defined in such a way that it can accommodate any other potential rule combination and its affects. Such conditions are often presented in the left-hand side of each rule in a grammar. The latter solution, the use of a formal guideline (which may be scripted using generative or optimising algorithms) remains the subject of more recent scrutiny. For example, recent research demonstrates the use of generative algorithms, stochastic search algorithms and optimisation methods to resolve this problem (Ahmad & Chase, 2012; Ang, Ng, & Pham, 2013; Franco, Duarte, Batista, & Landesmann, 2014; Kitchley & Srivathsan, 2014; J. Lee, Mueller, & Fivet, 2016; S. Ozdemir & Y. Ozdemir, 2017; Y. Ozdemir & S. Ozdemir, 2017; Ruiz-Montiel et al., 2013; Shea, Ertelt, Gmeiner, & Ameri, 2010; Youssef, Zhai, & Reffat, 2018). In a related way, the formal guideline can also be developed by capturing design knowledge (Hou & Stouffs, 2018; Kitchley & Srivathsan, 2014; Merrick et al., 2013; Ruiz-Montiel et al., 2014; Smith & Ceranic, 2008). For example, Smith and Ceranic (2008) develop a Shape Grammar and a set of functional logic rules incorporating design knowledge and guidance. Veloso, Celani and Scheeren (2018) use a shape-action graph to control automatically generated layouts to produce a useful result. In the shape-action graph, each state is a complete layout and a rule is described by a single directed edge. As a further variation of the second approach to increasing the usefulness of the generated outcome, reseachers have examined the syntactical properties of design instances generated by a grammar to select those that are most suitable for functional organisation (Eloy & Duarte, 2011, 2015). As revealed later in this book, a syntactically derived approach to grammatical analysis can also be used to eliminate unnecessary or unconventional design generation (J. H. Lee, Ostwald, & Gu, 2015, 2017, 2018). Despite all of the examples, the two common approaches to controlling design generation – employing detailed constraints and capturing design guidelines – require an often-complex analysis of a given set of designs, which can also result in an overly complicated generation system.

Rather than following either of these paths to resolving the problem, the present chapter adopts a mathematical approach (J. H. Lee & Gu, 2018; J. H. Lee, Gu, & Ostwald, 2016), using normalised distance (*ND*) and transition probability (*T*), to analyse and generate Palladio's architecture. This approach firstly measures the frequencies of the applied rules to generate a set of designs using a descriptive Shape Grammar. The frequencies not only serve as numerical data for describing an individual design and its style, but also provide a guide for design generation within that style. Thus, the information enables measuring and guiding the grammatical application of a set of rules for an architectural language or style. This mathematical approach to the analysis and generation of an architectural design is demonstrated in this chapter using the schematic planning (two dimensional drawings) of ten Palladian villas as encapsulated in a "Palladian Grammar".

Palladian Grammar

In Western architectural history, the villas of Andrea Palladio are famous for their geometric purity and consistency, often being regarded as one of the most important architectural style languages ever produced (Hersey, Freedman, & Palladio, 1992; Williams & Giaconi, 2003). As such, it is not surprising that one of the earliest examples of an architectural Shape Grammar was based on proportions in the planning of Palladio's villas (Stiny & Mitchell, 1978). Since then, multiple Palladian Shape Grammars have been developed for these seemingly simple, but actually quite complex plans. For example, Mitchell (1990) developed a more advanced Palladian Grammar encompassing rules for exterior wall definition and detailing, principal entrances and wall inflections, exterior columns, and windows and doors. George Hersey and Richard Freedman (Hersey et al., 1992) developed the first computer software for generating "possible Palladian villas" and Grasl (2012) presented a Palladian graph grammar to automate its application. Quattrini and Baleani (2015) present a framework for integrating a three-dimensional Palladian Grammar into a GIS model and Benrós, Duarte and Hanna (2012) develop an alternative version of the Palladian grammar originally proposed by Stiny and Mitchell. Benrós et al's grammar seeks to create a more economical production process as well as a means of generating a new corpus of Palladian designs, responding to his less well known "T'-shaped rooms and 3×2 and 3×4 planning grids. Seebohm and Chan (2001) investigate the design space of possible Palladian plans generated from the topologies of the villas *Angarano* and *Badoer*. They examine dimensionality and proportions as well as topology in schematic Palladian plans. While many variations of Palladian Grammars exist, the origins of these grammars, including which designs were used as the basis for their grammatical rules, are often not documented. For this reason, the present chapter develops a simple Palladian Grammar from a corpus of ten villas.

The Palladian Grammar developed in the present chapter follows in the footsteps of both Stiny and Mitchell's (1978) and Benrós et al.'s (2012) grammars. The grid systems that Palladio used to construct his architectural plans repeated a series of distinct ratios; 5×3, 5×4, 3×5, 3×3 and 5×6. While most Palladian plans employ the 5×3 grid system, the 5×4 grid is the second most dominant one, given the body of work typically used to define the Palladian style language. Nonetheless previous Palladian Grammars have largely ignored the 5×4 plans. Thus, the new Palladian Grammar developed in the present chapter differs from previous ones, as it is derived from his two most dominant planning grids (5×3 and 5×4) as recorded in *I Quattro Libri dell'Architettura*.

The ten Palladian villas from *I Quattro Libri dell'Architettura* that are the focus of the new grammar are: 1. *Villa Badoer* (XXXIII), 2. *Villa Zeno* (XXXIV), 3 *Villa Malcontenta* (XXXV), 4 *Villa Pisani* (XXXVII), 5. *Villa Emo* (XL), 6. *Villa Sarraceno* (XLI), 7. *Villa Ragona* (XLII), 8. *Villa Poiana* (XLIII), 9. *Villa Cornaro* (XXXVIII) and 10. *Villa Mocenigo* (XXXIX). The Roman number in capital letters after each villa refers to the plate number of the corresponding villa in *I Quattro Libri dell'Architettura* (Palladio, 1715). Figure 1 illustrates eight cases of Palladian villa plans designed on a 5×3 grid, while Figure 2 shows two cases of Palladian villa plans using a 5×4 grid.

Shape Grammars typically consist of at least three rules: a start rule, a transformational rule, and a termination rule. However, a Shape Grammar for a more detailed or complex set of shapes generally requires a larger number of transformational rules. For example, Hanson and Radford (1986) use more than 60 rules to generate their selected Murcutt designs, while Lambe and Dongre (2017) use 140 rules to generate the compositional form of the traditional India Pol house in Ahmedabad. The Pol Grammar has thirteen stages, from "placement of the chowk (courtyard)" to "rules for the roof". The first stage, as a starting rule, develops a courtyard from a single-point initial shape, with two rules defining two different boundary conditions. Its second stage has six rules to configure a living area, while the third stage consists of seven rules to place a veranda. Some stages of their grammar have more than ten rules. In another example, Eloy's transformation grammar (Eloy & Duarte, 2011, 2015) consists of ten stages, which span from "preparing the floor plan" to "integrating ICAT elements". The configuration of Eloy's grammar starts by defining the kitchen (five rules) and ends with defining the storage spaces (seven rules). In summary, categorising rules commonly follow spatial programs (functions) and the sequence of the rule applications depends on the first rule of each grammar and its design strategy.

In addition to the structure of the grammatical rules, there are two approaches to using the rules to define a design's shape. One commences

Figure 1. Eight cases of Palladian villa plans using a 5×3 grid

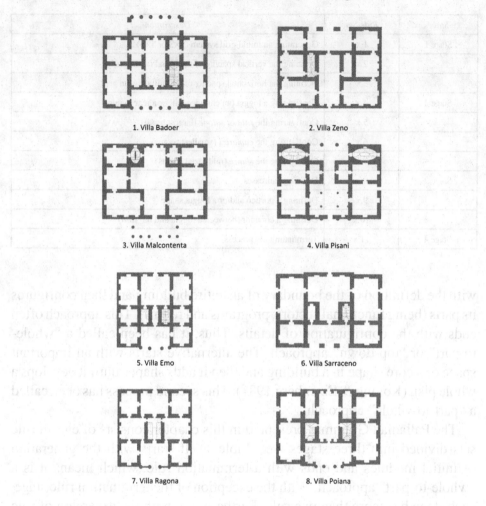

1. Villa Badoer   2. Villa Zeno

3. Villa Malcontenta   4. Villa Pisani

5. Villa Emo   6. Villa Sarraceno

7. Villa Ragona   8. Villa Poiana

Figure 2. Two cases of Palladian villa plans using a 5×4 grid

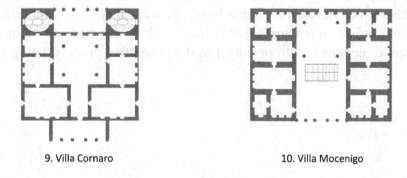

9. Villa Cornaro   10. Villa Mocenigo

Table 1. Four configurational stages of the Palladian Grammar

Stage	Rule Set	Description
Stage 1	1.x	Generating an initial grid system (5×3 or 5×4)
	2.x	Defining the vertical spacing of the initial tartan grid
	3.x	Defining the horizontal spacing of the initial tartan grid
Stage 2	4.x	Configuring a loggia (an entrance hall or a rear loggia)
	5.x	Configuring the *sala* or *salone* (largest room)
	6.x	Configuring the *camerini* (smallest rooms)
	7.x	Configuring the *stanze* (mid-sized rooms)
Stage 3	8.x	Defining staircases
	9.x	Defining a portico and/or a loggia shape
	10.x	Defining a corridor (between a loggia and the *sala*)
Stage 4	11.x	Terminating the process

with the definition of the boundary of an entire building and then configures its parts (being functional sectors, programs and rooms). This approach often ends with the configuration of details. Thus, it has been called a "whole-to-part" or "top-down" approach. The alternative starts with an important space or a core shape in a building and then it adds shapes until it develops a whole plan (Koning & Eizenberg 1981). This second process has been called a "part-to-whole" approach.

The Palladian Grammar presented in this chapter consists of eleven rule sets divided into three stages (see Table 1). It starts with the generation of initial modules and ends with a termination rule, which means it is a "whole-to-part" approach. With the exception of the termination rule stage, each stage has more than one rule. Furthermore, with the exception of rule sets 1, 2, and 4, each rule has multiple sub-rules. These sub-rules categorise topologically and functionally similar configurational rules. For example, rule 7.1 has two sub-rules (7.1.1 to 7.1.2) and rule 7.2 has three sub-rules (7.2.1 to 7.2.3), which develop the same topological configuration with different directions or in different grids (see Figure 7). These sub-rules accommodate different directions (south or north) in the generative process, being used, for example, to differentiate an entry loggia to the south (or front), from one to the north (or rear).

1. The first stage of the Palladian Grammar uses three rules to develop a grid system, to prepare the spatial configuration and define the proportional spacing between the grid lines. This stage creates a "tartan" gridded ordering system for the plan, along with the centre-lines of the potential walls of each villa. The spaces enclosed by the grid lines are called "room cells" and the grammar considers two constant values (a and b) to configure the vertical and horizontal spacing of a grid.

2. The second stage uses four rules to configure the spatial program of the plan. There are four functional room types in the Palladian Villa: the *loggia* (L), for a reception space or hall, *sala* (Sa) for formal gatherings (the largest room), *stanze* (St) for mid-size sitting rooms and the *camerini* (C) for the smallest rooms. The sequence of the rules models the formal growth of the villa plan, step-by-step from the *sala* at the centre to the *stanze* at the either side of a villa. The connections between rooms (doors) are not modelled in this grammar, although additional rules could be developed for this purpose.

3. The third stage, which has three rules, defines the major circulation of the villa. The three rules define: the nature of the loggia or portico, which is usually an extension from the main entrance; three types of staircases (oval, rectangle and open); and a corridor shape that provides a passage between a loggia and the *sala*. In each of these cases, the grammar considers only a simple version of Palladio's elements. For example, Palladio created loggias or porticos with three or five arches (supported on four or six columns), but the present grammar includes only a five-arch portico (supported on six circular columns). There are also small staircases in the villas *Malcontenta* and *Emo*, but the grammar considers only the primary staircases in Palladio's planning some of which are open and others enclosed.

4. The last stage terminates the generation process.

The six shapes that make up the vocabulary of the Palladian Grammar are: room cell, functional room, loggia, portico, staircase and corridor shapes (see Figure 3).

Figure 3. Palladian vocabulary

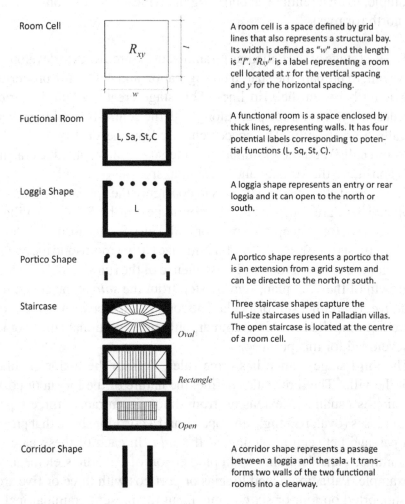

| Room Cell | A room cell is a space defined by grid lines that also represents a structural bay. Its width is defined as "w" and the length is "l". "R_{xy}" is a label representing a room cell located at x for the vertical spacing and y for the horizontal spacing. |

Fuctional Room — A functional room is a space enclosed by thick lines, representing walls. It has four potential labels corresponding to potential functions (L, Sq, St, C).

Loggia Shape — A loggia shape represents an entry or rear loggia and it can open to the north or south.

Portico Shape — A portico shape represents a portico that is an extension from a grid system and can be directed to the north or south.

Staircase — Three staircase shapes capture the full-size staircases used in Palladian villas. The open staircase is located at the centre of a room cell.

Corridor Shape — A corridor shape represents a passage between a loggia and the sala. It transforms two walls of the two functional rooms into a clearway.

Stage 1: Grid Configuration

The first stage of the grammar uses three rule sets to generate a grid system. The first rule set generates an initial grid from a labelled point (I) and with coordinates (x, y). Thereafter, two rules are used to generate two different grid systems (5×3 and 5×4). Figure 4 illustrates the two types of grids. A 5×3 grid has five vertical columns and values (x1 to x5) and three horizontal rows and values (y1 to y3). In the ten Palladian villas in *I Quattro Libri dell'Architettura*, the value of the vertical spacing is from 1/2a to 3a. In

Figure 4. Examples of 5×3 and 5×4 grid systems

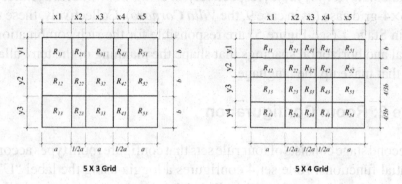

5 X 3 Grid   5 X 4 Grid

contrast, the 5×4 grid has four horizontal columns and values ($y1$ to $y4$) and the value of the horizontal spacing is from b to 2b. A "room cell" is labelled "R_{xy}", where x is the order number of the horizontal spacing of a grid and y is the vertical spacing. For, example, a room cell, R_{32}, is located at $x3$ vertically and $y2$ horizontally.

The Palladian Grammar begins by configuring a tartan grid using either a 5×3 (Rule1.1) or 5×4 grid (Rule1.2). The grid is a simplified rectangular grid, which conforms to the repetitive wall layout found in Palladio's domestic architecture. After the first rule set generates the initial grid, the second rule set configures the vertical spacing. While the dimensions of the enclosed spaces may vary in each of the Palladian villas, the wall layout captures the structural and proportional characteristics of each villa. For example, the villas *Badoer*, *Zeno* and *Malcontenta* (cases 1, 2 and 3 in Figure 1) consist of two types of spacing (a and $1/2a$) and the smaller spacing is used for $x2$ and $x4$, while in the villas *Pisani* and *Emo* (cases 4 and 5 in Figure 1) there are three smaller spacings ($x2$, $x3$ and $x4$). The exact dimensions of room cells are not considered in the grammar to simplify the number of variables used, and the dimensions depend on a variety of design contexts that are not part of the grammar developed at the conceptual design stage. Instead, the rules of the grammar consider Palladio's plan layouts in terms of two simplified constants (a for width, b for length).

There are three rules in the second rule set in Stage 1: Rule2.1 using a, $1/2a$, a, $1/2a$, a for the vertical spacing $x1, x2, x3, x4, x5$, respectively; Rule2.2 using a, $1/2a$, $1/2a$, $1/2a$, a; Rule2.3 using a, $3/2a$, $3a$, $3/2a$, a only for *Villa Mocenigo* (case 10). Next, the third rule set configures the horizontal spacing of the grid, and there are two rules: Rule3.1 using the equally distributed horizontal spacing with the value "b"; Rule3.2 using $b, b, 2b$ (Rule3.2.1) or $2b$,

b, b (Rule3.2.2) for $y1, y2, y3$, respectively, or using $4/3b, 4/3b, b, b$ (Rule3.2.3) for a 5×4-grid case (as in case 9, the *Villa Cornaro*). Collectively, these three rules in Stage 1 (see Figure 5) are responsible for the rich combinations of vertical and horizontal spacings that shape the planning of the ten Palladian villas that make up the language.

Stage 2: Room Configuration

The second stage consists of four rule sets that configure room types according to spatial functions. Rule set 4 configures a loggia using the label "L" as a starting point of the configuration. Rule4.1.1 develops an entrance hall as an entry loggia to the south of a building if Rule3.2 defines a rear loggia room to the north. In one case (*Villa Malcontenta*), the Palladian Grammar skips this fourth rule set. Three room cells in a horizontal spacing to the south or to the north (e.g., R_{23}, R_{33}, R_{43} or R_{21}, R_{31}, R_{41}) are merged into a loggia space (see Figure 6). Rule set 5 defines the *sala* as the largest room in a Palladian villa and consists of four rules. Rule5.1 defines three room cells (e.g., R_{23}, R_{33}, R_{43} or R_{21}, R_{31}, R_{41}) as the *sala* and has two sub-rules: Rule5.1.1 generates the southern *sala* that also functionally serves as a reception room, including a main entrance; Rule5.1.2 defines the northern *sala*. Rule5.2 merges two room cells at the centre horizontal spacing (e.g., R_{31}, R_{32} or R_{32}, R_{33}) into a *sala* and also has two sub-rules: Rule5.2.1 configuring the *sala* at the north of a loggia; Rule5.2.2 configuring the *sala* at the south of a loggia. Rule5.3 defines a "T'-shaped *sala* at the north of a loggia (5.3.1) or at the south of a loggia (5.3.2). In a unique case, *Villa Malcontenta*, Rule5.4 develops a cruciform *sala* across three vertical and horizontal spacings.

Rule set 6 defines the *camerini* (the smallest rooms) in a Palladian villa, which are usually located at both sides of the *sala* because the *camerini* are used for storage, washrooms, servants' rooms or staircases. Rule set 6 consists of five rules (Figure 6): Rule6.1 generating two *camerini* at R_{22} and R_{42} to serve the central *sala*; Rule6.2 generating four *camerini* along both sides of the *sala*; Rule6.3 executing *a skipping rule*; Rule6.4 generating two *camerini* at R_{21} and R_{41} in the northern side of a building; Rule6.5 generating four *camerini* at four corners of a 5×4 grid.

Rule set 7 (see Figure 7), defines the *stanze,* a mid-sized room often serving as a sitting room and usually occupying both sides of a Palladian villa plan. Rule set 7 consists of five rules. Rule7.1 generates four *stanze* by either Rule7.1.1 (two one-cell rooms and two southern two-cell rooms) or

Figure 5. Stage 1, generating a grid system

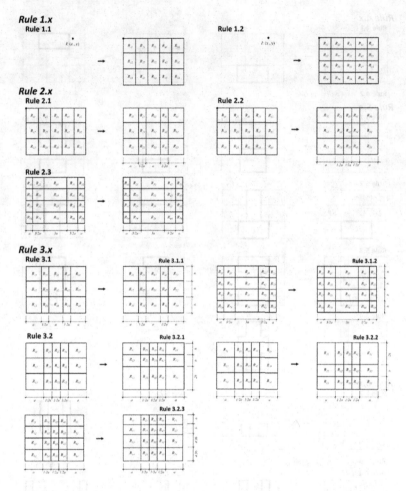

Rule7.1.2 (two one-cell rooms and two northern two-cell rooms). A two-cell room in Rule7.1 consists of two room cells in two horizontal bands of a grid. Rule7.2 generates six (a 5×3 grid) or eight (for a 5×4 grid) *stanze*. Rule7.2.1 generates four one-cell rooms and two southern two-cell rooms, while Rule7.2.2 generates four one-cell rooms and two northern two-cell rooms. Rule7.2.1 generates six one-cell rooms and two southern two-cell rooms for a 5×4-grid villa (*Villa Cornaro*). A two-cell room in Rule7.2 consists of two

Figure 6. Stage 2 (Rule 4.x to 6x), defining functional rooms

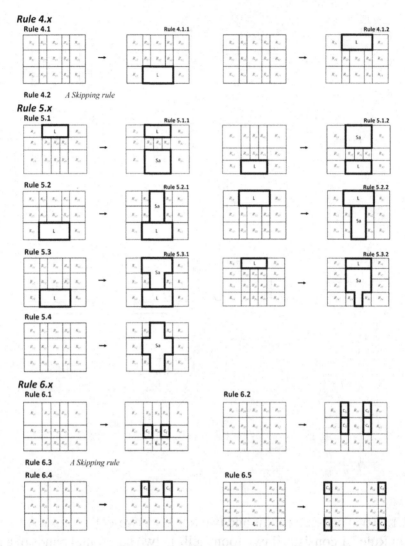

room cells in two vertical bands of a grid. Rule7.3 generates six equal-sized *stanze* along both sides of a building. As for two particular cases, Rule7.4 generates six *stanze*, including two, two-cell rooms at the middle horizontal band and Rule7.5 configures eight *stanze* between the central vertical band and four *camerini* at four corners (see Figure 7).

Figure 7. Defining the stanze (mid-sized rooms)

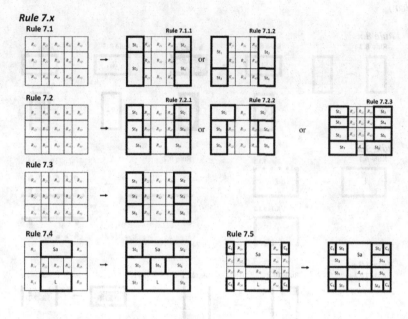

Stage 3: Circulation Definition

The third stage consists of three rule sets. First, defining staircases requires three rules: Rule8.1 defining a rectangular staircase in one of the *camerini*; Rule8.2 defining an oval staircase in one of the *stanze* (Rule8.2.1) or one of the *camerini* (Rule8.2.2); Rule8.3 defining an open staircase at the centre of a room cell. Many cases employ more than one rule in the eighth rule set, because "Palladio always placed stairs symmetrically about the central axis, although in practice both sets of stairs were not always built" (Seebohm & Chan, 2001, p.161). Rule set 9 defines a portico and/or a loggia and consists of two rules: Rule9.1 defining a loggia for a rear entrance (Rule9.1.1) or a front entrance (Rule9.1.2); Rule9.2 defining a portico for a rear façade (Rule9.2.1) or a front façade (Rule9.2.2). Rule set 10 defines a corridor between a loggia and the *sala*, but most of cases do not require this rule. Thus, Rule10.1 is "*a skipping rule*", while Rule10.2 defines this corridor as a room cell (Rule10.2.1) or as a room with an open staircase (Rule10.2.2).

Stage 4: Termination

The final stage of the grammar terminates the generation process, deleting unnecessary labels and lines.

Figure 8. Stage 3, configuring circulation shapes (portico, loggia, staircase, and corridor)

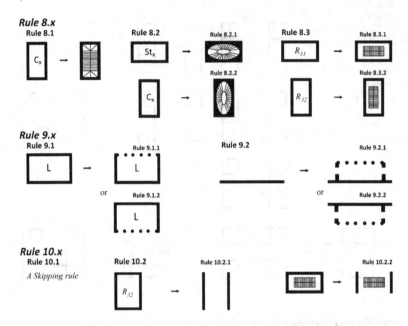

Ten Palladian Villas

The ten Palladian villas which are the basis for this grammar can be described using these rules and stages (Figures 3.9 – 3.13). For example, to describe the first case, *Villa Badoer*, the Palladian Grammar uses Rule1.1, Rule2.1, Rule3.1, Rule4.1, Rules 5.2 (*5.2.1*), Rule6.2, Rule7.1 (*7.1.1*), Rule8.1, Rule9.1 and Rule9.2, and Rule10.1(*a skipping rule*). The *Villa Mocenigo*, employs Rule1.2, Rule2.3, Rule3.1, Rule4.1, Rules 5.1, Rule6.5, Rule7.5, Rule8.3, Rule9.1 and Rule10.2.

The following section develops design knowledge based on these rule applications (frequencies) for generating a set of Palladian villas. The knowledge is developed using the frequencies of applied rules, which is mathematically significant for both design analysis and generation using a Shape Grammar.

Computational Analysis

The results of the Palladian Grammar can be used to mathematically analyse Palladio's designs and generate new designs within his particular style language.

Figure 9. Applied rule sets for generating Villa Badoer (Case 1) and Villa Zeno (Case 2)

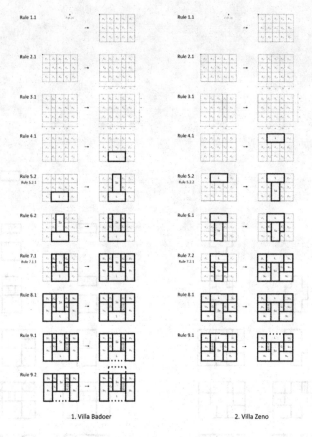

1. Villa Badoer   2. Villa Zeno

The first part of the analysis is concerned with the tendency of rules to be applied to generate the ten selected cases in *I Quattro Libri dell'Architettura* (Figures 3.1 and 3.2), and the second with an alternative way to characterise each case through a computational abstraction using the frequency of applied rule sets, or "normalised distance" (*ND*). This measure, in effect, determines the level of disparity in a design language. *ND* is used to visually illustrate the normalised value, which is an adjusted value to a notionally common scale. The frequencies of the applied rules for design generation are measured per rule in a rule set (or step). However, the number of rules in each rule set is different; that is, the frequencies are measured in different scales. For example, the Prairie grammar by Koning and Eizenberg (1981) uses two rules for locating the fireplace (rule schemata 1 and 2) and four rules for adding a living zone (3 to 6). Thus, the normalisation of the observed frequencies is

Figure 10. Applied rule sets for generating Villa Malcontenta (Case 3) and Villa Pisani (Case 4)

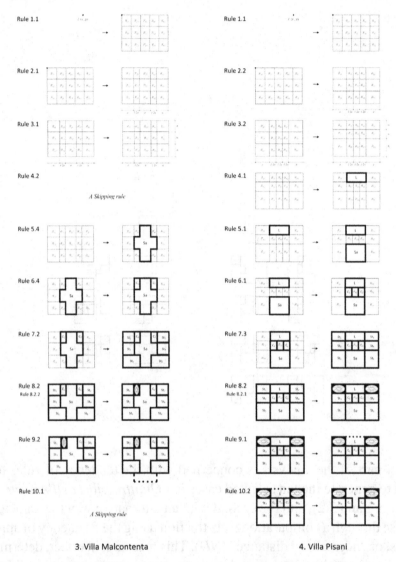

3. Villa Malcontenta

4. Villa Pisani

essential to reveal the level of similarity or disparity of each rule (or design) in a relationship between each rule (or design) and a dominant rule (or design). *ND* can also be used to identify a dominant design in a set of designs that can be understood as a standard language of a design style.

Figure 11. Applied rule sets for generating Villa Emo (Case 5) and Villa Sarraceno (Case 6)

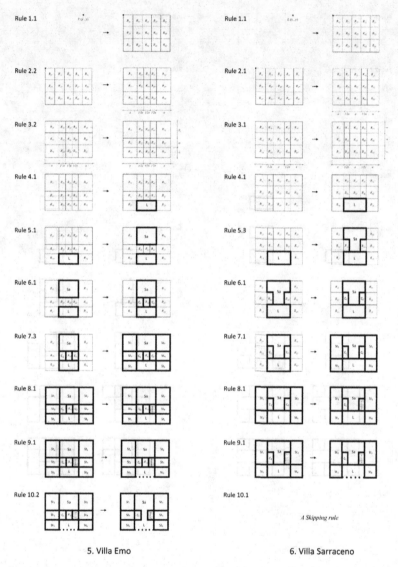

5. Villa Emo   6. Villa Sarraceno

Frequency of Applied Rules

Table 2 illustrates the rules used to generate the ten cases. For example, in order to generate the second case, the *Villa Zeno*, the Shape Grammar uses rules: 1.1, 2.1, 3.1, 4.1, 5.2, 6.1, 7.2, 8.1, 9.1 and 10.1. Across cases 1 to 8, Rule1.1 is applied in the first rule set to generate an initial grid system for a

Figure 12. Applied rule sets for generating Villa Ragona (Case 7) and Villa Poiana (Case 8)

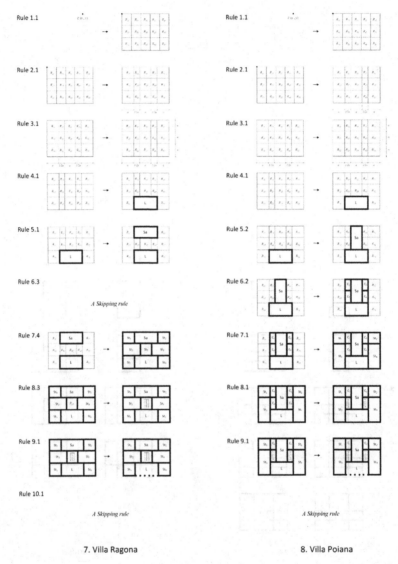

7. Villa Ragona   8. Villa Poiana

5×3-grid villa, while Rule1.2 is used for a 5×4-grid villa (as in cases 9 and 10). This table provides the core information needed to conduct a mathematical analysis of the application of the grammar.

The frequency of the applied rules can be determined within the set of the ten original designs. This information reflects Palladio's tendency to select a particular rule or pattern. In order to effectively investigate this tendency,

Figure 13. Applied rule sets for generating Villa Cornaro (Case 9) and Villa Mocenigo (Case 10)

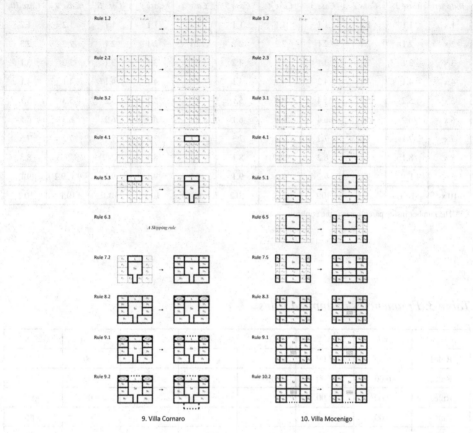

9. Villa Cornaro 10. Villa Mocenigo

the first sorted and applied rules at each step of the grammar are identified. Secondly, the frequency of each applied rule is calculated. Finally, the most frequently applied rule is located in the first sub-set rule (x.1) and the next frequently applied rule is set to the second sub-set rule (x.2). In this way, the research develops Table 3, which records the frequencies of each applied rule, showing that the first sub-set rule (x.1) is the most frequently applied rule in each set. This means the rules closer to the first sub-set rules in each set are more likely to generate archetypes in the original language of design.

Normalised Distance (*ND*)

Using the data in Table 3, it is possible to analyse the application of the grammar and visualise the characteristics of each case (in terms of the grammatical

Table 2. Rules used to generate the original ten cases

Rule set	Case 1	Case 2	Case 3	Case 4	Case 5	Case 6	Case 7	Case 8	Case 9	Case 10
1.x	1.1	1.1	1.1	1.1	1.1	1.1	1.1	1.1	1.2	1.2
2.x	2.1	2.1	2.1	2.2	2.2	2.1	2.1	2.1	2.2	2.3
3.x	3.1	3.1	3.1	3.2	3.2	3.1	3.1	3.1	3.2	3.1
4.x	4.1	4.1	4.2	4.1	4.1	4.1	4.1	4.1	4.1	4.1
5.x	5.2	5.2	5.4	5.1	5.1	5.3	5.1	5.2	5.3	5.1
6.x	6.2	6.1	6.4	6.1	6.1	6.1	6.3	6.2	6.3	6.5
7.x	7.1	7.2	7.2	7.3	7.3	7.1	7.4	7.1	7.2	7.5
8.x	8.1	8.1	8.2	8.2(2)	8.1	8.1	8.3	8.1(2)	8.2(2)	8.3
9.x	9.1, 9.2	9.1	9.2	9.1	9.1	9.1	9.1	9.1	9.1, 9.2	9.1
10.x	10.1	10.1	10.1	10.2	10.2	10.1	10.1	10.1	10.1	10.2

* The number inside parenthesis is the application number.

Table 3. Frequencies of applied rules

Rule set	x.1	x.2	x.3	x.4	x.5	Mean	SD
Rule1	8.00	2.00	-	-	-	5.00	4.24
Rule2	6.00	3.00	1.00	-	-	3.33	2.52
Rule3	7.00	3.00	-	-	-	5.00	2.83
Rule4	9.00	1.00	-	-	-	5.00	5.66
Rule5	4.00	3.00	2.00	1.00	-	2.50	1.29
Rule6	4.00	2.00	2.00	1.00	1.00	2.00	1.22
Rule7	3.00	3.00	2.00	1.00	1.00	2.00	1.00
Rule8	6.00	5.00	2.00	-	-	4.33	2.08
Rule9	9.00	3.00	-	-	-	6.00	4.24
Rule10	7.00	3.00	-	-	-	5.00	2.83

design process). Table 4 shows the *ND*s that are calculated using the applied rule's normalised frequency in relation to the rule that is most frequently applied. Each normalised value – normalised A = (A − mean)/SD) (Bilda & Gero, 2007; J. H. Lee & Gu, 2018) – indicates the standardised frequency based on each mean frequency.

Each rule's *ND* is then calculated using the absolute value of each normalised frequency subtracted from the normalised value of the most frequently applied

Table 4. Normalised distance (ND) of each applied rule set

Rule set	x.1	x.2	x.3	x.4	x.5
Rule1	0.00	1.41	-	-	-
Rule2	0.00	1.19	1.99	-	-
Rule3	0.00	1.41	-	-	-
Rule4	0.00	1.41	-	-	-
Rule5	0.00	0.77	1.55	2.32	-
Rule6	0.00	1.63	1.63	2.45	2.45
Rule7	0.00	0.00	1.00	2.00	2.00
Rule8	0.00	0.48	1.92	-	-
Rule9	0.00	1.41	-	-	-
Rule10	0.00	1.41	-	-	-

rule. The sub-set rules of each rule set are already ordered by the applied frequency in Palladio's ten houses (see Table 3). That is, sub-set rule $Rule_{x.1}$ is the most frequently applied rule in each rule set. Thus, the *ND* of the frequency of one of the rules $Rule_{x.y} \in Rule_x$ is:

$$ND\left(Rule_{x.y}\right) = \left| normalised\ value_{Rule_{x.y}} - normalised\ value_{Rule_{x.1}} \right|$$

Table 4 lists the *ND* of each applied rule. Since the first sub-set rule is the most frequently applied rule in the rule set, its *ND* is always zero. The farthest sub-set rules are Rule6.4 and 6.5, whose distance is 2.45. Thus, the *ND*s show the disparity of each rule, relative to a typical rule (being a dominant or standard component of the language) in the set. This also supports the process of visualising the application of the grammar to generate design instances.

Level of Disparity (*LoD*)

This section presents a mathematical approach to grammatically measuring the level of disparity of each Palladian villa through the normalised distance of each of the ten cases. Table 5 indicates the *ND* of the applied rules used to generate each case and the level of disparity (*LoD*) of each. The *ND*s of multiple applications at each rule set are averaged. The sum of the *ND* is regarded as an indicator of the *LoD* of each case, because it represents how far the applied rules are from the most typical ones. When viewed in this

Table 5. ND of each applied rule sets for generating each case and the level of disparity (LoD) of each case

	1.x	2.x	3.x	4.x	5.x	6.x	7.x	8.x	9.x	10.x	LoD
Case 1	0.00	0.00	0.00	0.00	0.77	1.63	0.00	0.00	0.71	0.00	3.11
Case 2	0.00	0.00	0.00	0.00	0.77	0.00	0.00	0.00	0.00	0.00	**0.77**
Case 3	0.00	0.00	0.00	1.41	2.32	2.45	0.00	0.48	1.41	0.00	8.07
Case 4	0.00	1.19	1.41	0.00	0.00	0.00	1.00	0.48	0.00	1.41	5.49
Case 5	0.00	1.19	1.41	0.00	0.00	0.00	1.00	0.00	0.00	1.41	5.01
Case 6	0.00	0.00	0.00	0.00	1.55	0.00	0.00	0.00	0.00	0.00	1.55
Case 7	0.00	0.00	0.00	0.00	0.00	1.63	2.00	1.92	0.00	0.00	5.55
Case 8	0.00	0.00	0.00	0.00	0.77	1.63	0.00	0.00	0.00	0.00	2.40
Case 9	1.41	1.19	1.41	0.00	1.55	1.63	0.00	0.48	0.71	0.00	8.38
Case 10	1.41	1.99	0.00	0.00	0.00	2.45	2.00	1.92	0.00	1.41	**11.18**
Mean	0.28	0.56	0.42	0.14	0.77	1.14	0.60	0.53	0.28	0.42	5.15
SD	0.5	0.75	0.68	0.45	0.82	1.03	0.84	0.77	0.49	0.68	3.33

way, Case 2, *Villa Zeno (LoD* = 0.77), is the most typical instance in terms of both its underlying grid system and the properties of functional rooms and circulation spaces. In contrast, Case 10, *Villa Mocenigo (LoD* = 11.18), may be the least typical of the entire group, or the most distinct case in this particular design language. This is because the rules it uses are, relatively, the most rarely applied (see also Figure 14). For example, employing the 5×4-grid system (Rule1.2); the unique vertical spacing (Rule2.3); a cruciform *sala* across three vertical and horizontal spacing (Rule5.4); four *camerini* at four corners of a building (Rule6.4); and eight *stanze* (Rule7.5).

Figure 14 illustrates the *LoD* graph, including the *ND* values of the applied rule sets used to generate the ten original cases. The *LoD* graph shows that Case 2 (*Villa Zeno*) is the closest to a typical instance of the language. The *LoD* graph also visually reveals that Cases 2 and 6, as well as Cases 4 and 5, could have similarities by observing the similar patterns of the graph bars.

Guided Design Generation

The design knowledge developed from the frequencies of the applied rules can also be used to guide design generation. The probability of the applied rule enables us to mathematically investigate the generation of design instances. This approach, furthermore, addresses the production on the right-hand side of a rule as a condition on the left-hand side of the following rule, in

Figure 14. LoD graphs of the ten selected case

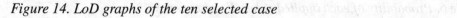

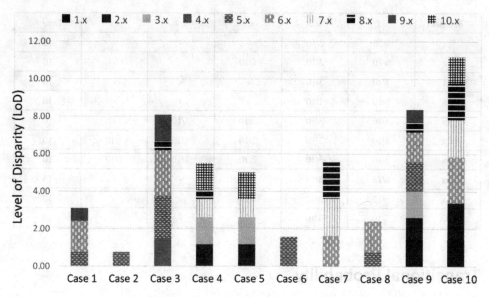

the sequential application of the Shape Grammar (as in most descriptive grammars). That is, it is possible to measure such conditional frequencies and utilise them for directing the Shape Grammar application. In this regard, transition probability is adopted to measure the probability of the occurrence of a transition between two states of a design.

Probability of Applied Rule Sets

As shown in Table 3, the application of the first sub-set rule in each rule set, as the dominant rule, may be used to generate the most typical instance of a Palladian villa. Thus, the probability of the applied rule enables us to guide or direct the generation of design instances (J. H. Lee, Gu, & Ostwald, 2016). Table 6 describes the probability of each applied rule being needed to generate a Palladian villa. For example, the probability of the application of Rule3.1 is 7/10, 70%, while for Rule3.2 it is 2/10 (20%). This means that the horizontal spacing of a Palladian grid tends to be equally distributed in terms of the value "*b*". The multiplication of the probabilities of applied rules also represents the probability of the generation of such a design instance developed by the rules.

Table 6. Probability of each applied rules (F = frequency).

Rule set	x.1	x.2	x.3	x.4	x.5	Total F
1.x	8/10	2/10	-	-	-	10
2.x	6/10	3/10	1/10	-	-	10
3.x	7/10	3/10	-	-	-	10
4.x	9/10	1/10	-	-	-	10
5.x	4/10	3/10	2/10	1/10	-	10
6.x	4/10	2/10	2/10	1/10	1/10	10
7.x	3/10	3/10	2/10	1/10	1/10	10
8.x	6/13	5/13	2/13	-	-	13
9.x	9/12	3/12	-	-	-	12
10.x	7/10	3/10	-	-	-	10

Transitional Probability

To generate new design instances in Palladio's design language, transition probability (T) can be used to determine the probability of transitioning from one rule to the following rule in the sequential step. Thus, generating a certain design can be understood as responding to the given contexts or constraints in the grammar. If a rule is currently in a rule set (state) $R_{x.a}$, it moves to Rule set $R_{y.b}$ at the next step with a probability denoted by $T_{x.a \to y.b}$ where $x, y, a, b > 1$.

$T_{x.a \to y.b}$ enables us to select more appropriate rules at each rule set in terms of the grammatical application. In addition, adopting a more likely rule at each sequential rule set generates typical designs in terms of Palladio's design styles (based on the ten houses that form the core knowledge ebase of the grammar). From the applied rules to the following rules, the transition probabilities are determined. For example, the transition probability from Rule set 1 to 2 ($R_{1.x}$ and $R_{2.x}$) is:

$$R_{2.1} \quad R_{2.2} \quad R_{2.3}$$

$$T_{x.a \to y.b} = \begin{array}{c} R_{1.1} \\ R_{1.2} \end{array} \begin{pmatrix} 6/8 & 2/8 & 0 \\ 0 & 1/2 & 1/2 \end{pmatrix}$$

Generally, both T and probability (P) are used for the grammar application. If there are more rules that have the maximum transition probability at each generation stage, the smaller numbered sub-set rule – the higher probability of the applied rule in Table 6 – is triggered. For example, the probabilities of the generation of two types of initial grid systems are respectively 8/10, 2/10. Thus, the application generally selects the first initial module (Rule1.1). In order to generate the following modules (Rule2.x), if the application chooses the dominant rule, Rule1.1, then it is followed by Rule2.1. Considering the maximum value of each transition probability, a new design instance can be generated. For example, "Rule1.1 → Rule2.1→ Rule3.1 → Rule4.1 → Rule5.1 → Rule6.1→ Rule7.3 → Rule8.1 (or Rule8.2) → Rule9.1 → Rule10.1" can be applied to generate a typical instance for a 5×3-grid villa, of which the *LoD* is 1.00 (or 1.48). However, it must be remembered that there is nothing absolute about the generative outcomes of a Shape Grammar. They reflect the set of works that were used to train or develop the grammar, and which in turn are a limited window into the style of a particular architect at a particular time (Seebohm & Chan, 2001). Thus, the dominant instance of the 5×3-grid villa generated using the transition probabilities in this section is an extrapolation of a language developed using only ten Palladian villas.

Design Generation Using *LoD*

Figure 15 illustrates an example of a variation of the typical instance of the Palladian Grammar identified in the previous section. This variation is generated by each rule set and the values that can suggest their *LoD*s in the design language. Since the first sub-set rule is the most frequently applied rule in the set, its *ND* is always zero. The farthest sub-set rule is either Rule6.4 or 6.5, whose distance is 2.45. Thus, the *ND*s demonstrate the disparity of each rule from a typical rule in the set. When we generate new design instances using the grammar, the values of these measurements can be used to guide the selection of rules, or the transition between rules, to suit different design purposes. The design instances generated using the grammar can freely scale from the most to the least consistent, relative to the original Palladian style. In other words, the values of the *ND*s of the applied rules can be used to support mathematical analysis as well as grammatical generation in the design language.

Figure 15. Design generation by each rule set and the values suggesting their LoDs

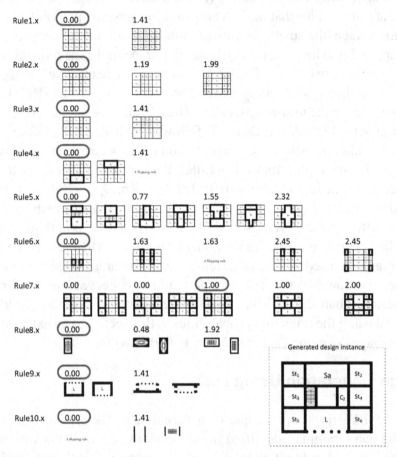

CONCLUSION

This chapter has described a design grammar (a schematic Palladian grammar) and presented a new approach for mathematically and visually analysing the properties of design instances and generating design variations within a style defined by rule sets. The Palladian Grammar introduced in this chapter features a sequential or linear process involving eleven steps over four stages, even though in practice a designer may not follow this sequence or may recursively revisit or vary steps. Nonetheless, selectively adopting sequential design steps can help to uncover a logical analogue of the grammatical design process embedded in an architectural style.

The Shape Grammar approach for design analysis and generation presented in this chapter, as it is enhanced with mathematical measurements, can also be applied to other design studies in the broader architectural and design context. This approach can be further articulated and adopted to consider the frequency of applied rules and the categorisation of rule sets that allow for the exploration of a particular architectural and design style. Thus, this research contributes to a better understanding of the grammatical design process implicit in the selected architecture or design language. In this mathematically supported Shape Grammar approach, the mathematical tendency of each rule is calculated and, more importantly, visualised, which can assist researchers to more effectively understand the properties of a specific language. The probability of the applied rules and the *LoD*s also enable us to mathematically investigate the generation of design instances in grammars. Subsequently, new design knowledge, based on the frequencies of applied rules, can be an effective aid for revealing possible design processes and thereby critically inform researchers and professionals when using a grammatical approach.

REFERENCES

Ahmad, S., & Chase, S. C. (2012). Style representation in design grammars. *Environment and Planning. B, Planning & Design*, *39*(3), 486–500. doi:10.1068/b37074

Ang, M. C., Ng, K. W., & Pham, D. T. (2013). Combining the Bees Algorithm and shape grammar to generate branded product concepts. *Proceedings of the Institution of Mechanical Engineers. Part B, Journal of Engineering Manufacture*, *227*(12), 1860–1873. doi:10.1177/0954405413494922

Benrós, D., Duarte, J. P., & Hanna, S. (2012). A new Palladian Shape Grammar: A subdivision grammar as alternative to the Palladian grammar. *International Journal of Architectural Computing*, *10*(4), 521–540. doi:10.1260/1478-0771.10.4.521

Bilda, Z., & Gero, J. S. (2007). The impact of working memory limitations on the design process during conceptualization. *Design Studies*, *28*(4), 343–367. doi:10.1016/j.destud.2007.02.005

Eilouti, B. H., & Hamamieh Al Shaar, M. J. (2012). Shape Grammars of traditional Damascene houses. *International Journal of Architectural Heritage*, *6*(4), 415–435. doi:10.1080/15583058.2011.575530

Eloy, S., & Duarte, J. (2011). A transformation grammar for housing rehabilitation. *Nexus Network Journal, 13*(1), 49–71. doi:10.100700004-011-0052-x

Eloy, S., & Duarte, J. P. (2015). A transformation-grammar-based methodology for the adaptation of existing housetypes: The case of the "rabo-de-bacalhau". *Environment and Planning. B, Planning & Design, 42*(5), 775–800. doi:10.1068/b120018p

Franco, J. M. S., Duarte, J. P., Batista, E. M., & Landesmann, A. (2014). Shape Grammar of steel cold-formed sections based on manufacturing rules. *Thin-walled Structures, 79*, 218–232. doi:10.1016/j.tws.2014.01.005

Grasl, T. (2012). Transformational Palladians. *Environment and Planning. B, Planning & Design, 39*(1), 83–95. doi:10.1068/b37059

Hanson, N. L. R., & Radford, A. D. (1986). Living on the edge: A grammar for some country houses by Glenn Murcutt. *Architecture Australia, 75*(5), 66–73.

Hersey, G. L., Freedman, R., & Palladio, A. (1992). *Possible Palladian villas (plus a few instructively impossible ones)*. Cambridge, MA: The MIT Press.

Hou, D., & Stouffs, R. (2018). An algorithmic design grammar for problem solving. *Automation in Construction, 94*, 417–437. doi:10.1016/j.autcon.2018.07.013

Hyun, K. H., Lee, J.-H., Kim, M., & Cho, S. (2015). Style synthesis and analysis of car designs for style quantification based on product appearance similarities. *Advanced Engineering Informatics, 29*(3), 483–494. doi:10.1016/j.aei.2015.04.001

Kitchley, J. J. L., & Srivathsan, A. (2014). Generative methods and the design process: A design tool for conceptual settlement planning. *Applied Soft Computing, 14*, 634–652. doi:10.1016/j.asoc.2013.08.017

Koning, H., & Eizenberg, J. (1981). The language of the prairie: Frank Lloyd Wright's prairie houses. *Environment & Planning B, 8*(3), 295–323. doi:10.1068/b080295

Lambe, N. R., & Dongre, A. R. (2017). A shape grammar approach to contextual design: A case study of the Pol houses of Ahmedabad, India. *Environment and Planning B. Urban Analytics and City Science, 2399808317734207*. doi:10.1177/2399808317734207

Lee, J., Mueller, C., & Fivet, C. (2016). Automatic generation of diverse equilibrium structures through shape grammars and graphic statics. *International Journal of Space Structures*, *31*(2-4), 147–164. doi:10.1177/0266351116660798

Lee, J. H., & Gu, N. (2018). A Design Grammar for Identifying Spatial Uniqueness of Murcutt's Rural Houses. In J.-H. Lee (Ed.), *Computational Studies on Cultural Variation and Heredity* (pp. 189–203). Singapore: Springer Singapore. doi:10.1007/978-981-10-8189-7_15

Lee, J. H., Gu, N., & Ostwald, M. J. (2016). Mathematical Analysis and Grammatical Generation of Design Instances of Murcutt's Domestic Architecture. In J. Zuo, L. Daniel, & V. Soebarto (Eds.), *Fifty years later: Revisiting the role of architectural science in design and practice: 50th International Conference of the Architectural Science Association 2006* (pp. 169-178). Adelaide, SA: The Architectural Science Association and The University of Adelaide, Adelaide.

Lee, J. H., Ostwald, M. J., & Gu, N. (2015). A syntactical and grammatical approach to architectural configuration, analysis and generation. *Architectural Science Review*, *58*(3), 189–204. doi:10.1080/00038628.2015.1015948

Lee, J. H., Ostwald, M. J., & Gu, N. (2017). A combined plan graph and massing grammar approach to Frank Lloyd Wright's Prairie Architecture. *Nexus Network Journal*, *19*(2), 279–299. doi:10.100700004-017-0333-0

Lee, J. H., Ostwald, M. J., & Gu, N. (2018). A Justified Plan Graph (JPG) grammar approach to identifying spatial design patterns in an architectural style. *Environment and Planning B. Urban Analytics and City Science*, *45*(1), 67–89. doi:10.1177/0265813516665618

Merrick, K. E., Isaacs, A., Barlow, M., & Gu, N. (2013). A shape grammar approach to computational creativity and procedural content generation in massively multiplayer online role playing games. *Entertainment Computing*, *4*(2), 115–130. doi:10.1016/j.entcom.2012.09.006

Ozdemir, S., & Ozdemir, Y. (2017). Prioritizing store plan alternatives produced with shape grammar using multi-criteria decision-making techniques. *Environment and Planning B. Urban Analytics and City Science*, *45*(4), 751–771. doi:10.1177/0265813516686566

Ozdemir, Y., & Ozdemir, S. (2017). Extended prioritizing of store plan alternatives produced with shape grammar using the generalized Choquet integral method. *Environment and Planning B. Urban Analytics and City Science, 2399808317739892*. doi:10.1177/2399808317739892

Palladio, A. (1715). The architecture of A. Palladio, in four books. London, UK: Printed by John Watts for the author. doi:10.5479il.395807.39088006535397

Quattrini, R., & Baleani, E. (2015). Theoretical background and historical analysis for 3D reconstruction model. Villa Thiene at Cicogna. *Journal of Cultural Heritage, 16*(1), 119–125. doi:10.1016/j.culher.2014.01.009

Ruiz-Montiel, M., Belmonte, M.-V., Boned, J., Mandow, L., Millán, E., Badillo, A. R., & Pérez-de-la-Cruz, J.-L. (2014). Layered shape grammars. *Computer Aided Design, 56*, 104–119. doi:10.1016/j.cad.2014.06.012

Ruiz-Montiel, M., Boned, J., Gavilanes, J., Jiménez, E., Mandow, L., & Pérez-de-la-Cruz, J.-L. (2013). Design with shape grammars and reinforcement learning. *Advanced Engineering Informatics, 27*(2), 230–245. doi:10.1016/j.aei.2012.12.004

Seebohm, T., & Chan, D. (2001). The design space of schematic Palladian plans for two villa topologies. In *Reinventing the Discourse – How Digital Tools Help Bridge and Transform Research, Education and Practice in Architecture: Proceedings of the Twenty First Annual Conference of the Association for Computer-Aided Design in Architecture* (pp. 156-165). Buffalo, NY: SUNY Buffalo.

Shea, K., Ertelt, C., Gmeiner, T., & Ameri, F. (2010). Design-to-fabrication automation for the cognitive machine shop. *Advanced Engineering Informatics, 24*(3), 251–268. doi:10.1016/j.aei.2010.05.017

Smith, G., & Ceranic, B. (2008). Spatial layout planning in sub-surface rail station design for effective fire evacuation. *Architectural Engineering and Design Management, 4*(2), 99–120. doi:10.3763/aedm.2008.0078

Stiny, G., & Mitchell, W. J. (1978). The Palladian grammar. *Environment & Planning B, 5*(1), 5–18. doi:10.1068/b050005

Tepavčević, B., & Stojaković, V. (2013). Procedural modeling in architecture based on statistical and fuzzy inference. *Automation in Construction, 35*, 329–337. doi:10.1016/j.autcon.2013.05.015

Veloso, P., Celani, G., & Scheeren, R. (2018). From the generation of layouts to the production of construction documents: An application in the customization of apartment plans. *Automation in Construction*, *96*, 224–235. doi:10.1016/j.autcon.2018.09.013

Williams, K., & Giaconi, G. (2003). *The villas of Palladio*. New York, NY: Princeton Architectural Press.

Youssef, A. M. A., Zhai, Z., & Reffat, R. M. (2018). Generating proper building envelopes for photovoltaics integration with shape grammar theory. *Energy and Building*, *158*, 326–341. doi:10.1016/j.enbuild.2017.09.077

Chapter 4
Space Syntax Approaches in Architecture

ABSTRACT

This chapter introduces three Space Syntax techniques – axial line analysis, convex space analysis, and visibility graph analysis (VGA). Conventional applications of the axial line technique typically range from domestic buildings to urban environments, providing a quantitative understanding of spatial configurations. Convex space analysis is typically used to capture relationships between human behaviour and the built environment, and VGA is used to reveal human spatial perceptions and responses in a specific built environment. This chapter provides a brief explanation of each technique before reviewing recent trends and developments in Space Syntax research. Two case studies are presented in the chapter to demonstrate axial line analysis and VGA for four urban neighbourhoods in Seoul (South Korea) and architectural plans for four aged care developments, two in Australia and two in South Korea.

INTRODUCTION

The canonical works of Space Syntax are *The Social Logic of Space* (Hillier & Hanson, 1984), *Space is the Machine* (Hillier, 1996) and *Decoding Houses and Homes* (Hanson, 1998). Collectively these three define the primary conceptual framework of the theory. In the first of these, Hillier and Hanson (1984) argue that spatial organisation has social consequences, and present a range of techniques for analysing the two-dimensional spatial properties

DOI: 10.4018/978-1-7998-1698-0.ch004

of built environments. In these techniques, the syntactic properties of an architectural or urban plan are abstracted, using various protocols, into a set of nodes and edges in a graph. Once converted in this way, the graph can be mathematically analysed, and the results are mapped back to the properties of the plan it was derived from. In this way, Space Syntax approaches are used to reveal the relationships between spaces and the social properties that necessitate or sustain these relationships (Hillier & Hanson, 1984).

Three basic correlations or mappings between human activities and spatial geometry are central to the majority of the Space Syntax techniques (Hillier & Vaughan, 2007). First, the movement of people through space can be conceptualised in terms of vectors or directions, leading to the proposition that "people move in lines". Second, people inhabit and interact in visually defined spaces, which, in geometric terms, are known as convex spaces. A convex space is one in which a straight line connecting any two points in the space does not cross a wall. Or, more intuitively, a convex room is one wherein, regardless of where you stand, the entire room is visible. Third, people understand the world, and find their way through it, using visual fields which change relative to the properties of the location they are in. These three correlations could be regarded as being between aspects of spatial topology and human behavioural, social and cognitive patterns, respectively (Figure 1).

The first of these three correlations or mappings is undertaken in Space Syntax using alpha analysis (employing an axial line map), the second, gamma analysis (using a convex space map), and the third uses isovists (or isovist fields). The first two of these, which rely on graph theory, are introduced in *The Social Logic of Space*, which also provides techniques for measuring and comparing the properties of graphs, including the extent to which nodes are integrated or segregated. Axial line analysis is ideally suited to studying street configurations in urban settlements, as streets could be regarded as primarily serving as spaces of movement. Convex space analysis is commonly used for studying the interior spatial configuration of buildings, as these are among the most important sites of social interaction and inhabitation. Hillier and Hanson (1984; Hanson, 1998), also introduce the concept of a building genotype, which can be uncovered using a "justified permeability map". This type of graph, which has had several different names over time, is called a justified plan graph (JPG) in the present book. The third approach, visibility analysis using isovists, was initially presented as an adjunct to convex and axial analysis, however, over time it has developed into an important technique in its

Figure 1. Three Space Syntax techniques that capture "intrinsic aspects of everything human beings do", adapted from (Hillier & Vaughan, 2007)

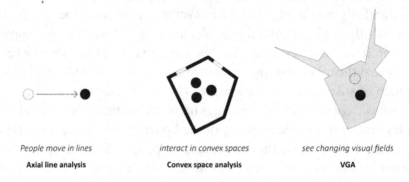

People move in lines	interact in convex spaces	see changing visual fields
Axial line analysis	**Convex space analysis**	**VGA**

own right. In particular, a considerable body of evidence has been developed demonstrating potential correlations between the mathematical properties of isovists and human spatial perceptions and responses (Stamps, 2005a, 2005b; Turner, Doxa, O'Sullivan, & Penn, 2001). The origins of isovist analysis are now more commonly traced to the work of Tandy (1967), whereas the Space Syntax technique known as visibility graph analysis (VGA) merges aspects of both isovist geometry and graph theory.

Regardless of which of these three approaches is adopted to abstract the features of the built environment into edges and nodes, graph mathematics is used to develop quantitative, mathematical descriptions of the properties of the graph structure. Common mathematical measures derived from the syntactic maps include connectivity (the number of direct connections to other spaces or movement paths), integration (the normalised mean depth when compared to an optimal D-value) and intelligibility (the correlation between connectivity and integration). Connectivity describes the mutual relationship between all movement paths or spaces, while integration indicates how well one space or path is connected to all others in a system (Hillier & Hanson, 1984). In practice, axial line analysis, convex space analysis and VGA are typically undertaken using software, of which *Depthmap* is the most well-known and accepted (Turner, 2001; Turner et al., 2001).

From this background it should be apparent that Space Syntax is neither a singular nor an independent approach; rather, it is a set of related techniques. These techniques draw on graph theory and spatio-visual geometry to investigate three basic types of human spatial relations – movement, interaction and cognition – as encapsulated in axial, convex and visibility analyses respectively (Vaughan, 2007). Space Syntax techniques are widely applicable to architectural design, urban analytics, transportation analysis and modelling, health care design, and even archaeology.

This chapter commences with a review of emerging Space Syntax research in architecture, with a focus on these three foundational techniques. This review is focused on Space Syntax research published between 2008 and 2018. Relevant research was identified using a keyword index search in three online journal databases: Taylor & Francis online, SAGE Journals, and ScienceDirect. These databases cover many of the major architectural and design journals, although there is one notable exception. The *Journal of Space Syntax* is not indexed in any of these online databases and therefore its 14 issues are not included in the present analysis. While it would have been possible to include these additional works, the desire to compare emerging Space Syntax and Shape Grammar research using a similar basis led to the decision to retain the three databases as the authoritative source. Other databases were also assessed for their capacity to broaden the scope to include conference papers. For example, the CumInCAD database indexes more than 12,000 research papers from the ACADIA, CAADRIA, eCAADe and CAAD futures conferences, but its coverage of Space Syntax and Shape Grammar research is limited. In the average year, only 2.17% of papers indexed in CumInCAD mention or use space syntax methods and only 0.91% refer to Shape Grammar or related methods (Ostwald, 2017). The review of emerging trends commences with an overview of the general characteristics of the papers identified in the three databases. An in-depth review then categorises the research in terms of the three major approaches: axial line analysis, convex space analysis and VGA. The first and third Space Syntax approaches are further discussed in this chapter using case studies, while convex space analysis and its mathematical measures are explained in detail in Chapter 5.

EMERGING SPACE SYNTAX RESEARCH DATA

The 206 separate research papers identified in the online database search include 61 in Taylor & Francis online, 50 in SAGE Journals and 95 in ScienceDirect. Notably, the total number of Space Syntax papers recorded across the three databases is almost triple the number of Shape Grammar papers (77) recorded in the same period in the same databases. This might suggest that Space Syntax methods have remained more useful than Shape

Figure 2. Space Syntax papers by publication year

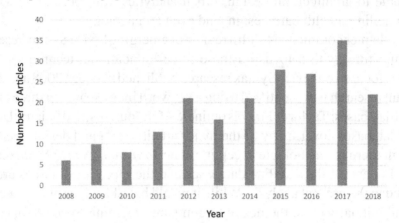

Grammar methods, or that they have continued to be updated in such a way as to remain relevant.

The number of Space Syntax papers published by year has grown since 2008 (Figure 2). For example, the number of papers published in 2017 is almost 6 times more than the number in 2008. However, some of this growth may be a by-product of the way database indexing has become more common throughout the period, along with international standards in archiving and key words use. Thus, in 2008 fewer journals may have been indexed in these databases.

Journals which published more than two Space Syntax papers in the last decade are listed in Table 1. The top 12 journals, each of which published five or more papers between 2008 and 2018, account for 54.6% of the total collected papers. The most significant of these is *Environment and Planning B: Urban Analytics and City Science* – which was previously *Environment and Planning B: Planning and Design* – which published 27 papers on Space Syntax (13%). *Environment and Planning B* also published the most Shape Grammar papers during the same period. The *Journal of Asian Architecture and Building Engineering* published the second most Space Syntax papers (16 papers, 7.7%) but only one Shape Grammar paper in the same period. Space Syntax techniques could be more relevant in Asia, with researchers during the focus decade investigating the growing problems of rapid urbanisation, transportation and new building types. The third dominant publishing outlet is *Procedia – Social and Behavioral Sciences* (11 papers, 5.3%), which is effectively a conference proceeding, and the next most significant is *HERD: Health Environments Research & Design Journal* (8 papers, 3.9%).

Table 1. Journals publishing more than two Space Syntax papers between 2008 and 2018

Journal	Number of Papers
Environment and Planning B: Urban Analytics and City Science	27 (13.0%)
Journal of Asian Architecture and Building Engineering	16 (7.7%)
Procedia – Social and Behavioral Sciences	11 (5.3%)
HERD: Health Environments Research & Design Journal	8 (3.9%)
Frontiers of Architectural Research	8 (3.9%)
Computers, Environment and Urban Systems	7 (3.4%)
International Journal of Geographical Information Science	6 (2.9%)
Environment and Behavior	5 (2.4%)
International Journal of Urban Sciences	5 (2.4%)
Automation in Construction	5 (2.4%)
Habitat International	5 (2.4%)
Cities	5 (2.4%)
Landscape and Urban Planning	5 (2.4%)
Journal of Anthropological Archaeology	4 (1.9%)
Architectural Science Review	3 (1.4%)
International Journal of Sustainable Transportation	3 (1.4%)
Journal of Urbanism: International Research on Placemaking and Urban Sustainability	3 (1.4%)
Transportation Research Part A: Policy and Practice	3 (1.4%)
Health & Place	3 (1.4%)
Building Research & Information	2 (1.0%)
Housing Studies	2 (1.0%)
International Journal of Urban Sustainable Development	2 (1.0%)
Journal of Architecture and Urbanism	2 (1.0%)
Town Planning and Architecture	2 (1.0%)
Transport Reviews	2 (1.0%)
Urban Studies	2 (1.0%)
Space and Culture	2 (1.0%)
American Journal of Alzheimer's Disease & Other Dementias	2 (1.0%)
Accident Analysis & Prevention	2 (1.0%)
Applied Geography	2 (1.0%)
Building and Environment	2 (1.0%)
Energy Procedia	2 (1.0%)
Journal of Science and Medicine in Sport	2 (1.0%)
Journal of Transport Geography	2 (1.0%)
Physica A: Statistical Mechanics and its Applications	2 (1.0%)
Procedia Engineering	2 (1.0%)
Urban Forestry & Urban Greening	2 (1.0%)
Sum	168 (81.2%)

Interestingly, syntactical studies in this health and design journal typically use VGA.

While many core architectural and urban design journals dominate Table 1 – including *Environment and Behavior*, *International Journal of Urban Sciences*, *Cities*, *Landscape and Urban Planning*, *Architectural Science Review*, *Journal of Architecture and Urbanism*, *Town Planning and Architecture*, *Urban Studies*, *Building and Environment* and *Automation in Construction* – there are also multiple journals focused on specific themes or issues. For example, research published in *HERD: Health Environments Research & Design Journal*, *Health & Place* and the *American Journal of Alzheimer's Disease & Other Dementias* applies Space Syntax techniques to health-related design and planning. Research published in the journal *Accident Analysis & Prevention* explores safety using Space Syntax approaches. As Hillier and Hanson (1984) also proposed archaeological and historical applications of their methods, it is not surprising that the *Journal of Anthropological Archaeology* (4), *Journal of Archaeological Science* (1), *Journal of Social Archaeology* (1), *Azania: Archaeological Research in Africa* (1) and *International Journal of Maritime History* (1) all feature in the complete list. Syntactic applications to transportation systems are also published in the *International Journal of Sustainable Transportation* (3), *Transportation Research Part A: Policy and Practice* (3), *Journal of Traffic and Transportation Engineering* (1), *Transportation Research Procedia* (1) and *Urban, Planning and Transport Research* (1). Furthermore, Space Syntax approaches are found in energy, policy, culture and physical activity (sport) journals. The following sections review these emerging studies in detail, thematically dividing them in terms of the specific techniques used: axial line analysis, convex space analysis, or VGA.

AXIAL LINE ANALYSIS

Axial line analysis was originally introduced as alpha-analysis, the syntactic analysis of settlements (Hillier & Hanson, 1984). An axial map is defined as the set of the longest lines of sight or movement that pass through and connect all of the habitable or accessible spaces of a plan (Hillier & Hanson, 1984). Axial maps capture two basic behavioural characteristics of environments: movement potential and navigational choice. In practice, an axial line map of an urban space consists of a matrix of the "longest and fewest" lines (Hillier, 1999), which represent an optimal or efficient set of movement

Figure 3. Example of an urban street network, its axial lines and axial map graph

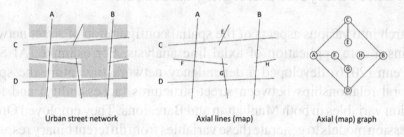

Urban street network   Axial lines (map)   Axial (map) graph

potentials on streets or paths. To analyse the axial map, the lines (streets, paths or movement vectors) are treated as nodes in a graph, and the points where these lines connect or cross, as edges or links in the graph (Figure 3). This topological representation enables various mathematical measures to be derived using graph theory.

Consider an example of an urban street plan (Figure 3) with four major axial lines (A, B, C and D), all of which have three connections (connectivity). Using relative asymmetry (or relative depth) it is possible to determine that these four lines have different levels of integration (A and D are higher than B and C). In this way, axial line analysis can begin to reveal the different properties or characteristics of spatial networks. In this example (Figure 3), assuming an even distribution of people, buildings and uses in this urban area, the topology of the city will ensure that people passing along streets A and D, are more likely to come in contact with others than people moving along streets B and C. Note that the words "even distribution" is a key part of the theory, as an analysis of a plan in this way cannot easily account for some three-dimensional factors. For example, if the city block bounded by lines E, C and B, is much higher density and has a commensurately larger residential population, and conversely, the blocks south of line D are a light industrial zone, integration might be a poor reflection of the reality of pedestrian movements (Netto, 2016; Ratti, 2004a, 2004b). Recognition of such issues has led to the development of new or more nuanced variations of axial line techniques. Nonetheless, this method for the topological analysis of space has been widely applied to both historic and modern urban and architectural plans.

Axial Line Analysis: Emerging Research

Research into various aspects of the spatial configuration of street networks remains a core application of axial line analysis. For example, Al Sayed and Penn (2016) developed a dependency network to capture the spatio-temporal relationships between street structures (accessibility) and form-function variables in both Manhattan and Barcelona. They employed Ordinal Regression models to generate these variables from different binary responses representing land use, high-rise development, street width and block density. Their results suggest that the dependency network can explain temporality in the relationships between the network structure of streets, street widths, building heights, land values and retail land uses. Marcus and Koch (2016) address the density and diversity of spatial morphology in smart city systems. Density is defined as accessibility in the street network to floor space, while diversity is defined as accessibility in the street network to building plots. They measure distance topologically using axial lines rather than traditional metrics, and suggest that the location-based measures can capture the human experience of the street. Ma, Omer, Osaragi, Sandberg and Jiang (2018) undertook a topological analysis of London streets, with a focus on "natural streets" and "natural street segments" modelled as axial lines and axial line segments. They suggest that natural streets – being those generated from individual street segments with the same names or clear continuity – are the best representation for predicting human activities or traffic movement. Omer and Kaplan (2018) investigate angular and metric centralities for modelling movements in street networks and conduct a correlation analysis between street network centralities and simulated movement flows. Their findings suggest that angular centralities are more suitable for describing pedestrian and vehicle movement flows, but the results can be affected by interrelated structural properties, agents and angular foreground sub-networks. Such research uses axial line analysis for the purpose of improving the traditional measures or models.

An alternative research direction develops new measures for axial line maps. For example, Barthelemy (2015) characterises and compares multiple street networks using new measures. To overcome the limitation of axial line measures (the difference between the Euclidean shortest path and the simplest path), Barthelemy's research suggests using spatial distribution embodied in the "betweenness centrality" measure for time-evolving road networks, which differs from conventional syntactic measures. After the statistical comparison of the lengths of the shortest and simplest paths, Barthelemy presents a simplicity index as the average ratio of these lengths, which allows for the quantitative properties on artificial (roads, highways, railways) and natural networks (leaves, insect wings) to be measured. The research also measures the conditional probability distribution of the shape factor of blocks to understand road networks in 130 major cities. This research direction suggests an interesting conceptual shift from paths to blocks. Pafka, Dovey and Aschwanden (2018) also explore several long-recognised problems of axial models, such as distance, scale and sinuous streetscapes. In spite of these limitations, they find that Space Syntax analysis remains a powerful tool for urban designers.

In another example of an advanced version of axial line analysis, di Bella, Corsi, Leporatti and Persico (2015) discuss the representation of space in statistical models of urban crime. To overcome a limitation of previous models of the dispersion of crime in a city, they suggest the use of alternative methods of analysis, including spatial configurational mapping using Space Syntax techniques. Their research adopts the angular segment technique (Dalton, 2001; Turner, 2007) to calculate three configurational properties of entire roads – permeability, integration and choice – which represent different forms of centrality. Permeability is configurationally interpreted as density of inbound and outbound connections, while integration is related to accessibility, being associated with the capacity to reach a destination from all origin points. The former relates to the concentrated behaviour of inbound flows and dispersion of outbound flows, while the latter is concerned with the attraction of destination movement flows and the modelling of shorter trips. The last property, choice, is regarded as the frequency of alternative shortest paths, which attract transit movement flows and also influence modelling of longer trips. In their study, no segment of an axial graph exceeds the boundary between two different roads. In a different type of methodological advance, Law (2017) presents the impact of Street-based Local Area (SLA) on house prices in London using a hedonic price approach. The definition of SLA employs a multi-level modularity optimisation algorithm on the street network dual graph developed from network science and Space Syntax research. Kim and Piao (2017) apply the concept of metric weighting to the issue of pedestrian density and closeness centrality distributions from axial maps. The metric weighting functions include square root function, square function of the distance, exponential function, and logarithmic function of a distance. Aschwanden, Haegler, Bosché, Van Gool and Schmitt (2011) propose a system to simulate, analyse and visualise occupant behaviour in urban environments. Their system automatically analyses functions of buildings and other urban elements, population density, utilisation and capacity of the public transport network, and congestion effect on the street network. They do not employ a traditional axial map, but use color-coded attribute maps to control the generation of street networks and building geometries.

Traditional Space Syntax techniques are also being used for the development of new models or methodologies. As an example, Morales, Flacke and Zevenbergen (2017) develop a multivariate regression model for land-value research, using geographic-access indices, geometric-access metrics (integration and choice) and a proposed geometric via geographic-access metric. The last is computed as potential access to network centrality. Geometric accessibility is calculated at neighbourhood and city-wide scales. Tsou and Cheng (2013) present a retail spatial integrated model for exploring the relationship between retail patterns and urban network structures. Using a case study of Taipei, Taiwan, they reveal the effect of multiple urban network structures on retail patterns. Urban network structures (street configuration, bus network and metro network) are described using syntactic values, such as connectivity, control, global integration and local integration. Choi, Kim and Byun (2013) develop a spatial configuration analysis model of apartment complexes using axial maps. They also present a one-way analysis of variance (ANOVA) using periodical indices of integration and standardised point depth for each spatial component. Hajrasouliha and Yin (2014) employ a structural equation modelling (SEM) technique using conventional metric-based and geometric-based variables for pedestrian counts of 302 street segments in Buffalo, New York. Their study of street network connectivity and pedestrian volume uses local integration (visual connectivity), intersection density (physical connectivity), population density, employment density and land use mix (entropy). Omer and Goldblatt (2016) adopt Q-analysis (multidimensional scaling methodology) to examine movement patterns and circulation systems within buildings. They present the potential of the conjunction between Q-analysis and Space Syntax (global integration, connectivity and intelligibility from axial lines). In their results, high spatial integration and intelligibility levels correlate to the spread of movement paths and their formation into integrated circulation systems.

Axial line analysis is also often used alongside other spatial information systems, including a geographic information system (GIS). For instance, Abune'meh, El Meouche, Hijaze, Mebarki and Shahrour (2016) develop a new methodology to evaluate risks within a construction site. The mean depth results of the spatial configuration are used to generate the spatial variability map of risk, which is integrated into GIS. They use the spatial analyst tools in ArcGIS and a differential evolution algorithm to minimise the global risk within the site. Scoppa and Peponis (2015) reveal that the syntactic measures of a street network have a significant relationship with commercial frontage density in the city of Buenos Aires, along with the analysis of the city's GIS database. The independent variables they use to describe the street network are metric reach, directional reach, street width, metric betweenness centrality, normalised angular choice, normalised angular integration, distance from nearest metro station, and distance from nearest railway station. The application of Space Syntax techniques in transportation research is often based on GIS (Helbich, 2017; Sooil Lee, Lee, Son, & Joo, 2013; Zaleckis, Kamičaitytė-Virbašienė, & Matijošaitienė, 2015). In a related way, Rashid (2012) examines a configurational theory of architecture which is framed from a situated observer's viewpoint, highlighting perceptual primitives (convex space and axial line) and their perceivable topological and projective relations. The research is an example of an attempt by Space Syntax researchers to integrate their approaches into a coherent mathematical system, wherein newly defined perceptual primitives are combined in a framework for configurational studies. Shen and Karimi (2016) present an interface graph (map) that describes the interplay between land-use points and co-visual paths, and characterise functional urban streets (Tianjin, China) using social media check-in data. They also introduce a model of the three principal dimensions of an urban function network: accessible density, accessible diversity and delivery efficiency. Tomé, Heitor and Nunes (2015) develop a computational tool, computer vision technology, that supports space-use analysis. They examine the relationship between movement and occupancy patterns (captured using video image processing) and spatial configuration (described in an axial map). Mavridou (2012) presents a qualitative study of three-dimensional urban scale in an immersive virtual environment. The integration values of axial lines and the perception of both geometrical and topological properties of space are examined with a focus on the dualism of form and space. The participants in Mavridou's study explore intelligible and non-intelligible planning layouts with different formal properties such as height and width of building and street. These are significant, because they are largely ignored in traditional Space Syntax approaches.

Historical analysis using axial line maps has remained a relatively consistent application since the 1980s. In a recent example, Thilagam and Banerjee (2015) investigate the morphological characteristics of the medieval temple towns of Tamilnadu in South India. They identify the temple town as a unique urban genotype using both traditional axial and convex maps. Three main characteristics of the seven medieval temple towns examined are a high degree of axiality, a higher level of spatial synchrony than in a regular settlement pattern and a high level of connectivity with integration cores. In another example, Chiang and Deng (2017) explore the spatial accessibility of the city gate of the ancient Gungnae city in Ji'an. Employing axial line analysis to calculate the average integration value for seven gate combination types, Chiang and Deng develop an evidence-based approach to historic spatial networks. D'Autilia and Spada (2017) present urban graphs of five historic cities and compare their syntactic properties of Real Relative Asymmetry (*RRA*), connectivity and accessibility, derived from axial line maps. Their research also measures the spectral gap, which is the first non-zero eigenvalue of the normalised Laplace matrix, to analyse the degree of connectivity. Önder and Gigi (2010) present a methodology to identify the social and physical problems of a historical urban space, the South Haliç area in Istanbul. Their axial line analysis (focusing on global and local integration values) is mainly used for analysing the historical urban area and offering design interventions.

Examining the historical stages of urban spatial configurations has also remained a strength of the axial line method since it was first proposed. For instance, Shpuza (2014) discusses urban growth using metric and topological space syntax measures to describe street networks. A unique database of historical maps and axial map representations enables the quantitative analysis of three historical stages of urban development. Importantly, Shpuza's research explores the allometric relationships between length, connectivity, depth, choice and entropy to size, to reveal the similarities and disparities between cities with and without gridiron street patterns. Zhu, Liu, Liu, Wang and Ma (2017) use axial maps of Qianmen, China, from 1950, 1990, 2002 and 2016 to investigate the spatial structure of the Recreational Business District development. Rashid and Alobaydi (2015) investigate the relationships between territorial practices and physical spatial networks in Baghdad, Iraq before and during the war. They highlight the significance of the mean integration (or closeness) and mean choice (or betweenness) values of the axial lines and segments. Jeong, Lee and Ban (2015) analyse the characteristics of spatial configurations in Pyongyang, North Korea over three periods – the 1930s, the 1970s, and beginning in 2010 – using angular segment analysis. Angular segment analysis breaks axial lines into segments and calculates the changes in direction from the starting segment to any other segment in a system. Kwon, Bonghee and Kim (2015) conduct an axial line analysis of Seoul's historic maps from 1751 and 1914 to reveal the transition of the city's spatial structure to functional pragmatism.

Axial line analysis is also used to understand spatial characteristics in architectural and urban design. Morgareidge, Cai and Jia (2014) conduct discrete event simulation and axial line analysis to optimise a care process in the emergency department and to design such environments to support enhanced visual surveillance and care coordination. Feng and Peponis (2018) identify three syntactic types for superblock designs: polarised, deformed, and regular grids. They then generate a universe of designs using these types and propose analytical and sorting algorithms to work with them. Prayitno (2017) discusses spatial and philosophical principles that relate to the phenomenon of change in the urban space in Yogyakarta, Indonesia, employing observation and axial line analysis. Yoo and Lee (2017) examine the transformation of the urban morphology of Barcelona, Spain, using axial line analysis (focusing on integration and choice). Their findings suggest that the integration between organic form and grid system may support urban regeneration in cities. Nam and Kim (2014) explore the relationship between spatial characteristics of parks in Seoul and their usages. Nam and Kim employ axial line analysis for this purpose, considering global and local integration measures and control value (developed using AXWOMAN 6.0 and Arc GIS 10.0 software). Choi (2018) proposes using individualism-collectivism cultural properties to differentiate between inhabitants and strangers using spatial "familiarity" – different wayfinding behaviour within a spatial configuration (axial map). The study of wayfinding behaviour in the built environment is a common application of Space Syntax techniques (Kalakou & Moura, 2014; Li & Klippel, 2012, 2014; Rybarczyk, 2014; Tzeng & Huang, 2009; Zamani, 2018).

Case Study 1

This case study uses axial line analysis to examine the spatial configurations of four "Design Seoul" streets – Daehak-ro in Jongno-gu (DJ), Namdaemun-ro in Jung-gu (NJ), Gangnam-daero in Gangnam-gu (GG), Cheonho-daero in gangdong-gu (CG) – in Seoul, South Korea. The four streets were redeveloped in 2008 to revitalise and promote cultural and social integration in the city. The focus of this case study is a comparison of "mixed" and "planned" urban street grids using axial line analysis. The first two streets (DJ and NJ) are classed as "mixed" urban street networks, as they formed naturally over time, before being partially redeveloped to support modern traffic and

Table 2. Average values of connectivity, global integration (Rn) and local integration (R3) of each neighbourhood area and target street (Daehak-ro in Jongno-gu (DJ); Namdaemun-ro in Jung-gu (NJ); Gangnam-daero in Gangnam-gu (GG); Cheonho-daero in gangdong-gu (CG))

Street	Neighbourhood area			Target street		
	Connectivity	Global integration	Local integration	Connectivity	Global integration	Local integration
DJ	6.78	1.3245	2.4497	57	2.2144	4.6265
NJ	6.31	1.4132	2.4221	24	2.3368	4.0404
GG	6.1	2.0935	2.6437	52	3.8606	4.8101
CG	6.82	2.0634	2.7089	43	3.6342	4.5609

infrastructure. These streets, near the royal palaces of the Chosun dynasty, are within the boundary of the old city of Seoul and thus they are part of a network of streets that can be traced to the fourteenth or fifteenth centuries. In contrast, the last two streets (GG and CG) were created as part of "planned" urban grid networks, which arose in the last century in response to new urban development (Figure 4).

To examine the properties of the four different streets, each of which have different lengths (550m – 760m), this case study considers an area or neighbourhood with a radius of 2km around each target street, which is also about 20 minutes' walking distance from the centre of the street to the boundary. These neighbourhoods are extracted from the Seoul GIS system (http://gis.seoul.go.kr/). The area images are then vectorized through image converter software to be imported into *Depthmap* software. Figure 4 illustrates four neighbourhood areas and axial maps (local integration) that include each target street. Table 2 records average values of connectivity, global integration (Rn) and local integration (R3) for each neighbourhood area (each target street). Connectivity measures the number of axial lines (spaces) connected to a certain axial line (space), while integration indicates easy access to the axial line (space), which is an indicator of its relative importance. Commonly, axial line analysis considers two integration values: global integration (the full range of the area of the analysis) and local integration (the inside area of depth 3 from a benchmark).

Namdaemun-ro in Jung-gu is the shortest street and it has the smallest number of connections or lowest connectivity (24), but its global integration (2.3368) is slightly higher than Daehak-ro in Jongno-gu (2.2144). Daehak-ro in Jongno-gu has 57 connections to other streets (being the longest axial line), but its integration values are relatively lower because many of these streets are dead ends or segregated. Conversely, the neighbourhood area around Gangnam-daero in Gangnam-gu, unexpectedly, has the lowest connectivity because it has a relatively well-planned urban grid, although the spaces within their larger grid comprise many small lanes or paths. The Gangnam-daero neighbourhood area has the highest global integration result and the second highest local integration, behind Cheonho-daero in gangdong-gu. In contrast, the Daehak-ro in Jongno-gu neighbourhood has the lowest global integration values, 2.2144 and 1.3245, respectively, while Namdaemun-ro in Jung-gu and its area are locally the least integrated, 4.0404 and 2.4221, respectively. These results reflect the fact that Daehak-ro and Namdaemun-ro are part of historic, *mixed* urban grids. Interestingly, the Cheonho-daero neighbourhood area has the highest local integration value (2.7089). This may be related to its smaller land parcels, but this interpretation would need further investigation to test.

In summary, axial line analysis allows for these four streets, and their associated urban neighbourhoods, to be quantitatively investigated to identify their properties or characteristics. The purpose of this short study is to demonstrate the particular syntactic approach, but the simple exploration of both a target street and its neighbourhood area raises multiple issues and interpretations that are worthy of further research.

Convex Space Analysis

Environmental and behavioural research identifies enclosure as an important property of a space, because it limits or shapes movement and perception (Alitajer & Molavi Nojoumi, 2016; Hayward & Franklin, 1974; Nasar & Jones, 1997; Stamps, 2005b). As such, convex space analysis is concerned with the relationship between human behaviour and the built environment (mostly represented in plan layouts). Convex space analysis involves the development of a convex map and its abstraction into a Justified Plan Graph (JPG). Convex maps allow for the analysis of enclosed or defined programmatic spaces and their connectivity, conceptualised, respectively as nodes and edges (or links). The JPG, which is a diagrammatic representation of the topological properties of the convex map and is used for analysing spatial configuration, has also been known as a "planar graph" or a "plan morphology" diagram (Steadman, 1983). The JPG was also described as a "justified permeability map" in *The Social Logic of Space* (Hillier & Hanson, 1984).

Figure 4a. Four neighbourhood areas and axial maps (local integration) with each target street (red rectangle around the centre of each neighbourhood area)

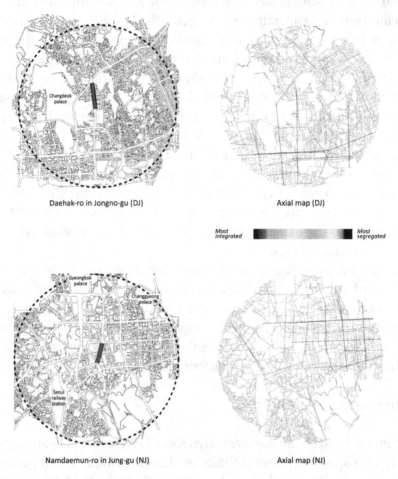

Daehak-ro in Jongno-gu (DJ)   Axial map (DJ)

Most integrated   Most segregated

Namdaemun-ro in Jung-gu (NJ)   Axial map (NJ)

Convex space analysis is typically used to examine building interiors or small, enclosed urban areas, and as such, it is not as susceptible to criticism (about long distances, scale, sinuosity and alternative pathways) as axial line analysis. Thus, the mathematical measures derived from nodes and edges in syntactical analysis are quite close to those of classical graph theory. Furthermore, topological configuration is a common stage in the architectural design process, making the connection between architectural configuration and convex mapping relatively intuitive.

Because convex space analysis is reliant on classical or basic graph theory, it cannot accommodate the properties of multigraphs without simplification. For example, Figure 5 illustrates four different spatial relations in an architecture

Figure 4b.

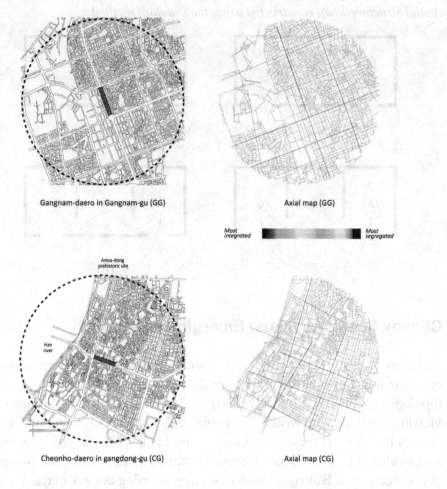

Gangnam-daero in Gangnam-gu (GG)   Axial map (GG)

Most integrated ▮▮▮▮▮▮▮▮▮ Most segregated

Cheonho-daero in gangdong-gu (CG)   Axial map (CG)

plan, which convex space analysis would treat as being identical. However, since there are two doors between each of the rooms in the top-left and bottom-right plans, they are potentially very different, in practical terms, from the relationships between rooms in the other two plans. For example, Room B at the bottom-left configuration suggests a circulation zone along an external wall, while the bottom-right configuration functions more as a single large room with some sub-divisions. Peponis, Bafna, Dahabreh and Dogan (2015, p. 218) suggest that "configuration is the entailment of a set of co-present relationships embedded in a design". This book partly deals with this issue through the use of centrality measures and a "Justified Plan Multigraph" (JPM) in the next chapter.

Figure 5. Four different spatial relations in a plan, each with an identical convex spatial structure when constructed using the standard method

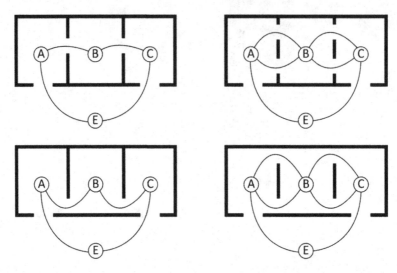

Convex Space Analysis: Emerging Research

A convex map and a JPG are often separately addressed in recent research, but their mathematical measures are the same because both use the same topological approach. Kim and Moon (2013) conduct a correlation analysis of viewing behaviours on weekdays or weekends in museums using integration and intelligibility values derived from convex maps. Maina (2013) examines socio-cultural factors (kinship, security and basic needs) for the design of public housing in Billiri, in north east Nigeria, using convex maps. Dawson (2008) analyses spatial layouts of Inuit houses of the Canadian Arctic using convex maps, focusing on the spatial distribution of activity categories by integration levels. Choi, Kim, Kang and Choi (2014) conduct a comparative analysis of the spatial structure of apartment unit plans in Asia to interpret the cultural properties embedded into the spatial structure. Yu, Ostwald and Gu (2016) describe a method for mathematically capturing and then parametrically generating new instances of traditional Chinese private gardens. Using a convex map, the total depth (*TD*), mean depth (*MD*) control value (*CV*), intelligibility (*I*) and integration (*i*) values are calculated for each node. The syntactic data are then used for a parametric system to generate new instances of the Suzhou type garden. Kishimoto and Taguchi (2014) investigate the spatial configuration of Japanese elementary schools using convex maps and

JPGs and then classify them into five types, considering mean integration, mean connectivity and intelligibility.

The JPG method is also widely applied to the analysis of domestic buildings (sometimes developing genotypes) and in archaeological studies. As an example of the latter, archaeological research, Edwards (2013) uses a JPG to examine Pataraya and Wari provincial administration in Nasca, and Fladd (2017) uses a similar approach to study Homol'ovi I, an ancestral Hopi village in north-eastern Arizona. In the former category, domestic architecture, França and Greene (2017) present a morphological analysis of the Isla Negra house using JPGs. Their research uses a configurational perspective to examine the totality and the historical process of the evolution of Nerudian space. The JPG graphs are used to reveal the parts and stages of growth of the house. Gao, Asami, Zhou and Ishikawa (2013) employ a JPG to express the depth of different spatial units in medium-sized apartments in Beijing, China. Jeong and Ban (2014) analyse the changes in the spatial configurations of apartment units in Cheongju, South Korea, built between 1972 and 2000. They use a J-SAP application to draw JPGs showing the spatial structure of housing units. Jeong and Ban (2011a) present algorithms to calculate the syntactic values of a JPG and develop J-Studio for Architectural Planning (J-SAP) software to draw JPGs and easily evaluate design solutions. Jeong and Ban (2011b) also develop a model (TIEM) that extracts topological information and recognises geometric and topological features of spaces. Their method, employing graph theory and a binary spatial partitioning (BSP) tree, automatically decomposes a concave space into optimal convex spaces and draws a JPG to measure spatial configurations.

Convex space analysis of building types or design languages often relies on the development of an "inequality genotype", being a list of programmatically defined spaces that are ordered in accordance with their integration values, as derived from a JPG (Bafna, 2001; Hillier & Hanson, 1984). Along with the statistical archetype (an average condition derived from a set of genotypes), the inequality genotype offers a means of understanding the recurring relationship between functional elements in a set of architectural plans (Bafna, 1999; Hillier, Hanson, & Graham, 1987; Ostwald, 2011a, 2011b). For example, Byun and Choi (2016) analyse the spatial structure in apartments by measuring the spatial configuration of JPGs and domestic space genotypes. Malhis (2008) explores the spatial properties of apartments in Jordan using integration order (genotype) and integration value.

The JPG's diagrammatic representation of spatial structure is also of interest in design-related research. For instance, Zadeh, Shepley and Waggener (2012) introduce a new design tool – the justified permeability diagram of spatial relationships – to increase the efficiency of acute care environments. Mustafa and Hassan (2013) explore the changes and transformations in the spatial configurations of mosque layouts, comparing the spatial structures of six types of layout using JPGs. Asif, Utaberta, Sabil and Ismail (2018) investigate the social information embedded in traditional architectural planning in the Malay Archipelago using JPG analysis. Wong (2014) investigates the spatial ring structures in Tadao Ando's museums, identifying such structures as a recurring theme in Ando's museum architecture. Wong's research proposes three new ring-based measures (d-ness, transcyclomatic number and ring-island ratio) and uses a second-order graph (a graph of a graph) to illustrate the relationships between the spatial rings in complicated plan layouts. Eloy and Duarte (2015) develop a transformation grammar to identify and encode the principles and rules behind the adaptation of existing house plans, and then evaluate the spatial properties of the proposed designs using JPG analysis. Finally, Lee, Ostwald and Gu (2015, 2016) present a hybrid approach, a JPG grammar, to identify spatial design patterns in an architectural style. They highlight the grammatical transformation of syntax, epistemological questions, similarity or disparity and the generation of JPG variations. This new combined method is introduced in detail in the latter chapters of the present book.

VISIBILITY GRAPH ANALYSIS (VGA)

In addition to axial and convex maps, a third approach, VGA, combines the concepts of isovists with visibility graphs. An isovist is defined as "the set of all points visible from a given vantage point in space" (Benedikt, 1979). The visibility graph was firstly introduced by Braaksma and Cook (1980) as "sight line analysis", but it became well known in architecture through Turner's research (Turner, 2001; Turner et al., 2001) and the development of *Depthmap*. The visibility graph is produced by calculating the co-visibility of various nodes (defined by a grid setting) within a plan layout and measuring the connectivity of such nodes. That is, it constructs a series of isovist polygons around a regular grid in space, and then compares the connectivity relationships between them. This isovist "field" is a representation of the spatio-visual properties of an environment. The properties of isovist geometry and construction are shown in Figure 6. This Space Syntax approach has been applied to predict patterns of pedestrian movement, improve surveillance,

Figure 6. Isovist viewshed (grey-shaded polygon) from a location in a plan, identifying some of the more commonly used properties

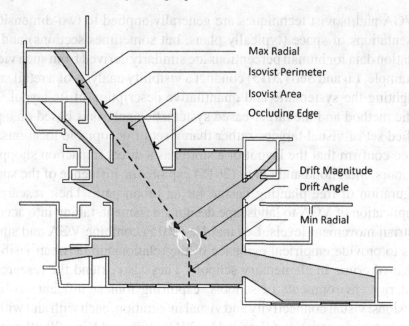

reduce crime through observation, and better understand access and control issues.

The measures derived from the isovist field for a plan effectively make up a visibility graph of its properties. Importantly, past research suggests that integration measures – including local and global integration – can be used to shape the design of healthcare facilities. "Visibility structures work together with and enhance permeability structures," and both influence how an environment functions spatially, as well as how it is experienced and understood (Guney, 2007, p. 038.10). While both methods are connected and related through the isovist field, they each have different levels of empirical evidence and different traditional applications (Braaksma & Cook, 1980; Turner et al., 2001). VGA seems to offer the potential for developing more holistic insights into the design of buildings that have particular visibility requirements. In contrast, particular isovists are effective for analysing spatial characteristics in terms of the perspectives of particular user groups.

VGA: Emerging Research

The VGA and isovist techniques are generally applied to two-dimensional representations of space (typically plans, but sometimes sections) and the correlation data for human perceptions are similarly derived from such views. For example, Lu and Seo (2015) conduct a visibility analysis of a retail store, highlighting the systematic and quantitative description of its layout. The analytic method and the target-based systematic analysis is based on a pre-specified set of visual targets, rather than a set of occupiable locations. Lu and Seo confirm that the layout of a store has a direct impact on shoppers' behaviours. Mahmoud and Omar (2015) explore the influence of the spatial configuration of tree planting design for an urban park. Their research is the application of VGA to landscape design assessment, taking into account pedestrian movement levels. Lee and Ha (2015) combine VGA and survey results to provide empirical evidence of the relationship between visibility and fear of crime in elementary schools. They also extend the research to the interior environments of schools, capturing four significant visibility dimensions: visual connectivity and visual integration, each with and without visible distance restrictions (Lee & Ha, 2016). Lim and Kim (2009) analyse the spatial characteristics of French mediatheques (public libraries) using convex space and VGA.

While VGA has often been combined with the other syntactic approaches in the past (axial line and convex space analysis), emerging research has identified new potential correlations. Choi (2013) develops evaluation data to support the remodelling of apartment units, comparing Post-Occupancy Evaluations (POE) with integration values from convex maps and isovist properties. Zamani (2018) examines the impact of emergency department design – security, wayfinding, visibility, privacy and efficiency – on staff satisfaction and performance. Zamani's research employs and combines the results of multiple methods: interviews, surveys, VGA and agent simulations. Alitajer and Molavi Nojoumi (2016) analyse behavioural patterns in the spatial configurations of traditional and modern houses in Hamedan, Iran, using VGA and agent count analysis. Lu and Peponis (2014) conduct a study of visitors' sensitivity to patterns of display co-visibility. Using *Depthmap* to estimate the size of visibility polygons, their research reviews existing measures of the objective co-visibility affordances of layouts, considering orientation, viewing angle and subtended angle. Their research suggests assessments of exhibition environments by co-visibility affordances. Lu, Gou, Ye and

Sheng (2017) develop three-dimensional visibility graphs from Space Syntax and social network theory to decode spatial cognition and behaviour. They also highlight a distinction between a generic visibility graph and a targeted visibility graph using visible locations instead of occupiable locations. In a related way, Tomé, Kuipers, Pinheiro, Nunes and Heitor (2015) propose a method for the analysis of space–use interactions. Their method includes various mobility indexes and maps: an occupancy map of the number of users, a flow map corresponding to movement flows, an encounter map and an average speed map. Spatial configuration and VGA are then correlated to those occupancy/co-presence patterns and movement/navigation patterns. The research of Amorim, Barros Filho and Cruz (2014) is concerned with complex intraurban socio-spatial patterns analysed using image textures and Space Syntax. Satellite image texture analysis identifies morphological patterns in urban areas, while the constitution map captures distinct patterns according to different social and urban dynamics. Their Space Syntax approaches include the public–private interface map or "constitution map" (Steadman, 1983) and VGA diagrams (Turner, 2001).

As an interdisciplinary study, Aknar and Atun (2017) analyse integration values derived from VGA using a Fibonacci mathematical sequence to differentiate the social importance of spaces (between segregated and integrated spaces). Kuipers, Tomé, Pinheiro, Nunes and Heitor (2014) propose a system combining the capacities of computer vision-based tracking and the identification capacities of radio frequency-based sensing (RFID). Their system aims to support the analytical procedures required for exploring the functional condition of architectural artefacts. It allows for a correlation to be made between occupancy/movement patterns and the configurational properties of space. Göçer et al. (2018) propose a new post-occupancy evaluation (POE) method – integrating user satisfaction, Space Syntax and behavioural mapping, biometeorological assessments, and user tracking – for outdoor spaces using spatio-temporal mapping. The configurational properties of a campus layout in İstanbul, Turkey, are explored through the visibility and accessibility values of outdoor spaces as well as spatio-temporal maps extending the use of GIS.

As previous examples in this section illustrate, multiple researchers have used Space Syntax techniques to support the analysis, optimisation and modelling of health facilities, including nurses' behaviours (walking patterns, entries to patient rooms and spatial positioning), patients' preferences and satisfaction levels (preference for bed privacy, perceived quality of care), and visitor movement in hospitals (Haq & Luo, 2012). For example, Seo,

Choi and Zimring (2011) observe that the spatial characteristics of routes taken by nurses from intensive care units (ICUs) to patient rooms and medication areas can contribute to behavioural patterns. Setola, Borgianni, Martinez and Tobari (2013) investigate the role of spatial layout in hospitals and analyse the integration of both public and staff spaces. They reveal the patterns of relationships between patient and medical staff (P-M) through the density of interactions and accessibility maps. Cai and Zimring (2017) conduct a comparative study of Chinese nursing unit typologies and their U.S. counterparts. By combining VGA and axial map analysis, they begin to develop an understanding of cultural differences in nursing unit design. Using these approaches, they translate abstract cultural schema, organisational constructs, and complex spatial relationships into quantitative spatial metrics.

In further examples, Sadek and Shepley (2016) examine various spatial measures to provide and facilitate accurate descriptions of different layout typologies in healthcare facilities. Haq and Luo (2012) review the use of syntactical techniques in modelling healthcare design, and Haq (2018) extends the review with a focus on the analytical techniques. Trzpuc and Martin (2010) explore nurses' communication in medical-surgical nursing units in urban hospitals using visibility and accessibility syntactical measures. Tzeng and Huang (2009) conduct both axial line and isovist analyses to investigate the influence of spatial forms and signage on wayfinding behaviours in hospitals. Axial maps, VGA and isovists are used to support van der Zwart's and van der Voordt's (2015) examination of the use of analytical drawing techniques to assess the attainment of pre-set objectives in hospital design. Setola et al. (2013) demonstrate the usefulness of VGA for understanding cultural differences in health care environments, and several related syntactical measures – including Target Visibility Analysis, Spatial Positioning Tool (SPOT), Weighted Isovist Area, Multi-Layered Network, Place Syntax, and Team-Base and Peer Distances – have been found effective in health care environments (Sadek & Shepley, 2016). Indeed, the investigation of both hospital planning and the correlation of computational measures for spatial visibility and accessibility with behavioural responses has become relatively common in recent years (Carranza, Koch, & Izaki, 2013; Yi Lu, 2010; Y. Lu, Peponis, & Zimring, 2009; Morgareidge et al., 2014).

Focusing on isovists, Knöll, Neuheuser, Cleff and Rudolph-Cleff (2017) conducted an empirical study measuring the environmental properties of open public space in the city of Darmstadt, Germany. In their research, public spatial typologies are the best predictors for perceived urban stress. They also identify, isovist visibility, vertices number and perimeter as being related to perceived urban stress in open public spaces. O'Hara, Klar, Patterson, Morris, Ascenzi, Fackler and Perry (2017) describe the interactions (formal and informal) in a pediatric intensive care unit, comparing distance matrices and isovist fields to panoramic photographs and ethnographic data. Space syntax constructs (openness, connectivity, and visibility) are often used to improve macrocognitive interactions. Lee, Ostwald and Lee (2017) measure the spatial and social characteristics of the architectural plans of aged care facilities, using visibility graph and isovist analyses. Their findings suggest that social and cultural factors may shape the design of aged care settings. Malhis (2016) investigates the spatial and formal properties of the layouts of Mamluk architecture to understand its historical design principles. Malhis' research analyses the data from fourteen Mamluk examples using axial analysis, global integration of VGA, and isovist visual fields. Kim and Jung (2014) develop a new method to calculate an isovist area weighted toward its origin point, a so-called "distance-weighted isovist area". Their method differs from the conventional isovist area and other isovist indices and offers a potential tool to investigate spatial cognition and human behaviour involving proximity.

Case Study 2

In this case study, VGA and isovist techniques are used to capture selected spatial and social properties of residential aged-care facilities. Aged care poses an interesting challenge for syntactical techniques, as such approaches often assume that human responses are relatively universal (or at least that mathematical patterns can be derived from them, which reflect universal tendencies). However, recent research suggests that the spatio-visual properties of physical environments have an impact on a variety of health-related outcomes (Hadi & Zimring, 2016; Hendrich et al., 2009; Pachilova & Sailer, 2013; Seo et al., 2011). While such studies demonstrate the usefulness of computational analysis in health care design, they are focused largely on functional planning and optimisation. In contrast, the challenges of designing for residential aged-care environments are not just functional, but social and cognitive. For example, past research has identified some of the most challenging factors in the design of aged-care centres, including isolation, loneliness and confusion (Gardner, 1994). As such, the problems of designing for aged-care are not only about surveillance and safety. The way a space is designed has a direct impact on the way people socialise, stay visually connected, avoid becoming lost, and can be visited by relatives and watched over by nurses, for care and safety. Aged-care facilities need to be designed to accommodate particular social and cognitive needs, in parallel with functional requirements. In response to this situation, this case study employs VGA to develop holistic measures for examining the spatio-visual properties of four plans for residential aged-care facilities, two in Australia and two in South Korea. In addition, individual isovist measures are used for analysing the difference between typical spaces for the resident, visitor and nurse in each facility.

For the first stage of the analysis, VGA, an isovist field is generated for all plans using a consistent 600mm grid, and all VGA calculations are completed using *Depthmap*. Measures for mean results for each plan for isovist area, isovist perimeter, drift angle, drift magnitude, maximum and minimum radial and occlusivity are then derived. These measures provide a holistic indication of various spatial properties of the plan. These measures are significant because they have been mapped to various cognitive and behavioural responses (Dawes & Ostwald, 2014a, 2014b). For the second stage of the analysis, specific isovists within each plan are used to examine the properties of different spaces and user-experiences. For this purpose, isovist area and perimeter measures are used to investigate four selected locations in each plan. The four locations are: lobby (representing the "visitor" perspective), common area (dining or lounge room, representing the "communal" perspective), nurse room (the "carer" perspective) and corridor in residential units (the "resident" perspective). After developing four isovists for each of the four cases, four properties – area, perimeter, maximum radial, and occlusivity – are measured for each location. These measures were chosen after a review of the results of past research that compares the mathematical properties of isovists with human spatial perceptions (Dawes & Ostwald, 2014a, 2014b; Stamps, 2005a). The analysis of the case study is only focused on interior spaces and views. Furthermore, for each plan, doors, low partitions and furniture below eye level were removed to conduct the VGA. This means that the results represent the inter-visibility properties of each layout (Cai & Zimring, 2013).

The first pair of plans are for Australian residential aged-care facilities, both of which were constructed in New South Wales in 2012. The second pair of plans are for South Korean residential aged-care facilities, one from 2004 and the other from 2015, both in Seoul. While these cases cannot be extrapolated to represent architectural design approaches to aged-care facilities in each nation, they can be regarded as contemporary designs that are shaped

Table 3. Four aged-care facilities in Australia and South Korea

Nation	Australia		South Korea	
Code	Au1	Au2	Ko1	Ko2
Name	Nambucca Head UnitingCare Ageing	Port Macquarie UnitingCare Ageing	Songpa Ageing Skilled-nursing home	Gangnam Happiness Nursing hospital
Date completed	January 2012	February 2012	March 2004	January 2015
No. of care units	86	110	93	307
Location	Nambucca Heads, NSW	Port Macquarie, NSW	Songpa-gu, Seoul	Gangnam-gu, Seoul
Site size	3,853 m^2	14,677 m^2	1,500 m^2	6,426 m^2
Building footprint	1,921 m^2	3,635 m^2	407 m^2	3,150 m^2
Building area	5,463 m^2	7,225 m^2	3,116 m^2	18,585 m^2

by socio-cultural characteristics and values. Across the two sets, the number of units ranges from 86 to 307 (Table 3). Because of these scale differences, the comparative study uses mean values of measures to allow for more useful comparisons to be made. The Australian cases typically adopt double-loaded corridors (a room on each side of a central corridor) and multi-level, two- or three-storey buildings, with the planning replicated on each floor. For this reason, only one level of each case needs to be examined. On the other hand, the Korean cases feature single-loaded corridors, in spite of the relatively high expense and lack of efficiency associated with this planning strategy. They are five and six storeys high, and the ground floors of the two Korean facilities differ from the upper levels, with the former containing extensive administration areas and a café. Thus, both the ground floor and a standard residential floor are examined for both Korean cases.

VGA results can be visualised by mapping various values (colour-coded from red for "very high" measures to dark blue for "very low" measures) to each grid square. Figure 7 contains the visibility graphs for each of the four designs, for visual integration measures. While each cell has a visual integration value assigned to it for more detailed numerical analysis, the colour coding allows for an early intuitive reading to be developed. The average values of integration and connectivity are also described in Figure 7. The visual integration values for Ko1 and Ko2 (ground floor: 6.6656 and 4.6261, respectively), with more extensive areas of warm colours (reds and oranges) in their graphs, are higher than in the Australian sets (2.8754 and 2.3889, respectively). This might be because the multi-storey Korean facilities

Figure 7. Visibility graphs (visual integration) of each case

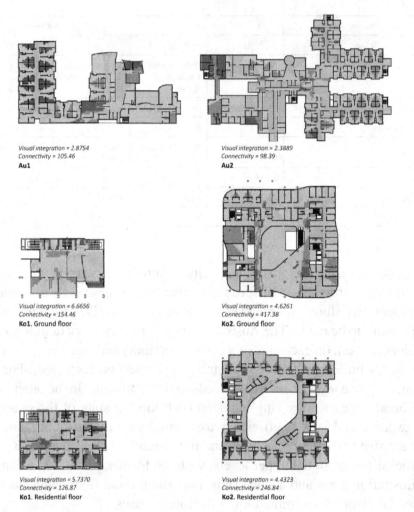

Visual integration = 2.8754
Connectivity = 105.46
Au1

Visual integration = 2.3889
Connectivity = 98.39
Au2

Visual integration = 6.6656
Connectivity = 154.46
Ko1. Ground floor

Visual integration = 4.6261
Connectivity = 417.38
Ko2. Ground floor

Visual integration = 5.7370
Connectivity = 126.87
Ko1. Residential floor

Visual integration = 4.4323
Connectivity = 246.84
Ko2. Residential floor

have a more focused circulation space and rely on single-loaded corridors. In contrast, the two Australian cases have relatively weak or low connectivity and integration measures. The results are unexpected because Australia has extensive experience in the aged-care domain and a higher mean integration level would be anticipated. The double-loaded corridors, interpenetration of landscaped courtyards, and greater reliance on horizontal circulation (rather than vertical) all shape this result. In general, a higher integration value represents a shallower or more accessible space (Hillier & Hanson, 1984). The connectivity ranges or values for the Australian cases are similar, although

Table 4. Isovist properties from four vantage points in Australian and Korean cases

Vantage point		IA(m²)	IAP (%)	IP (m)	IDM (m)	IMax (m)	IMin (m)	IO (m)
Au1	Lobby	81.21	1.49%	81.05	1.67	13.15	1.98	34.51
	Common	68.09	1.25%	51.47	0.57	10.29	3.33	17.21
	Nurse	59.93	1.10%	75.58	1.13	21.40	1.20	44.60
	Corridor	54.04	0.99%	69.89	0.89	14.81	0.75	29.24
Au2	Lobby	73.55	1.02%	79.22	0.81	8.94	1.81	43.09
	Common	58.63	0.81%	43.63	0.44	7.78	2.04	11.07
	Nurse	21.98	0.30%	41.37	1.68	9.01	1.30	22.65
	Corridor	74.10	1.03%	122.76	0.60	19.30	0.78	65.53
Ko1	Lobby	98.79	3.17%	112.94	0.73	10.09	3.82	68.03
	Common	59.44	1.91%	61.58	3.24	14.40	2.69	30.44
	Nurse	80.40	2.58%	101.27	3.24	11.08	1.28	65.07
	Corridor	72.53	2.33%	132.23	0.51	13.66	1.11	87.01
Ko2	Lobby	384.31	2.07%	303.48	9.02	33.62	3.49	217.07
	Common	124.82	0.67%	150.67	1.89	21.43	1.61	99.70
	Nurse	173.21	0.93%	222.40	0.80	21.83	2.07	146.28
	Corridor	183.98	0.99%	180.43	1.83	28.38	1.07	110.14
Mean		104.31	1.42%	114.37	1.82	16.20	1.90	68.23
SD		85.87	0.78%	71.45	2.12	7.49	0.97	54.52

(IA: Isovist Area, IAP: Isovist area proportion (= (IA/Building area) × 100), IP: Isovist Perimeter, IDA: Isovist Drift Angle, IDM: Isovist Drift Magnitude, IMax: Isovist Max Radial, IMin: Isovist Min Radial, IO: Isovist Occlusivity)

the design with the larger footprint (Au2) has a lower level of connectivity. In contrast, in the Korean set, Ko2 has the highest level of connectivity.

For the second stage of the case study, isovists in four distinct locations on each plan are developed, which represent three different users (residents, visitors and nurses) and a more general communal space. The results of this process are in Table 4 and isovists maps are in Figures 4.8 and 4.9.

Since isovist area can be affected by building area, and the buildings differ in size, the proportion of the total area that is taken up by a given isovist is also calculated by isovist area proportion (*IAP*). The lobbies in both Korean cases have a higher area and occlusivity than in the Australian cases. The nurse room and residential corridor in Ko1 also have relatively higher *IAP*. This is because it has the smallest building footprint, even though it has a "group home" layout with only south-facing resident units, which is reminiscent of a traditional Korean housing configuration. Au1's *IA* and *IAP* feature a clear hierarchy, wherein Lobby > Common > Nurse > Corridor. Visitors also have a distinctive spatial experience, with highest levels of visible space (outlook) and closest distance from walls (*IMin*). All common areas have the lowest levels of mystery (*IO*). This may be because the Australian cases are closer to a typical "double-loaded corridor" type, which is a traditional western typology for aged-care facilities. The isovist area proportions (*IAP*) confirm that the Korean cases do feature a large volume of visible space in the visitor's lobby, but a small volume in the common area. The different isovist properties may also reflect the difference between these spatial configurations in cultural terms.

This brief case study is designed to demonstrate the use of VGA and isovist analysis for measuring and extrapolating the spatial and social properties of an architectural plan. Acknowledging the small sample size, the data derived from the demonstration begins to provide an insight into the spatial and social patterns of each case, including both similarities and differences. These spatial differences may be related to the design typologies the architects have adopted, either shaped by policy guides or drawn from a priori knowledge or reasoning.

CONCLUSION

This chapter introduces three Space Syntax techniques – axial line, convex space and visibility graph analysis – before reviewing emerging trends in their use and development. Significantly, while some new techniques, such as angular segmentation and agent analyses, are emerging, the three basic approaches continue to be explored and applied in many fields. Furthermore, the quantitative results of Space Syntax approaches can be easily used as independent or dependant variables for new computational models or applications. In this way, they have become part of a design or information system that can be used to support generative designs and a systematic understanding of the built environment.

This chapter presents two case studies to demonstrate axial line and visibility graph analyses. The first case study is an application of axial line analysis to four different streets and their associated neighbourhood areas in Seoul. The results are interpreted in terms of the degree to which these streets and neighbourhoods are planned or have evolved over time. The second case study uses VGA and isovists to capture a holistic insight into the design of a building type and to reveal different spatial characteristics of the experience of particular user groups. Acknowledging their limited sample sizes, these

Figure 8. Isovists maps from four selected points of Australian cases

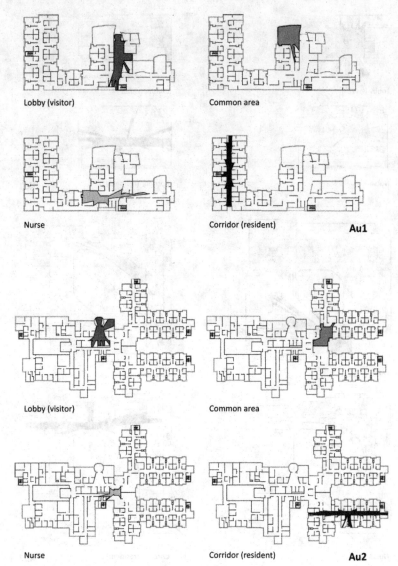

Lobby (visitor)

Common area

Nurse

Corridor (resident)   **Au1**

Lobby (visitor)

Common area

Nurse

Corridor (resident)   **Au2**

Figure 9. Isovists maps from four selected points of Korean cases

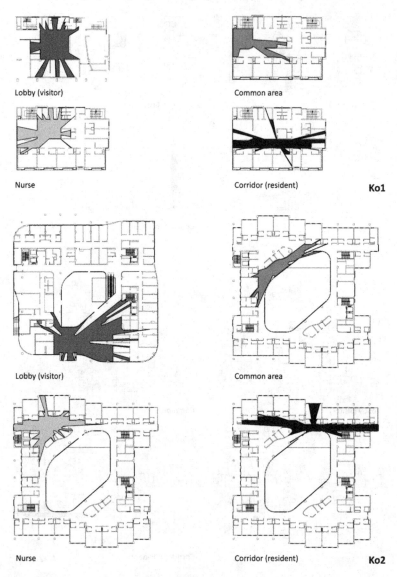

Lobby (visitor)

Common area

Nurse

Corridor (resident)   **Ko1**

Lobby (visitor)

Common area

Nurse

Corridor (resident)   **Ko2**

case studies extend the conventional applications of Space Syntax approaches and identify areas of further investigation. The next chapter explains and demonstrates the convex space analysis technique, focusing on the JPG and its mathematical measures.

REFERENCES

Abune'meh, M., El Meouche, R., Hijaze, I., Mebarki, A., & Shahrour, I. (2016). Optimal construction site layout based on risk spatial variability. *Automation in Construction*, *70*, 167–177. doi:10.1016/j.autcon.2016.06.014

Aknar, M., & Atun, R. A. (2017). Predicting movement in architectural space. *Architectural Science Review*, *60*(1), 78–95. doi:10.1080/00038628 .2016.1254594

Al-Sayed, K., & Penn, A. (2016). On the nature of urban dependencies: How Manhattan and Barcelona reinforced a natural organisation despite planning intentionality. *Environment and Planning B: Planning and Design*, *43*(6), 975-996. doi:10.1177/0265813516650200

Alitajer, S., & Molavi Nojoumi, G. (2016). Privacy at home: Analysis of behavioral patterns in the spatial configuration of traditional and modern houses in the city of Hamedan based on the notion of space syntax. *Frontiers of Architectural Research*, *5*(3), 341–352. doi:10.1016/j.foar.2016.02.003

Amorim, L. M. E., Barros Filho, M. N. M., & Cruz, D. (2014). Urban texture and space configuration: An essay on integrating socio-spatial analytical techniques. *Cities (London, England)*, *39*, 58–67. doi:10.1016/j. cities.2014.02.001

Aschwanden, G. D. P. A., Haegler, S., Bosché, F., Van Gool, L., & Schmitt, G. (2011). Empiric design evaluation in urban planning. *Automation in Construction*, *20*(3), 299–310. doi:10.1016/j.autcon.2010.10.007

Asif, N., Utaberta, N., Sabil, A. B., & Ismail, S. (2018). Reflection of cultural practices on syntactical values: An introduction to the application of space syntax to vernacular Malay architecture. *Frontiers of Architectural Research*, *7*(4), 521–529. doi:10.1016/j.foar.2018.08.005

Bafna, S. (1999). The morphology of early modernist residential plans: Geometry and genotypical trends in Mies van der Rohe's designs. In *Proceedings of the Second International Symposium on Space Syntax* (pp. 01.01-01.12). Brasília, Brazil: University of Brasilia.

Bafna, S. (2001). Geometric intuitions of genotypes. In J. Peponis, J. Wineman, & S. Bafna (Eds.), *Proceedings of the Third International Symposium on Space Syntax* (pp. 20.21-20.16). Ann Arbor, MI: University of Michigan.

Barthelemy, M. (2015). From paths to blocks: New measures for street patterns. *Environment and Planning B. Urban Analytics and City Science, 44*(2), 256–271. doi:10.1177/0265813515599982

Benedikt, M. L. (1979). To take hold of space: Isovists and isovist fields. *Environment and Planning. B, Planning & Design, 6*(1), 47–65. doi:10.1068/b060047

Braaksma, J. P., & Cook, W. J. (1980). Human orientation in transportation terminals. *Transportation Engineering Journal, 106*(2), 189–203.

Byun, N., & Choi, J. (2016). A typology of Korean housing units: In search of spatial configuration. *Journal of Asian Architecture and Building Engineering, 15*(1), 41–48. doi:10.3130/jaabe.15.41

Cai, H., & Zimring, C. (2013). Understanding cultural differences in nursing unit design with the support of space syntax analysis: Are Chinese nursing units designs different from their U.S. counterparts? In Y. O. Kim, H. T. Park, & K. W. Seo (Eds.), *Proceedings of the Ninth International Space Syntax Symposium* (pp. 014:1-24). Seoul, South Korea: Sejong University.

Cai, H., & Zimring, C. (2017). Cultural impacts on nursing unit design: A comparative study on Chinese nursing unit typologies and their U.S. counterparts using space syntax. *Environment and Planning B. Urban Analytics and City Science, 2399808317715639.* doi:10.1177/2399808317715639

Carranza, P. M., Koch, D., & Izaki, A. (2013). SPOT with paths, and interactive diagram with a low complexity isovist algorithm. In Y. O. Kim, H. T. Park, & K. W. Seo (Eds.), *Proceedings of the Ninth International Space Syntax Symposium* (pp. 062:1-13). Seoul, South Korea: Sejong University.

Chiang, Y.-C., & Deng, Y. (2017). City gate as key towards sustainable urban redevelopment: A case study of ancient Gungnae City within the modern city of Ji'an. *Habitat International, 67,* 1–12. doi:10.1016/j.habitatint.2017.06.007

Choi, J., Kim, M., & Byun, N. (2013). Quantitative analysis on the spatial configuration of Korean apartment complexes. *Journal of Asian Architecture and Building Engineering, 12*(2), 277–284. doi:10.3130/jaabe.12.277

Choi, J., Kim, Y., Kang, J., & Choi, Y. (2014). Comparative analysis of the spatial structure of apartment unit plans in Asia – Apartments in Korea, Vietnam, and Kazakhstan. *Journal of Asian Architecture and Building Engineering, 13*(3), 563–569. doi:10.3130/jaabe.13.563

Choi, Y. (2013). Comparative evaluation of unit layout alternatives in plan-extension remodeling of domestic Korean apartments. *Journal of Asian Architecture and Building Engineering, 12*(2), 205–212. doi:10.3130/jaabe.12.205

Choi, Y. (2018). Identifying the individualist / collectivist cultural dimension in space. *Journal of Asian Architecture and Building Engineering, 17*(2), 337–344. doi:10.3130/jaabe.17.337

D'Autilia, R., & Spada, M. (2017). Shaping ideal cities: The graph representation of the urban utopia. *Environment and Planning B. Urban Analytics and City Science.* doi:10.1177/2399808317716163

Dalton, N. (2001). Fractional configurational analysis and a solution to the Manhattan problem. In *Proceedings of the 3rd International Symposium on Space Syntax (Vol. 26,* pp. 1-13). Atlanta, GA: Georgia institute of Technology.

Dawes, M. J., & Ostwald, M. J. (2014a). Prospect-Refuge theory and the textile-block houses of Frank Lloyd Wright: An analysis of spatio-visual characteristics using isovists. *Building and Environment, 80,* 228–240. doi:10.1016/j.buildenv.2014.05.026

Dawes, M. J., & Ostwald, M. J. (2014b). Testing the "Wright Space': Using isovists to analyse prospect-refuge characteristics in Usonian architecture. *The Journal of Architecture, 19*(5), 645–666. doi:10.1080/13602365.2014.965722

Dawson, P. C. (2008). Unfriendly architecture: Using observations of Inuit spatial behavior to design culturally sustaining houses in Arctic Canada. *Housing Studies, 23*(1), 111–128. doi:10.1080/02673030701731258

di Bella, E., Corsi, M., Leporatti, L., & Persico, L. (2015). The spatial configuration of urban crime environments and statistical modeling. *Environment and Planning B. Urban Analytics and City Science, 44*(4), 647–667. doi:10.1177/0265813515624686

Edwards, M. J. (2013). The configuration of built space at Pataraya and Wari provincial administration in Nasca. *Journal of Anthropological Archaeology, 32*(4), 565–576. doi:10.1016/j.jaa.2013.09.004

Eloy, S., & Duarte, J. P. (2015). A transformation-grammar-based methodology for the adaptation of existing housetypes: The case of the "rabo-de-bacalhau". *Environment and Planning. B, Planning & Design, 42*(5), 775–800. doi:10.1068/b120018p

Feng, C., & Peponis, J. (2018). The definition of syntactic types: The generation, analysis, and sorting of universes of superblock designs. *Environment and Planning B. Urban Analytics and City Science.* doi:10.1177/2399808318813576

Fladd, S. G. (2017). Social syntax: An approach to spatial modification through the reworking of space syntax for archaeological applications. *Journal of Anthropological Archaeology, 47*, 127–138. doi:10.1016/j.jaa.2017.05.002

França, F. C. d., & Greene, M. (2018). The poet Neruda's environment: The Isla Negra house. *Environment and Planning B. Urban Analytics and City Science, 45*(4), 713–732. doi:10.1177/0265813516685566

Gao, X., Asami, Y., Zhou, Y., & Ishikawa, T. (2013). Preferences for floor plans of medium-sized apartments: A survey analysis in Beijing, China. *Housing Studies, 28*(3), 429–452. doi:10.1080/02673037.2013.759542

Gardner, I. L. (1994). Why people move to retirement villages: Home owners and non-home owners. *Australian Journal on Ageing, 13*(1), 36–40. doi:10.1111/j.1741-6612.1994.tb00632.x

Göçer, Ö., Göçer, K., Başol, A. M., Kıraç, M. F., Özbil, A., Bakovic, M., ... Özcan, B. (2018). Introduction of a spatio-temporal mapping based POE method for outdoor spaces: Suburban university campus as a case study. *Building and Environment, 145*, 125–139. doi:10.1016/j.buildenv.2018.09.012

Guney, Y. I. (2007). Analyzing visibility structures in Turkish domestic spaces. In *Proceedings, 6th International Space Syntax Symposium* (pp. 038.1-038.12). İstanbul, Turkey: Istanbul Technical University.

Hadi, K., & Zimring, C. (2016). Design to improve visibility: Impact of corridor width and unit shape. *HERD: Health Environments Research & Design Journal, 9*(4), 35–49. doi:10.1177/1937586715621643 PMID:26747840

Hajrasouliha, A., & Yin, L. (2014). The impact of street network connectivity on pedestrian volume. *Urban Studies (Edinburgh, Scotland)*, *52*(13), 2483–2497. doi:10.1177/0042098014544763

Hanson, J. (1998). *Decoding homes and houses*. Cambridge, UK: Cambridge University Press.

Haq, S. (2018). Where we walk is what we see: Foundational concepts and analytical techniques of space syntax. *HERD: Health Environments Research & Design Journal*. doi:10.1177/1937586718812436 PMID:30523701

Haq, S., & Luo, Y. (2012). Space syntax in healthcare facilities research: A review. *HERD: Health Environments Research & Design Journal*, *5*(4), 98–117. doi:10.1177/193758671200500409 PMID:23224810

Hayward, S. C., & Franklin, S. S. (1974). Perceived openness-enclosure of architectural space. *Environment and Behavior*, *6*(1), 37–52. doi:10.1177/001391657400600102

Helbich, M. (2017). Children's school commuting in the Netherlands: Does it matter how urban form is incorporated in mode choice models? *International Journal of Sustainable Transportation*, *11*(7), 507–517. doi:10.1080/15568 318.2016.1275892

Hendrich, A., Chow, M. P., Bafna, S., Choudhary, R., Heo, Y., & Skierczynski, B. A. (2009). Unit-related factors that affect nursing time with patients: Spatial analysis of the time and motion study. *HERD: Health Environments Research & Design Journal*, *2*(2), 5–20. doi:10.1177/193758670900200202 PMID:21161927

Hillier, B. (1996). *Space is the machine: A configurational theory of architecture*. Cambridge, UK: Cambridge University Press.

Hillier, B. (1999). The hidden geometry of deformed grids: Or, why space syntax works, when it looks as though it shouldn't. *Environment and Planning. B, Planning & Design*, *26*(2), 169–191. doi:10.1068/b4125

Hillier, B., & Hanson, J. (1984). *The social logic of space* (Vol. 1). Cambridge, UK: Cambridge University Press. doi:10.1017/CBO9780511597237

Hillier, B., Hanson, J., & Graham, H. (1987). Ideas are in things: An application of the space syntax method to discovering house genotypes. *Environment and Planning. B, Planning & Design*, *14*(4), 363–385. doi:10.1068/b140363

Hillier, B., & Vaughan, L. (2007). The city as one thing. *Progress in Planning, 67*(3), 205–230.

Jeong, S.-K., & Ban, Y.-U. (2011a). Computational algorithms to evaluate design solutions using space syntax. *Computer Aided Design, 43*(6), 664–676. doi:10.1016/j.cad.2011.02.011

Jeong, S.-K., & Ban, Y.-U. (2011b). Developing a topological information extraction model for space syntax analysis. *Building and Environment, 46*(12), 2442–2453. doi:10.1016/j.buildenv.2011.05.024

Jeong, S. K., & Ban, Y. U. (2014). The spatial configurations in South Korean apartments built between 1972 and 2000. *Habitat International, 42*, 90–102. doi:10.1016/j.habitatint.2013.11.002

Jeong, S. K., Lee, T. H., & Ban, Y. U. (2015). Characteristics of spatial configurations in Pyongyang, North Korea. *Habitat International, 47*, 148–157. doi:10.1016/j.habitatint.2015.01.010

Kalakou, S., & Moura, F. (2014). Bridging the gap in planning indoor pedestrian facilities. *Transport Reviews, 34*(4), 474–500. doi:10.1080/0144 1647.2014.915441

Kim, M., & Moon, J. (2013). A study on the correlation between viewing behavior and exhibiting methods in museums – Focusing on viewing behavior on weekdays and weekends in medium sized history museums in Korea. *Journal of Asian Architecture and Building Engineering, 12*(2), 173–180. doi:10.3130/jaabe.12.173

Kim, M., & Piao, G. (2017). A study on the applying concept of metric weighting to space syntax. *Journal of Asian Architecture and Building Engineering, 16*(3), 447–454. doi:10.3130/jaabe.16.447

Kim, Y., & Jung, S. K. (2014). Distance-weighted isovist area: An isovist index representing spatial proximity. *Automation in Construction, 43*, 92–97. doi:10.1016/j.autcon.2014.03.006

Kishimoto, T., & Taguchi, M. (2014). Spatial configuration of Japanese elementary schools: Analyses by the space syntax and evaluation by school teachers. *Journal of Asian Architecture and Building Engineering, 13*(2), 373–380. doi:10.3130/jaabe.13.373

Knöll, M., Neuheuser, K., Cleff, T., & Rudolph-Cleff, A. (2017). A tool to predict perceived urban stress in open public spaces. *Environment and Planning B. Urban Analytics and City Science*, *45*(4), 797–813. doi:10.1177/0265813516686971

Kuipers, M., Tomé, A., Pinheiro, T., Nunes, M., & Heitor, T. (2014). Building space-use analysis system – A multi location/multi sensor platform. *Automation in Construction*, *47*, 10–23. doi:10.1016/j.autcon.2014.07.001

Kwon, Y., Bonghee, J., & Kim, S. (2015). The seventeenth-century transition of Seoul's spatial structure to functional pragmatism. *Journal of Asian Architecture and Building Engineering*, *14*(2), 419–426. doi:10.3130/jaabe.14.419

Law, S. (2017). Defining street-based local area and measuring its effect on house price using a hedonic price approach: The case study of Metropolitan London. *Cities (London, England)*, *60*, 166–179. doi:10.1016/j.cities.2016.08.008

Lee, J. H., Ostwald, M. J., & Gu, N. (2015). A syntactical and grammatical approach to architectural configuration, analysis and generation. *Architectural Science Review*, *58*(3), 189–204. doi:10.1080/00038628.2015.1015948

Lee, J. H., Ostwald, M. J., & Gu, N. (2016). A justified plan graph (JPG) grammar approach to identifying spatial design patterns in an architectural style. *Environment and Planning B. Urban Analytics and City Science*, *45*(1), 67–89. doi:10.1177/0265813516665618

Lee, J. H., Ostwald, M. J., & Lee, H. (2017). Measuring the spatial and social characteristics of the architectural plans of aged care facilities. *Frontiers of Architectural Research*, *6*(4), 431–441. doi:10.1016/j.foar.2017.09.003

Lee, S., & Ha, M. (2015). The duality of visibility: Does visibility increase or decrease the fear of crime in schools' exterior environments? *Journal of Asian Architecture and Building Engineering*, *14*(1), 145–152. doi:10.3130/jaabe.14.145

Lee, S., & Ha, M. (2016). The effects of visibility on fear of crime in schools' interior environments. *Journal of Asian Architecture and Building Engineering*, *15*(3), 527–534. doi:10.3130/jaabe.15.527

Lee, S., Lee, S., Son, H., & Joo, Y. (2013). A new approach for the evaluation of the walking environment. *International Journal of Sustainable Transportation*, *7*(3), 238–260. doi:10.1080/15568318.2013.710146

Li, R., & Klippel, A. (2012). Wayfinding in libraries: Can problems be predicted? *Journal of Map & Geography Libraries*, *8*(1), 21–38. doi:10.10 80/15420353.2011.622456

Li, R., & Klippel, A. (2014). Wayfinding behaviors in complex buildings: The impact of environmental legibility and familiarity. *Environment and Behavior*, *48*(3), 482–510. doi:10.1177/0013916514550243

Lim, H., & Kim, S. (2009). Changes in spatial organization in French public libraries. *Journal of Asian Architecture and Building Engineering*, *8*(2), 323–330. doi:10.3130/jaabe.8.323

Lu, Y. (2010). Measuring the structure of visual fields in nursing units. *HERD: Health Environments Research & Design Journal*, *3*(2), 48–59. doi:10.1177/193758671000300205 PMID:21165869

Lu, Y., Gou, Z., Ye, Y., & Sheng, Q. (2017). Three-dimensional visibility graph analysis and its application. *Environment and Planning B. Urban Analytics and City Science*. doi:10.1177/2399808317739893

Lu, Y., & Peponis, J. (2014). Exhibition visitors are sensitive to patterns of display covisibility. *Environment and Planning. B, Planning & Design*, *41*(1), 53–68. doi:10.1068/b39058

Lu, Y., Peponis, J., & Zimring, C. (2009). Targeted visibility analysis in buildings: Correlating targeted visibility analysis with distribution of people and their interactions within an intensive care unit. In D. Koch, L. Marcus, & J. Steen (Eds.), *Proceedings of the Seventh International Space Syntax Symposium* (pp. 0.681-0.6810). Stockholm, Sweden: KTH.

Lu, Y., & Seo, H.-B. (2015). Developing visibility analysis for a retail store: A pilot study in a bookstore. *Environment and Planning. B, Planning & Design*, *42*(1), 95–109. doi:10.1068/b130016p

Ma, D., Omer, I., Osaragi, T., Sandberg, M., & Jiang, B. (2018). Why topology matters in predicting human activities. *Environment and Planning B. Urban Analytics and City Science*, *2399808318792268*. doi:10.1177/2399808318792268

Mahmoud, A. H., & Omar, R. H. (2015). Planting design for urban parks: Space syntax as a landscape design assessment tool. *Frontiers of Architectural Research*, *4*(1), 35–45. doi:10.1016/j.foar.2014.09.001

Maina, J. J. (2013). Uncomfortable prototypes: Rethinking socio-cultural factors for the design of public housing in Billiri, north east Nigeria. *Frontiers of Architectural Research*, *2*(3), 310–321. doi:10.1016/j.foar.2013.04.004

Malhis, S. (2008). The new upper-middle class residential experience: A case study of apartment flats in Jordan using the logics of Burden, Hillier and Hanson. *Architectural Science Review*, *51*(1), 71–79. doi:10.3763/asre.2008.5110

Malhis, S. (2016). Narratives in Mamluk architecture: Spatial and perceptual analyses of the madrassas and their mausoleums. *Frontiers of Architectural Research*, *5*(1), 74–90. doi:10.1016/j.foar.2015.11.002

Marcus, L., & Koch, D. (2016). Cities as implements or facilities – The need for a spatial morphology in smart city systems. *Environment and Planning B. Urban Analytics and City Science*, *44*(2), 204–226. doi:10.1177/0265813516685565

Mavridou, M. (2012). Perception of three-dimensional urban scale in an immersive virtual environment. *Environment and Planning. B, Planning & Design*, *39*(1), 33–47. doi:10.1068/b34049

Morales, J., Flacke, J., & Zevenbergen, J. (2017). Modelling residential land values using geographic and geometric accessibility in Guatemala City. *Environment and Planning B. Urban Analytics and City Science*, *2399808317726332*. doi:10.1177/2399808317726332

Morgareidge, D., Cai, H., & Jia, J. (2014). Performance-driven design with the support of digital tools: Applying discrete event simulation and space syntax on the design of the emergency department. *Frontiers of Architectural Research*, *3*(3), 250–264. doi:10.1016/j.foar.2014.04.006

Mustafa, F. A., & Hassan, A. S. (2013). Mosque layout design: An analytical study of mosque layouts in the early Ottoman period. *Frontiers of Architectural Research*, *2*(4), 445–456. doi:10.1016/j.foar.2013.08.005

Nam, J., & Kim, H. (2014). The correlation between spatial characteristics and utilization of city parks: A focus on neighborhood parks in Seoul, Korea. *Journal of Asian Architecture and Building Engineering*, *13*(2), 515–522. doi:10.3130/jaabe.13.515

Nasar, J. L., & Jones, K. M. (1997). Landscapes of fear and stress. *Environment and Behavior*, *29*(3), 291–323. doi:10.1177/001391659702900301

Netto, V. M. (2016). "What is space syntax not?" Reflections on space syntax as sociospatial theory. *URBAN DESIGN International*, *21*(1), 25–40. doi:10.1057/udi.2015.21

O'Hara, S., Klar, R. T., Patterson, E. S., Morris, N. S., Ascenzi, J., Fackler, J. C., & Perry, D. J. (2017). Macrocognition in the healthcare built environment (mHCBE): A focused ethnographic study of "neighborhoods" in a pediatric intensive care unit. *HERD: Health Environments Research & Design Journal*, *11*(2), 104–123. doi:10.1177/1937586717728484 PMID:29243506

Omer, I., & Goldblatt, R. (2016). Using space syntax and Q-analysis for investigating movement patterns in buildings: The case of shopping malls. *Environment and Planning B. Urban Analytics and City Science*, *44*(3), 504–530. doi:10.1177/0265813516647061

Omer, I., & Kaplan, N. (2018). Structural properties of the angular and metric street network's centralities and their implications for movement flows. *Environment and Planning B. Urban Analytics and City Science*. doi:10.1177/2399808318760571

Önder, D. E., & Gigi, Y. (2010). Reading urban spaces by the space-syntax method: A proposal for the South Haliç Region. *Cities (London, England)*, *27*(4), 260–271. doi:10.1016/j.cities.2009.12.006

Ostwald, M. J. (2011a). Examining the relationship between topology and geometry: A configurational analysis of the rural houses (1984-2005) of Glenn Murcutt. *Journal of Space Syntax*, *2*(2), 223–246.

Ostwald, M. J. (2011b). A justified plan graph analysis of the early houses (1975-1982) of Glenn Murcutt. *Nexus Network Journal*, *13*(3), 737–762. doi:10.100700004-011-0089-x

Ostwald, M. J. (2017). Digital research in architecture: Reflecting on the past, analysing the trends and considering the future. *Architectural Research Quarterly*, *21*(4), 351–358. doi:10.1017/S135913551800009X

Pachilova, R., & Sailer, K. (2013). The effect of hospital layout on caregiver-patient communication patterns. In A. Yoxall, & K. Christer (Eds.), *Proceedings of the Second European Conference on Design 4 Health* (pp. 174-184). Sheffield, UK: Sheffield Hallam University.

Pafka, E., Dovey, K., & Aschwanden, G. D. P. A. (2018). Limits of space syntax for urban design: Axiality, scale and sinuosity. *Environment and Planning B. Urban Analytics and City Science*, 2399808318786512. doi:10.1177/2399808318786512

Peponis, J., Bafna, S., Dahabreh, S. M., & Dogan, F. (2015). Configurational meaning and conceptual shifts in design. *The Journal of Architecture, 20*(2), 215–243. doi:10.1080/13602365.2015.1025814

Prayitno, B. (2017). Co-habitation space: A model for urban informal settlement consolidation for the heritage city of Yogyakarta, Indonesia. *Journal of Asian Architecture and Building Engineering, 16*(3), 527–534. doi:10.3130/jaabe.16.527

Rashid, M. (2012). On space syntax as a configurational theory of architecture from a situated observer's viewpoint. *Environment and Planning. B, Planning & Design, 39*(4), 732–754. doi:10.1068/b37071

Rashid, M., & Alobaydi, D. (2015). Territory, politics of power, and physical spatial networks: The case of Baghdad, Iraq. *Habitat International, 50*, 180–194. doi:10.1016/j.habitatint.2015.08.031

Ratti, C. (2004a). Rejoinder to Hillier and Penn. *Environment and Planning. B, Planning & Design, 31*(4), 513–516. doi:10.1068/b3019b

Ratti, C. (2004b). Space syntax: Some inconsistencies. *Environment and Planning. B, Planning & Design, 31*(4), 487–499. doi:10.1068/b3019

Rybarczyk, G. (2014). Simulating bicycle wayfinding mechanisms in an urban environment. *Urban, Planning and Transport Research, 2*(1), 89–104. doi:10.1080/21650020.2014.906909

Sadek, A. H., & Shepley, M. M. (2016). Space syntax analysis: Tools for augmenting the precision of healthcare facility spatial analysis. *HERD: Health Environments Research & Design Journal, 10*(1), 114–129. doi:10.1177/1937586715624225 PMID:26747842

Scoppa, M. D., & Peponis, J. (2015). Distributed attraction: The effects of street network connectivity upon the distribution of retail frontage in the city of Buenos Aires. *Environment and Planning. B, Planning & Design, 42*(2), 354–378. doi:10.1068/b130051p

Seo, H.-B., Choi, Y.-S., & Zimring, C. (2011). Impact of hospital unit design for patient-centered care on nurses' behavior. *Environment and Behavior*, *43*(4), 443–468. doi:10.1177/0013916510362635

Setola, N., Borgianni, S., Martinez, M., & Tobari, E. (2013). The role of spatial layout of hospital public spaces in informal patient-medical staff interface. In Y. O. Kim, H. T. Park, & K. W. Seo (Eds.), *Proceedings of the Ninth International Space Syntax Symposium* (pp. 025.1-11). Seoul, South Korea: Sejong University.

Shen, Y., & Karimi, K. (2016). Urban function connectivity: Characterisation of functional urban streets with social media check-in data. *Cities (London, England)*, *55*, 9–21. doi:10.1016/j.cities.2016.03.013

Shpuza, E. (2014). Allometry in the syntax of street networks: Evolution of Adriatic and Ionian coastal cities 1800–2010. *Environment and Planning. B, Planning & Design*, *41*(3), 450–471. doi:10.1068/b39109

Stamps, A. E. III. (2005a). Isovists, enclosure, and permeability theory. *Environment and Planning. B, Planning & Design*, *32*(5), 735–762. doi:10.1068/b31138

Stamps, A. E. III. (2005b). Visual permeability, locomotive permeability, safety, and enclosure. *Environment and Behavior*, *37*(5), 587–619. doi:10.1177/0013916505276741

Steadman, P. J. (1983). *Architectural morphology*. London, UK: Pion.

Tandy, C. R. V. (1967). The isovist method of landscape survey. In H. C. Murray (Ed.), *Symposium: Methods of Landscape Analysis* (pp. 9-10). London, UK: Landscape Research Group.

Thilagam, N. L., & Banerjee, U. K. (2015). The morphological characteristics of medieval temple towns of Tamilnadu. *Environment and Planning. B, Planning & Design*, *43*(1), 7–33. doi:10.1177/0265813515603869

Tomé, A., Heitor, T., & Nunes, M. (2015). Computer vision of mobility: Towards a space-use analysis method. *Environment and Planning. B, Planning & Design*, *42*(5), 830–856. doi:10.1177/0265813515599512

Tomé, A., Kuipers, M., Pinheiro, T., Nunes, M., & Heitor, T. (2015). Space-use analysis through computer vision. *Automation in Construction*, *57*, 80–97. doi:10.1016/j.autcon.2015.04.013

Trzpuc, S. J., & Martin, C. S. (2010). Application of space syntax theory in the study of medical-surgical nursing units in urban hospitals. *HERD: Health Environments Research & Design Journal*, *4*(1), 34–55. doi:10.1177/193758671000400104 PMID:21162428

Tsou, K.-W., & Cheng, H.-T. (2013). The effect of multiple urban network structures on retail patterns – A case study in Taipei, Taiwan. *Cities (London, England)*, *32*, 13–23. doi:10.1016/j.cities.2013.02.003

Turner, A. (2001). Depthmap: A program to perform visibility graph analysis. In *Proceedings 3rd International Symposium on Space Syntax* (pp. 31.31-31.39). Atlanta, GA: Georgia Institute of Technology.

Turner, A. (2007). From axial to road-centre lines: A new representation for space syntax and a new model of route choice for transport network analysis. *Environment and Planning. B, Planning & Design*, *34*(3), 539–555. doi:10.1068/b32067

Turner, A., Doxa, M., O'Sullivan, D., & Penn, A. (2001). From isovists to visibility graphs: A methodology for the analysis of architectural space. *Environment and Planning. B, Planning & Design*, *28*(1), 103–121. doi:10.1068/b2684

Tzeng, S.-Y., & Huang, J.-S. (2009). Spatial forms and signage in wayfinding decision points for hospital outpatient services. *Journal of Asian Architecture and Building Engineering*, *8*(2), 453–460. doi:10.3130/jaabe.8.453

van der Zwart, J., & van der Voordt, T. J. M. (2015). Pre-occupancy evaluation of patient satisfaction in hospitals. *HERD: Health Environments Research & Design Journal*, *9*(1), 110–124. doi:10.1177/1937586715595506 PMID:26338307

Vaughan, L. (2007). The spatial syntax of urban segregation. *Progress in Planning*, *67*(3), 205–294. doi:10.1016/j.progress.2007.03.001

Wong, J. F. (2014). Conceptual engawa: The experience of ring-based circulation in Tadao Ando Museums. *Environment and Planning. B, Planning & Design*, *41*(2), 229–250. doi:10.1068/b39012

Yoo, C., & Lee, S. (2017). When organic urban forms and grid systems collide: Application of space syntax for analyzing the spatial configuration of Barcelona, Spain. *Journal of Asian Architecture and Building Engineering*, *16*(3), 597–604. doi:10.3130/jaabe.16.597

Yu, R., Ostwald, M., & Gu, N. (2016). Mathematically defining and parametrically generating traditional chinese private gardens of the Suzhou region and style. *Environment and Planning B. Urban Analytics and City Science*, *45*(1), 44–66. doi:10.1177/0265813516665361

Zadeh, R. S., Shepley, M. M., & Waggener, L. T. (2012). Rethinking efficiency in acute care nursing units: Analyzing nursing unit layouts for improved spatial flow. *HERD: Health Environments Research & Design Journal*, *6*(1), 39–65. doi:10.1177/193758671200600103 PMID:23224842

Zaleckis, K., Kamičaitytė-Virbašienė, J., & Matijošaitienė, I. (2015). Using space syntax method and GIS-based analysis for the spatial allocation of roadside rest areas. *Transport*, *30*(2), 182–193. doi:10.3846/16484142.2015.1045026

Zamani, Z. (2018). Effects of emergency department physical design elements on security, wayfinding, visibility, privacy, and efficiency and its implications on staff satisfaction and performance. *HERD: Health Environments Research & Design Journal*. doi:10.1177/1937586718800482 PMID:30231637

Zhu, H., Liu, J., Liu, H., Wang, X., & Ma, Y. (2017). Recreational business district boundary identifying and spatial structure influence in historic area development: A case study of Qianmen area, China. *Habitat International*, *63*, 11–20. doi:10.1016/j.habitatint.2017.03.003

Chapter 5
Syntactical and Mathematical Measures of Spatial Configuration

ABSTRACT

This chapter presents a detailed explanation of the construction and analysis of a justified plan graph (JPG) of a building plan. It introduces the classic syntactical and mathematical measures derived from a JPG and discusses their interpretation in terms of the original architectural plan the results are derived from. Thereafter, an alternative weighted and directed JPG is introduced which uses four measures: centrality, degree centrality, centrality closeness, and betweenness. The mathematical measures introduced in this chapter are applied in Section 3 of this book to examine two syntactical and grammatical applications. Throughout the present chapter, three "Palladian" villas—Villa Saraceno, Villa Sepulveda, and Villa Poiana—are used as examples to explain and demonstrate the concepts.

INTRODUCTION

As discussed in the previous chapter, Space Syntax techniques typically commence with the abstraction of the spatial properties of a plan (or section) into a set of nodes and edges (or links), which collectively form a graph. This abstraction process relies on a conceptual shift in our understanding of architecture. Instead of seeing architecture in terms of formal, dimensional or

DOI: 10.4018/978-1-7998-1698-0.ch005

"geographic" properties, the abstraction that is at the heart of Space Syntax views architecture solely in terms of spatial, relational or "topological" properties. This shift occurs in the process of translating architecturally defined space (or convex space) and the connections between spaces, into the nodes and edges of a graph. Once converted into a graph, the shape-based, dimensional and geographic properties are stripped away from the plan, and all that remains is topology, which can be mathematically analysed. This chapter explains the syntactical and mathematical measures that can be derived from spatial configurations in architecture. More specifically, this chapter describes the justified plan graph (JPG) technique in detail, and its use to analyse or explore enclosed or defined programmatic spaces (nodes) with the connections between them (links).

Graph theory is conventionally regarded as originating in the seventeenth century paradox of the Bridges of Königsberg, a mathematical puzzle about seven bridges separating four landmasses and a Knight's desire to cross each bridge only once while moving in a continuous sequence (Harary, 1960; Hopkins & Wilson, 2004). In mathematics, this problem became known as the "Euler characteristic', as the Swiss mathematician Leonhard Euler used a graphical method (comprising nodes and connections) to prove that it was not possible to complete the Knight's desired journey for the particular set of spatial conditions. While isolated examples of graph theory may be traced in nineteenth century mathematics, it was not until the 1960s and early 1970s that there was a growth in interest in graph theory and its capacity to explain a variety of geographic and spatial phenomena (Harary, 1960). Furthermore, by the 1970s, graph theorists had begun to apply simple mathematical calculations to their node and line (or vertex and edge) diagrams to calculate the relative depths of these structures (Seppänen & Moore, 1970; Taaffe & Gauthier, 1973). These same formulas provided the mathematical basis for Space Syntax research a decade later, and in the intervening years they were responsible for encouraging a range of mathematical applications in architecture. For example, Christopher Alexander (1964) developed a variation of graph theory to explain urban connectivity before combining graph theory and a rule-based grammar to define a pattern-based approach to design (Alexander, Ishikawa, & Silverstein, 1977). However, within a few years of this publication Alexander rejected the mathematics of graph theory, preferring instead to seek geometric or relational systems in graphs. It was Lionel March and Philip Steadman (1971) who collaboratively developed the early stages of a syntactical model of architectural form that drew on graph theory, before later separately extrapolating this idea in different ways

(March, 1976; Steadman, 1983). Their work at this time was largely focused on architectural form, and despite their efforts, this application of graph theory was never developed in a productive way. It wasn't until the 1980s that Hillier, Hanson, and their colleagues suggested to architectural researchers that graph theory was more useful in spatial analysis.

The first essential work of Space Syntax, *the Social Logic of Space* (Hillier & Hanson, 1984), describes the use of a convex map, a chart of visually defined space, to generate a graph of spatial configuration. Called "gamma analysis" at the time, the method and its graph-based representations have since been known by various titles, including "planar graphs" (March & Steadman, 1971, p. 242), "plan morphology" (Steadman, 1983, p. 209), "node analysis" (Manum, 2009), and a "justified permeability map" (Hillier & Hanson, 1984, p. 151). The convex map has been described as producing a "justified graph", a "justified permeability graph" (Hanson, 1998, pp. 27, 247), a "plan graph", an "access graph" (Stevens, 1990, p. 208) and a "justified access graph" (Shapiro, 2005, p. 114). While Steadman (1983) provides different definitions for a plan graph and an access graph, the two concepts have been largely melded in subsequent use. Recent research has tended to emphasise the "justified" nature of the graph, using titles like "J-graph" (Jeong & Ban, 2011b), "Justified graph" (Wong, 2014), and "justified plan graph" (Lee, Ostwald, & Gu, 2015, 2017, 2018; Ostwald, 2011a, 2011b, 2011c). For consistency, in this chapter the method is described as producing a "justified plan graph" (JPG).

The JPG method was the first practical analytical technique developed as part of the theory of Space Syntax, and for introducing syntactic genotypes (Hillier & Hanson, 1984). It purported to provide both a graphical and a mathematical model for analysing the spatial configuration of a building's plan. This method was adopted by a range of researchers throughout the 1980s and 1990s, being applied to the analysis of more than twenty primitive or historic communities and over 100 individual buildings. In recent years, the JPG method has been continuously applied to domestic architecture plans, spanning from historic times to the present day (Asif, Utaberta, Sabil, & Ismail, 2018; Byun & Choi, 2016; Edwards, 2013; Eloy & Duarte, 2015; Fladd, 2017; Gao, Asami, Zhou, & Ishikawa, 2013; Jeong & Ban, 2014; Kishimoto & Taguchi, 2014; Malhis, 2008; Zadeh, Shepley, & Waggener, 2012).

Several software tools are available to support the creation of the JPG and its mathematical analysis, including AGRAPH (Manum, 2009) and J-SAP (Jeong & Ban, 2011a). Such tools have automated the use of the JPG, making the method more accessible, but also reducing the average researcher's knowledge of how the method actually works. The situation is worsened by the fact that the construction and analysis of the JPG is rarely explained in its totality, and when it is the descriptions are often inconsistent or obtuse. Dovey (1999) is particularly critical of the lack of clarity in explanations of the mathematics underlying the technique, and even suggests that this opacity may be deliberate as it shields the technique from serious and objective critique. Dovey further comments that once the mathematical analysis of the graph has been completed there is a marked lack of consistency in how the results are interpreted.

Taking into account Dovey's criticism of the way the JPG has been presented in previous works, and the fact that it plays a key role in the new method developed in later chapters in the present book, it is important to provide a detailed account of its use here. This chapter provides such an account, along with a worked example of its application in the analysis of the *Villa Saraceno* in Agugliaro (Vincenzo, Italy), which was designed by Andrea Palladio in the 1540s. In order to interpret the mathematical results of the syntactical analysis, a second "Palladian" design is used for comparative purposes, the *Villa Sepulveda*. This villa plan was generated by George Stiny (1985) using a Palladian Shape Grammar. Finally, the *Villa Poiana* in Maggiore (Vincenzo, Italy), which was designed by Andrea Palladio in the 1540s, is used to explain an alternative weighted and directed JPG construction. In each of the three Palladian villas, only the main building is considered. That is, the connections between the central building and colonnaded wings or *barchesse* (rural service buildings) are excluded from the analysis.

While it could be said that most of the stages of the JPG method presented here have been recorded in some form in previous research, e.g., Ostwald's works (2011a; 2011c), the construction of a consistent theoretical and mathematical framing is the initial aim of this chapter. The chapter then identifies some important interpretative limits for the method and uses the new Palladian examples to explain its potential use in design analysis. Furthermore, the alternative weighted and directed JPG with centrality measures is presented as a means to overcome some limitations of the method.

Constructing a JPG

The first step in the construction of a JPG is typically the production of a convex map or boundary map. A convex map is a way of partitioning an architectural plan into a diagram of defined spaces or nodes and the connections between them. There are a number of alternative variations of this process, ranging from the highly proscribed to the very general (Hillier & Hanson, 1984; Markus, 1993). The particular method chosen for producing the convex map has a direct impact on the JPG and its results. For example, it is possible for an irregular plan for a small house to require as many as 50 separate convex spaces to fulfil the precise requirements of the original convex map definition (Hillier & Hanson, 1984). But the subsequent JPGs are typically over-convoluted and can be mathematically dominated by the influence of often quite small architectural features. For example, a convex map produced by Major and Sarris (2001) of Peter Eisenman's *House 1* has 39 nodes or spaces, although Eisenman actually identifies only seven functional rooms in the house. By counting every alcove for a built-in bookcase, display stand or wardrobe, and by dividing every section of space visually occluded by, or separated from, another space by a change in corridor width, or location of a blade column or open stair, the number of spaces is increased times six. This rigorous convex mapping process artificially inflates the program and alters the actual, inhabited and experienced, structure of the house. More recent approaches to constructing a permeably map tend to directly associate spaces with functional zones, thus reducing the number of nodes and more clearly aligning the JPG with inhabitation patterns (Bafna, 2003; Peponis, Wineman, Rashid, Kim, & Bafna, 1997). Indeed, given the almost complete lack of advice on how to consistently convert a concave space into a convex space, it is not surprising that subsequent works have tended to ignore this process. For example, if the original definition of a convex map is followed, the "T-shaped" room at the centre of the *Villa Saraceno* (Figure 1) must be broken down into two convex spaces before analysis can commence (Hillier & Hanson, 1984; Markus, 1993). To complicate matters, there are several possible ways this particular space can be subdivided and arguably the thick walls of the villa produce additional convex spaces in every doorway. Rather than subdivide spaces in this way, the more contemporary JPG technique identifies most "T-shaped" or "L-shaped" rooms as a single node.

As shown in Figure 1, the JPG method commences with an architectural plan that records the relative size, shape, location and orientation of rooms within an overall building footprint; this could be considered the geography of the building. The connections between these rooms are simply delineated by icons for doors or openings. The construction of a plan graph involves an inversion of the hierarchy implicit in this conventional representational schema. The plan graph emphasises, at the expense of all other information, the number of spaces and the connections between them. In order to do this,

Figure 1. Villa Saraceno, an architectural plan and its defined space plan

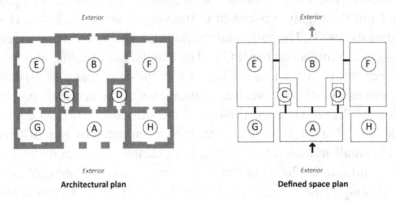

a "defined space" plan is constructed, describing functional spaces (nodes) and the connections between them (links) (Figure 1). The defined space plan also captures access to the exterior of a building like a traditional architectural bubble diagram.

The defined space plan serves to assist in the identification of spaces and connections. For simple architectural plans this step is often unnecessary, as the spaces and connections are already visually well-defined. However, for complex buildings, and those with more intricate connections between interior and exterior spaces, the defined space plan can be a useful precursor to the construction of the JPG. When used in this way, the plan graph is simply drawn over the top of the defined space plan. This process does not differentiate between spaces that are large or small, high or low, it simply records the existence of a defined space, which is also a node. The nature of the connection, be it a door, opening, or ladder, is not recorded, only the fact that a connection exists. Graphically this process converts the defined space plan into a diagram of circular nodes (rooms) and lines (connections between rooms) in the plan graph (Figure 2). The exterior is typically represented in the graph as a crossed circle, and many previous researchers, such as Hillier, Hanson and Ostwald, use the graphical symbol "⊕" to indicate the exterior, while it can also be denoted as "E" for algebraic expressions. This chapter uses the ⊕ symbol for the exterior, as it supports a better intuitive reading of the graph, and employs "E" for algebraic grammars in the following chapters. The newly produced connectivity diagram is then arrayed across a number of levels, starting with zero at the base, regardless of the actual orientation of space in the original building (Hillier & Hanson, 1984). Once arrayed in this way, the graph displays levels of connectivity and separation between

Figure 2. Villa Saraceno, a plan graph and its JPG

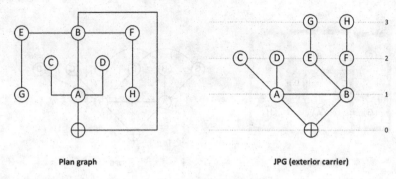

Plan graph   JPG (exterior carrier)

the root or carrier space (or node) at the bottom of the graph and all other spaces (or nodes).

A JPG can be graphically or visually analysed to uncover a range of properties of the spatial structure, including relative asymmetry, spatial hierarchy (arborescent qualities) and permeability (rhizomorphous qualities). A small number of examples of qualitative visual analysis of this type have used multiple carriers and visual archetypes to investigate the properties of space (Alexander, 1966; Ostwald, 1997). The majority of the examples of this approach to the JPG (Dovey, 1999; Markus, 1987, 1993; Ostwald, 2011b, 2011c) are concerned with "inhabitant-visitor relations". For example, in the *Villa Saraceno,* let us imagine that the doorway at the rear (top) side of the villa is a visitor entrance. The space "B" (Figure 1) is then connected to the exterior and therefore serves as a key zone for "inhabitant-visitor relations". Moreover, this places the visitor who gains entry to B just two spaces away from all of the most private or isolated parts of the plan (Figure 2).

Because the lengths of the lines in the graph are unimportant – a fact that is responsible for some of the ongoing controversy surrounding syntactical techniques (Hillier & Penn, 2004; Ratti, 2004) – the line and node graph may then be removed from the plan and justified. The word "justified" refers to the process of arranging the graph by the relative depth of nodes from a given starting point, generally known as the "carrier" or "root" node (Klarqvist, 1993). Thus, the JPG is constructed around a series of depths (often graphically represented as horizontal, dotted lines) numbered consecutively from 0; the lowest line. Each depth (dotted line) represents a level of separation between rooms. The carrier node, often the outside world, is located on the lowest line on the chart (marked 0). Those nodes, which are directly connected to the carrier, are located on the line above (marked 1). Further nodes directly

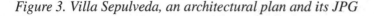

Figure 3. Villa Sepulveda, an architectural plan and its JPG

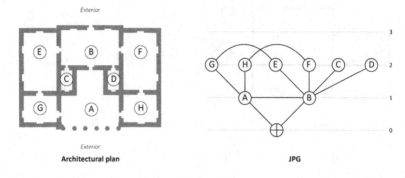

connected to those on line 1 are placed on line 2, and so on. Whereas the exterior is represented as a crossed circle, other nodes are typically given letters (or less often numbers) that can be keyed to particular programmatic functions (Figure 2).

In order to understand the way a JPG can capture the subtleties of spatial connectivity, compare the plans of the *Villa Saraceno* (Figure 1) and *Villa Sepulveda* (Figure 3). At first glance they might look identical. Now compare the JPGs of the *Villa Saraceno* (Figure 2) and *Villa Sepulveda* (Figure 3) and several substantial differences are apparent. Each of these villas possess the same building footprint and the same number of rooms. The sizes of rooms and relative locations of each are also almost identical. Thus, from a geographic or geospatial perspective these buildings are largely the same. However, the way in which rooms are connected differs in each villa, changing the spatial morphology in terms of permeability and depth. For example, consider a JPG, with the exterior as carrier, for each of the two villas. From this perspective it quickly becomes apparent that despite similar plans, the spatial configuration present, including the degree of connectivity and depth, varies greatly (Figure 2 and 3). From the example of the two villas it is possible to see that while the architectural plans are superficially similar, the spatial configuration of each is quite distinctive. For instance, both villas have a "ring-like" structure due to the two entrances of the conventional Palladian plan. But after that, the spatial configuration of the *Villa Saraceno* has a more arborescent or "bush-like" structure – and if the rear access is ignored, this villa could have an even deeper (more linear) structure. Conversely, the *Villa Sepulveda* features a rhizomorphous or "lattice-like" structure in plan, which suggests a high degree of permeability or flexibility of use. Figure 4 identifies the four

Figure 4. Archetypal arborescent and rhizomorphous configurations

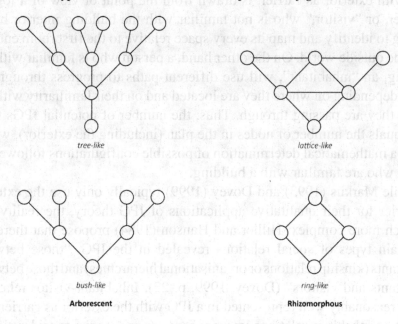

classic archetypal arborescent and rhizomorphous configurations, which are often used in syntactical analysis to characterise particular planning patterns.

Further differences between the two plans are apparent if we focus on some of the major spaces. For example, while node A (entrance hall) in the *Villa Saraceno* controls the primary passage to the T-shaped salon (B) and two small service nodes, in the *Villa Sepulveda* there are three accesses to the salon (B), as well as two rooms at the front (G and H). Therefore, the salon in the *Villa Sepulveda* has six links, including the two side chambers and two small service spaces. Finally, some qualities may be discerned from a comparison between the two villa plans. First, relative to houses of this size, the *Villa Saraceno* has a three-layered plan and the *Villa Sepulveda* has a shallower, two-layered plan. What this implies is that, just by looking at a plan graph, some potential qualities may be uncovered, in this case being relative depth/shallowness, control/permeability and symmetry/asymmetry. The first two of these categories have been used for the graphic analysis of power structures implicit in a range of building types (Dovey, 1999; Markus, 1987, 1993; Ostwald, 2011b, 2011c).

While JPGs are often drawn, for ease of visual comparison, with the exterior node as carrier, a separate JPG representation exists for each node in a plan. One way of understanding this is to imagine that the conventional

JPG, with exterior as carrier, is drawn from the point of view of a logical explorer, or "visitor," who is not familiar with the building interior but is seeking to identify and map its every space relative to the first room entered from the outside world. On the other hand, a person who is familiar with the building, an "inhabitant", will use different paths to progress through the space, depending on where they are located and on their familiarity with the spaces they are passing through. Thus, the number of potential JPGs for a plan equals the number of nodes in the plan (including the exterior), which is also a mathematical determination of possible configurations followed by people who are familiar with a building.

While Markus (1993) and Dovey (1999) typically only use the exterior as carrier for their qualitative applications of JPG theory, the reality can be much more complex. Hillier and Hanson (1984) propose that there are two main types of social relations revealed in the JPG, "those between inhabitants (kinship relations or organisational hierarchies) and those between inhabitants and visitors" (Dovey, 1999, p. 22). Inhabitant-visitor relations can be reasonably well represented in a JPG with the exterior as carrier, but inhabitant-inhabitant relations are more complex and require consideration of multiple additional JPGs. For example, a close review of the other eight JPGs for the *Villa Saraceno* (Figure 5) shows that, while from the point of view of a visitor (carrier ⊕, Figure 2) the plan is slightly linear and symmetrical, from the point of view of an inhabitant (carriers C, D, G or H, Figure 5) the plan is more linear and much deeper. The reality that multiple parallel interpretations of the JPGs for a given building are possible is often forgotten in graphical analysis, a fact that can have significant analytical consequences. This is why, despite the usefulness of the JPG as a qualitative or visual tool, a quantitative, mathematical approach is ultimately more valuable.

Mathematical Measures of a JPG

A JPG is mathematically analysed as a complete system. The formulas for this process may be found in a range of places (Hanson, 1998; Hillier & Hanson, 1984; Ostwald, 2011a) as well as in several software tools, such as *Depthmap, AGRAPH* (Manum, 2009) and *J-SAP* (Jeong & Ban, 2011a). Using mathematical analysis, it is possible to develop a set of values describing the JPG from the point of view of total depth (*TD*), mean depth (*MD*), relative asymmetry (*RA*), integration (*i*), real relative asymmetry (*RRA*), control value (*CV*) and difference factor (*H* and *H**) (Table 1). The integration value is

Figure 5. Villa Saraceno, eight possible JPGs and an alternative JPG without a rear entrance

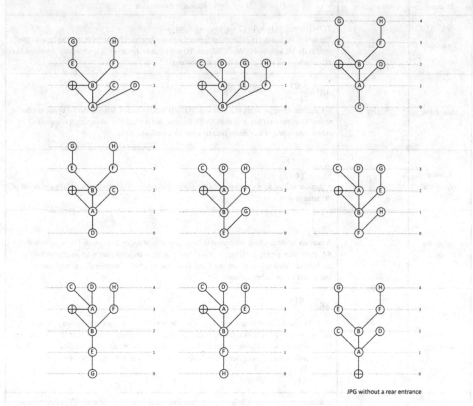

JPG without a rear entrance

probably the most common measure used in many studies and it is also central to the development of an "inequality genotype" in architectural analysis.

While the previous section described the graphical formation of the JPG and its use in qualitative interpretation, the present section explains the mathematics of the JPG using Ostwald's approach (2011c) and the *Villa Saraceno* as an example, The process for mathematically analysing the JPG of an architectural plan typically involves at least the first five steps, and possibly all nine steps, of the sequence that follows.

Step 1.

The total number (K) of nodes (or spaces) in a set is determined. The depth of each node, relative to a carrier, is also calculated; that is, how many levels (L) deep in the JPG is the node. The number of nodes at a given level and for a given carrier is also recorded (n_x). The number of levels is counted in the

Table 1. Various mathematical measures of a JPG Ostwald, 2011c

Measure	Abbreviation	Formula / Explanation
Total depth	TD	$TD = (0 \times n_x) + (1 \times n_x) + (2 \times n_x) + \ldots + (X \times n_x)$ The sum of the number of connections between a particular node (the carrier or root) and every other node in the set, weighted by depth. Because TD is relative to the carrier, it is sometimes abbreviated to TD_n which means the TD value for a particular node.
Mean depth	MD	$MD = \dfrac{TD}{(k-1)}$ The average degree of depth of a node in a JPG. *MD* is calculated by dividing the *TD* by the number of nodes (*K*) minus one (that is, without itself). Because *MD* is relative to the carrier, it is sometimes abbreviated to MD_n which means the *MD* value for a particular node.
Relative asymmetry	RA	$RA = \dfrac{2(MD-1)}{(k-2)}$ A measure of how deep a system is (for a given carrier) relative to a symmetrical or balanced model of the same system.
Integration value	i	$i = \dfrac{1}{RA}$ A measure of the degree of integration (relative centrality of nodes) in a system. *i* is the reciprocal of *RA*. Some older papers use *In* (upper case i, lowercase N) as the abbreviation for integration but this has been confused with *In* (lower case L and lowercase N) which conventionally, in both mathematics and in JPG theory, means *natural log*.
Real relative asymmetry	RRA	$RRA = \dfrac{RA}{D_k}$ Describes the degree of isolation or depth of a node, not only in comparison to its own system or set, but also in comparison with a suitably scaled and idealised benchmark configuration, *D*. The idealised building (*D*) is always relative to a particular *K* value (Table 2 provides part of the values for D_k from Hillier and Hanson's (1984) chart). The *i* value for RRA is calculated using either of the following: $i_{RRA} = \dfrac{D_k}{RA}$ or $i_{RRA} = \dfrac{1}{RRA}$
Control value	CV	A measure of the degree of influence each node has in a system. To calculate the CV, a determination of the NC_n and *CVe* of each node needs to be made, as follows. NC_n (node connection number) is the number of nodes directly connected to a node. *CVe* (control value distributed to each node) is a redistribution of the set of relations in a JPG relative to a particular node.
Unrelativised difference factor	H	$H = -\sum \left[\dfrac{a}{t} In\left(\dfrac{a}{t}\right) \right] + \left[\dfrac{b}{t} In\left(\dfrac{b}{t}\right) \right] + \left[\dfrac{c}{t} In\left(\dfrac{c}{t}\right) \right]$ Calculated using the above formula, wherein: *a* = the maximum RA. *b* = mean *RA* and *c* = minimum *RA*. The sum of results *a*, *b* and *c* is *t* (ie. *a+b+c=t*). *In* is natural logarithm to base *e*.
Relativised difference factor	H*	$H^* = \dfrac{(H - In2)}{(In3 - In2)}$

JPG from the lowest, the carrier at 0, nodes directly connected to the carrier at 1, and so on. For example, for the *Villa Saraceno* there are 9 nodes, that is, $K = 9$ (⊕, A, B, C, D, E, F, G, H) and these nodes are spread over 3 levels (0, 1, 2, 3) when arrayed with ⊕ as carrier. Thus, for the JPG of the *Villa Saraceno* with the exterior as carrier, the *L* value for node G = 3 (Figure 2).

Step 2.

Calculate the total depth (*TD*) of the graph for a given carrier. *TD* is the sum of the number of connections between a particular node and every other node in the set, weighted by level (*L*). It is calculated by adding together, for each level of the justified graph, the number of nodes (n_x) at that level of justification multiplied by the *L* (0, 1, 2, 3, 4, …). Thus:

$$TD = (0 \times n_x) + (1 \times n_x) + (2 \times n_x) + \ldots + (X \times n_x)$$

For the *Villa Saraceno*:

$$TD = (0 \times 1) + (1 \times 2) + (2 \times 4) + (3 \times 2)$$

$$TD = 0 + 2 + 8 + 6$$

$$TD = 16$$

Thus, with the exterior as carrier, the *Villa Saraceno* has a *TD* = 16.

Step 3.

The mean depth (*MD*) is the average degree of depth of a node in a justified plan graph. A room depth that is higher than the mean is therefore more isolated than a room depth that is lower than the mean. *MD* is calculated by dividing the total depth (*TD*) by the number of rooms (*K*) minus one (that is, without itself). Therefore:

$$MD = \frac{TD}{(k-1)}$$

For the *Villa Saraceno*:

$$MD = \frac{16}{(9-1)}$$

$MD = 2$

This outcome suggests that, for the *Villa Saraceno* and with the exterior as carrier, nodes A (L=1) and B (L=1) are all more accessible than nodes G (L=3) and H (L=3).

Step 4a.

Relative asymmetry (RA) involves a comparison between a node in a target system and a node in a similar but more symmetrical system (sometimes incorrectly called an optimal system). Symmetry in this instance simply refers to a balanced or evenly distributed quality in a hypothetical system. Thus, asymmetry is a measure of how much a node in a target system differs from a similar node in a more balanced or equally integrated system. This could be rephrased as suggesting that RA is a measure of *the degree of isolation of a node* in a target system, in comparison with that same node in a more balanced version of the same system.

RA is valuable because it effectively normalises the range of possible results to between 0.0 and 1.0. This is possible because the method places the comparison in a range between a perfectly shallow system where all nodes are connected to the carrier and the most depth when all nodes are linearly arrayed. RA is calculated with the following formula:

$$RA = \frac{2(MD-1)}{(k-2)}$$

Thus, for the example of the *Villa Saraceno* and using the exterior as carrier:

$$RA = \frac{2(2-1)}{(9-2)}$$

$$RA = \frac{2}{7}$$

$$RA = 0.2857$$

148

When this calculation is repeated for all of the carriers for the *Villa Saraceno,* a sequence can be constructed from the most isolated node to the least isolated: "most isolated" > G (0.57), H (0.57), C (0.46), D (0.46), E (0.32), F (0.32), ⊕ (0.29), B (0.21) and A (0.14) > least isolated.

Because the *RA* results are normalised to a range between 0.0 and 1.0, *RA* results for nodes in different buildings may only be directly compared if they have a similar *K* value (total number of nodes). Thus, the *RA* values of two houses, each with 9 rooms, may be directly compared. The *RA* values for two houses with, say, *K* values of 9 and 11 might also be compared, but the larger the differential between *K* values, the less valid or useful the comparison. In order to make a valid comparison between different size sets, an idealised benchmark must be used. For a comparative variation suitable for unequal *K* values, see *Step 4b*.

Step 5a.

If the *RA* for a carrier node reflects its relative *isolation*, then the degree of *integration* (*i*) of that node in the JPG can be calculated by taking its reciprocal:

$$i = \frac{1}{RA}$$

The integration value for the exterior node in relation to the *Villa Saraceno* is therefore:

$$i = \frac{1}{0.2857}$$

$$i = 3.50$$

In isolation, this value is relatively meaningless, but when compared with integration measures for the other nodes in the same graph, or, alternatively, with those in an ideally distributed benchmark plan, it can be very informative. In the first instance, for the *Villa Saraceno,* a comparison between *i* results for each room reveals a hierarchy of space from least integrated to most integrated as follows: least integrated < G (1.75), H (1.75), C (2.15), D (2.15), E (3.11), F (3.11), ⊕ (3.50), A (4.67) and B (7.00) < most integrated. Because of the reciprocal relationship between *i* and *RA,* this is simply the reverse order of the previous result recorded in *Step 4a*. However, whereas *RA* results were limited to a range between 0.0 and 1.0, *i* results start at 1.0 and have no upper limit. Nevertheless, in order to use this data to construct a comparison with a building of a radically different size, a comparison must be constructed against an optimal benchmark (see *Step 5b*).

Step 4b.

This is an alternative to *Step 4a*, which was focused on relative asymmetry (*RA*). Real relative asymmetry (*RRA*) describes the degree of isolation, or depth, of a node, not only in comparison to the complete set of results for the graph, but also in comparison with a suitably scaled and idealised benchmark configuration. *RRA* results are useful for comparisons between buildings with radically different *K* values. It should be noted that in much contemporary scholarship (Shapiro, 2005; Thaler, 2005) *RRA* is sometimes completely ignored in favour of *RA*, and while most scholars in this field agree that a comparative basis is necessary, they are not all convinced by the original logic of Hillier and Hanson's method (Asami, Kubat, Kitagawa, & Iida, 2003; Krüger, 1989; Thaler, 2005) or even necessarily understand how it works, Hillier and Hanson's explanation being, according to Manum, "not absolutely clear" (Manum, 2009, p. 4). Hillier and Hanson describe the construction of the idealised benchmark at the centre of the *RRA* stage as a diamond JPG "in which there are *K* spaces at mean depth level, *K/2* at one level above and below, *K/4* at two levels above and below, and so on until there is one space at the shallowest [...] and deepest points" (1984, pp.111-112). They then provide a table of "*D*-values for *K* spaces", partly repeated in Table 2. For the purposes of comparison, *RRA* is produced by dividing the subject *RA* by the optimised or idealised *RA*, called a *D*-Value after its diamond shape. Thus, the *RRA* of a carrier node is calculated as follows:

$$RRA = \frac{RA}{D_k}$$

This approach may appear reasonable if the argument that a diamond plan is a balanced, symmetrical configuration is accepted, and therefore provides a potential universal point of comparison. However, the process soon becomes more complex if the *K* values being considered, like those of the *Villa Saraceno*, are not neatly divisible into a continuous sequence (like

Table 2. D-values for k spaces extracted from Hillier and Hanson (1984, p.112

k	D-value	k	D-value
5	0.352	15	0.259
6	0.349	16	0.251
7	0.340	17	0.244
8	0.328	18	0.237
9	0.317	19	0.231
10	0.306	20	0.225
11	0.295	21	0.220
12	0.285	22	0.214
13	0.276	23	0.209
14	0.267	24	0.205

1, 2, 4, 8, 16, 32, etc). The difficulty arises because while Hillier and Hanson provide a table of *D*-Values for every number of *K* above 4 (1984, p.112), they do not explain where these are sourced from. As such, some scholars have rejected *RRA* in favour of *RA* as, despite the latter's known limitations, its origins are more transparent (Manum, 2009).

Despite ongoing debate about Hillier and Hanson's D-values, the present chapter accepts these as a reasonable approximation. Therefore, the *RRA* for the *Villa Saraceno*, using Hillier and Hanson's *D*-value for a *K* of 9, is as follows:

$$RRA = \frac{0.2857}{0.317}$$

$$RRA = 0.9013$$

Step 5b.

This is an alternative to *Step 5a*, which was focused on relative asymmetry (*RA*). If the *RRA* for a carrier node is a reflection of the relative isolation of a node in a JPG (in comparison with an otherwise optimal and symmetrical JPG system), then the degree of integration (*i*) of the JPG can be calculated by taking the reciprocal of the *RRA*.

$$i_{RRA} = \frac{D_k}{RA}$$

or, alternatively,

$$i_{RRA} = \frac{1}{RRA}$$

The *i* value for the *Villa Saraceno*, with exterior as carrier, and in comparison with a symmetrical configuration of the same *K* value, is therefore:

$$i_{RRA} = \frac{0.317}{0.2857}$$

$$i_{RRA} = 1.11$$

Step 6.

To this point, the majority of the steps have been focused on calculations for a single carrier, $\oplus$. In *Step 6*, all of the previous steps – 2, 3, 4a and 5a (or alternatively, 4b and 5b) – are repeated for each other potential carrier, producing a "distance data" table (Table 3). In this table for the *Villa Saraceno*, the top row of italic cells, starting from 0 and $\oplus$ (i.e. below the column titles), records the set of results developed in the previous steps in this chapter for the exterior carrier graph. Repeating this process for each node as carrier fills the remainder of the cells. The simplest way to do this is to produce a distance matrix in the chart, where each of the six nodes and the exterior (making seven) are placed in a matrix opposite the same node, and the number of connections needed to pass from each node to each other node is recorded. Thus, there will always be a set of cells with 0 in them where the matrix crosses. Finally, the mean results for the *Villa Saraceno*, for *TD*, *MD*, *RA* and *i* are recorded in Table 3.

Step 7.

The control value (*CV*) of a JPG is typically described as being a reflection of the degree of influence exerted by a space in a network (Jiang, Claramunt,

Table 3. Distance data table for Villa Saraceno

#	Node	⊕	A	B	C	D	E	F	G	H	TD_n	MD_n	RA	i
0	⊕	0	1	1	2	2	2	2	3	3	16	2.00	0.29	3.50
1	A	1	0	1	1	1	2	2	3	3	14	1.75	0.21	4.67
2	B	1	1	0	2	2	1	1	2	2	12	1.50	0.14	7.00
3	C	2	1	2	0	2	3	3	4	4	21	2.63	0.46	2.15
4	D	2	1	2	2	0	3	3	4	4	21	2.63	0.46	2.15
5	E	2	2	1	3	3	0	2	1	3	17	2.13	0.32	3.11
6	F	2	2	1	3	3	2	0	3	1	17	2.13	0.32	3.11
7	G	3	3	2	4	4	3	1	0	4	24	3.00	0.57	1.75
8	H	3	3	2	4	4	1	3	4	0	24	3.00	0.57	1.75
Mean											18.44	2.31	0.37	3.24

& Klarqvist, 2000; Zheng, Zhao, Fu, & Wang, 2008). For example, Klarqvist describes it as "a dynamic local measure" that determines "the degree to which a space controls access to its immediate neighbours" (Klarqvist, 1993, p. 11). In reality, any room in a plan has the potential to be a site of control, and certain spatial configurations may increase that potential, but otherwise the *CV* has relatively little to do with power or control. If the equation that generates the *CV* is examined in detail, the closest explanation for what it actually does is offered by Asami et al. (2003), who propose that control must be "thought of as a measure of relative strength … in pulling the potential of the system from its immediate neighbours" (Asami et al., 2003, p. 6). While this is a reasonable explanation of the machinations of the formula, there is a notion in network theory entitled "distributed equilibrium" that also comes close.

The concept of distributed equilibrium is founded on the assumption that a network has "capacity" of some sort, and that without outside influence this network will strive for equilibrium by automatically passing that capacity from one node equally to all adjacent nodes in the system (but no further). Once all of the capacity in the system has been simultaneously divided among its immediate neighbouring nodes in this way, the system will have achieved a state of equilibrium through the unequal distribution of its capacity. The difference between nodes in this balanced state with more or less capacity is simply a factor of adjacent network configuration. Viewed in this way, the *CV* value should be thought of as signifying sites of attraction, "pulling" potential or capacity, like whirlpools that retain their position in a stream. Attractors are naturally occurring patterns in otherwise complex systems (Hofstadter, 1981; Stewart, 1989). There are many types of attractors, from single point geometric ones (Thom, 1975, 1983) to Chaos Theory's strange attractors (Casti, 1995; Lewin, 1993). Attractors do not possess any specific spatial properties, but assuming that all other things are equal, they may designate stable zones of high energy in otherwise seemingly disordered, low energy systems. In socio-spatial terms, a high *CV* result might designate an area where people naturally congregate and interact, and a low *CV* is more likely to identify a space for solitary activities or relations.

Shapiro describes the construction of the *CV* value as beginning with "counting the number of neighbours of each space" in the JPG. That is, "the spaces with which it has a direct connection"; this is called the NC_n value. Then, "each space gives to its neighbours a value equal to 1/n of its control" (Shapiro, 2005, p. 52). The distributed, or shared, value of each node is known as *CVe*, thus, $CVe = 1/NC_n$. Once the complete set of *CVe* values have been shared across the JPG, then the *CV* value for each node can be calculated. Calculating *CV* values therefore requires a holistic approach that methodically traces where every node is influenced by every connection it has. Thus, in the case of the *Villa Saraceno,* the following are three example calculations of *CV* values.

In the first example, node $\oplus$ has two connections, node A and B, so it must distribute 1/2 or 0.50 *CVe* to the node it is connected to, leaving it with an interim *CV* of 0. However, node A is connected to four nodes, including $\oplus$, and so it must distribute 1/4, or 0.25 *CVe,* to each of these nodes. Node B is also connected to four nodes, and so it distributes 1/4, or 0.25 *CVe.* Thus, the *CV* for $\oplus$ is 0+0.25+0.25 = 0.50. In the second example, the *CV* for node A is calculated by taking 1/n for each of nodes $\oplus$ (1/2 = 0.50), B (1/4 = 0.25), C (1.00) and D (1.00). Therefore, the *CV* for node A is (0.50+0.25+1.00+1.00) = 1.75.

The complete set of NC_n, *CVe* and *CV* results for the *Villa Saraceno* are contained in Table 4. They reveal that node A, with a *CV* of 2.75 has the greatest natural attraction or pulling power, followed by node B, with a $CV = 1.75$. Shapiro (2005) suggests that control values above 1.00 are considered relatively high and typically define rooms that permit or enable access. Certainly, node A is a pivotal space from the point of view of access and security and has full control of two small service spaces (C and D). Node B (the second highest) also has a rear access and a shared control of two chambers (E and F) but looks more influential as the salon of the Palladian villa. This is why the simple definition of a *CV* value as pertaining to control is less convincing than seeing it as a site of natural influence or, even better, of natural congregation.

Table 4. Connection Data Table for the Villa Saraceno

#	Node	⊕	A	B	C	D	E	F	G	H	NC_n	CVe	CV
0	⊕	0	1	1	0	0	0	0	0	0	2.00	0.50	0.50
1	A	1	0	1	1	1	0	0	0	0	4.00	0.25	2.75
2	B	1	1	0	0	0	1	1	0	0	4.00	0.25	1.75
3	C	0	1	0	0	0	0	0	0	0	1.00	1.00	0.25
4	D	0	1	0	0	0	0	0	0	0	1.00	1.00	0.25
5	E	0	0	1	0	0	0	0	1	0	2.00	0.50	1.25
6	F	0	0	1	0	0	0	0	0	1	2.00	0.50	1.25
7	G	0	0	0	0	0	1	0	0	0	1.00	1.00	0.50
8	H	0	0	0	0	0	0	1	0	0	1.00	1.00	0.50

Step 8.

In this step, the difference factor (*H*) is calculated for the complete set of results for a building. Hanson describes the difference factor as an "entropy-based measure" because it assumes that the location of rooms in a building is a deliberate strategy and not a default position arising from a minimal investment in energy. The difference factor measures "the spread or degree of configurational differentiation across a set of integration values" (Hanson, 1998, p.30). Results closer to one are so "homogenised" that all nodes "have equal integration values and hence no configurational differences exist between them" while those closer to zero are "more differentiated", "structured" or deliberate (Hanson, 1998, pp.30-31). It is assumed that in a set of similar projects, for example houses with the same number of rooms, the distribution of space is intentional and therefore similar configurational strategies will be uncovered through the analysis of the difference factor.

As a precursor to calculating *H*, three *RA* values must first be identified for the complete set of results for a building: the maximum *RA* (*a*), the mean *RA* (*b*) and the minimum *RA* (*c*). The sum of results *a*, *b* and *c*, known as *t*, is also required (ie. *a+b+c=t*). Therefore, for the *Villa Saraceno a*=0.57, *b*=0.37, *c*=0.14 and *t*=1.08 (see Table 5). The unrelativised *H* is calculated as follows (note that *In* in the formula is natural logarithm to base *e*):

$$H = -\sum \left[\frac{a}{t} In\left(\frac{a}{t}\right) \right] + \left[\frac{b}{t} In\left(\frac{b}{t}\right) \right] + \left[\frac{c}{t} In\left(\frac{c}{t}\right) \right]$$

Therefore, for the *Villa Saraceno* the calculation is:

$$H = -\sum\left[\frac{0.57}{1.08}In\left(\frac{0.57}{1.08}\right)\right]+\left[\frac{0.37}{1.08}In\left(\frac{0.37}{1.08}\right)\right]+\left[\frac{0.14}{1.08}In\left(\frac{0.14}{1.08}\right)\right]$$

$$H = -\sum\left[0.5278\times-0.6391\right]+\left[0.3426\times-1.0712\right]+\left[0.1296\times-2.0431\right]$$

$$H = -\sum-0.3373-0.3670-0.2648$$

$$H = 0.9691$$

The relative difference factor is calculated as follows:

$$H* = \frac{\left(H-In2\right)}{\left(In3-In2\right)}$$

For the *Villa Saraceno* this results in:

$$H* = \frac{\left(0.9691-0.693\right)}{\left(1.0986-0.693\right)}$$

With $H* = 0.6806$ for the *Villa Saraceno,* the planning is slightly unstructured or does not appear to possess a definitive purpose.

Step 9.

Finally, the complete set of data for the building is tabled, recording mean, high and low results for *TD, MD, RA, i* and *CV* as well as results for *H* and *H**. For the *Villa Saraceno*, Table 5 records the complete set of results.

A methodological problem that is not mentioned in the literature on JPGs occurs when the total depth of a node equals the number of rooms, minus one. That is, $MD = 1.00$; a room that is connected to every other room. This is not as uncommon as it sounds, as open plan houses are structured in precisely this way. The problem occurs because the relative asymmetry calculation (*Step 4a*) produces an irrational result for the special case of a room that connects to every other room. This is a problem because the following stage

Table 5. Data Summary for the Villa Saraceno

#	Node	TD_n	MD_n	RA	i	CV
0	⊕	16	2.00	0.29	3.50	0.50
1	A	14	1.75	0.21	4.67	2.75
2	B	12	1.50	0.14	7.00	1.75
3	C	21	2.63	0.46	2.15	0.25
4	D	21	2.63	0.46	2.15	0.25
5	E	17	2.13	0.32	3.11	1.25
6	F	17	2.13	0.32	3.11	1.25
7	G	24	3.00	0.57	1.75	0.50
8	H	24	3.00	0.57	1.75	0.50
Minimum		24.00	3.00	0.57	7.00	2.75
Mean		18.44	2.31	0.37	3.24	1.00
Maximum		12.00	1.50	0.14	1.75	0.25
H						0.9691
H*						0.6806

(*Step 5a*) seeks the reciprocal of the irrational number, often incorrectly listed by software programs as zero. This then leads to *H* and *H** values being impossible to calculate for the chosen dwelling.

Interpretation of the Results of JPG measures

Osman and Suliman argue that while the "analytical procedure" to derive measures from the JPG "is simple, objective, and replicable, the interpretation process of the numerical results remains complex, subjective and [...] controversial" (Osman & Suliman, 1994, p. 190). Leach (1978) similarly suggests that while the results of the mathematical analysis may be used to make simple distinctions, the bigger question remains, what does this really say about social patterns in space? In the present section, the mathematical results for Palladio's *Villa Saraceno* (Table 5) are compared with those of Stiny's *Villa Sepulveda* (Table 6). The purpose of this comparison is to test whether the mathematical results, and their standard or anticipated interpretation, are supported by a simple comparison between two different spatial configurations of the same size (*K*). These two structures also possess several different configurational archetypes, identified in JPG theory (Figure 6); *Villa Saraceno* has a "bush-like" or shallow hierarchical structure with

Table 6. Data Summary for the Villa Sepulveda

#	Node	TD_n	MD_n	RA	i	CV
0	⊕	14	1.75	0.21	4.67	0.42
1	A	15	1.88	0.25	4.00	1.67
2	B	11	1.38	0.11	9.33	3.75
3	C	18	2.25	0.36	2.80	0.17
4	D	18	2.25	0.36	2.80	0.17
5	E	15	1.88	0.25	4.00	0.67
6	F	15	1.88	0.25	4.00	0.67
7	G	17	2.13	0.32	3.11	0.75
8	H	17	2.13	0.32	3.11	0.75
Minimum		18.00	2.25	0.36	9.33	3.75
Mean		15.56	1.94	0.27	4.20	1.00
Maximum		11.00	1.38	0.11	2.80	0.17
H						0.9993
H*						0.7550

Figure 6. JPGs of the Villa Saraceno and Villa Sepulveda

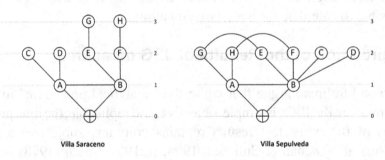

Villa Saraceno   Villa Sepulveda

a high degree of control, while *Villa Sepulveda* has a "ring-like" or "lattice-like" spatial configuration with a high degree of permeability, relatively low control, and medium relative depth.

The shallowness or depth of a spatial configuration can be quantified from two perspectives: *relative* to the *system* (by developing a *TD* value) or *relative* to the *node* (by calculating an *MD* value); remembering that the *MD* is just *TD* divided by the number of nodes but not counting the carrier (*K*-1). Starting with the calculation relative to the system: for the *Villa Saraceno* the deepest nodes (G and H) have a *TD* of 24 and for the *Villa Sepulveda*, the deepest nodes (C and D) have a *TD* of 18. This suggests that the villa with the deepest rooms is *Saraceno*, which aligns with a common sense reading of the plans. However, it is possible for an otherwise shallow plan to have one deep space or node, and thus it may be more informative to compute and report the mean or average *TD* results for comparison between the two buildings. The mean *TD* results of *Villa Saraceno* and *Villa* Sepulveda are 18.44 and 15.56, respectively. Given the same *K* values for each (that is, they have the same number of nodes) it is not surprising that the degree of difference is reduced when the average weighted depth for the spatial configuration is determined. Furthermore, since *MD* is just *TD* averaged for the total number of rooms (but without the carrier) rather than the system, the *MD* results will not change the order; it will simply present the data relative to nodes. The mean *MD* values for the *Villa Saraceno* and *Villa* Sepulveda are 2.31 and 1.94, respectively. So far, all of this is in accord with the anticipated results and the standard reading of the architectural qualities of such spaces. The question of what these results are useful for is slightly more difficult to answer with just two simple cases. Certainly, by identifying the average result for some quality in a system it is immediately possible to classify nodes into "above" or "below" average (in this case depth). While of only minimal interest in the case of the two Palladian villas, it can be a useful quantity to know for larger buildings; for example, Hanson (1998) uses the JPG method to examine *Bearwood Hall* a nineteenth century English manor house with 134 rooms.

Just as *TD* and *MD* are effectively two versions of the same thing, so too are *RA* and *i*. *RA* is a measure of the degree of isolation of a node in a target system in comparison with that same node in a more balanced version of the same system. *RA* is much more interesting and controversial than *TD* and *MD* because it can, purportedly, be used to suggest something about both the apparent seclusion of a node in a system and the degree of conscious decision making invested in the location of that node. However, a close review of the formula reveals that *RA* can only reasonably be claimed to provide an abstract measure of the unbalanced positioning of a node in a system relative to the same node in a more balanced system. In a way, Hillier and Hanson's (1984) name, relative asymmetry, is a closer description of what the mathematics measures than any of the later interpretations. Certainly, any reading of an *RA* measure of the degree of either relative isolation or design deliberation is founded on a range of complex and shifting assumptions about the relationship between configuration and intent.

According to the theory (Hillier & Hanson, 1984) a perfect shallow and symmetrical composition should have an *RA* close to 0.00 (representing spatial integration), while a perfectly linear, enfilade structure should have an *RA* close to 1.00 (representing spatial isolation). The *Villa Sepulveda* is a shallow configuration with a high degree of symmetry and the resulting *RA* is 0.27. The *Villa Saraceno* is both slightly more linear with a single ring and its result, *RA* = 0.37, seems to confirm this.

The reciprocal of *RA* is *i*, the integration dimension that is central to so much analysis using the JPG method (Shapiro, 2005). Typically, *i* is used to identify spaces, or sequences of spaces, that are pivotal to a spatial configuration and those which are not. For the *Villa Saraceno*, the sequence from most integrated to least integrated (or most isolated) is: B (7.00) > A (4.67) > ⊕ (3.50) > E (3.11), F (3.11) > C (2.15), D (2.15) > G (1.75) and H (1.75). Hanson (1998) suggests that this sequence is a record of "inhabitant-visitor" relations, and that it may be more important for a house to just consider "inhabitant-inhabitant" relations. When the JPG data for the *Villa Saraceno* is recalculated without the presence of an exterior node, then the following is the integration sequence: A and B (3.50) > E and F (2.63) > C and D (1.75) > G and H (1.50). This change marginally flattens the results for the *Villa Saraceno*, identifying two clear zones of integration and replicating the visual effect of the JPG produced with A (and B) as carrier (Figure 4). Similar patterns of results are developed for the *Villa Sepulveda* when a comparison is constructed between *i* for the whole set and *i* just for the interior set. For the *Villa Sepulveda*, a range of 2.80 to 9.33 is reduced to a range of 2.33 to 7.00, once again flattening the results into a tighter range of values but not otherwise changing anything. For the *Villa Sepulveda*, with its ringed, permeable structure, node B, has the least depth and the salon space (being the only direct path to spaces C and D), has the most elevated level of influence or attraction (3.75), although space A also has an influential level (1.67). All of the other nodes have similar results (a range from 0.75 to 0.17). The *H** value for the *Villa Saraceno* was discussed in the previous section. For the *Villa Sepulveda*, the *H** result is 0.7550, which is just marginally less deliberative or structured than the result for the *Villa Saraceno*.

Fundamentally, the interpretation of mathematical measures derived from a JPG must be undertaken with some care and in parallel with a common-sense reading of the properties of the architectural plan it is derived from. Furthermore, scholars developing JPG data using software should do so with some awareness of what the graph mathematics is actually doing. For example, *TD* and *MD* are parallel perspectives on the same theme, and *RA* and *i* are literally two sides of the same idea. *CV* is a different measure, and as the scale of the JPG increases it becomes more difficult to intuitively determine the result, and thus it remains potentially useful. Conversely, the JPG method and its mathematical measures – based on the topological length of a simple graph – have some limitations, including those relating to multiple connections (or links) and distance between spaces (or nodes). The following section discusses an alternative method and centrality measures for such situations.

WEIGHTED, DIRECTED JPG AND CENTRALITY

This section presents a new way of addressing three potentially problematic issues in JPGs using centrality measures. The three issues are the handling of multiple links, directed links and "distance" between spaces. While the JPG method remains invaluable for many purposes, there are some situations in building plans that it cannot easily accommodate. For example, a common feature of many Palladian villas, like the *Villa Poiana*, is that they have two entrances; a formal entrance through a large portico or loggia at the front for visitors and inhabitants, and the rear entrance solely intended for inhabitants and people who have already been formally introduced to them (see Figure 7). These two features raise interesting questions about the JPG's capacity to capture more complex spatial connections.

A characteristic of the formal entrance of a Palladian villa is that it often has multiple links between the entrance hall (A) and the exterior ($\oplus$). Interestingly, Hillier and his colleagues capture and graphically represent this type of situation in JPGs (Hillier, Hanson, & Graham, 1987), but these additional connections have no impact on the calculated measures. In essence, if two spaces have multiple direct connections between them, they are treated in the same way as two spaces which have a single direct connection between them. This might be reasonable in some circumstances, but in others, including the Palladian villa, it might be significant that multiple major portals connect one space to another. The rear entrance to the Palladian villa poses another dilemma, as, from the visitor's perspective, it is effectively a one-way pathway from the interior to the exterior but not back again. Visitors do not enter through the rear of the house, but they may depart that way, meaning that the door has a directionality implicit in its use. These two situations are described, in graph terminology, as multiple and directed links, and they are significant because they can change the spatial properties of the JPG in terms of inhabitant-visitor relations. However, the conventional JPG method using a simple graph cannot distinguish between these different types of pathways to the exterior.

Figure 7. Villa Poiana, architectural plan and its plan graph

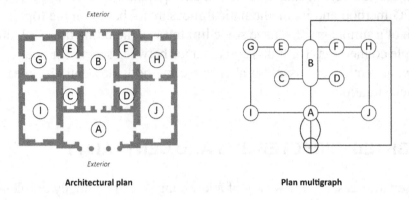

Architectural plan   Plan multigraph

A further challenge for JPG analysis is *distance,* an ongoing source of criticism of Space Syntax approaches (Netto, 2016; Pafka, Dovey, & Aschwanden, 2018; Ratti, 2004). The mathematical measures of a JPG are only based on the topological length between nodes, and, as such, the JPG ignores the actual metric distance between spaces. Although the method is typically used to investigate building layouts or small urban spaces, which generally do not develop very long edges, the JPG's lack of capacity to model distance remains a weakness for some applications. For example, in the *Villa Poiana,* movement from space B to space H, and from space A to space H, is identical in a topological sense (traversing two depths). But the former of these is much shorter (by a factor of four) than the latter, which might be significant for some purposes or applications.

Centrality Measures

The notion of centrality was introduced in the late 1940s by Alex Bavelas at the Group Networks Laboratory, Massachusetts Institute of Technology (Freeman, 1978). Centrality indices were first applied in the analysis of communication networks as a means of identifying the most important nodes in a graph. As such, centrality is a graph theory measure that can be used to determine, for example, who is an important (or influential) person in a social communication network. Equally, it can be used to calculate which road is most critical for a transportation network or, most significantly in the present context, which room is most important in a building. Thus, while centrality measures were originally developed for social network analysis (Borgatti, 2005; Freeman, 1978; Scott, 1988), they have since been used for a variety of purposes in other fields. As a result of this, multiple new centrality measures have been developed, including degree centrality, closeness, betweenness, eigenvector centrality, information centrality, flow betweenness and the rush index, along with various influence measures (Borgatti, 2005). The present chapter deals with only three centrality indices and their use in JPGs: degree centrality (C_D), closeness centrality (C_C) and betweenness centrality (C_B).

Centrality measures have been used in syntactical analysis in the past, and particularly to address the problems of urban street networks. For example, Barthelemy (2015) proposes using the spatial distribution of C_B for time-evolving road networks to overcome the limitations of axial line measures (the difference between the Euclidean shortest path and the simplest path). Crucitti, Latora and Porta (2006b) propose a set of four centrality indices – closeness, betweenness, straightness and information centralities – to investigate the urban street patterns of world cities. However, there appears to be no application of centrality measures to the exploration of interior spatial configurations.

Interestingly, closeness centrality (C_C) and betweenness centrality (C_B) are sometimes used interchangeably for "integration" and "choice" values in axial line analysis (di Bella, Corsi, Leporatti, & Persico, 2015; Jayasinghe, Sano, & Rattanaporn, 2017; Jiang & Jia, 2011; Morales, Flacke, & Zevenbergen, 2017; Omer & Goldblatt, 2016; Omer & Jiang, 2015). Pafka et al. (2018) also indicate that C_C and C_B are sometimes misnamed in space syntax research, leading to additional confusion. Furthermore, permeability (or connectivity) is described as "nodal degree centrality" (di Bella et al., 2015) and "global integration" as C_C (Jiang & Jia, 2011). Pafka et al. summarise the difference as being that whereas integration is used to measure " the least number of axes or segments encountered in moving from any single axis to all of the others in the network; choice analysis measures the degree to which each axis lies on the simplest path between all possible pairs of axes (all possible trips) within that network" (Pafka et al., 2018, p. 6). Therefore, measuring "integration" (to-movement) and "choice"(through-movement) is based on angular distance and angular segment analysis (Omer & Kaplan, 2018; Serra & Hillier, 2018; Turner, 2007). In contrast, Crucitti, Latora and Porta (2006a) use primal graphs (rather than dual) and metric distance (rather than topologic) to calculate centrality indices. Hillier and Vaughan (2007) further indicate that the syntactic measures (integration and choice) are calculated in a slightly different way from C_C and C_B in mathematics. Serra and Hillier (2018) claim that "angular distance" (paths with minimal sum of angular change) is superior to "metric distance" (paths with minimal sum of metric

163

length) in term of the road network analysis. However, they also argue that at local radii, "angular C_B" is strongly correlated with "metric C_B", which has a strong value at the most local radius (1 km). In summary, the syntactic versions of closeness and betweenness centralities are usually based on segmentation and radius (Pafka et al., 2018). However, centrality measures can adopt a "metric framework" (not topological terms or steps) (Crucitti et al., 2006b, p. 1), wherein the shortest path (geodesic) can be dependent on metric distance. This section of the chapter addresses this issue of different distances between nodes through the use of a weighted JPG, where the weight is the inverse value of the metric length of a link. But first, three centrality measures are introduced.

Degree centrality (C_D), is the degree of a node (or point), which is the number of other nodes that are adjacent to it and with which it is in direct contact (Freeman, 1978). It is also defined as "the number of ties incident upon a node" (Borgatti, 2005). Thus, the definition parallels that of "connectivity" in Space Syntax research. For example, "axial connectivity is the number of other lines with which an axial line intersects" (Hillier & Hanson, 1984, p. 103) and "connectivity measures the number of immediate neighbours that are directly connected to a space" (Klarqvist, 1993, p. 11). C_D is the simplest and the most intuitively concept of centrality, and it is also regarded as a measure of immediate influence. The C_D of node i is given by:

$$C_D(i) = \sum a_{ij}$$

where $a_{ij} = 1$ if i is adjacent to j and 0, when this is not the case. Degree centrality can be normalised if divided by the maximum possible degree of a network $(n - 1)$, where n is the number of nodes, to compare the relative centrality of nodes from different graphs.

Figure 8 is an example of a simple JPG to demonstrate centrality measures. The C_D of node $\oplus$ is two (because two edges of links connect to it), while A has the highest C_D of four. The C_D values of nodes C and F are one, as they are dead-end spaces.

Closeness centrality (C_C) is the sum of graph-theoretic distances from all other nodes, where the distance from one node to another is defined as the length (in links) of the shortest path from one to the other (Borgatti, 2005; Freeman, 1978). Freeman notes that a "message originating in the most central position in a network would spread throughout the entire network in minimum time." As such, "a point (or node) is central to the degree that the

Figure 8. Example of a simple JPG

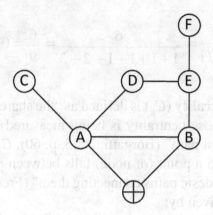

distances associated with all its geodesics are minim[ised]. Short distances mean fewer message transmissions, shorter times and lower costs"(Freeman, 1978, p. 225). Thus, C_c measures the extent to which a node i is near to all the other nodes along the shortest paths (Crucitti et al., 2006b). Closeness is the inverse of "farness". The C_C of node i is given by:

$$C_C(i) = \frac{1}{\sum_{i \neq j} d(i,j)}$$

where $d(i, j)$ is the distance of a geodesic from i to j. The C_c can be normalised, multiplied by $(n - 1)$ where n is the number of nodes. Thus,

$$C_C'(i) = \frac{(n-1)}{\sum_{i \neq j} d(i,j)}$$

For example, the sum of graph-theoretic distances from all other nodes to node A (or vice versa) in Figure 8 is:

$$\sum_{A \neq j} d(A, j) = d(\oplus, A) + d(B, A) + d(C, A) + d(D, A) + d(E, A) + d(F, A)$$

$$\sum_{A \neq j} d(A, j) = 1 + 1 + 1 + 1 + 2 + 3$$

Thus,

$$C_c{}'(A) = \frac{(7-1)}{\sum_{A \neq j} d(A, j)} = \frac{6}{1+1+1+1+2+3} = \frac{6}{9} = 0.67$$

Betweenness centrality (C_B) is defined as "the share of times that a node j needs a node i (whose centrality is being measured) in order to reach a node k via the shortest path" (Borgatti, 2005, p. 60). C_B is based upon "the frequency with which a point (or node) falls between pairs of other points on the shortest or geodesic paths connecting them" (Freeman, 1978, p. 221). The C_B of node i is given by:

$$C_B(i) = \sum_{i \neq j \neq k} \frac{g_{jk(i)}}{g_{jk}}$$

where g_{jk} is the number of geodesic paths from j to k, and $g_{jk}(i)$ is the number of these geodesics that pass through node i. That is, betweenness basically counts the number of geodesic paths that pass through a node i. C_B can be normalised by dividing it by the number of pairs of vertices not including i, which is $(n-1)(n-2)$ for directed graphs and $(n-1)(n-2)/2$ for undirected graphs. Thus,

$$C_B{}'(i) = \frac{2 \sum_{i \neq j \neq k} \dfrac{g_{jk(i)}}{g_{jk}}}{(n-1)(n-2)}$$

For example, the C_B of node A (the sum of the number of geodesics that pass through node A divided by the number of geodesic paths from j to k) is:

$$C_B(A) = \sum_{A \neq j \neq k} \frac{g_{jk(A)}}{g_{jk}} = g_{C,\oplus}(A)/ g_{C,\oplus} + g_{C,B}(A)/ g_{C,B} + g_{C,D}(A)/ g_{C,D} + g_{C,E}(A)/$$

$$g_{C,E} + g_{C,F}(A)/ g_{C,F} + g_{D,\oplus}(A)/ g_{D,\oplus} + g_{D,B}(A)/ g_{D,B}$$

$$C_B(A) = \sum_{A \neq j \neq k} \frac{g_{jk(A)}}{g_{jk}} = 1+1+1+\frac{2}{2}+\frac{2}{2}+1+\frac{1}{2} = 6.5$$

Thus,

$$C'_B(A) = \frac{2 \times 6.5}{(7-1)(7-2)} = 0.43$$

The C_B values of two dead-end nodes (C and F) are 0. The C_B of node $\oplus$ is also zero because there is no geodesic passing through the node. In this way, the centrality values of all nodes of the JPG in Figure 8 can be calculated (Table 7).

Weighted JPGs

The centrality measures in the previous section were presented using a simple graph (Figure 8), while this section proposes a new graph that is used for situations where multiple links, directed links and distances between spaces have an impact on spatial configuration. For the present purposes, this new graph is called a "weighted and directed JPG".

The concept of a network that is weighted in some way (say, to model the existence of multiple major doors between two spaces) is sometimes described as being a factor of the "tie strength" between nodes. This idea that different edges in a graph have different strengths (regardless of innate topology) has been widely explored by social network researchers (Barrat, Barthélemy, Pastor-Satorras, & Vespignani, 2004; Newman, 2001; Opsahl, Agneessens, & Skvoretz, 2010). In social network theory, the weight of a link (or tie) can be a function of duration, emotional intensity, intimacy or exchange of service (Granovetter, 1973). In architecture, the level of physical connectivity or the extent of metric distance between spaces are the most logical determinants of link strength or weighting. For example, the left JPG of Figure 9 depicts a situation where multiple links occur between node A and the exterior ($\oplus$), while the second and third graphs are weighted versions of the JPG taking into consideration connectivity and distance. Focusing on the multiple links in the first JPG, the C_D values of node A and $\oplus$ are increased to 6 and 4, respectively, but the C_C and C_B values are not changed and are the same as the values of the simple JPG in Figure 8. This is because the theoretical distance of the geodesic and the ratio of the number of geodesic paths passing through a node are unchanged.

The middle JPG of Figure 9 represents a weighted link between node A and $\oplus$, which is valued as 3 (being simply the number of links), and the other

Table 7. Centrality indices of the JPG in Figure 8 C" means normalised centrality

Node	C_D	C'_D	C_C	C'_C	C_B	C'_B
⊕	2.00	0.33	0.09	0.55	0.00	0.00
A	4.00	0.67	0.11	0.67	6.50	0.43
B	3.00	0.50	0.11	0.67	4.00	0.27
C	1.00	0.17	0.07	0.43	0.00	0.00
D	2.00	0.33	0.10	0.60	2.00	0.13
E	3.00	0.50	0.10	0.60	5.50	0.37
F	1.00	0.17	0.07	0.40	0.00	0.00
Minimum	1.00	0.17	0.07	0.40	0.00	0.00
Mean	2.29	0.38	0.09	0.56	2.57	0.17
Maximum	4.00	0.67	0.11	0.67	6.50	0.43

links have the theoretical distance of 1. There is another way to calculate these binary distances using a "tuning parameter" – the relative importance of the number of ties (links) compared to tie weights (Opsahl et al., 2010). However, calculating the number of links as a weighted value is a simpler way to explore the spatial configuration of an architectural plan. The weighed centrality degree (C^w_D) of node i is given by

$$C^w_D(i) = \sum w_{ij}$$

, where w_{ij} is the value represents the weight of the link between nodes i and j, and w_{ij} is greater than 0 if the node if i is adjacent to j and 0, if this is not the case. Each link generally (if no other indication is given) has a weight of 1 (the middle JPG of Figure 9). In this way, the C^w_D values of node A and ⊕ are 6 (1 + 1 + 1 + 3) and 4 (3 + 1), respectively, in the weighted JPG for multiple link.

C_C is the sum of graph-theoretic distances from all other nodes, while weighed centrality closeness (C^w_C) considers a weighted distance (d^w).

$$d^w(i,j) = \min\left(\frac{1}{w_{ih}} + \ldots + \frac{1}{w_{hj}}\right)$$

, where h are intermediary nodes on paths between node i and j. Thus, the d^w is still identifying as the length of the shortest path from one to the other node. For example, the d^w between node C and $\oplus$ in the middle JPG of Figure 9 is:

$$d^w (C, \oplus) = \left(\frac{1}{1} + \frac{1}{3}\right) = \qquad\qquad 1.333$$

In this way, the C_c^w of node i is given by:

$$C_c^w (i) = \frac{1}{\sum_{i \neq j} d^W (i, j)}$$

where $d^w(i, j)$ is the distance of a geodesic from i to j. The C_c^w can be normalised, divided by $(n - 1)$ where n is the number of nodes. Thus,

$$C_c^w{}'(i) = \frac{(n-1)}{\sum_{i \neq j} d^w (i, j)}$$

For example, the sum of weighted distances from node A to all other nodes in Figure 9 is:

$$\sum_{A \neq j} d^w (A, j) = d^w(A, \oplus) + d^w(A, B) + d^w(A, C) + d^w(A, D) + d^w(A, E) +$$
$d^w(A, F)$

$$\sum_{A \neq j} d^w (A, j) = 1/3 + 1 + 1 + 1 + 2 + 3$$

Thus,

$$C_c^w{}'(A) = \frac{(7-1)}{\sum_{A \neq j} d(A, j)} = \frac{6}{1/3 + 1 + 1 + 1 + 2 + 3} = \frac{6}{8.333} = 0.72$$

The normalised C_c^w value of node A (0.72) is slightly increased from its $C_c{}'$ (0.67). In contrast, the normalised C_c^w value of node B is the same value of its $C_c{}'$ (0.67). Thus, the normalised C_c^w better captures node A (for example, as in the main entrance hall of a Palladian villa) which provides a faster circulation flow to the other nodes (spaces) than node B (the rear entrance of a Palladian villa) for visitors. In addition, the weight of a link can describe a metric distance. w_{ij} (the weight of the link between nodes i and j) is

$$w_{ij} = \frac{1}{d^m(i,j)}$$

, where d^m is the metric length of a link between i to j. That is, the weight is the inverse value of the metric length of a link. For example, if a long distance between A and B in the third JPG of Figure 9 is 2, then w_{AB} is ½. Thus, the sum of weighted distances from node A to all other nodes in Figure 9 is:

$$\sum_{A \neq j} d^w(A, j) = d^w(A, \oplus) + d^w(A, B) + d^w(A, C) + d^w(A, D) + d^w(A, E) + d^w(A, F)$$

$$\sum_{A \neq j} d^w(A, j) = 1/3 + (1+1/3) + 1 + 1 + 2 + 3$$

$$C_c^w{}'(A) = \frac{(7-1)}{\sum_{A \neq j} d(A, j)} = \frac{6}{0.333 + 1.333 + 1 + 1 + 2 + 3} = \frac{6}{8.666} = 0.69$$

There are two geodesic paths from A to E in the simple JPG in Figure 8, but the path passing through node D is only one geodesic from A to E in the last JPG in Figure 9. The geodesic from A to B is a path passing-through $\oplus$. Thus, C_B values of the weighed JPG are also changed from those of a simple JPG. Please note that the numbers near links in the weighted JPG are not distances but their weights.

The C_B^w of node i is given by:

$$C_B^w(i) = \sum_{i \neq j \neq k} \frac{g_{jk(i)}^w}{g_{jk}^w}$$

Figure 9. A JPG with multiple links and weighted JPGs

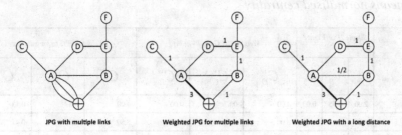

JPG with multiple links	Weighted JPG for multiple links	Weighted JPG with a long distance

where g^w_{jk} is the number of weighted geodesic paths from j to k, and g^w_{jk} *(i)* is the number of these weighted geodesics that pass through node *i*. For example, the C^w_B of node A in the right JPG of Figure 9 is

$$C^w_B(A) = 1+1+1+1+1+1+1 = 7$$

This is because the path passing through node D is only one geodesic from A to E in the weighted JPG. Thus, the normalised C^w_B of node A is:

$$C^w_B{}'(A) = \frac{2 \times 7}{(7-1)(7-2)} = 0.47$$

In this way, the weighted centrality measures can be used to quantify the two different types of entrances in the *Villa Poiana* as well as different metric distances between nodes. Table 8 reports centrality indices of the JPG in Figure 8 and two weighed JPGs in Figure 9. The weighted link between node A and ⊕ captures the different closeness centralities ($C^w_c{}'$) between two nodes, A (0.72) and B (0.67), while accommodating a longer distance between A and B, which develops different closeness and betweenness indices for most of the nodes due to many changes of geodesics in the graph. Thus, the Weighted JPG considering metric distances can identify more detailed spatial configurations.

Weighted And Directed JPGS

The last alternative measure is for accommodating a directed JPG. For example, there is a directed link in Figure 10 from node B to ⊕. This directed link captures the rear exit in the *Villa Poiana* that is used for an inhabitant's

Table 8. Centrality indices of the JPG in Figure 8 and two weighed JPGs in Figure 9 C" means normalised centrality

Node	Simple JPG (Figure 8)			Weighted JPG (multi-links)			Weighted JPG (a long distance)		
	C_D	C'_C	C'_B	C_D^W	$C_C^{W'}$	$C_B^{W'}$	C_D^W	$C_C^{W'}$	$C_B^{W'}$
⊕	2.00	0.55	0.00	4.00	0.67	0.00	4.00	0.67	0.13
A	4.00	0.67	0.43	6.00	0.72	0.43	5.50	0.69	0.47
B	3.00	0.67	0.27	3.00	0.67	0.27	2.50	0.62	0.13
C	1.00	0.43	0.00	1.00	0.45	0.00	1.00	0.44	0.00
D	2.00	0.60	0.13	1.00	0.64	0.13	1.00	0.64	0.27
E	3.00	0.60	0.37	2.00	0.60	0.37	2.00	0.60	0.40
F	1.00	0.40	0.00	1.00	0.40	0.00	1.00	0.40	0.00
Minimum	1.00	0.40	0.00	1.00	0.40	0.00	1.00	0.40	0.00
Mean	2.29	0.56	0.17	2.57	0.59	0.17	2.43	0.58	0.20
Maximum	4.00	0.67	0.43	6.00	0.72	0.43	5.50	0.69	0.47

pathway from inside to outside (but is not for a visitor to return by way of this path). In order to measure centrality indices of this directed graph (or digraph), two separate measures of degree centrality are employed: indegree and outdegree. "Indegree is a count of the number of ties directed to the node, and outdegree is the number of ties that the node directs to others" (He & Petoukhov, 2011, p. 145). Calculating indegree and outdegree of a node results in double the potential number of values of centrality indices (White & Borgatti, 1994). Thus, for example, both indegree and outdegree of node A are 5.5 (1 + 1 + ½ + 3) because all links of the node are undirected. Therefore, considering indegree and outdegree, the C_D of node A is 11 (5.5 + 5.5), which is double its C_D^W in Table 8. The indegree of node B is 1.5 (1 + ½) in the JPG of Figure 10, while its outdegree is 2.5 (1 + ½ + 1). Thus, the centrality measures of a digraph are the average values of additions of incoming and outgoing centrality indices. That is, the C_D^W of node B is:

$$C_D^W(B) = \frac{1.5 + 2.5}{2} = 2$$

The centrality measures of a digraph are slightly more complex. One way of understanding them is to use an "adjacency matrix for a weighted and directed graph". Table 9 is the adjacency matrix of the weighted JPG with a

Figure 10. A weighted JPG with a directed link

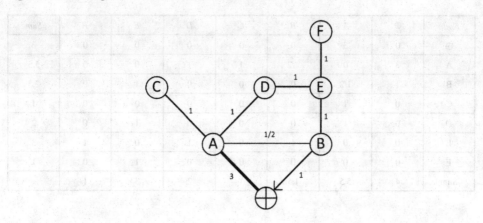

directed link (Figure 10). As observed, due to a directed link, the upper diagonal and lower diagonals are not equal (unlike the matrix of an undirected graph). The sum of all entries in a column is the indegree of a node and the sum of all entries in a row is the outdegree of the node. Thus, the C_D^w of a node is the average value of the sum of all entries in the column and the row of the node.

In contrast, measuring C_C^w and C_B^w of a digraph is more complicated. For example, the shortest path from A to B uses the link between the two nodes ($d^w = \dfrac{1}{1/2} = 2$), but the geodesic from B to A passes through $\oplus$ ($d^w = \dfrac{1}{1} + \dfrac{1}{3} = 1.333$). In this way, the sum of weighted distances from all other nodes to node A (for incoming C_C^w) in Figure 10 is:

$$\sum_{j \neq A} d^w(j, A) = d^w(\oplus, A) + d^w(B, A) + d^w(C, A) + d^w(D, A) + d^w(E, A) + d^w(F, A)$$

$$\sum_{j \neq A} d^w(j, A) = 1/3 + 1.333 + 1 + 1 + 2 + 3$$

The incoming C_C^w (C_C^{w-}) is:

Table 9. Adjacency matrix of the weighted and directed JPG in Figure 9

Node	⊕	A	B	C	D	E	F	Sum
⊕	0	3	0	0	0	0	0	3
A	3	0	1/2	1	1	0	0	5.5
B	1	1/2	0	0	0	1	0	2.5
C	0	1	0	0	0	0	0	1
D	0	1	0	0	0	1	0	2
E	0	0	1	0	1	0	1	3
F	0	0	0	0	0	1	0	1
Sum	4	5.5	1.5	1	2	3	1	

$$C_c^{w-}(A) = \frac{1}{\sum_{A \neq j} d(A,j)} = \frac{1}{1/3 + 1.333 + 1 + 1 + 2 + 3} = \frac{1}{8.666} = 0.1154$$

Simultaneously, the sum of weighted distances from A to all other nodes (for outgoing C_c^w) is

$$\sum_{A \neq j} d^w(A,j) = d^w(A, ⊕) + d^w(A, B) + d^w(A, C) + d^w(A, D) + d^w(A, E) + d^w(A, F)$$

$$\sum_{A \neq j} d^w(A,j) = 1/3 + 2 + 1 + 1 + 2 + 3$$

The outgoing C_c^w (C_c^{w+}) is:

$$C_c^{w+}(A) = \frac{1}{\sum_{A \neq j} d(A,j)} = \frac{1}{1/3 + 2 + 1 + 1 + 2 + 3} = \frac{1}{9.333} = 0.1071$$

Thus, the C_c^w node A is:

$$C_c^w(A) = \frac{C_c^{w-}(A) + C_c^{w+}(A)}{2} = \frac{0.1154 + 0.1071}{2} = 0.1113$$

Thus, the normalised C_C^w of node A is:

$$C_c^{w'}(A) = C_c^w(A) \times (n-1) = 0.1113 \times 6 = 0.67$$

This value is the same as the $C_C^{w}{}'$ of node A in a weighted JPG (having a longer distance) in Table 8. Even if the calculation is rounded to four decimal places, the difference is only 0.002. That is, the directed link is not a strong influence on the centrality closeness of node A. However, the $C_C^w{}'$ of node B in the weighted JPG with a directed link is 0.55, which is different from the value without the directed link (0.62). This is because the incoming C_C^w is significantly reduced due to the one-way path. This sort of detail identification can raise interesting interpretations of spatial configuration in a building program or an urban system, taking into account, for example, public and private entrances, one-way roads or paths, and controlled systems for security and safety. Measuring C_B^w for the weighted, directed JPG also considers two-way geodesic paths. As a result, the C_B^w values of node B and $\oplus$ are changed from 0.13 to 0.07 because one of the two-way geodesic paths is blocked. The final centrality indices are described in Table 10.

In axial line analysis, C_C and C_B tend to be used almost interchangeably with "integration" and "choice" values. In the mathematical measures of a JPG, integration value (i) and control value (CV) would be conceptually similar to C_C and C_B. Table 10 reports the i and CV values and centrality indices. The order of integration values is quite similar to the orders of all different types of centrality closeness. The hierarchy of CV is quite similar to centrality betweenness, but the latter cannot distinguish three nodes ($\oplus$, C and F) because there is no geodesic passing through these nodes. The $C_C^w{}'$ of the weighted, directed JPG is better at capturing two different types of links, ($\oplus$, A) and ($\oplus$, B), as well as considering the different distances between nodes. Thus, the new JPG method using centrality measures can be used to address multiple links, directed links and "distance" between spaces that could not be explored in the conventional method.

CONCLUSION

This chapter started by presenting the classical mathematical techniques for deriving measures of spatial connectivity from a standard JPG. In the latter part of the chapter a weighted, directed JPG method was presented, which proposed an alternative way of exploring specific design properties.

Table 10. Integration value i and control value CV with centrality indices C' means normalised centrality

Node	Simple JPG						Weighted, directed JPG	
	i	CV	C_C	C_B	C'_C	C'_B	$C_C^{w}{}'$	$C_B^{w}{}'$
⊕	3.00	0.58	0.09	0.00	0.55	0.00	0.61	0.07
A	5.00	2.33	0.11	6.50	0.67	0.43	0.69	0.47
B	5.00	1.08	0.11	4.00	0.67	0.27	0.55	0.07
C	1.88	0.25	0.07	0.00	0.43	0.00	0.43	0.00
D	3.75	0.58	0.10	2.00	0.60	0.13	0.64	0.27
E	3.75	1.83	0.10	5.50	0.60	0.37	0.59	0.40
F	1.67	0.33	0.07	0.00	0.40	0.00	0.40	0.00
Minimum	5.00	2.33	0.07	0.00	0.40	0.00	0.40	0.00
Mean	3.43	1.00	0.09	2.57	0.56	0.17	0.56	0.18
Maximum	1.67	0.25	0.11	6.50	0.67	0.43	0.69	0.47

It introduced various centrality measures that capture different features of a network and demonstrates how graph centralisation can be calculated. This new approach can be used to overcome some current limitations of the JPG method; however, the classical JPG approach is still able to quantitatively capture spatial configurations and characteristics based on the spatial topology of the built environment.

Throughout this chapter, as in most space syntax research, the focus has been on topological relationships. However, there is a dimension to JPG research that has never been adequately developed. While the JPG has been used to compare social patterns in a range of historic and vernacular homes or villages and in some modern housing estates, there are relatively few examples of the method being used to analyse the body of work of an individual architect. Thus, these techniques are used in Section 3 of this book to examine two syntactical and grammatical applications (the language of Glenn Murcutt's Domestic Architecture and Frank Lloyd Wright's Prairie Houses). Through the focused analysis on an architect's work it would be possible to not only interrogate their actual social and cultural values, and compare them with their espoused views, but it may be possible to trace the development of their design approaches throughout their careers. It is this territory of design analysis, previously largely ignored by proponents of the JPG method, which is potentially most relevant for its revival.

REFERENCES

Alexander, C. (1964). *Notes on the Synthesis of Form.* Cambridge, MA: Harvard University Press.

Alexander, C. (1966). A city is not a tree. *Design, 206,* 46–55.

Alexander, C., Ishikawa, S., & Silverstein, M. (1977). *A pattern language: Towns, buildings, construction.* New York, NY: Oxford University Press.

Asami, Y., Kubat, A. S., Kitagawa, K., & Iida, S.-i. (2003). Introducing the third dimension on space syntax: Application on the historical Istanbul. In J. Hanson (Ed.), *Proceedings: 4th International Space Syntax Symposium* (pp. 48.01 – 48.18). London, UK: University College London.

Asif, N., Utaberta, N., Sabil, A. B., & Ismail, S. (2018). Reflection of cultural practices on syntactical values: An introduction to the application of space syntax to vernacular Malay architecture. *Frontiers of Architectural Research, 7*(4), 521–529. doi:10.1016/j.foar.2018.08.005

Bafna, S. (2003). Space syntax: A brief introduction to its logic and analytical techniques. *Environment and Behavior, 35*(1), 17–29. doi:10.1177/0013916502238863

Barrat, A., Barthélemy, M., Pastor-Satorras, R., & Vespignani, A. (2004). The architecture of complex weighted networks. *Proceedings of the National Academy of Sciences of the United States of America, 101*(11), 3747–3752. doi:10.1073/pnas.0400087101 PMID:15007165

Barthelemy, M. (2015). From paths to blocks: New measures for street patterns. *Environment and Planning B. Urban Analytics and City Science, 44*(2), 256–271. doi:10.1177/0265813515599982

Borgatti, S. P. (2005). Centrality and network flow. *Social Networks, 27*(1), 55–71. doi:10.1016/j.socnet.2004.11.008

Byun, N., & Choi, J. (2016). A typology of Korean housing units: In search of spatial configuration. *Journal of Asian Architecture and Building Engineering, 15*(1), 41–48. doi:10.3130/jaabe.15.41

Casti, J. L. (1995). *Complexification: Explaining a paradoxical world through the science of surprise.* London, UK: Abacus.

Crucitti, P., Latora, V., & Porta, S. (2006a). Centrality in networks of urban streets. *Chaos (Woodbury, N.Y.), 16*(1), 015113. doi:10.1063/1.2150162 PMID:16599779

Crucitti, P., Latora, V., & Porta, S. (2006b). Centrality measures in spatial networks of urban streets. *Physical Review. E, 73*(3), 036125. doi:10.1103/PhysRevE.73.036125 PMID:16605616

di Bella, E., Corsi, M., Leporatti, L., & Persico, L. (2015). The spatial configuration of urban crime environments and statistical modeling. *Environment and Planning B. Urban Analytics and City Science, 44*(4), 647–667. doi:10.1177/0265813515624686

Dovey, K. (1999). *Framing places: Mediating power in built form.* London, UK: Routledge. doi:10.4324/9780203267639

Edwards, M. J. (2013). The configuration of built space at Pataraya and Wari provincial administration in Nasca. *Journal of Anthropological Archaeology, 32*(4), 565–576. doi:10.1016/j.jaa.2013.09.004

Eloy, S., & Duarte, J. P. (2015). A transformation-grammar-based methodology for the adaptation of existing housetypes: The case of the "rabo-de-bacalhau'. *Environment and Planning. B, Planning & Design, 42*(5), 775–800. doi:10.1068/b120018p

Fladd, S. G. (2017). Social syntax: An approach to spatial modification through the reworking of space syntax for archaeological applications. *Journal of Anthropological Archaeology, 47*, 127–138. doi:10.1016/j.jaa.2017.05.002

Freeman, L. C. (1978). Centrality in social networks conceptual clarification. *Social Networks, 1*(3), 215–239. doi:10.1016/0378-8733(78)90021-7

Gao, X., Asami, Y., Zhou, Y., & Ishikawa, T. (2013). Preferences for floor plans of medium-sized apartments: A survey analysis in Beijing, China. *Housing Studies, 28*(3), 429–452. doi:10.1080/02673037.2013.759542

Granovetter, M. S. (1973). The strength of weak ties. *American Journal of Sociology, 78*(6), 1360–1380. doi:10.1086/225469

Hanson, J. (1998). *Decoding homes and houses.* Cambridge, UK: Cambridge University Press.

Harary, F. (1960). Some historical and intuitive aspects of graph theory. *SIAM Review, 2*(2), 123–131. doi:10.1137/1002023

He, M., & Petoukhov, S. (2011). *Mathematics of bioinformatics: Theory, methods and applications*. Hoboken, NJ: John Wiley and Sons.

Hillier, B., & Hanson, J. (1984). *The social logic of space* (Vol. 1). Cambridge, UK: Cambridge University Press. doi:10.1017/CBO9780511597237

Hillier, B., Hanson, J., & Graham, H. (1987). Ideas are in things: An application of the space syntax method to discovering house genotypes. *Environment and Planning. B, Planning & Design, 14*(4), 363–385. doi:10.1068/b140363

Hillier, B., & Penn, A. (2004). Rejoinder to Carlo Ratti. *Environment and Planning. B, Planning & Design, 31*(4), 501–511. doi:10.1068/b3019a

Hillier, B., & Vaughan, L. (2007). The city as one thing. *Progress in Planning, 67*(3), 205–230.

Hofstadter, D. R. (1981). Strange attractors: Mathematical patterns delicately poised between order and chaos. *Scientific American, 245*, 16–29.

Hopkins, B., & Wilson, R. J. (2004). The truth about Königsberg. *The College Mathematics Journal, 35*(3), 198–207.

Jayasinghe, A., Sano, K., & Rattanaporn, K. (2017). Application for developing countries: Estimating trip attraction in urban zones based on centrality. *Journal of Traffic and Transportation Engineering, 4*(5), 464–476. doi:10.1016/j.jtte.2017.05.011

Jeong, S.-K., & Ban, Y.-U. (2011a). Computational algorithms to evaluate design solutions using space syntax. *Computer Aided Design, 43*(6), 664–676. doi:10.1016/j.cad.2011.02.011

Jeong, S.-K., & Ban, Y.-U. (2011b). Developing a topological information extraction model for space syntax analysis. *Building and Environment, 46*(12), 2442–2453. doi:10.1016/j.buildenv.2011.05.024

Jeong, S.-K., & Ban, Y. U. (2014). The spatial configurations in South Korean apartments built between 1972 and 2000. *Habitat International, 42*, 90–102. doi:10.1016/j.habitatint.2013.11.002

Jiang, B., Claramunt, C., & Klarqvist, B. (2000). Integration of space syntax into GIS for modelling urban spaces. *International Journal of Applied Earth Observation and Geoinformation, 2*(3), 161–171. doi:10.1016/S0303-2434(00)85010-2

Jiang, B., & Jia, T. (2011). Agent-based simulation of human movement shaped by the underlying street structure. *International Journal of Geographical Information Science, 25*(1), 51–64. doi:10.1080/13658811003712864

Kishimoto, T., & Taguchi, M. (2014). Spatial configuration of Japanese elementary schools: Analyses by the space syntax and evaluation by school teachers. *Journal of Asian Architecture and Building Engineering, 13*(2), 373–380. doi:10.3130/jaabe.13.373

Klarqvist, B. (1993). A space syntax glossary. *Nordisk Arkitekturforskning, 2*, 11–12.

Krüger, M. (1989). *On node and axial grid maps: Distance measures and related topics.* London, UK: University College London.

Leach, E. (1978). Does space syntax really "constitute the social"? In D. Green, C. Haselgrove, & M. Spriggs (Eds.), *Social Organization and Settlement: Contributions from Anthropology, Archaeology, and Geography* (Vol. 2, pp. 385–401). Oxford, UK: British Archaeological Reports.

Lee, J. H., Ostwald, M. J., & Gu, N. (2015). A syntactical and grammatical approach to architectural configuration, analysis and generation. *Architectural Science Review, 58*(3), 189–204. doi:10.1080/00038628.2015.1015948

Lee, J. H., Ostwald, M. J., & Gu, N. (2017). A combined plan graph and massing grammar approach to Frank Lloyd Wright's Prairie architecture. *Nexus Network Journal, 19*(2), 279–299. doi:10.100700004-017-0333-0

Lee, J. H., Ostwald, M. J., & Gu, N. (2018). A justified plan graph (JPG) grammar approach to identifying spatial design patterns in an architectural style. *Environment and Planning B. Urban Analytics and City Science, 45*(1), 67–89. doi:10.1177/0265813516665618

Lewin, R. (1993). *Complexity: Life on the edge of chaos.* London, UK: Dent.

Major, M. D., & Sarris, N. (2001). Cloak-and-dagger theory: Manifestations of the mundane in the space of eight Peter Eisenman houses. *Environment and Planning. B, Planning & Design, 28*(1), 73–88. doi:10.1068/b2671

Malhis, S. (2008). The new upper-middle class residential experience: A case study of apartment flats in Jordan using the logics of Burden, Hillier and Hanson. *Architectural Science Review, 51*(1), 71–79. doi:10.3763/asre.2008.5110

Manum, B. (2009). AGRAPH: Complementary software for axial-line analysis. In D. Koch, L. Marcus, & J. Steen (Eds.), *Proceedings of the 7th International Space Syntax Symposium.* (pp. 0701-0709). Stockholm, Sweden: KTH.

March, L. (Ed.). (1976). *The architecture of form.* Cambridge, UK: Cambridge University Press.

March, L., & Steadman, P. (1971). *The geometry of environment: An introduction to spatial organization in design.* London, UK: RIBA Publications.

Markus, T. A. (1987). Buildings as classifying devices. *Environment and Planning. B, Planning & Design, 14*(4), 467–484. doi:10.1068/b140467

Markus, T. A. (1993). *Buildings and power: Freedom and control in the origin of modern building types.* London, UK: Routledge.

Morales, J., Flacke, J., & Zevenbergen, J. (2017). Modelling residential land values using geographic and geometric accessibility in Guatemala City. *Environment and Planning B. Urban Analytics and City Science, 2399808317726332.* doi:10.1177/2399808317726332

Netto, V. M. (2016). "What is space syntax not?" Reflections on space syntax as sociospatial theory. *URBAN DESIGN International, 21*(1), 25–40. doi:10.1057/udi.2015.21

Newman, M. E. J. (2001). Scientific collaboration networks II. Shortest paths, weighted networks, and centrality. *Physical Review. E, 64*(1), 016132. doi:10.1103/PhysRevE.64.016132 PMID:11461356

Omer, I., & Goldblatt, R. (2016). Using space syntax and Q-analysis for investigating movement patterns in buildings: The case of shopping malls. *Environment and Planning B. Urban Analytics and City Science, 44*(3), 504–530. doi:10.1177/0265813516647061

Omer, I., & Jiang, B. (2015). Can cognitive inferences be made from aggregate traffic flow data? *Computers, Environment and Urban Systems, 54,* 219–229. doi:10.1016/j.compenvurbsys.2015.08.005

Omer, I., & Kaplan, N. (2018). Structural properties of the angular and metric street network's centralities and their implications for movement flows. *Environment and Planning B. Urban Analytics and City Science, 2399808318760571.* doi:10.1177/2399808318760571

Opsahl, T., Agneessens, F., & Skvoretz, J. (2010). Node centrality in weighted networks: Generalizing degree and shortest paths. *Social Networks, 32*(3), 245–251. doi:10.1016/j.socnet.2010.03.006

Osman, K. M., & Suliman, M. (1994). The space syntax methodology: Fits and misfit. *Architecture & Comportement /Architecture & Behaviour, 10*(2), 189 – 204.

Ostwald, M. J. (1997). Structuring virtual urban space: Arborescent schemas. In P. Droege (Ed.), *Intelligent environments – spatial aspects of the information revolution* (pp. 451–482). Amsterdam, The Netherlands: Elsevier. doi:10.1016/B978-044482332-8/50026-3

Ostwald, M. J. (2011a). Examining the relationship between topology and geometry: A configurational analysis of the rural houses (1984-2005) of Glenn Murcutt. *Journal of Space Syntax, 2*(2), 223–246.

Ostwald, M. J. (2011b). A justified plan graph analysis of the early houses (1975-1982) of Glenn Murcutt. *Nexus Network Journal, 13*(3), 737–762. doi:10.100700004-011-0089-x

Ostwald, M. J. (2011c). The mathematics of spatial configuration: Revisiting, revising and critiquing justified plan graph theory. *Nexus Network Journal, 13*(2), 445–470. doi:10.100700004-011-0075-3

Pafka, E., Dovey, K., & Aschwanden, G. D. P. A. (2018). Limits of space syntax for urban design: Axiality, scale and sinuosity. *Environment and Planning B. Urban Analytics and City Science, 2399808318786512.* doi:10.1177/2399808318786512

Peponis, J., Wineman, J., Rashid, M., Kim, S. H., & Bafna, S. (1997). On the description of shape and spatial configuration inside buildings: Convex partitions and their local properties. *Environment and Planning. B, Planning & Design, 24*(5), 761–781. doi:10.1068/b240761

Ratti, C. (2004). Space syntax: Some inconsistencies. *Environment and Planning. B, Planning & Design, 31*(4), 487–499. doi:10.1068/b3019

Scott, J. (1988). Social network analysis. *Sociology, 22*(1), 109–127. doi:10.1177/0038038588022001007

Seppänen, J., & Moore, J. M. (1970). Facilities planning with graph theory. *Management Science, 17*(4), 242–253. doi:10.1287/mnsc.17.4.B242

Serra, M., & Hillier, B. (2018). Angular and metric distance in road network analysis: A nationwide correlation study. *Computers, Environment and Urban Systems, 74,* 194–207. doi:10.1016/j.compenvurbsys.2018.11.003

Shapiro, J. S. (2005). *A space syntax analysis of Arroyo Hondo Pueblo, New Mexico.* Santa Fe, NM: School of American Research Press.

Steadman, P. J. (1983). *Architectural morphology.* London, UK: Pion.

Stevens, G. (1990). *The reasoning architect: Mathematics and science in design.* New York, NY: McGraw Hill.

Stewart, I. (1989). *Does God play dice? The new mathematics of chaos.* London, UK: Penguin.

Stiny, G. (1985). Computing with Form and Meaning in Architecture. *Journal of Architectural Education, 39*(1), 7-19.

Taaffe, E. J., & Gauthier, H. L. (1973). *Geography of transportation.* Upper Saddle River, NJ: Prentice Hall.

Thaler, U. (2005). Narrative and syntax, new perspectives on the Late Bronze Age palace of Pylos, Greece. In A. v. Nes (Ed.), *5th International Space Syntax Symposium, Proceedings* (vol. 2, pp. 323-339). Delft, The Netherlands: Techne Press.

Thom, R. (1975). *Structural stability and morphogenesis.* Reading, MA: Addison-Wesley.

Thom, R. (1983). *Mathematical models of morphogenesis.* New York, NY: Halsted Press.

Turner, A. (2007). From axial to road-centre lines: A new representation for space syntax and a new model of route choice for transport network analysis. *Environment and Planning. B, Planning & Design, 34*(3), 539–555. doi:10.1068/b32067

White, D. R., & Borgatti, S. P. (1994). Betweenness centrality measures for directed graphs. *Social Networks, 16*(4), 335–346. doi:10.1016/0378-8733(94)90015-9

Wong, J. F. (2014). Conceptual engawa: The experience of ring-based circulation in Tadao Ando Museums. *Environment and Planning. B, Planning & Design, 41*(2), 229–250. doi:10.1068/b39012

Zadeh, R. S., Shepley, M. M., & Waggener, L. T. (2012). Rethinking efficiency in acute care nursing units: Analyzing nursing unit layouts for improved spatial flow. *HERD: Health Environments Research & Design Journal, 6*(1), 39–65. doi:10.1177/193758671200600103 PMID:23224842

Zheng, X., Zhao, L., Fu, M., & Wang, S. (2008). Extension and application of space syntax: A case study of urban traffic network optimizing in Beijing. In Q. Luo, & W. Zheng (Eds.), *2008 Workshop on Power Electronics and Intelligent Transportation System* (pp. 291-295). Guangzhou, China: IEEE. 10.1109/PEITS.2008.22

Section 3

Chapter 6
A Combined Grammatical and Syntactical Method

ABSTRACT

This chapter presents a method that combines Shape Grammar and Space Syntax approaches to offer a rigorous way of understanding an architectural style and then producing variations of that style. The two approaches have only rarely been connected in the past, and the relationship between them has never been fully developed. The method commences with a justified plan graph (JPG) grammar and illustrates the grammatical interpretation of the structure of this syntax. The JPG technique is then followed by a massing grammar, which adds a consideration of architectural form. A significant strength of this method is that it encapsulates both the formal and functional properties of architecture. As part of the introduction to this method, the chapter employs two generic grammars, drawn from the combined method, along with their abstraction, measures, and configurations.

INTRODUCTION

This chapter explains and demonstrates a grammatically interpolated and syntactically derived method for architectural design analysis and generation. The first of the two approaches, the grammatical, is associated with the logical relationships that exist between elements (Stiny & Gips, 1972). In architecture, this usually refers to the form-generating rules that describe the two or three-dimensional shape of a building. The second of the approaches,

DOI: 10.4018/978-1-7998-1698-0.ch006

the syntactical, focuses on spatial relations that may in turn be mapped to various functional considerations (Hillier & Hanson, 1984), leading to its use to describe the functional structure of space. Applications of the two approaches – Shape Grammar and Space Syntax – are similarly diverse. Fundamentally, in its conventional architectural use, the former develops a set of rules to describe or generate a corpus of designs (*form*), while the latter is used to investigate spatial topologies and social relations (*function*). This combination is significant, as traditionally architecture has been defined, at least in part, as being made up of *form* and *function*, which, when combined in the right way, achieves a level of poetic or aesthetic appeal. Early twentieth century Modernist architects even argued that form necessarily follows function, although subsequent architectural movements challenged this simple, if powerful, proposition. Because of the importance of form and function in architecture, and the fact that their relationship has often been viewed as reciprocal (form shapes function, and in turn, function shapes form), it is natural that grammatical and syntactical approaches would be conceptualised as potentially offering a powerful analytical combination. Nonetheless, despite some isolated attempts, they have rarely been successfully combined to consider both the grammatical and syntactical features of architecture.

Several past studies (Eloy, 2012; Heitor, Duarte, & Pinto, 2004; March, 2002) have proposed combining the strengths of both Shape Grammar and Space Syntax approaches. Such works have typically connected the insights developed separately in these fields, and have tended to generate design instances using a grammatical process and then evaluated them using graph theory. Thus, in such examples, a Space Syntax technique is used to decide which applications of the grammatical rules are most valuable in the set of design productions. By developing shape as the starting point, this particular combined approach privileges form over function. In contrast, the combined grammatical and syntactical method introduced in the present chapter commences with a consideration of functional issues, identifying the syntactical properties of a design through a special type of Justified Plan Graph (JPG). By commencing with a JPG grammar in the first stage, the method is able to capture a variety of syntactical values in an architectural plan layout (Lee, Ostwald, & Gu, 2015a, 2018). After defining the spatial and syntactic relations implicit in a design, the method then derives a set of shape-based rules to illustrate the overall form of the design using a descriptive grammar, in this case called "a massing grammar" (Lee, Ostwald, & Gu, 2017). In this method, the configuration of functional spaces precedes the generation of forms, meaning that, conceptually, form follows function. While past research in architectural theory has demonstrated that form and function do not necessarily exist in such a fixed relationship, in general, for both practical and aesthetic reasons, functional thinking tends to precede formal resolution in the classical design process and in much architectural practice.

The proposed conceptual framework for understanding the combined grammatical and syntactical method is developed from our previous works (Lee, Ostwald, & Gu, 2015a; 2015b; 2017; 2018). The framework highlights three different components – node, link and shape – that encapsulate different types of spatial and formal information and provide a conceptual foundation for understanding the overall method. The method is then used to identify both the grammatical patterns and the syntactical properties of two design examples. The two configurational grammars that make up the method, the JPG grammar and the massing grammar, are also introduced. The former addresses the functional structure of architectural space (insofar as the connectivity or permeability of an architectural plan defines its practical use), while the latter illustrates the form-generating rules underlying its three-dimensional expression.

The presentation of the grammatical and syntactical method in this chapter is framed around its use for the analysis of formal and spatial properties in a set of existing or proposed architectural designs. The method can then be used to either analyse the properties of these works or generate new designs that possess the same social and formal characteristics. However, parts of the chapter also discuss possible broader applications of the method in, for example, mapping design processes and decisions.

NODE, LINK AND SHAPE

The combined grammatical and syntactical method introduced in this chapter relies on three connected processes. Each of these can also be conceptualised in terms of the conventional linguistic analogies common in computational design and then expressed in the algebraic form used in conventional graph

Figure 1. Node, link and shape (Common (C), Private (P), Hall (H), Transit (T), Exterior (E))

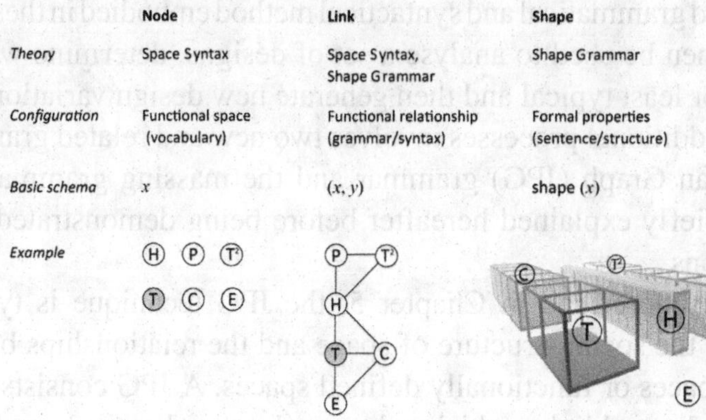

	Node	**Link**	**Shape**
Theory	Space Syntax	Space Syntax, Shape Grammar	Shape Grammar
Configuration	Functional space (vocabulary)	Functional relationship (grammar/syntax)	Formal properties (sentence/structure)
Basic schema	x	(x, y)	shape (x)
Example	Ⓗ Ⓟ Ⓣ Ⓣ Ⓒ Ⓔ		

grammars (Figure 1). The three processes are introduced hereafter, along with their linguistic and algebraic equivalents.

1.   The first process identifies each functionally defined group or sector of spaces in a design and defines them as nodes. This first process effectively defines the architectural "vocabulary" of the style (its functional spaces). In algebraic notation, each node is coded as "x", where x represents the name of the space associated with the node or its functional type.

2.   The second process links these nodes in a particular sequence, based on relative adjacency. Thus, both the "grammar" (sequence) and "syntax" (adjacency) of the nodes are configured in the second process. This relates to the social structure or connectivity of these functional spaces. In algebraic notation, the connection between a node x and a node y, is expressed as "(x, y)".

3.   The third process associates formal properties (shape) with each node. This could be conceptualised as completing the "sentence structure" or "phraseology" of the design, being the way the combination of spaces and forms is arranged and expressed. In algebraic notation, the shape associated with node x *is* expressed as "shape (x)".

    Thus, the newly combined grammatical and syntactical method uses three basic schemas, "x", "(x, y)" and "shape (x)", to describe node, link and shape, respectively. Collectively, these three processes develop syntactical knowledge, along with topological and formal constraints, as precursors to undertaking computational analysis and generation processes.

The combined grammatical and syntactical method embodied in these three processes can then be used to analyse a set of designs, determine which in the set is most or least typical and then generate new design variations. The basis for these additional processes involves two new and related grammars, the Justified Plan Graph (JPG) grammar and the massing grammar, each of which are briefly explained hereafter before being demonstrated in the following sections.

As previously described in Chapter 5, the JPG technique is typically used to identify the social structure of space and the relationships between either convex spaces or functionally defined spaces. A JPG consists of two components, nodes and links, which, when analysed collectively, reveal the range of mathematical properties of the spatial structure. For example, total depth (*TD*), relative asymmetry (*RA*), real relative asymmetry (*RRA*), and integration (*i*), along with many other values, can be developed to compare different types of graphs and the social structures they encapsulate. Many studies (Hanson, 1998; Hillier & Hanson, 1984; Ostwald, 2011) have developed detailed approaches to constructing a permeability graph from a plan layout. Using such a predetermined protocol, these approaches partition a plan into a series of spaces (nodes) and the connections (links) between them. In the traditional Space Syntax approach to the analysis of architectural plans, each node typically represents either a convex space or a functionally defined room. For example, Hillier and Hanson (1984) develop rigorously defined convex spaces as a precursor to developing a plan graph, while Bafna (1999) uses programmatically defined areas for a similar purpose. The latter of these two methods has become more common in recent years as researchers have identified that a JPG of functionally defined spaces may produce more robust results.

In contrast to these standard approaches, the method introduced in the present chapter defines a node as both a set of similarly defined spaces and a corresponding three-dimensional (3D) modular form, as shown in Figure 2 (a). That is, the definition of a node is associated with the functional and formal module of the design. Amorim's concept of "dwelling sectors" (Amorim, 1999) has similarities to this definition, as it identifies a functionally defined group of spaces. For Amorim, a dwelling sector is a zone comprised of programmatically related rooms. Grouping such rooms into a so-called "sector-based node" (Lee, Ostwald, & Gu, 2015b) is one of the first means architects have for designating initial functional requirements and their associated 3D shapes. While a convex-plan-based JPG could more explicitly consider visually defined spaces or permeability, the method is less concerned with the precise modelling of spatial visibility than with the connectivity relationships that exist between functional sectors and forms.

The first part of the grammatical and syntactical method requires identification of the complete set of functionally defined sectors in a plan and their algebraic expression as nodes. After developing the complete set of nodes, their links are identified, capturing the functional relationships presented in the structure of their planning. The links represent the practical "adjacency" or "connectivity" between "functional sectors". For example, the line (link) in Figure 2 (b) between the two nodes represents connections between the adjacent rooms. In this way, the connectivity results in a joint form of the two 3D shapes, A and B, in the figure. That is, the sector nodes and links are not only used to generate a graph accommodating both permeability and adjacency, but also to generate the logic of shape composition. Furthermore, whereas in the traditional syntactical analysis of convex spaces the graph is always presented in its complete form, the combined grammatical and syntactical method has an additional property: it is sequentially evolved. Thus, by following a protocol that identifies a carrier around which the graph is justified, the plan graph is effectively grown step by step. Consequently, this special type of JPG has grammatical properties embedded in its formation.

In a sense, the JPG grammar serves as an analogue of the stage in the design process where "bubble diagrams" or "proximity matrixes" are used to determine the basic spatio-functional relationships in a plan (Balmer & Swisher, 2012; Seonwook, 2012). Indeed, the process of sequentially generating and defining a set of functional spaces (nodes) in a plan, along with their levels of connectivity (links), could be regarded as a general design stage. The JPG grammar can also be understood as a variation of a graph grammar that generates planar mechanisms. Graph grammars (Freudenstein & Maki, 1979; Li & Schmidt, 2004; Schmidt & Cagan, 1997) are illustrated with vertices (links) and edges (joints), and mechanical components and functional relationships can also be represented as graphs (Grasl & Economou, 2013; Schmidt & Cagan, 1997). For example, Grasl and Economou (2013) introduce a part-relation graph consisting of maximal lines and points to nodes (two different types of nodes), and relations to edges. In this way, these graphs are regarded as a source of information which can be used to generate plans and 3D shapes. Like graph grammars, which are often described using algebraic expressions, the starting point for a JPG consists of two nodes and a topological link between then. In Figure 2 (b) this relationship is described as {A, B, (A,

B)}, where A and B are nodes and (A, B) is a link between the two nodes. Thus, nodes and links in a sector-adjacency JPG can be represented as a collection of non-terminal symbols and terminal symbols that are assigned to spatial or formal entities.

The second grammar of the method is a massing grammar, which provides the basis for shape-based configurational processes. Shape Grammars, regardless of their variations, can be thought of as providing both a system for the analysis of a corpus of designs and a production process for generating new ones with similar properties (Stiny & Gips, 1972). Importantly, as shown in Figure 2 (a), nodes in the method represent functional spaces or sectors as well as their forms (in 3D) or shapes (in 2D). To do this, the massing grammar simplifies the forms used in architecture and decomposes them using a modular system. Like Koning and Eizenberg's grammar (Koning & Eizenberg, 1981), the massing grammar conceptually follows the production system of assembling blocks (much like Lego, Froebel and Cuisenaire blocks) as a useful analogical basis for a simplified modular system. Furthermore, the rule basis of the massing grammar is determined by the spatial and social structure of the space expressed in the JPG. That is, the massing grammar adopts the definitions of the basic modules (structural or functional bays) in a design from the JPG grammar. Thus, the first rule of the massing grammar is the transformation of a sector node into a shape. The following two sections describe the process of developing a JPG grammar and a massing grammar in more detail.

A (GENERIC) JPG GRAMMAR

Sector-Based JPGs

As a precursor to describing the development of sector node graphs, it is important to clarify that the plan graphs that make up the basic JPG grammar are all "simple graphs" or "strict graphs". This means that two nodes are connected by only one link or, conversely, that multiple links between nodes of the graph are not permitted. This is important for three reasons. First, it allows users to employ standard graph mathematics, most of which is intended for use in simple graphs. Second, the links in the JPG are also related to the formal joints in the massing grammar at the later stage, and third, the JPG grammar has a sequential process consisting of addition rather

Figure 2. Node and link corresponding shape

a. Two disconnected nodes corresponding to convex spaces as well as forms (the three-dimensional shapes of the rooms)

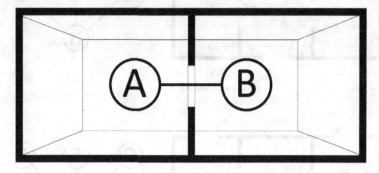

b. Two nodes and a link reflecting a connected spatial and formal relationship

than subtraction rules, both of which require simple graphs. While a later section in this chapter briefly considers multi-graphs in the context of JPG grammars, the majority of applications in this book are for simple graphs.

Consider the simple example of a plan for a house with three functional sectors – hall (H), common (C) and private (P) – and an exterior (E). Three variations of spatial relationships between these sections are depicted in Figure 3, along with sector-based JPGs to represent their plan layouts. The different connections between the nodes in the JPGs reflect different planning functions or priorities. For example, Figure 3 shows that the private sector node in JPG A is two sector depths from the hall sector, while in JPGs B and C there is only one sector depth between the hall and private sectors. As a result, each JPG reflects a different spatial relationship from which various syntactic values may be calculated. But such JPGs also contain within them the seeds of a simple sequential process of development that commences with an important entry and hall node (H) and then grows additional nodes,

Figure 3. Sector-based justified plan graphs

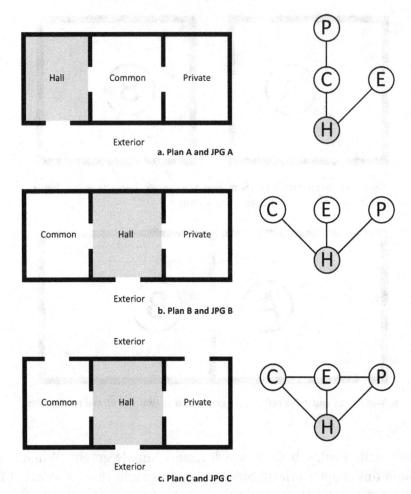

a. Plan A and JPG A

b. Plan B and JPG B

c. Plan C and JPG C

first inside (C and P) and then outside (E). For example, to build JPG A, the common node is the first link added to the hall (H, C) and the private node is then added to the common node (C, P), completing the interior. Finally, the exterior node is linked to the hall, completing the graph (H, E). In contrast, JPG B is developed first by the common and private nodes directly linking to the hall (H, C and H, P), and then by completing the graph with the hall connecting to the exterior (H, E). JPG C has an additional sequential generation stage that connects common, private and exterior sectors. While the logic underpinning the rules used in this example is not developed until later in the chapter, it should be apparent that a JPG can be used to identify a sequence of spatial operations. This special type of generative process produces the JPG grammar.

A basic JPG can express a range of topological types in a design. For example, Hillier (1999) argues that the a-type or "cut-link" is associated with occupation, whilst the b-type or "tree-link" is more relevant to movement. Ring-link nodes are divided into c-type or "single ring-link" and d-type or "multiple ring-link". For example, JPG A and JPG B in Figure 3 consist of a- and b-type links, while all nodes in JPG C are ring-links, with two nodes (E and H) being multiple ring-links. Once the graph of functional sector nodes and adjacent links is prepared, its syntactical properties are calculated. Mathematical values such as mean depth (*MD*) and integration (*i*) can also be calculated to describe the characteristics of various sectors. For example, the most isolated spaces in JPG A are the private and exterior sectors (*MD* = 2.00 and *i* =3.00), while the common and hall sectors are relatively more accessible (*MD* = 2.00 and *i* =1.00). In contrast, the hall sector in JPG B is more accessible (MD = 1.00) than the other three sectors (*MD* = 1.67). With the connections of C and P to E, the exterior sector in JPG C has the same *MD* as the hall sector, and the others (C and P) also become more accessible (*MD* = 1.33), revealing the shallow structure of JPG C. The JPGs for plans B and C in Figure 3 are similar, with the exception of additional links to the exterior (E), but these differences are readily apparent in the mathematical results. Following such a syntactical review of the JPG, it is possible to derive a series of rules that describe the graph grammatically. This is the subject of the next section.

G-JPG Grammar

In essence, a JPG grammar uses the graph-based (node and link) logic of a graph grammar, wherein the symbol of a vertex represents a sector node and the edge of a graph grammar corresponds to a link that connects nodes in a plan layout. Importantly, the JPG grammar introduced in this chapter could also be regarded as a "generic Shape Grammar", in line with the definitions of Costa and Duarte (2015). A "generic" Shape Grammar is represented by a set of algebraic rules that are used to create any type of plan graph. A "specific" Shape Grammar is then developed through the customisation of the generic grammar to capture a distinct set of designs. Two specific JPG (s-JPG) grammars are presented in Chapters 7 and 8, whereas the present section describes a "generic JPG (g-JPG) grammar" as a syntactically derived and grammatical approach that uses the method.

A JPG is a set of nodes and links and any graph, g_a, generated by applying the JPG grammar is represented by:

$$g_a = (N, L),$$

where N is a set of nodes and L is a set of links represented as (i, j) when i and j are nodes of the graph. For example, the three JPGs in Figure 3 are represented by:

$$g_{JPG\,A} = (\{H, C, P, E\}, \{(H, C), (C, P), (H, E)\}),$$

$$g_{JPG\,B} = (\{H, C, P, E\}, \{(H, C), (H, P), (H, E)\}),$$

$$g_{JPG\,C} = (\{H, C, P, E\}, \{(H, C), (H, P), (H, E), (P, E), (C, E)\}),$$

where the first bracketed group $\{x, y, z\}$ is the set of sector nodes, and the second comprises the connections between the nodes $\{(x, y), (x, z)\}$.

The JPG grammar uses algebra to describe a plan graph consisting of sector nodes and topological links. For example, the rule that a node (y) and a link (x, y) are added adjacent to a node (x) can be described as:

$$x \rightarrow x, y, (x, y),$$

where x and y are nodes and (x, y) is a link between the two nodes. Using this method, the typological links between every node in the sector-adjacency JPG can be encoded as a series of rules. In this way, the JPG grammar has parallels with the production rules of a "context-free grammar" (Hopcroft, Motwani, & Ullman, 2006). To encode such a generic grammar, four components are developed from graph grammars: Grammar $G = (V, T, P, S)$, where V is the set of variables (non-terminal), T is the terminals, P is the set of production (rules), and S is the start symbol.

The JPG grammar in the architectural design domain is represented by:

$$G_{JPG} = (\{x, y\}, \{N, c, E\}, P, S),$$

where x and y are non-terminal symbols. As in a traditional graph grammar, P is the set of rules and S is the start symbol. Terminal symbol N denotes a set of nodes and terminal symbol "c" denotes a "core node" that is used to identify the first node generation from a start symbol. Terminal symbol "E" denotes an exterior node. The terminal symbols should be clearly defined before developing the production rules for the JPG grammar. Importantly, four schemas defining the sectors are used to identify a set of nodes *N*. They are: (i) identifying a set of functional sectors; (ii) grouping "visually enclosed" convex spaces into a sector; (iii) configuring transit sectors; and (iv) configuring second functional sectors.

The JPG grammar starts by identifying the set of functional sectors, taking into account spatial and formal modules. For example, for the upper plan in Figure 4, the 1975 *Marie Short House* by Glenn Murcutt, five sector nodes are identified. By grouping "visually enclosed" convex spaces into a sector node, the LDK (Living, Dining, Kitchen) room and the utility room are merged into a common node (C). Two en-suite bedrooms including WIRs (Walk in Robes) are merged into a private node (P). The sector nodes defined in this way consist of four functional modules that are visually captured with dot-dashed lines in Figure 4 (a). In contrast, for the 1902 *Francis W. Little House* by Frank Lloyd Wright (Figure 4 (b)), both a living room and a dining room are identified as a living sector node (L) and a dining sector node (D), respectively. A kitchen is identified as a service node (K) that often includes pantries and small rooms for servants. An entry node (N) includes the entry and reception spaces in the plan as a combined functional and formal module. In this way, each functional sector can include multiple small spaces (alcoves, bathrooms, toilets, utility cupboards) within its larger grouping.

After identifying the set of sector nodes, transit (T) nodes are configured. Transit spaces are typically intermediate zones between interior and exterior. Additional functional sector nodes are also considered in the set of sectors. For example, if there are two or more spatially separated instances of the same functional sectors, each is separately numbered. Thus, the *Marie Short House* has two transit nodes (T, T^2) and the *Little House* has two living sector nodes (L, L^2) and two dining sector nodes (D, D^2) (Figure 4).

The second terminal symbol "c" is used to distinguish a core node from the other sector nodes in the JPG grammar. The core node in the JPG grammar is similar to the "core unit" in Koning and Eizenberg's grammatical research (1981). The core node is first generated by the JPG grammar, playing a significant role in configuring spatial programs as well as generating forms for the massing grammar. Past research identifies two logical types of core nodes, the first being the central social space of the plan, and the second the primary entry to the plan. Both of these spaces are socially, symbolically

Figure 4. Defining sector and core nodes

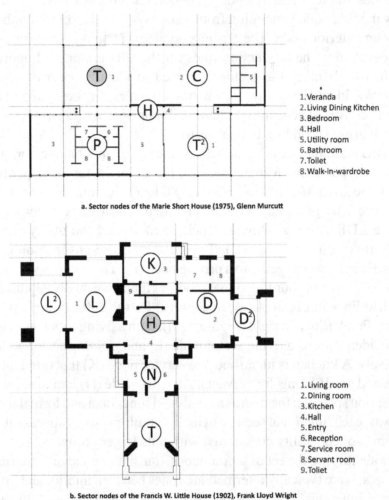

1. Veranda
2. Living Dining Kitchen
3. Bedroom
4. Hall
5. Utility room
6. Bathroom
7. Toilet
8. Walk-in-wardrobe

a. Sector nodes of the Marie Short House (1975), Glenn Murcutt

1. Living room
2. Dining room
3. Kitchen
4. Hall
5. Entry
6. Reception
7. Service room
8. Servant room
9. Toliet

b. Sector nodes of the Francis W. Little House (1902), Frank Lloyd Wright

and functionally significant, although the entry is arguably a more practical starting point, as its primary role is to define inhabitant-visitor relations. For example, in the *Marie Short House* in Figure 4 (a), the transit node (T), including the main entrance, is the logical core node. Given the long narrow forms often found in Murcutt's architecture, and his focus on creating an architecture that mediates between the interior and exterior, the entry transit space is the obvious core node. In contrast, a hall sector node is the core node for the *Little House* in Figure 4 (b), because it is commonly located in the middle of the cruciform plan of the Prairie style, and Wright argued that such central spaces evoked greater feelings of safety and contentment (Ostwald & Dawes, 2018).

The configuration of terminal symbols differs from the traditional graph grammar approach, which is used to solve mechanical design problems. To develop JPGs representing the spatial structures of architectural designs, decisions about a set of nodes and a core node need additional configurational processes and will also affect the application of the following rules. Thereafter, the g-JPG grammar consists of three production stages (comprising eight general rule sets): (i) core configuration ($L_n R_1$ to $L_n R_2$); (ii) local configuration ($L_n R_3$ to $L_n R_5$); and (iii) global configuration ($L_n R_6$ to $L_n R_8$). The g-JPG grammar can produce multiple levels of s-JPG grammars by the use of "n", which is the location of a level, with the default value for the ground floor being 0. The construction of the g-JPG starts with the production of plan graphs on the ground level (L_0) and then moves on to subsequent levels (L_1, L_2, and so on).

The eight rule sets for constructing a g-JPG grammar are presented in Table 1. The first rule set generates the core node. For example, the first production rules for JPGs for two plans in Figure 4 are $S_0 \rightarrow T_{c0}$ for the *Marie Short House* and $S_0 \rightarrow H_{c0}$ for the ground floor of the *Little House*. That is, using the first rule set, two specific JPG (s-JPG) grammars generate the transit node and the hall node as a core node, respectively. The second rule set ($L_n R_2$) then adds nodes and links adjacent to a core node.

The local configuration ($L_n R_3$ to $L_n R_5$) in Table 1 addresses the relationship between inhabitants. It adds nodes and links adjacent to a core node and then configures additional nodes and links adjacent to the non-core node(s). At the fourth rule set ($L_n R_4$), a link between non-core nodes is also added. In the rare case of a locally isolated but formally connected sector in a level, the fifth rule set ($L_n R_5$) considers a node without a link. For example, a transit sector (veranda) without a local connection can be added at the fifth rule set. The global configuration ($L_n R_6$ to $L_n R_8$) connects different levels or storeys. This global connection stage also commonly deals with the relationships between the exterior and interior topologies. In the grammar, an exterior sector node (E) represents the outside world, signifying the potential for ingress and egress relationships. Thus, the global configuration commences by adding the exterior node (E) and a link between a node (core node or non-core node) at the ground level and E. The seventh rule set ($L_n R_7$) then develops a link between a node(s) at the ground level and E, if necessary and also considers a link addition between two nodes on two different topological levels, L_n and L_{n-1}. Finally, at the eighth rule set, the production system moves to the next

Table 1. A generic JPG grammar (S: start symbol, c: core node symbol, N: a set of nodes) (Lee, Ostwald, & Gu, 2018)

Rule set (L: level)	Description	Schema	Rule diagram
$L_n R_1$	Transform a start symbol into a core node.	$S_n \rightarrow x_{cn}$ where $x \in N(L_n)$	$S_n \rightarrow$ (x)
$L_n R_2$	Add node and link adjacent to a core node.	$x_{cn} \rightarrow x_{cn}, y, (x_{cn}, y)$ where $x, y \in N(L_n)$	(x) $\rightarrow$ (x)—(y)
$L_n R_3$	Add node and link adjacent to a non-core node(s).	$x \rightarrow x, y, (x, y)$ where $x, y \in N(L_n)$	(x) $\rightarrow$ (x)—(y)
$L_n R_4$	Add link between non-core nodes.	$x, y \rightarrow x, y, (x, y)$ where $x, y \in N(L_n)$	(y) (x) $\rightarrow$ (x)—(y)
$L_n R_5$	Add node without a link (locally isolated but formally connected node in the level).	$x \rightarrow x, y$ where $x, y \in N(L_n)$	(x) $\rightarrow$ (x) (y)
$L_n R_6$	Add the exterior node (E) and add link between a core node at the ground level and E. Or: Add the exterior node (E) and add link between	$x_{cn} \rightarrow x_{cn}, E, (x_{cn}, E)$ where $x \in N(L_n)$ $x \rightarrow x, E, (x, E)$	(x) $\rightarrow$ (x)—(E) (x) $\rightarrow$ (x)

n: the location of a level, with the default value for the ground floor being 0.
(i) Core configuration: $L_n R_1$ to $L_n R_2$, (ii) local configuration: $L_n R_3$ to $L_n R_5$, (iii) global configuration: $L_n R_6$ to $L_n R_8$.

level (L_{n+1}), when there is a further topological level to configure as JPGs, otherwise the process is terminated. In this way, the grammar facilitates the development of three syntactic phrases – the "head" of a graph, and "local" and "global" syntax – that may not be easily discerned in a more straightforward graph developed from plan layouts only.

Figure 5 illustrates the rules in the s-JPG grammars used to generate the JPGs for the two plans in Figure 4, the *Marie Short House* and *Little House* (ground level only). The full sets of the s-JPG grammars are presented in the following chapters. The *Marie Short House* and *Little House* examples also demonstrate that the core node can be understood as the "head" of a phrase (Chomsky, 1995; Corbett, Fraser, & McGlashan, 1993) because it usually shapes the basic structure of the JPG. Consequently, the grammar develops local connectedness at a topological level and then through global configurations. Thus, this JPG grammar allows for two different types of social relations to be captured by considering the relationship between the local and global syntax of the graph (Hillier & Hanson, 1984), as shown in Figure 5.

Figure 5. Rule sets and JPG growths for the s-JPG grammars

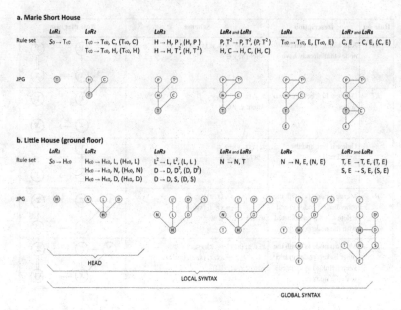

a. Marie Short House

	LoR₁	LoR₂	LoR₃	LoR₄ and LoR₅	LoR₆	LoR₇ and LoR₈
Rule set	$S_O \to T_{c0}$	$T_{c0} \to T_{c0}, C, (T_{c0}, C)$ $T_{c0} \to T_{c0}, H, (T_{c0}, H)$	$H \to H, P, (H, P)$ $H \to H, T^2_c (H, T^2_c)$	$P, T^2_c \to P, T^2_c (P, T^2_c)$ $H, C \to H, C, (H, C)$	$T_{c0} \to T_{c0}, E, (T_{c0}, E)$	$C, E \to C, E, (C, E)$

b. Little House (ground floor)

	LoR₁	LoR₂	LoR₃	LoR₄ and LoR₅	LoR₆	LoR₇ and LoR₈
Rule set	$S_O \to H_{c0}$	$H_{c0} \to H_{c0}, L, (H_{c0}, L)$ $H_{c0} \to H_{c0}, N, (H_{c0}, N)$ $H_{c0} \to H_{c0}, D, (H_{c0}, D)$	$L^2 \to L, L^2, (L, L)$ $D \to D, D^2, (D, D^2)$ $D \to D, S, (D, S)$	$N \to N, T$	$N \to N, E, (N, E)$	$T, E \to T, E, (T, E)$ $S, E \to S, E, (S, E)$

HEAD

LOCAL SYNTAX

GLOBAL SYNTAX

A Variation of the JPG Grammar

The g-JPG grammar has several practical limitations, including its focus on the analysis of architectural plans, although the following massing grammar deals with the three-dimensional formal aspects of a design. Moreover, the full social implications of the syntactical approach are not developed to the same level they would be using a rigorous convex space analysis. While in theory it is possible to substitute convex spaces for sector nodes in the application of the g-JPG grammar, in practice this would require an overly laborious application of the method which would not necessarily produce better results. Despite these limitations, the method's strength is that it offers a way of working computationally with both topology and geometry in a design, and it develops a sequential set of production rules which captures both properties. A further strength of the method is that if the production of the graph requires multiple links or edges between nodes (effectively being a multigraph), the JPG grammar enables a further configuration of nodes and links capturing such a recursive model of design. This variation adds more than one link between two nodes as well as modifying a node and/or a link. These alternative configurations of the JPG grammar can encapsulate or model modification activities that occur in the early conceptual design

Table 2. Examples of rule sets for the variation of the JPG grammar (N: a set of nodes)

Rule set	Description	Schema	Rule diagram
R_1	Add a link between two nodes that already have a link.	$x, y, (x, y) \rightarrow x, y, (x, y), (x, y)$ where $x, y \in N$	
R_2	Delete a link between two nodes	$x, y, (x, y) \rightarrow x, y$ where $x, y \in N$	
R_3	Delete a link and the linked node	$x, y, (x, y) \rightarrow x$ where $x, y \in N$	
R_4	Merge a node (x) with the other linked node (y) and delete a link(s) associated with the node (x)	$x, y, z, (x, y), (x, z), (y, z)$ $\rightarrow xy, z, (xy, z)$ where $x, y, z \in N$	
R_5	Merge a node (x) with the other linked node (y) and keep a link(s) associated with the node (x)	$x, y, z, (x, y), (x, z), (y, z)$ $\rightarrow xy, z, (x, z), (xy, z)$ where $x, y, z \in N$	

stage, when decisions are made about sector node connectivity. Thus, for example, the classic early design stage in architecture is the production of "bubble diagrams", wherein circles representing functional sectors in a plan are sketched on paper, along with the connections between them. At this early design stage, it is common for connections or links to be added and then removed as different functional uses and relations are tested. The adding and then removing of links, like the sketching and then erasing of forms, is often thought of as a "working-forward" and "working-backward" design process. The multigraph variation of the JPG grammar enables modelling of this design approach, which could help to support design thinking processes identified by Jones' Analysis-Synthesis-Evaluation model (Jones, 1992). Table 2 shows examples of rule sets for the multi-graph variation of the JPG grammar.

Since this chapter is focussed on the basic combined grammatical and syntactical method, the multi-graph variation of the JPG grammar is not fully developed here. However, the application of the two modification rule sets (R_4 and R_5) in Table 2 is illustrated in Figure 6 to show the potential of this variation. In this example – consisting of four functional spaces: living room (L), dining room (D), kitchen (K) and hall (H) – the rules for the standard JPG grammar application cannot capture the formal productions in the plan layout. In contrast, the multigraph variation of the JPG grammar in Table

Figure 6. The application of two modification rule sets

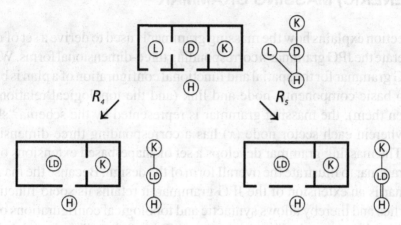

2 has rules which can merge two functional spaces into one. For example, if a designer wants to merge a living room and a dining room into a living-dining room (LD), the two modification rule sets (R_4 and R_5) can be applied according to this intention. After combining the two spaces, R_4 deletes all links associated with the living room, while R_5 keeps a link between the living room and the hall. Consequently, the application of R_5 results in two links between "LD" and "H" in Figure 6. R_4 and R_5 are used to develop different social and functional relationships, but the traditional syntactical measures based on relative depths do not reveal these subtleties. In such a case, a measure like centrality betweenness or centrality closeness would be more useful for uncovering the social properties in the spatial structure, including multiple links between nodes (as discussed in the previous chapter). Again, the detail application of this variation of the JPG grammar is beyond the scope of the present chapter, which is primarily concerned with the use of the method for exploring the combined social and formal properties of a set of existing or proposed designs. The following section describes the development of a formal massing grammar as an extension of the JPG grammar.

A (GENERIC) MASSING GRAMMAR

This section explains how the massing grammar is used to derive a set of rules to generate the JPG grammar's corresponding three-dimensional forms. Whilst the JPG grammar for the spatial and functional configuration of a plan is based on two basic components, node and link (and the topological relationship between them), the massing grammar is represented by the schema "shape (x)", wherein each sector node (x) has a corresponding three-dimensional form. The massing grammar develops a set of shape-based extensions of the JPG grammar to illustrate the overall form of the design. Because the massing grammar is an extension of the JPG grammar, it retains its socio-functional properties and thereby allows syntactic and topological configurations of the massing to inform analysis and generation. Table 3 describes the rule sets of the generic massing grammar, which commence with the transformation of sector nodes into 3D modular blocks and ends with a termination rule. As discussed in the previous section, the basic plan modules are identified first.

The conceptual foundation for configuring a massing grammar has two parts. First is the simplification of architectural forms and the second is their decomposition using a modular system. In this way, the massing grammar starts by defining the basic modules (structural or functional bays) in a design, which are used to standardise and delineate enclosed spaces. For orthogonal designs, the bays can be simplified using a rectangular grid (Figure 4), which often conforms to the repetitive column layout or modular construction systems found in many designs. A variation of the decomposition process for non-orthogonal plans could readily be developed, if needed, using arc-based modules for curved sections and secondary grids for buildings with forms that intersect at non-right-angled junctions.

While the dimensions of the enclosed spaces will vary from one building to another, the module, regardless of its shape, is a major characteristic of most designs. Thus, the first stage of the grammar develops blocks from sector nodes. The first shape rule set (SR_1) is

$x \rightarrow$ shape (x), where x is a node.

The generic massing grammar is used to develop a specific descriptive grammar involves three processes, with relevant configurations for defining: (a) block properties, (b) composition and (c) roof types. That is, configuring 3D blocks consists of applying three of the shape rule sets $(SR_2, SR_3$ and $SR_4)$ in Table 3. In the massing grammar, any form $(SHAPE_a)$ is represented by

Table 3. A generic massing grammar (N: a set of nodes)

Shape rule set	Description	Schema
SR_1	Transform sector nodes into 3D modular blocks.	$x \rightarrow$ shape (x) where $x \in N$
SR_2	Configure block properties – size and wall type (both sets of block sizes and wall types depend on a set of designs being described in the specific massing grammar).	shape $(x) \rightarrow$ shape $(x, size.type)$ where $x \in N$
SR_3	Identify block composition – formal relationships between blocks: *Direction* = {east, west, north, south, northeast, northwest, southeast, southwest}, *Alignment* = {equal, centre, left, right and interleaving}.	If x is a core node (block) then shape $(x, size.type) \rightarrow$ shape $(x, size.type, coreblock)$ otherwise shape $(x, size.type)$ $\rightarrow$ shape $(x, size.type, y.direction.alignment)$ where $x, y \in N$
	If there is more than one level, use Level composition – joining two formal levels, L_n and L_{n-1}.	shape $(x_n, size.type, coreblock)$, shape $(y_{n-1}, size.type, coreblock) \rightarrow$ shape $(x_n, size.type, coreblock)$, shape $(y_{n-1}, size.type, x_n.top.alignment)$
SR_4	Configure a roof type that depends on a set of designs being described in the specific massing grammar.	shape $(x, size.type, y.direction.alignment)$ $\rightarrow$ shape $(x, size.type, y.direction.alignment, roof\text{-}type)$ where $x, y \in N$
SR_5	Terminate the process.	Termination

$$\text{SHAPE}_a = \text{shape } (x, size.type, y.direction.alignment, roof\text{-}type)$$

where x and y are nodes (blocks). The "block properties" consist of block (module) size and wall type. "Composition" is the relationship between adjacent blocks in terms of direction and alignment, and "roof type" is the form of any capping to the blocks.

Block Properties

In this part of the configuration process in the massing grammar, the sectored modules are elaborated to identify the appropriate block (module) size and wall type. Size is a multiple of the dominant planning module and the exact dimensions of modules are not considered in the grammar because of the need to simplify the number of variables and dimensions used. In terms of size, for example, the *Marie Short House* uses a six-bay structure which consists of two types of modules: a wide room-type module (represented by "*R*") which features habitable spaces, and a narrow hall-type module (represented by "*H*") for circulation (Figure 7 (a)). The common sector of the

Figure 7. Configuration of block properties

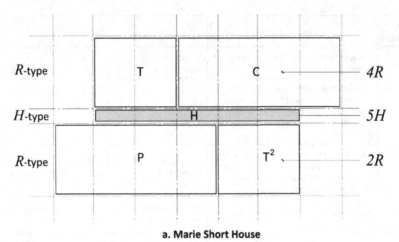

a. Marie Short House

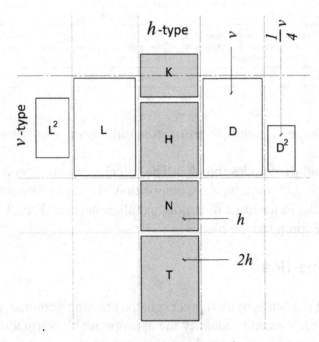

b. Little House (ground floor)

house consists of four room-type modules (*4R*), while the hall is composed of five hall-type modules (*5H*). In this way, the modular blocks are generated by the combination of two basic modules (room-type and hall-type modules). In contrast, there are two different types of modules, horizontal (*h*-type) and vertical (*v*-type), in Frank Lloyd Wright's Prairie architecture. Figure 7 (b) displays the ground floor of the Little House, with sector nodes transformed into modular blocks and each annotated in accordance with the grammar. For example, the transit block (T) is double the normal horizontal module and its size is therefore *2h*. The dining block is a single vertical module (*v*) while the second dining (D^2) is a quarter of this, still vertically arrayed. Once all of the nodes have been interpreted in this way, the massing grammar configures the wall type of each 3D block.

The grammar captures the overall shapes of the modular blocks by adding walls and specifying their properties. Thus, it is not only the shape of the plan that determines how their forms will look and be used, but also the degree to which the boundaries of each block are transparent, opaque or an intermediate mixture of these two. A block is typically regarded as a rectangular prism, having four faces for walls. The bottom face of the block is solid, like a slab-on-ground, while the top face can be open or solid, being eventually covered in a roof form. While the four wall faces may be different, those in Figure 8 are the same for each block because the architects used a consistent material and formal approach for each design. For example, in Murcutt's architecture the transit modules have no wall and are usually roofed and semi-enclosed. Thus, they act as intermediate zones between interior and exterior spaces. Common modules often have a transparent wall to the exterior, while private modules have a higher proportion of solid walls to the exterior. "Open" and "transparent" blocks are often adopted in Murcutt's architecture, which famously accommodates uninterrupted visual connections to the surrounding landscape. A transparent block tends to employ a curtain wall (glass wall) with internal and/or external louvres. The grammar could, in theory, identify Murcutt's sliding walls, which provide an adjustable building skin, but this example is only concerned with base wall types, not transient ones. The designation "solid" can include small windows, while "semi-transparent" occurs when over half of a wall is openable. For the Prairie houses, a transit module is also roofed and visually defined by columns at the edges, but it is open to the weather. For this reason, it is classed as "open". All of the rest of the spaces are enclosed and have small glazed openings, and their massing expression is therefore classified as "solid". Thus, four types of blocks: "open", "transparent", "semi-transparent" and "solid", are considered in the configuration of block properties, although their precise definition depends on the set of designs being analysed in a massing grammar. In this way, the massing grammar configures block properties, size and wall type. The generic rule for the second shape rule set (SR_2) is:

shape (x) → shape $(x, size.type)$, where x is a node.

A specific massing grammar can develop appropriate rule sets through this generic rule. For example, to configure the properties of the five blocks of Murcutt's *Marie Short House* in Figure 7 (a), a specific massing grammar uses five rules: shape (T) → shape (T, *2R.open*); shape (C) → shape (C, *4R.transparent*); shape (H) → shape (H, *5H.transparent*); shape (P) → shape (P, *4R.transparent*); and shape (T^2) → shape (T^2, *2R.open*). For the ground floor of Wright's *Little House*, the eight modular blocks of Figure 7 (b) are configured using eight rules: shape (H) → shape (H, *1h.solid*); shape (D) → shape (D, *1v.solid*); shape (L) → shape (L, *1v.solid*); shape (N) → shape (N, *1h.solid*); shape (K) → shape (K, *1h.solid*); shape (L^2) → shape (L^2, *1/4.solid*); shape (D^2) → shape (D^2, *1/4.solid*); and shape (T) → shape (T, *2h.open*).

Composition

The compositional process, as part of the massing grammar, describes the direction and alignment of each block relative to an adjacent one. The composition connects modular blocks into overall massing relationships. That is, the modular blocks are connected to generate the three-dimensional form of the design. The connection logic is derived from the JPG grammar, which defines the first set of links starting from a core node (block) to functionally adjacent nodes (blocks). In a similar way, the core block, as the first segment of the massing in the massing grammar, provides possible directions for the "growth" of the massing. Thus, the composition has a direct relationship to the JPG grammar. Although the detailed composition varies in ways that correspond to a variety of building designs or architectural styles, the generic rule of the composition is:

shape (x, size.type) → shape (x, size.type, y.direction.alignment),

where *x*, *y* are nodes, and *direction* is one of eight cardinal and sub-cardinal directions – east, west, north, south, northeast, northwest, southeast, southwest. The grammar also distinguishes five types of *alignment* relationships: equal, centre, left, right and interleaving. The interleaving alignment refers to the diagonal relationship between nodes. Like the linguistic structure of Space Syntax, the spatial relationship between two nodes is describe by a *locatum* (a

Figure 8. Shape composition

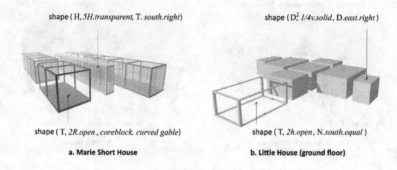

shape (H, *5H.transparent*, T. *south.right*)

shape (D²ᵢ *1/4v.solid*, D.*east.right*)

shape (T, *2R.open* , *coreblock, curved gable*)

shape (T, *2h.open*, N.*south.equal*)

a. Marie Short House

b. Little House (ground floor)

given entity, *x*) and a *relatum*, which is *y* here, and the particular descriptions (*direction* and *alignment*). In this way, the composition configures spatial relationships. Since the functional and formal modules topologically "touch" each other (they do not overlap and are not disjointed), the massing grammar only configures the direction and alignment. When overlapping two different wall types in the compositions, the face follows the thicker types from open to solid. For example, merging "transparent" with "solid" results in a "solid" wall. Figure 8 illustrates examples of the composition of 3D modular blocks. As observed in the *Marie Short House*, the transit block (T) is described as a core block in this configuration and the hall block (H) is located at the south of the transit block (T) and is right-aligned. These compositions are configured by two shape rules: shape (T, *2R.open*) → shape (T, *2R.open*, *coreblock*) and shape (H, *5H.transparent*) → shape (H, *5H.transparent*, T.*south.right*). For the *Little House*, the transit block is to the south of the primary hall block (N) and is equally aligned. The second dining-room block (D²) is located to the east of the dining block (D) and is aligned to the right. In addition, if there are two topological levels, L_n and L_{n-1}, the massing grammar also joins the two formal levels by a specific rule: shape (x_n, *size.type*, *coreblock*), shape (y_{n-1}, *size.type*, *coreblock*) → shape (x_n, *size.type*, *coreblock*), shape (y_{n-1}, *size.type*, x_n.*top.alignment*). In this case, two coreblocks work as a formal joint between two levels. These configurations are supported by the outcome of the JPG grammar because the composition deals with the links in the JPG grammar.

Figure 9. Configuration of roof types

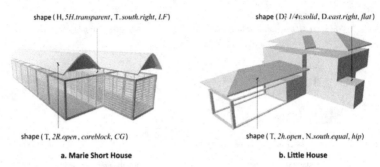

shape (H, *5H.transparent*, T.*south.right*, *LF*)

shape (D? *1/4v.solid*, D.*east.right*, *flat*)

shape (T, *2R.open* , *coreblock*, *CG*)

shape (T, *2h.open*, N.*south.equal*, *hip*)

a. Marie Short House

b. Little House

Roof Types

The final stage of the massing grammar caps the upper surface of the blocks with a roof. There are many possible roof shapes, including flat, shed, gable, hipped and butterfly roofs. Although the roof shapes depend on the actual design being analysed and its context, this final process uses some common three-dimensional roof forms corresponding to the defined blocks. They can be combined, expanded and transformed for different scenarios. The generic rule for the roof type configuration is:

shape (x, size.type, y.direction.alignment) → shape (x, size.type, y.direction. alignment, roof-type),

where *x*, *y* are nodes. This last configuration process determines roof types depending on a set of designs being described in the specific massing grammar. For example, the roof designs of Murcutt's domestic buildings can be categorised into six types: curved shed (CS), linear shed (LS), curved gable (CG), linear gable (LG), curved flat (CF) and linear flat (LF). In the case of the Prairie houses, there are only two types: hip and flat. Figure 9 shows the configurations of roof types. For the *Marie Short House*, curved-apex gable roofs are applied to the transit block, while the hall block is covered by a flat-type roof. For the *Little House*, the transit block uses a hipped roof and the other blocks at the ground floor have flat-type roofs. After this final configuration process, the massing grammar is completed with a termination rule, and the corresponding topological and geometrical properties of the design are complete.

CONCLUSION

The method presented in this chapter is ideally intended, like many other applications of syntactical and grammatical research, to be applied to the analysis of characteristic sets of buildings. Such sets might, for example, be the works of individual architects or vernacular building types from a particular region or era, but they must all have a clear rationale for being combined into a set (Ostwald & Vaughan, 2016). Once the set is identified, the aim of the method is to capture both the spatial and formal properties of a building. From this point it is possible to analyse the outcome and determine which designs in the set are most or least typical, or generate new designs which replicate characteristics of the set.

The conceptual framework for the method described herein consists of three components, node, link and shape, which allow for the spatial and syntactic relations implicit in a design to be defined, expressed algebraically and then used to develop mathematical measures. Significantly, the combined method conceptually privileges the functional or spatio-structural properties of the design by starting with the JPG grammar and thereafter derives corresponding forms using the massing grammar. The two *generic* grammars (the JPG grammar and the massing grammar) use algebraic expression to facilitate *specific* design grammars and explore the characteristics of a particular set of designs.

What is significant about the method is that it is the first time that both the spatial and formal properties of architecture have been simultaneously captured and then retained through the process of generating, or identifying, what is effectively a new design. For this reason, the applications of the method in the following chapters involve a close relationship between social patterns, functional spaces and their associated forms. The next chapter develops an s-JPG grammar and massing grammar for Glenn Murcutt's domestic architecture that demonstrates the analytical and generative capability of the method. In the final chapter of this book, the method is used to study Wright's Prairie architecture.

REFERENCES

Amorim, L. M. D. E. (1999). *The sectors' paradigm: A study of the spatial and functional nature of modernist housing in Northeast Brazil* (Doctoral thesis). University of London, London, UK.

Bafna, S. (1999). The morphology of early modernist residential plans: Geometry and genotypical trends in Mies van der Rohe's designs. In *Proceedings of the Second International Symposium on Space Syntax* (pp. 01.01-01.12). Brasília, Brazil: Academic Press.

Balmer, J., & Swisher, M. T. (2012). *Diagramming the big idea: Methods for architectural composition.* London, UK: Routledge. doi:10.4324/9780203103593

Chomsky, N. (1995). *The minimalist program.* Cambridge, MA: The MIT Press.

Corbett, G. G., Fraser, N. M., & McGlashan, S. (Eds.). (1993). *Heads in grammatical theory.* Cambridge, UK: Cambridge University Press. doi:10.1017/CBO9780511659454

Costa, E. C., & Duarte, J. P. (2015). Generic shape grammars for mass customization of ceramic tableware. In J. S. Gero & S. Hanna (Eds.), *Design computing and cognition "14* (pp. 437–454). London, UK: Springer International Publishing. doi:10.1007/978-3-319-14956-1_25

Eloy, S. (2012). *A transformation grammar-based methodology for housing rehabilitation* (PhD thesis). Universidade Técnica de Lisboa, Lisbon, Portugal.

Freudenstein, F., & Maki, E. R. (1979). The creation of mechanisms according to kinematic structure and function. *Environment & Planning B, 6*(4), 375–391. doi:10.1068/b060375

Grasl, T., & Economou, A. (2013). From topologies to shapes: Parametric shape grammars implemented by graphs. *Environment and Planning. B, Planning & Design, 40*(5), 905–922. doi:10.1068/b38156

Hanson, J. (1998). *Decoding homes and houses.* Cambridge, UK: Cambridge University Press.

Heitor, T., Duarte, J., & Pinto, R. (2004). Combing grammars and space syntax: Formulating, generating and evaluating designs. *International Journal of Architectural Computing, 2*(4), 492–515. doi:10.1260/1478077042906221

Hillier, B. (1999). *Space is the machine: A configurational theory of architecture*. Cambridge, UK: Cambridge University Press.

Hillier, B., & Hanson, J. (1984). *The social logic of space* (Vol. 1). Cambridge, UK: Cambridge University Press. doi:10.1017/CBO9780511597237

Hopcroft, J. E., Motwani, R., & Ullman, J. D. (2006). *Introduction to automata theory, languages, and computation* (3rd ed.). Boston, MA: Pearson Addison-Wesley.

Jones, J. C. (1992). *Design methods*. New York, NY: Van Nostrand Reinhold.

Koning, H., & Eizenberg, J. (1981). The language of the prairie: Frank Lloyd Wright's Prairie houses. *Environment & Planning B, 8*(3), 295–323. doi:10.1068/b080295

Lee, J. H., Ostwald, M. J., & Gu, N. (2015a). A syntactical and grammatical approach to architectural configuration, analysis and generation. *Architectural Science Review, 58*(3), 189–204. doi:10.1080/00038628.2015.1015948

Lee, J. H., Ostwald, M. J., & Gu, N. (2015b). Using a JPG grammar to explore the syntax of a style: An application to the architecture of Glenn Murcutt. In J. S. Gero & S. Hanna (Eds.), *Design computing and cognition "14* (pp. 589–604). Cham, Switzerland: Springer International Publishing. doi:10.1007/978-3-319-14956-1_33

Lee, J. H., Ostwald, M. J., & Gu, N. (2017). A combined plan graph and massing grammar approach to Frank Lloyd Wright's Prairie architecture. *Nexus Network Journal, 19*(2), 279–299. doi:10.100700004-017-0333-0

Lee, J. H., Ostwald, M. J., & Gu, N. (2018). A justified plan graph (JPG) grammar approach to identifying spatial design patterns in an architectural style. *Environment and Planning B. Urban Analytics and City Science, 45*(1), 67–89. doi:10.1177/0265813516665618

Li, X., & Schmidt, L. (2004). Grammar-based designer assistance tool for epicyclic gear trains. *Journal of Mechanical Design, 126*(5), 895–902. doi:10.1115/1.1767823

March, L. (2002). Architecture and mathematics since 1960. In K. Williams & J. F. Rodrigues (Eds.), Nexus IV: Architecture and mathematics (pp. 7-33). Fucecchio (Florence), Italy: Kim Williams Books.

Ostwald, M. J. (2011). A justified plan graph analysis of the early houses (1975-1982) of Glenn Murcutt. *Nexus Network Journal, 13*(3), 737–762. doi:10.100700004-011-0089-x

Ostwald, M. J., & Dawes, M. (2018). *The mathematics of the modern villa: An analysis using space syntax and isovists.* Basel, Switzerland: Birkhäuser.

Ostwald, M. J., & Vaughan, J. (2016). *The fractal dimension of architecture.* Basel, Switzerland: Birkhäuser. doi:10.1007/978-3-319-32426-5

Schmidt, L., & Cagan, J. (1997). GGREADA: A graph grammar-based machine design algorithm. *Research in Engineering Design, 9*(4), 195–213. doi:10.1007/BF01589682

Seonwook, K. (2012). *Architectural and program diagrams.* Berlin, Germany: DOM Publishers.

Stiny, G., & Gips, J. (1972). Shape grammars and the generative specification of painting and sculpture. In C. V. Freiman (Ed.), *Information processing 71* (pp. 1460–1465). Amsterdam, The Netherlands: North-Holland.

Chapter 7
The Language of Glenn Murcutt's Domestic Architecture

ABSTRACT

This chapter presents a JPG grammar and massing grammar for Glenn Murcutt's domestic architecture, demonstrating the analytical and generative capability of the combined grammatical and syntactical method. The chapter commences with a JPG-grammar-based analysis of 10 of Murcutt's rural domestic designs. Using this as a starting point, the chapter then describes the massing grammar that configures the form of each design, defining block properties, composition, and roof types. Throughout this process, the new method is used to develop the mathematical indicators of the properties of each house that are most similar or disparate. This information supports the generation of a "dominant design" as well as potential new variations that are consistent with the language of Murcutt's domestic architecture. Thus, the combined grammatical and syntactical method contributes to a deeper and more rigorous understanding of an architectural style and its design instances.

DOI: 10.4018/978-1-7998-1698-0.ch007

INTRODUCTION

This chapter demonstrates the use of two specific grammars – JPG and massing grammars – for analysing the combined grammatical and syntactical properties of Glenn Murcutt's rural domestic architecture. As discussed in Chapter 6, a "generic" JPG grammar consists of a set of algebraic rules that are customised to create a "specific" JPG grammar and associated formal massing for a family of designs or architectural language. Pritzker prize winning architect Glenn Murcutt's designs are the subject of the present chapter and the specific JPG grammar. Murcutt's designs have been described as possessing a distinct and highly consistent architectural language of space and form (Baker, 1996; Fromonot, 1995). His rural domestic buildings typically have a modernist, linear pavilion plan with extensive visual and physical connections to the landscape (Spence, 1986). Indeed, each of these houses could be regarded as a local variant of a more universal type (Ostwald, 2011b), and his early rural domestic architecture has been identified as an exemplar of Arcadian minimalism and described as a rigorous modern evocation of the form and tectonics of the "primitive hut" (Ostwald, 2011c).

The seemingly close relationship between form and spatial structure in Murcutt's architecture has been extensively documented in past research, although there is ongoing debate about the extent to which these works constitute either a largely static or an evolving architectural language. Indeed, such is their apparent consistency and rigour that multiple authors have used computational approaches to examine the properties of Murcutt's architecture. For example, Hanson and Radford (1986a, 1986b) analysed Murcutt's early houses using a variation of the Shape Grammar approach to attempt to understand their formal properties, while Ostwald (2011a, 2011b) used a syntactical technique to undertake visual, mathematical and theoretical analysis of Murcutt's architecture. Despite such examples, Murcutt's work has only rarely been the subject of any attempt to understand both its formal and spatial properties and the interplay between the two.

Our previous research (Lee, Ostwald, & Gu, 2015, 2018) investigates the results of a syntactically-derived grammatical analysis to characterise the combined spatial and formal properties of a set of potential design outcomes in the particular style of Glenn Murcutt's domestic architecture. This chapter presents a detailed exploration of the language of Murcutt's architecture through the combined method. Furthermore, because the method is innately grammatical, the chapter provides a generative sequence, or logic, for the language of Murcutt's architecture. The chapter commences by describing a specific JPG (s-JPG) grammar for Glenn Murcutt's domestic architecture and then applies this to a distinct stylistic set of his works. This set comprises ten houses that were constructed between 1975 and 2005 on isolated rural sites in Australia. The houses are: the *Marie Short House, Nicholas House, Carruthers House, Fredericks House, Ball-Eastaway House, Magney House, Simpson-Lee House, Fletcher-Page House, Southern Highlands House* and *Walsh House*. Collectively, these designs are regarded as comprising the canon of Murcutt's regional works. For each of the designs the chapter provides a brief background, including its date of construction, location and any special programmatic features. This is accompanied by a figure which has three parts. The first is a cutaway axonometric of the design and its planning, showing the way spaces and forms are related (or not related) in Murcutt's architecture. This is annotated with sector nodes and specific functional space labels. The second is a list of the s-JPG grammar rule set, which replicates the spatial structure of the design – i.e., rule sets, L_0R_1 (Level 0 Rule 1) to L_0R_8 (Level 0 Rule 8). The last is the corresponding grammar of the spatial structure, which represents the stages in the evolution of the plan graph. Thereafter the syntactical measures for the spatial structure are tabulated, presented and discussed and sector-based inequality genotypes are provided. The second half of the chapter demonstrates the use of a specific massing grammar to generate a corresponding three-dimensional (3D) form for each of the ten designs developed using the s-JPG grammar. These hybrid grammatical analyses provide a unique insight into the functional and formal design operations and outcomes that were available to the architect.

THE JPG GRAMMAR AND ITS APPLICATIONS

The S-JPG Grammar of Murcutt's Domestic Architecture

In this section, the JPG grammar for a distinct set of Murcutt's architectural works is developed from the g-JPG grammar. It commences by defining a complete set of sector nodes found in the ten cases by Murcutt, taking into account both spatial and formal modules. The section then summarises the complete set of rules required to generate the JPG grammar for Murcutt's works and the rule paths followed for each design. The following sections examine each case in detail, tracing all of the JPG grammars, syntactical measures and design features. First, however, the cases are examined collectively as a complete language.

Murcutt's rural domestic architecture has six types of sector nodes: common (C), private (P), hall (H), garage (G), transit (T) and exterior (E). The common node (C), typically consists of living rooms, dining rooms, foyers and kitchens. The private sector node (P) includes bedrooms and bathrooms. The hall sector node (H) includes corridors and linking spaces. The garage sector node (G) is for the storage of cars, but also typically includes workshops, laundries and service areas. In addition to these four "enclosed" or internal sectors (C, P, H, G), there are two types of "open" sectors: transit (T) and exterior (E). The transit sector node is an intermediate zone between interior and exterior, which in Murcutt's architecture is often a veranda. The exterior is simply the outside world, and it is most closely associated with ingress and egress relationships. Sectors that have a similar functional grouping but are disconnected from each other in the plan are numbered. Thus, a second bedroom and bathroom sector that is not physically connected to other bedrooms and bathrooms in a plan is treated as a second private node (P^2). Similarly, if a plan has a primary living room and music room (C) common sector, and a dining room and kitchen sector in a separate part of the plan, this is regarded as a second common node (C^2). In summary, for Murcutt's domestic architecture, including the second functional sector nodes, the node set, N, which is used to generate the ten cases, is represented by:

$$N = \{E, H, C, P, T, G, C^2, P^2, T^2\}.$$

Importantly each sector node can include multiple small spaces (alcoves and open storage and shelves) within its larger grouping. For example, a common node (C) could be made up of a grouping of entry foyer, living room, gallery and display nook. Not only is this a practical response to the grouping of similarly socially defined or delineated spaces in a floor plan, but it allows for comparisons to be made between houses that have different numbers of rooms but similar planning strategies. For example, Murcutt's *Southern Highlands House* has twenty-five spaces, whereas his *Carruthers House* has only seven. While, for instance, the specific way he accommodates five bedrooms in the plan of one house may appear completely different from the way he accommodates one bedroom in another, the general zoning strategy he adopts may be completely consistent. This is one of the advantages in taking a sector-based approach to spatial topology.

In addition, three of the ten cases examined this chapter – *Nicholas House, Carruthers House* and *Fredericks House* – have small mezzanine or loft levels that are accessible by ladders or steep stairs. In all three cases, these have been merged into the appropriate functional sector node they are connected to. In two cases this is the private sector, as these loft spaces serve as temporary bedrooms. As such, these spaces do not separately appear in the JPGs or any of the analysis.

The complete s-JPG grammar of Murcutt's rural domestic architecture is recorded in Table 1. That is, for each generic rule set, the specific rule variations required to generate the ten designs studied in this chapter are listed. The generic rules are transformed into specific rules for Murcutt's ten design as follows.

1. The first rule set (L_0R_1) of the s-JPG grammar transforms a start symbol (S_0) into a core node at the ground level (L_0). In the case of Murcutt's domestic architecture, the core node is the sector that includes the main entrance. There are three reasons for this. First, because it is commonly located in the middle of Murcutt's long, narrow building forms (being the formal core). Second, it is often the functional connection between two sectors (being the functional core). Third, Murcutt claims that his architecture seeks to mediate between external and internal environmental conditions (meaning the entry is the core transition point). Only three variations of this rule occur across the ten cases. Transforming a hall sector (H) into a core node, which is $S_0 \rightarrow H_{c0}$, dominates in the first rule set (50%). A transit sector (T) functions as the core node in three cases. A common sector (C) is regarded as the core node in two cases. In summary, L_0R_1 consists of three rules: $S_0 \rightarrow H_{c0}$, $S_0 \rightarrow T_{c0}$, and $S_0 \rightarrow C_{c0}$. The second rule set (L_0R_2) generates nodes and links adjacent to a core node. Applying the first and second rule sets can be regarded as defining a syntactic head in a graph, which is one of the topologically significant processes in the grammar application. There are three sets of rules that generate nodes and links from three core nodes, H_{c0}, T_{c0} and C_{c0}, respectively.

2. The second rule set (L_0R_2) of this s-JPG grammar tends to form a tree-like structure in the resultant JPG because it frequently generates two or more links. The two most frequently applied rules to develop JPGs for the ten houses are $H_{c0} \rightarrow H_{c0}$, C, ($H_{c0}$, C) and $H_{c0} \rightarrow H_{c0}$, P, ($H_{c0}$, P), five and four times, respectively. That is, a hall sector node as a circulation zone tends to link to both common and private sector nodes. This would

be a common pattern in domestic buildings, but the fact that many links are generated from the common and transit sectors at the second rule set illuminates a more distinctive pattern, which may begin to characterise Murcutt's domestic architectural design language.

3. The third rule set (L_0R_3) generates nodes and a second set of links starting from a node generated by the previous rule set to the adjacent nodes at the next depth, while L_0R_4 adds only links between non-core nodes at the same depth. L_0R_3 deals with seven sets of derivations, including 17 nodes and links.

4. The fourth rule set (L_0R_4) develops only four rule variations: H, C → (H, C); P, T^2 → (P, T^2); P, H → (P, H); and C^2, H → (C^2, H). In addition, both L_0R_3 and L_0R_4 require a skipping rule that goes to the next rule set. Two cases (the *Carruthers House* and the *Walsh House*) skip both rule sets, while a total of 21 links are generated in the other eight cases. Eleven links generated by L_0R_3 start from a common sector, because the common sector, like a hall sector, is generally used as a circulation zone. The hall and common sectors naturally link to the other nodes and often develop a chain or loop structure. It is interesting that these features are revealed sequentially through applying the s-JPG grammar. JPGs developed through L_0R_3 and L_0R_4 are ideal for investigating local relations between inhabitants. L_0R_5 adds nodes that are locally isolated but formally connected in the level.

5. The fifth rule set (L_0R_5) develops only three rules: P → P, P^2; P^2 → P^2, G and it is skipped in eight cases. The local configuration ends with the fifth rule set.

6. The sixth rule set (L_0R_6) adds the exterior node (E) and a link between a core node at the ground level and the exterior node by way of three rules: H_{c0} → H_{c0}, E, (H_{c0}, E); T_{c0} → T_{c0}, E, (T_{c0}, E); C_{c0} → C_{c0}, E, (C_{c0}, E).

7. The seventh rule set (L_0R_7) generates links between non-core nodes at the ground level and the exterior node. To generate these for the ten houses, L_0R_7 develops specific links from five nodes (G, P^2, C^2, C, H) to an exterior sector node. L_0R_7 is concerned with inserting a sub-entrance into a node or a garage sector node at the first depth. L_0R_7 develops 17 links altogether in eight cases by five rules: H, E → H, E, (H, E); C, E → C, E, (C, E); C^2, E → C^2, E, (C^2, E); G, E → G, E, (G, E); and P^2, E → P^2, E, (P^2, E). In the three most recent houses (*Fletcher-Page, Southern Highlands* and *Walsh* houses), L_0R_7 develops three links, producing {(C, E), (P^2, E), (G, E)} or {(C^2, E), (H, E), (G, E)}.

8. Finally, the eighth rule set $(L_0 R_8)$ terminates the production process.

When viewed collectively, these Murcutt-specific rule variations articulate the common grammatical and syntactical characteristics of his rural domestic works (Figure 1). Moreover, the rules can be visualised as a series of decision paths, commencing with the key decision about which of three sector nodes will become the core $(L_0 R_1)$, then moving to one of seven groups of decisions $(L_0 R_2)$ about interior connectedness, and finally exterior connections. For example, the JPG of the *Marie Short House* (named $g_{case1,}$ in the figure in accordance with standard graph grammar notation), is generated by the rules on the heavier weighted path in Figure 1. This figure also summarises the syntax derivations that are grammatically segmented and generated through the use of the s-JPG grammar. The nodes or links produced by each rule can include the previous results, which are a conditional part of each rule, but the figure only shows the derivations emerging from that rule to simplify it. The JPGs of cases that are produced in the specific rule sets are illustrated in the bottom of the figure, with some variations potentially generated by the s-JPG grammar.

The following sections present the results of the grammatical and syntactical analysis of the ten rural domestic designs by Murcutt. The rule variations developed for each house are the ones combined in Table 1 and Figure 1.

Marie Short House

The *Marie Short House* was constructed in 1975 and it is located on a raised floodplain near Kempsey, in New Sales Wales, Australia. This twin-pavilion house with a six-bay structural module is the first of Murcutt's famous rural houses. The first pavilion contains a veranda, which functions as an entry or transit node (T), and a common node (C), made up of a combined living-dining-kitchen space and several small utility rooms and cupboards. The second pavilion consists of a private node (P), containing two bedrooms, a toilet, a bathroom and walk-in-wardrobes (WIRs). An additional private veranda, coded here as a second transit zone (T^2), completes the second pavilion (Figure 2). A corridor (H) both divides and connects the two pavilions.

The grammatical analysis of the JPG (Figure 2) reveals that a "tree-like" structure, which evolves over the second and third rule sets $(L_0 R_2 - L_0 R_3)$, is then converted into two "ring-like" structures for the common and private pavilions at the fourth rule set $(L_0 R_4)$. The hall node provides a constant point of connection and passage in the building, while the transit node (T)

Table 1. Murcutt's specific JPG grammar (S: start symbol, C: common, P: private, H: hall, G: garage, T: transit, E: exterior node)

Rule set	Generic Description	Specific Rule Variations Required for Murcutt's Architecture
$L_0 R_1$	Transform a start symbol into a core node.	$S_0 \to H_{c0}$ $S_0 \to T_{c0}$ $S_0 \to C_{c0}$
$L_0 R_2$	Add node and link adjacent to a core node.	$H_{c0} \to H_{c0}, C, (H_{c0}, C); H_{c0} \to H_{c0}, P, (H_{c0}, P); H_{c0} \to H_{c0}, T^2, (H_{c0}, T^2)$ $T_{c0} \to T_{c0}, C, (T_{c0}, C); T_{c0} \to T_{c0}, C^2, (T_{c0}, C^2); T_{c0} \to T_{c0}, H, (T_{c0}, H)$ $C_{c0} \to C_{c0}, C^2, (C_{c0}, C^2); C_{c0} \to C_{c0}, H, (C_{c0}, H); C_{c0} \to C_{c0}, P (C_{c0}, P)$
$L_0 R_3$	Add node and link adjacent to a non-core node(s).	$H \to H, T^2, (H, T^2); H \to H, P, (H, P); H \to H, C^2 (H, C^2);$ $H \to H, G, (H, G); H \to H, P^2, (H, P^2)$ $C \to C, P, (C, P); C \to C, H, (C, H); C \to C, T, (C, T); C \to C, P^2, (C, P^2)$ $C^2 \to C^2, P^2, (C^2, P^2); C^2 \to C^2, P, (C^2, P)$ $P \to P, G, (P, G)$ Skipping and going to the next rule set
$L_0 R_4$	Add link between non-core nodes.	$H, C \to (H, C)$ $P, T^2 \to (P, T^2)$ $P, H \to (P, H)$ $C^2, H \to (C^2, H)$ Skipping and going to the next rule set
$L_0 R_5$	Add node without a link	$P \to P, P^2$ $P^2 \to P^2, G$ Skipping and going to the next rule set
$L_0 R_6$	Add the exterior node (E) and add link between a node at the ground level and E.	$H_{c0} \to H_{c0}, E, (H_{c0}, E)$ $T_{c0} \to T_{c0}, E, (T_{c0}, E)$ $C_{c0} \to C_{c0}, E, (C_{c0}, E)$
$L_0 R_7$	Add link between a node(s) at the ground level and E.	$H, E \to H, E, (H, E)$ $C, E \to C, E, (C, E)$ $C^2, E \to C^2, E, (C^2, E)$ $G, E \to G, E, (G, E)$ $P^2, E \to P^2, E, (P^2, E)$ Skipping and going to the next rule set
$L_0 R_8$	Terminate the process.	Terminaton

(i) Core configuration: $L_0 R_1$ to $L_0 R_2$, (ii) local configuration: $L_0 R_3$ to $L_0 R_5$, (iii) global configuration: $L_0 R_6$ to $L_0 R_8$.

acts as a bridge between the common node and the exterior. This spatial pattern is a direct reflection of the functional program of the house, with its separated zones for private activities and for common and service activities. Rules $L_0 R_6$ and $L_0 R_7$, which add two further links, develop Hillier's "d-type" structures globally, minimising the depths of the plan. As an aside, in 1980 Murcutt purchased this house and expanded it to a nine-bay scheme, where it has an additional connection between the second transit node (T^2) and the exterior. In that revised plan, additional "ring-like" structures create a highly integrated system.

Figure 1. The syntax tree generated by each rule set of the s-JPG grammar of Murcutt's ten houses

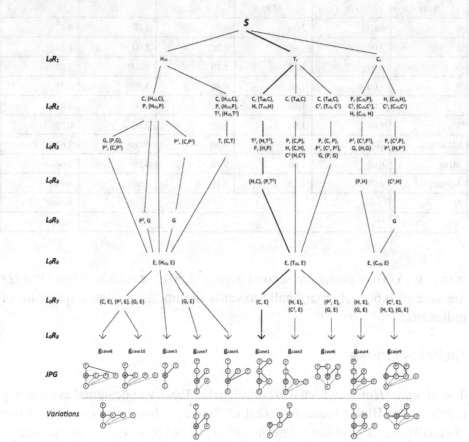

The sector node graph of the *Marie Short House* (Table 2) has a mean total depth (*TD*) of 8.00 and the mean depth (*MD*) of rooms in the house is 1.60. The most isolated nodes in the configuration are, in order, the exterior node (*MD* = 2.00), the private node (*MD* = 1.80) and the second transit node (*MD* = 1.80). Conversely, the more accessible nodes are the hall (*MD* = 1.20), the transit node (*MD* = 1.40) and the common node (*MD* = 1.40). The integration results for the graph indicate that the hallway (*i* = 10.00) is double the level of the next most integrated pair of nodes, the transit and the common node (both, *i* = 5.00). The remainder of the rooms, including the exterior, are all relatively isolated (ranging from 2.00 to 2.50). Finally, and not surprisingly, the hall exerts the highest spatial influence (*CV* = 1.67). The inequality genotype of the *Marie Short House* is: hall (10.00) > common

Table 2. Marie Short House, syntactical data

Node	TD_n	MD_n	RA	i	CV
E	10.00	2.00	0.50	2.00	0.67
T	7.00	1.40	0.20	5.00	1.08
H	6.00	1.20	0.10	10.00	1.67
P	9.00	1.80	0.40	2.50	0.75
C	7.00	1.40	0.20	5.00	1.08
T^2	9.00	1.80	0.40	2.50	0.75
Maximum	10.00	2.00	0.50	10.00	1.67
Mean	8.00	1.60	0.30	4.50	1.00
Minimum	6.00	1.20	0.10	2.00	0.75
H					0.9369
H*					0.6011

= transit (5.00) > private = second transit (2.50) > exterior (2.00). The $H*$ measure of 0.6011 is marginally towards the undifferentiated spectrum of indicators.

Nicholas House

The *Nicholas House*, which was completed in 1980, was designed as a country retreat in the Blue Mountains, west of Sydney. This house consists of two unequally sized pavilions. The larger north pavilion (with five structural modules) has a veranda, semi-open plan living and dining room and two ground floor bedrooms (Figure 3). A small third bedroom, which is rarely annotated on any plan of this house, is located in a loft space and accessed by a narrow ladder in the larger pavilion. In the present analysis it is merged into the private (P) sector node. The south pavilion (with three structural bays) includes a kitchen and bathroom. The north edge of the house is clad in timber boards and lined with glass louvres and cedar external blinds, while the south edge has a distinctive solid wall, clad in corrugated iron, and with a curved roof.

The planning structure of the *Nicholas House*, like the *Marie Short House* before it, is centred around a corridor that connects the two pavilions. The grammatical analysis of the JPG in Figure 3 reveals that a "tree-like" structure, which evolves from the fourth (L_0R_4) and sixth rule set (L_0R_6), is then developed into two "ring-like" structures for the two pavilions at the

Figure 2. Marie Short House, annotated axonometric view and JPG productions by the s-JPG grammar

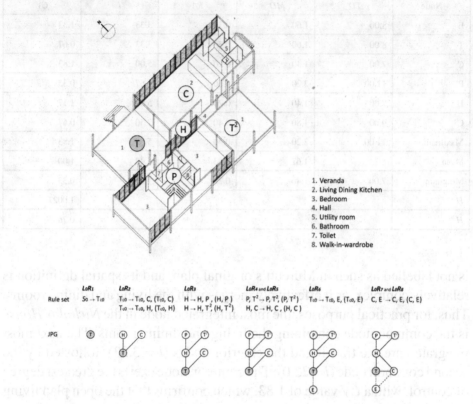

1. Veranda
2. Living Dining Kitchen
3. Bedroom
4. Hall
5. Utility room
6. Bathroom
7. Toilet
8. Walk-in-wardrobe

seventh rule set (L_0R_7) by H, E → H, E, (H, E) and C^2, E → C^2, E, (C^2, E). The four-level deep structure produced at the end of the sixth rule is then changed into three levels deep when the exterior carrier is added. That is, the process of connecting to the exterior creates a shallower structure for the JPG, with the private node (P) remaining as an "a-type" node, or dead-end space.

The mean total depth (*TD*) of the house is 8.33 and the mean depth (*MD*) of rooms in the house is 1.67 (Table 3), both of which are marginally higher than the equivalent *Marie Short House* results. The most isolated nodes in the configuration are, in order, the private node (*MD* = 2.20) and the second common node (*MD* = 1.80). This outcome arises from the "tree-like" structure, which is developed at the sixth rule set (L_0R_6) in Figure 3. Conversely, the more accessible nodes are the common and the hall (*MD* = 1.40). The integration values for the common and the hall nodes (both, *i* = 5.00) are triple the level of the private node (*i* = 1.67). However, the hall node

Table 3. Nicholas House, syntactical data

Node	TD_n	MD_n	RA	i	CV
E	8.00	1.60	0.30	3.33	1.33
T	8.00	1.60	0.30	3.33	0.67
C	7.00	1.40	0.20	5.00	1.83
P	11.00	2.20	0.60	1.67	0.33
H	7.00	1.40	0.20	5.00	1.17
C^2	9.00	1.80	0.40	2.50	0.67
Maximum	11.00	2.20	0.60	5.00	1.83
Mean	8.33	1.67	0.33	3.47	1.00
Minimum	7.00	1.40	0.20	1.67	0.33
H					1.0027
H*					0.7635

is not labelled as such in Murcutt's original plan, and its spatial definition is relatively complex, as it effectively merges with the living and dining rooms. Thus, for practical purposes, the most integrated node in the *Nicholas House* is the common node containing the living and dining rooms. The next most integrated are the transit and the exterior nodes ($i = 3.33$), followed by the second common node ($i = 2.50$). The common node exerts the greatest degree of control, with a *CV* value of 1.83, which confirms that the open plan living and dining room is the most important space in the structure of the house. The inequality genotype of the *Nicholas House* is: common = hall (5.00) > = transit = exterior (3.33) > second common (2.50) > private (1.67). The *H** measure of 0.7635 suggests a low level of determination or deliberation.

Carruthers House

Built in 1980, the *Carruthers House* is located on the site adjacent to the *Nicholas House*. This house is a single pavilion building (with a seven-bay modular schema), which is internally divided into two sections, the northern and southern parts. The former contains the main circulation space, with a sitting room open to the landscape, while the latter consists of two bedrooms, a bathroom and a kitchen (Figure 4). There is a small loft bedroom at the first floor level over the private (P) and the hall (H) nodes, while the living area has a large, double height space. A visual analysis of the JPG for the *Carruthers House* reveals a simple "tree-like" structure reflecting its simplified,

Figure 3. Nicholas House, annotated axonometric view and JPG productions by the s-JPG grammar

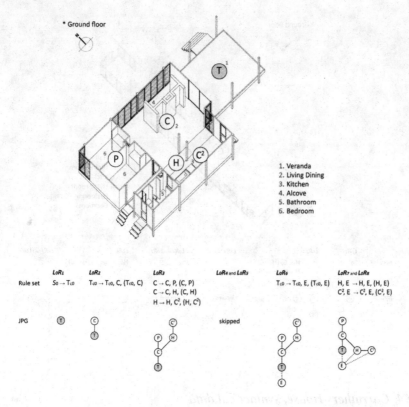

modular sectored nodes. The hall node (H) provides a connection between two main interior sector nodes (C and P) and links to the exterior (E). The JPG grammar for this design is relatively limited as, with the exception of the start (L_0R_1) and termination rules (L_0R_8), only three transformation rules, $H_{c0} \rightarrow H_{c0}, C, (H_{c0}, C); H_{c0} \rightarrow H_{c0}, P, (H_{c0}, P)$ and $H_{c0} \rightarrow H_{c0}, E, (H_{c0}, E)$, are applied at L_0R_2 and L_0R_6 to generate the final JPG (Figure 4).

The mathematical analysis (Table 4) of the syntactic data of the *Carruthers House* has several practical limitations because of the irrational result that occurs when $MD = 1.00$ in a plan. To accommodate this, the maximum integration value of the other cases is used for the hall of the *Carruthers House* as the best approximation ($i = 10.00$). This solution to the irrational number problem results in a highly differentiated graph, with $H^* = 0.0184$. That is, because the integration value of the hall node is much higher than the remainder, the graph appears more differentiated than it is in reality.

Figure 4. Carruthers House, annotated axonometric view and JPG productions by the s-JPG grammar

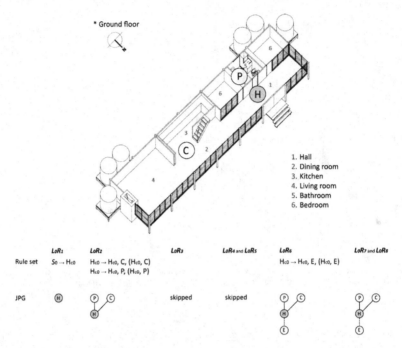

Table 4. Carruthers House, syntactical data

Node	TD_n	MD_n	RA	i	CV
E	5.00	1.67	0.67	1.50	0.33
H	3.01	1.00	0.00	10.00**	3.00
P	5.00	1.67	0.67	1.50	0.33
C	5.00	1.67	0.67	1.50	0.33
Maximum	5.00	1.67	0.67	10.00	3.00
Mean	4.50	1.50	0.50	3.63	1.00
Minimum	3.01	1.00	0.00	1.50	0.33
H					0.7006
H*					0.0184

(**denotes a value used to replace an irrational result that occurs when MD = 1.00 in a plan)

Fredericks House

The *Fredericks House* was constructed in 1982 in Jambaroo, New South Wales, Australia. This twin-pavilion building is reminiscent of the *Marie Short House* in its planning, but the two pavilions are unequally sized, as they are in the *Nicholas House* (Figure 5). The larger pavilion of the *Fredericks House* (which has a long, nine-bay structural module) has two private nodes, including a bathroom, a WIR and a storage area at its two ends, and two central common nodes. The southern (smaller) pavilion functions primarily as a garage node, although there is also a small room in its loft space. The hall node (a corridor), which is not separately annotated in Murcutt's original plan, connects the two pavilions, as it does in the previous two-pavilion designs.

The *Fredericks House* is not physically the largest of the ten cases reviewed in this chapter, but its sector node graph is among the most complex, with seven nodes (Table 5). The mean total depth (*TD*) of the house is 11.14 and the most integrated node is the common node ($i = 7.50$), followed by the hall ($i = 5.00$) and the exterior ($i = 3.75$). The least integrated nodes are the private ($i = 1.50$) and the garage ($i = 2.14$). These groupings by integration have clear similarities to those seen in Murcutt's previous works in this chapter. The control value results further conform to this dominant structural type, with the most significant nodes being the common and hall nodes ($CV = 1.58$). The inequality genotype of the *Fredericks House* is: common (7.50) > hall (5.00) > exterior (3.75) > second common = second private (3.00) > garage (2.14) > private (1.50). However, the H^* measure of 0.5749 shows the JPG is more balanced in its level of differentiation than the results for the previous houses.

The JPG grammar in Figure 5 shows that the first rule set transforms a start symbol into a core node, which is the common node including a main entrance, i.e., $S_0 \rightarrow C_{CO}$. Three rules are then applied as part of the second rule set; $C_{CO} \rightarrow C_{CO}, C^2, (C_{CO}, C^2)$; $C_{CO} \rightarrow C_{CO}, P (C_{CO}, P)$; $C_{CO} \rightarrow C_{CO}, H, (C_{CO}, H)$. L_0R_3 develops nodes and links adjacent to the second common and the hall nodes by $C^2 \rightarrow C^2, P^2, (C^2, P^2)$; $H \rightarrow H, G, (H, G)$. L_0R_4 adds a link between the private and the hall node through P, $H \rightarrow (P, H)$, which develops a "ring-like" structure. L_0R_5 is skipped and the sixth rule set (L_0R_6) connects the common node to the exterior by $C_{CO} \rightarrow C_{CO}, E, (C_{CO}, E)$. L_0R_7 develops two "ring-like" structures and the second private node generated at the third rule set (L_0R_3) remains the deepest space from the exterior.

Table 5. Fredericks House, syntactical data

Node	TD_n	MD_n	RA	i	CV
E	10.00	1.67	0.27	3.75	1.00
C	8.00	1.33	0.13	7.50	1.58
C^2	11.00	1.83	0.33	3.00	1.25
P	16.00	2.67	0.67	1.50	0.50
H	9.00	1.50	0.20	5.00	1.58
P^2	11.00	1.83	0.33	3.00	0.50
G	13.00	2.17	0.47	2.14	0.58
Maximum	16.00	2.67	0.67	7.50	1.58
Mean	11.14	1.86	0.34	3.70	1.00
Minimum	8.00	1.33	0.13	1.50	0.50
H					0.9263
H*					0.5749

Ball-Eastaway House

Constructed in 1982, the *Ball-Eastaway House*, which was designed as a house and small private gallery, is sited on top of a series of sandstone ledges near a wooded reserve in Glenorie, New South Wales. This single pavilion house has a linear plan with metal cladding and detailing that makes it visually reminiscent of a train carriage. When it was completed, it was one of Murcutt's most high profile and awarded works, but in more recent years it has tended to be omitted from monographs or treated as an outlier in his canon. Despite this, its planning and singular pavilion form appear very similar to his other works. Indeed, except for two transit nodes (verandas), the simple "tree-like" spatial structure of the *Ball-Eastaway House* is very similar to that of the *Carruthers House* (Figure 6). Considering the functional sectors in this design, the hall node (H) includes a hall, a bathroom and a laundry, while the common node (C) consists of a living, dining and kitchen area. The hall node provides an important point of connection and passage in the building and connects to the exterior. There is a single private (P) sector node with two bedrooms and a bathroom.

In the JPG grammar for this design, rule L_0R_2 confirms the generation of three sets of nodes and links adjacent to the core node (H). The "tree-like" structure, consisting of hall, common, private and second transit nodes, continues to the final production of the JPG at the sixth rule set (L_0R_6) without

Figure 5. Fredericks House, annotated axonometric view and JPG productions by the s-JPG grammar

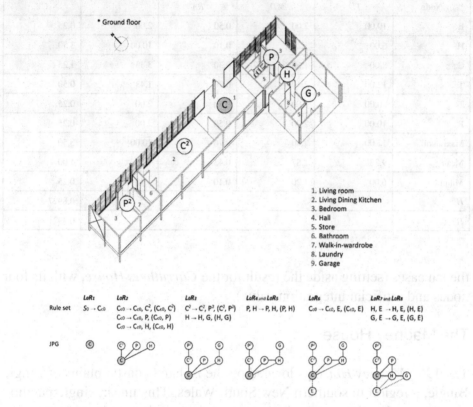

* Ground floor

1. Living room
2. Living Dining Kitchen
3. Bedroom
4. Hall
5. Store
6. Bathroom
7. Walk-in-wardrobe
8. Laundry
9. Garage

any "ring-like" structure. Similarly, the generative process of the JPG in Figure 6 skips L_0R_4 and L_0R_7, which normally develops a circulation loop. As a result, the transit node is the deepest space from the exterior.

The *Ball-Eastaway House* has a mean structural depth of 9.33, which is slightly deeper than that of the *Marie Short House* (8.00), both of which have the same set of nodes (Table 6). Just as the spatial graph for the exterior suggests, the hall is the most important room in the spatial configuration. It has an integration value of 10 and a control value of 3.50. This hall node is the most important in the everyday use of the house. The remainder of the nodes are controlled by the hallway/room structure. The least integrated node is the transit ($i = 1.43$), while the exterior, the second transit and the private node ($i = 2.00$) are also isolated in the graph. The inequality genotype of the *Ball-Eastaway House* is: hall (10.00) > common (3.33) > exterior = second transit = private (2.00) > private (1.43). The H* measure of 0.4921 for the JPG is marginally less than 0.5, confirming it is the most differentiated of

Table 6. Ball-Eastaway House, syntactical data

Node	TD_n	MD_n	RA	i	CV
E	10.00	2.00	0.50	2.00	0.25
H	6.00	1.20	0.10	10.00	3.50
C	8.00	1.60	0.30	3.33	1.25
T	12.00	2.40	0.70	1.43	0.50
T^2	10.00	2.00	0.50	2.00	0.25
P	10.00	2.00	0.50	2.00	0.25
Maximum	12.00	2.40	0.70	10.00	3.50
Mean	9.33	1.87	0.43	3.46	1.00
Minimum	6.00	1.20	0.10	1.43	0.25
H					0.8927
H^*					0.4921

the ten cases (setting aside the result for the *Carruthers House*, with its four nodes and artificial integration value).

The Magney House

The 1984 *Magney House* is located on the isolated coastal plains of Bingie Bingie, a region in southern New South Wales. This linear, single pavilion building is visually open to the north and the east, but enclosed to the west and south to protect the rear from harsh winter winds. A similar organisational strategy is found in many of Murcutt's rural domestic designs, which are often sited on dramatic, windswept sites. Interestingly, although the Magney House is a single long, narrow building (Figure 7), it has an undulating, partial butterfly roof form and an adjoining access corridor connecting the entire house. Thus, this house can be divided into three layers (a service zone along the solid south façade, a corridor, and a main functional zone which is more open). The horizontal formal modules of the *Magney House* are based on the six-bay structural schema. In the sector node analysis, a court, as an intermediate space between interior and exterior, is defined as a transit node as well as a core node. The left side of the courtyard includes a second common node and a second private node, while the right side consists of a common, a private (two bedrooms, a bathroom and a toilet) and a garage node. The grammatical analysis of the JPG in Figure 7 reveals that a long "tree-like" structure evolves up to the sixth rule set (L_0R_6), and then is transformed into

Figure 6. Ball-Eastaway House, annotated axonometric view and JPG productions by the s-JPG grammar

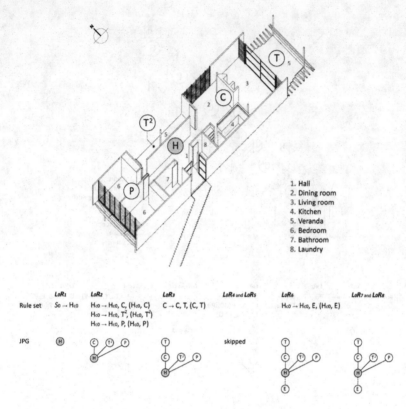

1. Hall
2. Dining room
3. Living room
4. Kitchen
5. Veranda
6. Bedroom
7. Bathroom
8. Laundry

two "ring-like" structures at the seventh rule set (L_0R_7) for two clustered spaces (the left and right spaces of the transit node). As a result, the five-level deep structure for the exterior carrier becomes three levels during the final configuration of the JPG.

With seven nodes (Table 7), the mean total depth (*TD*) of the JPG is 10.86. The most integrated nodes are the exterior and the transit nodes ($i = 5.00$). The least integrated nodes are the common and the two private nodes ($i = 2.50$). The control value results also suggest that the most significant nodes are the exterior and the transit ($CV = 1.33$). The inequality genotype of the *Magney House* is: exterior = transit (5.00) > second common = garage (3.00) > common = private = second private (2.50). The H^* result of 0.9077 signifies a plan with a very low level of determination or deliberation.

Figure 7. Magney House, annotated axonometric view and JPG productions by the s-JPG grammar

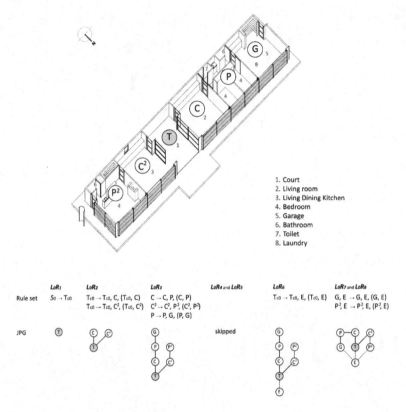

1. Court
2. Living room
3. Living Dining Kitchen
4. Bedroom
5. Garage
6. Bathroom
7. Toilet
8. Laundry

Simpson-Lee House

The 1994 *Simpson-Lee House* is located at Mount Wilson, overlooking an escarpment of the Blue Mountains, north-west of Sydney. The house, which consists of two separated pavilions, is a variation on Murcutt's linear planning typology (Figure 8) and it has mono-pitch roofs which lift up toward the views and to capture winter sunlight. The larger building (with a six-bay structural module) is located to the east and contains two bedrooms that are separated by a central living area. A long, narrow space connecting two hallways is reminiscent of the corridor/hall planning often found in Murcutt's domestic architecture. In addition, the hall node merges two hall spaces and the northern part of the living and dining rooms (see Figure 8), because the structural bay defines the spatial and formal modular nodes in this way. That is, the northern façade can be interpreted as a long hallway (corridor), which is clearly shown

Table 7. Magney House, syntactical data

Node	TD_n	MD_n	RA	i	CV
E	9.00	1.50	0.20	5.00	1.33
T	9.00	1.50	0.20	5.00	1.33
C	12.00	2.00	0.40	2.50	0.83
P	12.00	2.00	0.40	2.50	1.00
P^2	12.00	2.00	0.40	2.50	0.83
C^2	11.00	1.83	0.33	3.00	0.83
G	11.00	1.83	0.33	3.00	0.83
Maximum	12.00	2.00	0.40	5.00	1.33
Mean	10.86	1.81	0.32	3.36	1.00
Minimum	9.00	1.50	0.20	2.50	0.83
H					1.0612
H*					0.9077

in his two-pavilion houses. The smaller building at the western site combines the garage with a pottery studio. The simple, arborescent JPG structure is shown evolving across the eight rule sets in Figure 8, which leaves the two private (P, P^2) nodes and the garage (G) "a-type" spaces.

The total depth of the deepest nodes in the *Simpson-Lee House* is 13.00 (P^2 and G) while the relatively accessible nodes are the hall ($MD = 1.40$), the common ($MD = 1.80$) and the exterior nodes ($MD = 1.80$). Similarly, the hall node is the most integrated space ($i = 5.00$), while the second private and the garage nodes are the least integrated spaces ($i = 1.25$). Finally, and not surprisingly, the hall exerts the highest spatial influence ($CV = 2.00$). The H^* measure of 0.6888 suggests a relative looseness of the planning structure and a low level of determination or deliberation.

Fletcher-Page House

Constructed in 1998, the *Fletcher-Page House* is located on sloping grasslands in the hills of Kangaroo Valley, south of Sydney. This design is another narrow, linear building that can be interpreted as a nine-bay structural module scheme. The left side of the core node (H) includes a private node (P) consisting of a bedroom, a bathroom and a studio, and a garage node (G), with a garage and laundry. The right side consists of a common (C) and a second private node (P^2), made up of a bedroom, a bathroom and a

Table 8. Simpson-Lee House, syntactical data

Node	TD_n	MD_n	RA	i	CV
E	9.00	1.80	0.40	2.50	1.33
H	7.00	1.40	0.20	5.00	2.00
C	9.00	1.80	0.40	2.50	1.33
P	11.00	2.20	0.60	1.67	0.33
P^2	13.00	2.60	0.80	1.25	0.50
G	13.00	2.60	0.80	1.25	0.50
Maximum	13.00	2.60	0.80	5.00	2.00
Mean	10.33	2.07	0.53	2.36	1.00
Minimum	7.00	1.40	0.20	1.25	0.33
H					0.9724
H*					0.6888

WIR. The hall node connects both sides. While there are many similarities between this design and Murcutt's typical corridor planning strategy, there are also some departures. In particular, a series of connecting doors along the southern length of the house potentially enclose each room with its own air-lock corridor. The grammatical analysis of the JPG in Figure 9 reveals that the long "tree-like" structure, which has developed over the first five rules, transforms at the sixth rule set (L_0R_6) into Hillier's "d-type" structures, and at the seventh rule set (L_0R_7) three links to the exterior are generated. As a result, the four-level arborescent structure for the exterior carrier transforms into a shallow structural plan, wherein every space is topologically close to the transition between interior and exterior.

The syntactical data in Table 9 confirms that the exterior, with four exterior connections (including the garage door), is the most important node in the JPG. This is also the case in five of the ten cases examined. The most integrated space is the exterior $(i = 10)$, followed by the other four nodes $(i = 5.00)$. This result reflects the close connection between the functional areas and the landscape. The lowest integration result is for the garage $(i = 3.33)$, although bathroom 2 and the study are also quite low (respectively, $i = 2.25$ and $i = 2.40$). The control value result also confirms the most significant node is the exterior $(CV = 1.67)$. The H* result of 0.7849 is suggestive of a lack of configurational determination.

Figure 8. Simpson-Lee House, annotated axonometric view and JPG productions by the s-JPG grammar

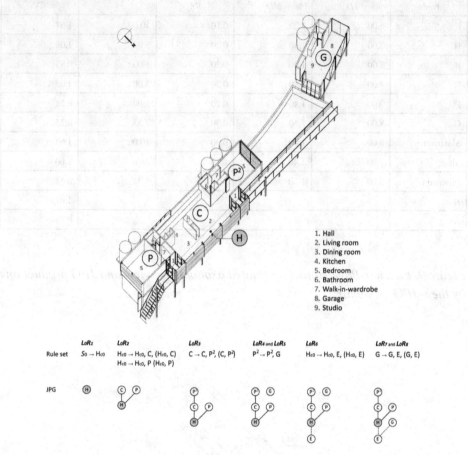

1. Hall
2. Living room
3. Dining room
4. Kitchen
5. Bedroom
6. Bathroom
7. Walk-in-wardrobe
8. Garage
9. Studio

	LoR₁	LoR₂	LoR₃	LoR₄ and LoR₅	LoR₆	LoR₇ and LoR₈
Rule set	So → Hco	Hco → Hco, C, (Hco, C) Hco → Hco, P (Hco, P)	C → C, P², (C, P²)	P² → P², G	Hco → Hco, E, (Hco, E)	G → G, E, (G, E)

Southern Highlands House

The *Southern Highlands House*, which was built in 2001, is sited on agricultural land in Kangaloon, New South Wales. The entire length of the southern façade takes the form of a curved metal plane to protect against severe winds. This house is one of the largest of Murcutt's residential buildings, with a complex program for 24 habitable spaces, including ten exterior doors (Figure 10). The western side of the core node (C) is a children's area, including a family room and two bedrooms with two bathrooms. The main functions of the eastern area are a living room, dining-kitchen, a music room, a parent bedroom (P²), and a garage. Like the *Fredericks House*, the common node includes a lobby space located between the two areas, but an additional long hallway at the south of

Table 9. Fletcher-Page House, syntactical data

Node	TD_n	MD_n	RA	i	CV
E	6.00	1.20	0.10	10.00	1.67
H	7.00	1.40	0.20	5.00	1.08
P	7.00	1.40	0.20	5.00	0.83
C	7.00	1.40	0.20	5.00	1.08
P^2	7.00	1.40	0.20	5.00	0.58
G	8.00	1.60	0.30	3.33	0.75
Maximum	8.00	1.60	0.30	10.00	1.67
Mean	7.00	1.40	0.20	5.56	1.00
Minimum	6.00	1.20	0.10	3.33	0.58
H					1.0114
H*					0.7849

Figure 9. Fletcher-Page House, annotated axonometric view and JPG productions by the s-JPG grammar

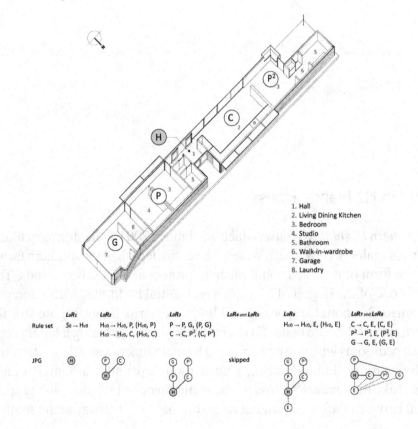

1. Hall
2. Living Dining Kitchen
3. Bedroom
4. Studio
5. Bathroom
6. Walk-in-wardrobe
7. Garage
8. Laundry

the plan connects a series of rooms in the eastern area. Thus, the circulation system in this house can be interpreted as comprising two dominant strategies: one is a long corridor (hallway) providing a constant point of connection and passage (typical of the two-pavilion houses), the other uses the central core node connecting two separated areas. In other words, despite its linear plan, many rooms are connected by the single-loaded corridor.

Figure 10 shows how the sector planning graph is generated by applying all the rule sets of the s-JPG grammar. The first rule set transforms a start symbol into a core node, which is the common node, including a lobby space, using "$S_0 \rightarrow C_{c0}$". The second rule set (L_0R_2) adds nodes and links adjacent to the core node. Generating the JPG of the *Southern Highlands House* employs two rules, $C_{C0} \rightarrow C_{C0}$, C^2, (C_{C0}, C^2) and $C_{C0} \rightarrow C_{C0}$, H, ($C_{C0}$, H). L_0R_3 develops nodes and links adjacent to the second common and the hall nodes by $C \rightarrow C, P^2, (C, P^2)$ and $H \rightarrow H, P^2, (H, P^2)$. L_0R_4 adds a link between the second common and the hall through $C^2, H \rightarrow (C^2, H)$, which develops a "ring-like" structure. L_0R_5 adds the garage node by $P^2 \rightarrow P^2$, G. The sixth rule set (L_0R_6) connects the core node to the exterior by $C_{C0} \rightarrow C_{C0}$, E, ($C_{C0}$, E), while the seventh rule set (L_0R_7) linking three nodes to the exterior, transforms the graph into a shallower system. Finally, the generating process is terminated by L_0R_8.

The *Southern Highlands House* (Table 10) sector plan graph has a mean total depth (*TD*) of 10.29 and the mean depth (*MD*) of rooms in the house is 1.71. The most accessible nodes are the exterior, the hall, and the second common node (*MD* = 1.33), followed by the core node (*MD* = 1.50). The integration values confirm this, showing the most accessible nodes are the most integrated spaces (i = 7.50). They also exert the highest spatial influence (*CV* = 1.83). In contrast, the private nodes and the garage are the least integrated spaces (i = 2.14). The *H** measure of 0.7263 is again towards the undifferentiated spectrum of indicators, confirming a similar looseness in the planning.

Walsh House

The 2005 *Walsh House,* which is located on a gently sloping site in the Kangaroo Valley, has been designed with minimal window openings and it is constructed from rustic materials. This mono-pitch roof building addresses prominent views, and its extended roofline protects the high northern windows from the harsh summer sun. Like Murcutt's other long, narrow houses, the *Magney House* and the *Fletcher-Page House*, the core node in the *Walsh*

Table 10. Southern Highlands House, syntactical data

Node	TD_n	MD_n	RA	i	CV
E	8.00	1.33	0.13	7.50	1.83
C	9.00	1.50	0.20	5.00	0.75
C^2	8.00	1.33	0.13	7.50	1.83
P	13.00	2.17	0.47	2.14	0.25
H	8.00	1.33	0.13	7.50	1.83
P^2	13.00	2.17	0.47	2.14	0.25
G	13.00	2.17	0.47	2.14	0.25
Maximum	13.00	2.17	0.47	7.50	1.83
Mean	10.29	1.71	0.29	4.85	1.00
Minimum	8.00	1.33	0.13	2.14	0.25
H					0.9876
H*					0.7263

House connects the left side and the right side of the building (Figure 11), but the second private node and the garage are only accessible from the exterior. Thus, the isolated nodes belong to a separate pavilion, like the structure of the *Simpson-Lee House*, although they are contained in the same volume of linear architecture.

The first rule set (Figure 11) transforms a start symbol into a core node, which is the hall node, through $S_0 \rightarrow H_{c0}$. Two nodes (the private and the common) and the corresponding two links with the hall node are then added by two rules at the second rule set (L_0R_2), $H_{c0} \rightarrow H_{c0}$, P, (H_{c0}, P) and $H_{c0} \rightarrow H_{c0}$, C, (H_{c0}, C). L_0R_3 and L_0R_4 are skipped, and L_0R_5 adds the second private sector node and the garage node by $P \rightarrow P$, P^2 and $P^2 \rightarrow P^2$, G. The sixth rule set (L_0R_6) connects the core node to the exterior by $H_{C0} \rightarrow H_{C0}$, E, (H_{C0}, E). Three nodes are connected to the exterior by the seventh rule set (L_0R_7): C, E $\rightarrow$ C, E, (C, E); P^2, E $\rightarrow$ P^2, E, (P^2, E); and G, E $\rightarrow$ G, E, (G, E). As a result, the most integrated space is the exterior ($i = 10.00$), which also has the highest spatial influence ($CV = 2.83$) in the syntactical data of the JPG (Table 11). The next most integrated is the hall ($i = 5.00$), followed by the common node ($i = 3.33$). The inequality genotype of the *Walsh House* is: exterior (10.00) > hall (5.00) > common (3.33) > second private = garage (2.00) > private (1.67). The genotype shows a dominant hierarchical structure of the last five cases out of the ten cases reviewed in this chapter. The $H*$ measure of 0.5413 is in the middle range.

Figure 10. Southern Highlands House, annotated axonometric view and JPG productions by the s-JPG grammar

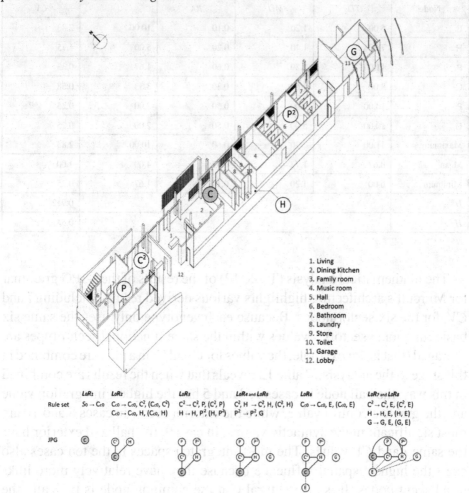

1. Living
2. Dining Kitchen
3. Family room
4. Music room
5. Hall
6. Bedroom
7. Bathroom
8. Laundry
9. Store
10. Toilet
11. Garage
12. Lobby

COMPARATIVE ANALYSIS

The floor plan of a building could be regarded as a reflection of the needs or values of the building's users. As such, the comparative analysis of a set of floor plans allows for the development of a spatio-functional typology of design solutions (van der Voordt, Vrielink, & van Wegen, 1997). The JPGs created by applying the s-JPG grammar can thus be compared using both mathematical and graphical approaches to develop a deeper understanding of the results.

Table 11. Walsh House, syntactical data

Node	TD_n	MD_n	RA	i	CV
E	6.00	1.20	0.10	10.00	2.83
H	7.00	1.40	0.20	5.00	1.75
P	11.00	2.20	0.60	1.67	0.33
C	8.00	1.60	0.30	3.33	0.58
P^2	10.00	2.00	0.50	2.00	0.25
G	10.00	2.00	0.50	2.00	0.25
Maximum	11.00	2.20	0.60	10.00	2.83
Mean	8.67	1.73	0.37	4.00	1.00
Minimum	6.00	1.20	0.10	1.67	0.25
H					0.9126
H*					0.5413

The mathematical analysis (Table 12) of the results of the s-JPG grammar for Murcutt's architecture highlights various derived results, including i and CV, for the six sector nodes. Because each genotype only uses the same six basic functional sectors, i values within the same functional sector types are averaged (that is, for example, the values for C and C^2 in a plan are combined in this stage of the analysis). Table 12 reveals that when the results are combined in this way, the hall node in cases 1, 3 and 5 has the highest integration value and the greatest control value, while the exterior sector in cases 8 and 10 are most significant in the syntactic values. In case 9, the hall and exterior have the same i and CV values. The most integrated spaces in the ten cases also exert the highest spatial influence because they have relatively more links to adjacent nodes. It is also natural that the common node is typically the second most integrated space.

The grammatical analysis in the previous sections confirms that syntactic patterns could arise from the most frequently generated links, in particular from L_0R_2 and L_0R_7. For example, adding multiple nodes and links from each core node in L_0R_2 develops the most integrated spaces in four cases (3, 4, 5, 6). Cases 4 and 5 apply L_0R_2 three times to generate three different links connecting the core node. The generated JPGs therefore have a "tree-like" structure, which results in the most integrated node ($i = 7.50$ and 10.00, respectively) and the greatest degree of control (CV $= 1.67$ and 3.50, respectively) among other nodes. In the last three cases (8, 9, 10), by applying L_0R_7 three times the exterior sector becomes the most integrated space. That is, the repetitive

Figure 11. Walsh House, annotated axonometric view and JPG productions by the s-JPG grammar

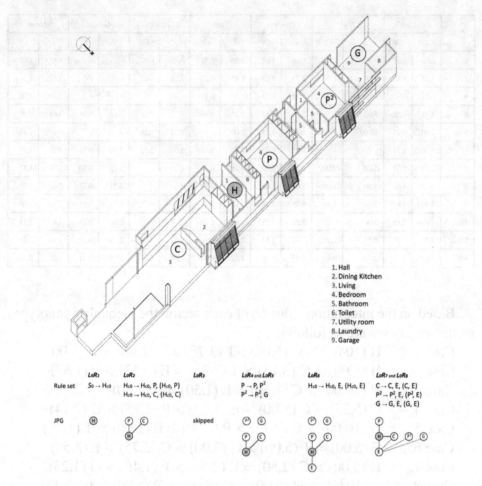

1. Hall
2. Dining Kitchen
3. Living
4. Bedroom
5. Bathroom
6. Toilet
7. Utility room
8. Laundry
9. Garage

application of rules two or seven (L_0R_2 or L_0R_7) plays an important role in the formation of the syntactic patterns. The nodes of the seventh case, the *Simpson-Lee House*, are comparatively less integrated (average i value = 2.54) while the eighth case, the *Fletcher-Page House*, has the highest average i value (5.67).

Ten cases: 1. *Marie Short House*, 2. *Nicholas House*, 3. *Carruthers House*, 4. *Fredericks House*, 5. *Ball-Eastaway House*, 6. *Magney House*, 7. *Simpson-Lee House*, 8. *Fletcher-Page House*, 9. *Southern Highlands House*, 10. *Walsh House*.

Table 12. Summary of syntactic analysis results (*denotes a value used to replace an irrational result that occurs when MD = 1.00 in a plan)

Case	Exterior		Hall		Common		Private		Transit		Garage		Mean	
	i	*CV*	*i*	*CV*	*i*	*CV*	*i*	*CV*	*i*	*CV*	*i*	*CV*	*i*	*CV*
1	2.00	0.67	10.00	1.67	5.00	1.08	2.50	0.75	3.75	0.92	-	-	4.65	1.02
2	3.33	1.33	5.00	1.17	3.75	1.25	1.67	0.33	3.33	1.67	-	-	3.42	1.15
3	1.50	0.33	10.00*	3.00	1.50	0.33	1.50	0.33	-	-	-	-	1.50	1.00
4	3.75	1.00	5.00	1.58	5.25	1.42	2.25	0.50	-	-	2.14	0.58	3.68	1.02
5	2.00	0.25	10.00	3.50	3.33	1.25	2.00	0.25	1.71	0.38	-	-	3.81	1.13
6	5.00	1.33	-	-	2.75	0.83	2.50	0.92	5.00	1.33	3.00	0.83	3.65	1.05
7	2.50	1.33	5.00	2.00	2.50	1.33	1.46	0.42	-	-	1.25	0.50	2.54	1.12
8	10.00	1.67	5.00	1.08	5.00	1.08	5.00	0.71	-	-	3.33	0.75	5.67	1.06
9	7.50	1.83	7.50	1.83	6.25	1.29	2.14	0.25	-	-	2.14	0.25	5.11	1.09
10	10.00	2.83	5.00	1.75	3.33	0.58	1.83	0.29	-	-	2.00	0.25	4.43	1.14
Mean	4.76	1.26	6.56	1.95	3.87	1.04	2.29	0.48	3.45	1.08	2.31	0.53	3.84	1.08
SD	3.27	0.77	2.29	0.80	1.47	0.36	1.02	0.24	1.36	0.56	0.75	0.24	1.22	0.06

Based on the integration value (*i*) of each sector, the inequality genotypes of the ten houses are as follows:

Case 1:   H (10.00) > C (5.00) >T (3.75) > P (2.50) > E (2.00)

Case 2:   H (5.00) > C (3.75) > T (3.33) = E (3.33) > P (1.67)

Case 3:   H (10.00) > C (1.50) = E (1.50) = P (1.50)

Case 4:   C (5.25) > C (5.00) > E (3.75) > P (2.25) > G (2.14)

Case 5:   H (10.00) > C (3.33) > P (2.00) = E (2.00) > T (1.71)

Case 6:   E (5.00) = T (5.00) > G (3.00) > C (2.75) > P (2.50)

Case 7:   H (5.00) > C (2.50) = E (2.50) > P (1.46) > G (1.25)

Case 8:   E (10.00) > H (5.00) = C (5.00) = P (5.00) > G (3.33)

Case 9:   H (7.50) = E (7.50) > C (6.25) > G (2.14) = P (2.14)

Case 10:   E (10.00) > H (5.00) > C (3.33) > G (2.00) > P (1.83)

The integration value of each node is sequenced broadly in line with the concept of "intimacy gradients" (Alexander et al., 1997; Ostwald 2011b), starting with the most public and ending with the most private. In seven cases (1, 2, 3, 4, 5, 7, 9) the hall node dominates the genotype as the most integrated space, while the private node of five cases (2, 3, 6, 9, 10) is the least integrated space. Another pattern revealed from the data is that most nodes in the more recent houses (1984-2005) tend to connect directly to the exterior. This is a by-product of the long, narrow forms often found in Murcutt's architecture, and one of the notable findings of this chapter. Figure 12 uses radar charts to represent the inequality genotypes of the ten houses. The charts illustrate similarities and disparities between the syntactical structures of the ten plans. For example, the inequality genotype of the first case, the *Marie Short House*, is hierarchically similar to that of the fifth case, the *Ball-Eastaway House*. Although the first case consists of two pavilions and the fifth case forms one pavilion, the topological configuration of both is similar to a genotype (H > C > P, T, E). In addition, it is evident that the eighth case (*Fletcher-Page House*) and the tenth case (*Walsh house*) have a similar topological configuration (E > H, C > G, P). Conversely, the ninth case, with its four exterior connections, two of which are directly through common areas and two of which loop through common and hallway zones, represents a clear doubling of this design strategy in the same house; something which would be rare in a more conventional design.

There are several notable differences between the fifth and sixth cases, the *Ball-Eastaway House* and the *Magney House*. The exterior and transit nodes dominate the sixth genotype as the most integrated space and the common node has a relatively low i value compared to the other cases. The sixth case is also an interesting genotype that shows the least range of fluctuation between the maximum and minimum i values. In the sixth case, the grammar configures a transit node that functions as a core node and it directly links to common sectors. Links with T, C, C^2 and P are generated, rather than those with H that are dominant in the fifth case. The application of L_0R_7 results in three links to the exterior in the eighth case, while it is not used in the third and fifth cases. Thus, two different applications of rules produce the two dissimilar JPGs (tree-type and two-ring-type) and their genotypes.

The analysis of the four topological types of spaces (Hillier, 1999) is shown in Table 13. The distributions of the overall sector nodes of the ten houses in relation to Hillier's categorisation of basic types are as follows: a-type 29.5%, b-type 11.5%, c-type 31.1% and d-type 27.9%. Therefore, the ring-type (including c- and d-type) nodes are the dominant ones in these selected houses. In three cases (1, 6 and 8) only ring-type nodes are identified. Except for two tree-like complexes (cases 3 and 5), the exterior, hall and common nodes are typically arranged as a ring type (c-, d-type), which also collectively have higher i and CV results than other sectors (such as the private sector). The exterior nodes tend to be d-type (50.0%) and there is one instance of a b-type (10.0%). The hall nodes are mostly d-type (55.6%), while c- and d-types are dominant in the common nodes. In contrast, the distributions of the private nodes are: a-type 62.5% and c-type 37.5%. Thus, the pattern wherein a hall

Figure 12. Charts representing the inequality genotypes of Murcutt's houses

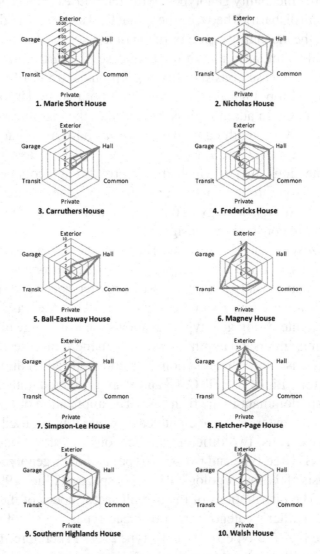

and a common node link to the exterior, as a core node, provides a starting point for the generation of the house plans, while it ends with a private node.

While applying L_0R_2 often produces a pair of links that transform the core node into a b-type (tree-type) node, the use of L_0R_3 develops a node at a much deeper level, up to the third depth in the graph (see cases 2 and 6). This process leads to the identification of another feature of Murcutt's domestic designs: they rely on the use of long corridors or passages in parallel to generate circulation loops. The particular application of L_0R_7 is divided

Table 13. Four topological types of spaces

Case	Exterior	Hall	Common	Private	Transit	Garage
1	c-type	d-type	d-type	c-type	c-type, d-type	-
2	d-type	d-type	c-type, c-type	a-type	c-type	-
3	a-type	b-type	a-type	a-type	-	-
4	d-type	d-type	b-type, d-type	a-type, c-type	-	c-type
5	a-type	b-type	b-type	a-type	a-type, a-type	-
6	d-type	-	c-type, c-type	c-type, c-type	d-type	c-type
7	b-type	b-type	b-type	a-type, a-type	-	a-type
8	d-type	d-type	d-type	c-type, c-type	-	c-type
9	d-type	d-type	d-type, d-type	a-type, a-type	-	a-type
10	c-type	c-type	c-type	a-type, a-type	-	a-type
Summary	d-type (50.0%) c-type (20.0%) b-type (10.0%) a-type (20.0%)	d-type (55.6%) b-type (33.3%) c-type (11.1%)	c-type (35.7%) d-type (35.7%) b-type (21.4%) a-type (7.1%)	a-type (62.5%) c-type (37.5%)	a-type (33.3%) c-type (33.3%) d-type (33.3%)	c-type (50.0%) a-type (50.0%)

Ten cases: 1. *Marie Short House*, 2. *Nicholas House*, 3. *Carruthers House*, 4. *Fredericks House*, 5. *Ball-Eastaway House*, 6. *Magney House*, 7. *Simpson-Lee House*, 8. *Fletcher-Page House*, 9. *Southern Highlands House*, 10. *Walsh House*.

between (C or C^2, E), five times, and (G, E), five times. This is reasonable in domestic planning, because a common sector and a garage often link to the exterior. However, applying $L_0 R_6$ and $L_0 R_7$ of the s-JPG grammar significantly changes the syntactic feature of each JPG. Most b-type (tree-type) nodes are transformed into the ring-type (c-, d-type) nodes after the global connection.

This detailed analysis of Murcutt's architecture using the s-JPG grammar is initially founded on a clearly delineated space of movement (associated with the hall node), which in turn provides a means of accessing a set of common or public spaces. This is not only a dominant pattern, but the significance of these sector pairings is also reinforced by turning this simple structure into a ring or loop by, for example, connecting H to C, before finally linking to E. While this loop may evolve in the penultimate stage of the design process to include tree-like or secondary ring-like planning structures (often founded on H and which encompass private zones), the significance of the original ring-type is preserved by the number of exterior connections through $L_0 R_7$. It is the combination of these factors, not any one of them in isolation, that is central to the sector-adjacency decision-making process in Murcutt's architecture. Based on this model, Murcutt's architecture is characterised by

Figure 13. JPGs at three grammatical stages, head, local and global syntax

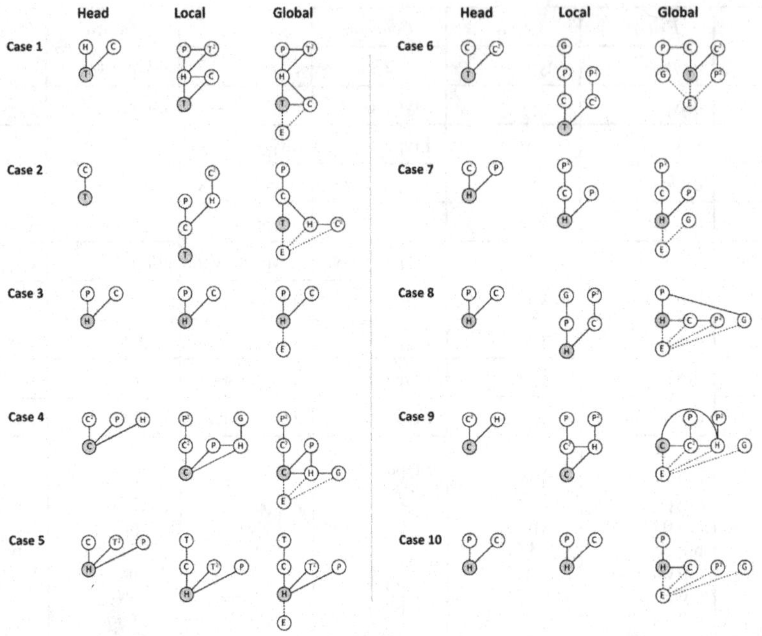

a clear programmatic and functional pattern of relationships between just three key parts of the plan, and a similarly strong relationship between these and the exterior.

Grammatical Generation

Shape Grammars typically have two significant applications. First, they can be used to simulate a version of the design process (Economou, 2000) and, second, the application of rules in a Shape Grammar provides a means to dissect and analyse a design (Knight, 2003). The s-JPG grammar presented in this chapter has a similar dual prupose. In particular, it highlights three design stages that develop three syntactic patterns: the head of a graph, local syntax and global syntax. Figure 13 depicts JPGs generated at the three grammatical stages to address these syntactic patterns.

Although the generative process illustrated in Figure 13 may not reveal the actual process used by the architect, it does provide an effective approach for revealing and exploring the formal possibilities that may have contributed to, or could contribute to, the architect-specific language of design. It is also possible to hypothesise from the data that each core node acts as the head of a graph and thereby determine the syntactic type of the graph. For example, L_0R_2 initiates the tree structures of the syntax by generating more than two links in eight cases. The s-JPG grammar identifies a sector that includes the main entrance as a core node, but a hall sector may be regarded as a core node because in many cases the hall sector dominates the genotype as the most integrated space (also see the discussion in Chapter 8). In spite of that, many core nodes are at the centre of the tree structures of the local syntax of the JPGs (Figure 13) and they also have the highest integration value among the local nodes (cases 3, 4, 5, 6, 7, 8, 10). However, the links to an exterior sector node (E) by L_0R_6 and L_0R_7 of the s-JPG grammar change the syntactic features of each JPG into the ring-type structures. Thus, the final inhabitant-visitor relations (the global topology) of Murcutt's domestic designs evolve from the local relations shown in the local configuration stage of the s-JPG grammar. The local relations are isolated through L_0R_2 and L_0R_3 in the long-narrow forms of the plans, while the final syntax of each JPG becomes more integrated through L_0R_6 and L_0R_7, which increases inhabitant-visitor relations.

The s-JPG grammar also enables the generation of JPG variations through the derivation tree (see Figure 1), and four examples of this are illustrated in Figure 14. The first variation has nodes and links similar to that of the *Nicholas House* (case 2), but its exterior link, generated by L_0R_7, is only (C, E) instead of two links of the house, (H, E) and (C², E). The result is, however, an unconventional structure that locates the second common sector at the deepest depth. In contrast, the second and third variations are more acceptable in terms of their syntax. The second variation in Figure 14 is also developed by a different application of L_0R_7. The same node and link generation in the ninth case (*Southern Highlands House*) occurs before L_0R_7, but only two links are developed by H → H, E, (H, E); G → G, E, (G, E). That is, two rules used for the *Fredericks House* are employed. Conversely, the node and link generation in the fourth case with three links by L_0R_7, {(H, E), (G, E), (C², E)} will also develop another variation (see Figure 1). The third variation employs the rule sets to generate the JPG of the *Simpson-Lee House*, while the fourth variation follows the rule sets applied in the generation of the JPG of the last case. Both cases employ the hall node as a core node. That is, L_0R_1 generates H_{C0} through S_0 → H_{c0}. The second rule set (L_0R_2) generates the private and the common nodes, and the related links, (H_{c0}, P) and (H_{c0}, C). L_0R_7 develops the second private node (P²) and a link (C, P²) from the common node for the third variation, while it is skipped for the fourth variation. In this way, two variations adopt the same rules used for the two cases, but applying the different rule sets at L_0R_7 develops the JPG variations in Figure 14.

Krstic (1999) argues that a grammar establishes the limits of the style. The s-JPG grammar has the beneficial property that it can be employed to examine possible alternatives using a holistic application of the rule sets as well as to generate design instances in the style. Thus, Shape Grammars provide a parsimonious or efficient means for constructing designs in specific languages (Economou, 2000). Furthermore, a JPG can be identified as a representative graph showing the syntactic style of the JPGs generated in the case study. It is developed by the dominant productions of each rule during the generation of the ten cases. Therefore, applying the dominant rules identified from each step allows a dominant JPG to be generated, which arguably encapsulates most of the spatial relationships present in Murcutt's architecture. Since the s-JPG grammar uses a sequential generative procedure, the rules applied in the previous rule sets must be considered to produce such a dominant JPG. It is also possible to calculate the mathematical likelihood of certain rule combinations being used for the transition probabilities and conditions (see "rule transition paths" in Chapter 3). For example, L_0R_1 generates H_{C0}, which is the most dominant node in the ten JPGs generated by the s-JPG grammar for Murcutt's ten cases. It is followed by L_0R_2 which produces the most frequent two pairs of nodes and links, P, (H_{c0}, P) and C, (H_{c0}, C). L_0R_3 is skipped (66% transition probability) and L_0R_4 is consequently skipped. L_0R_5 develops two nodes, P^2 and G, which are unlinked. After generating E and (H_{c0}, E) by L_0R_6, the s-JPG grammar generates $\{(C, E), (P^2, E), (G, E)\}$ through L_0R_7. Finally, by applying the termination rule L_0R_8, the final JPG of the last case is constructed (see Figure 11). This implies that, of the complete set of ten selected designs, the last case (the *Walsh House*), best encapsulates the way Murcutt creates functional relationships in space. Of course, calculating the transition probability and frequency indicators ideally needs a larger sample group to allow for the generation of a more precise dominant JPG.

THE MASSING GRAMMAR AND ITS APPLICATIONS

Block Properties

This section uses the massing grammar to capture the combined formal and spatial properties of the set of Murcutt's architectural works. The massing grammar requires three configuration processes for defining (a) block properties, (b) composition, and (c) roof types. This descriptive grammar

Figure 14. JPG variations generated by the s-JPG grammar

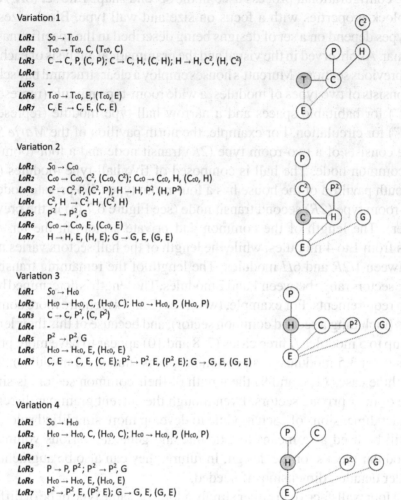

Variation 1

LoR1	$S_0 \rightarrow T_{co}$
LoR2	$T_{co} \rightarrow T_{co}$, C, (T_{co}, C)
LoR3	$C \rightarrow C, P, (C, P); C \rightarrow C, H, (C, H); H \rightarrow H, C^2, (H, C^2)$
LoR4	-
LoR5	-
LoR6	$T_{co} \rightarrow T_{co}$, E, (T_{co}, E)
LoR7	$C, E \rightarrow C, E, (C, E)$

Variation 2

LoR1	$S_0 \rightarrow C_{co}$
LoR2	$C_{co} \rightarrow C_{co}, C^2, (C_{co}, C^2); C_{co} \rightarrow C_{co}, H, (C_{co}, H)$
LoR3	$C^2 \rightarrow C^2, P, (C^2, P); H \rightarrow H, P^2, (H, P^2)$
LoR4	$C^2, H \rightarrow C^2, H, (C^2, H)$
LoR5	$P^2 \rightarrow P^2, G$
LoR6	$C_{co} \rightarrow C_{co}, E, (C_{co}, E)$
LoR7	$H \rightarrow H, E, (H, E); G \rightarrow G, E, (G, E)$

Variation 3

LoR1	$S_0 \rightarrow H_{co}$
LoR2	$H_{co} \rightarrow H_{co}, C, (H_{co}, C); H_{co} \rightarrow H_{co}, P, (H_{co}, P)$
LoR3	$C \rightarrow C, P^2, (C, P^2)$
LoR4	-
LoR5	$P^2 \rightarrow P^2, G$
LoR6	$H_{co} \rightarrow H_{co}, E, (H_{co}, E)$
LoR7	$C, E \rightarrow C, E, (C, E); P^2 \rightarrow P^2, E, (P^2, E); G \rightarrow G, E, (G, E)$

Variation 4

LoR1	$S_0 \rightarrow H_{co}$
LoR2	$H_{co} \rightarrow H_{co}, C, (H_{co}, C); H_{co} \rightarrow H_{co}, P, (H_{co}, P)$
LoR3	-
LoR4	-
LoR5	$P \rightarrow P, P^2; P^2 \rightarrow P^2, G$
LoR6	$H_{co} \rightarrow H_{co}, E, (H_{co}, E)$
LoR7	$P^2 \rightarrow P^2, E, (P^2, E); G \rightarrow G, E, (G, E)$

configures a set of shape-based extensions from the s-JPG grammar. Thus, the first shape rule (SR_1) in any specific massing grammar transforms a programmatic area (a functional node) into a functionally-sectored modular block in the plan using a basic schema, $x \rightarrow$ shape (x). That is, the sector nodes of the JPG are transformed into shapes. In this way, the massing grammar produces modular blocks and then configures each sectored block with an appropriate property.

The configurational process used in the second shape rule set (SR_2) deals with block properties with a focus on size and wall type. Block sizes and wall types depend on a set of designs being described in the specific massing grammar. As observed in the visual and the grammatical analysis of each case in the previous sections, Murcutt's houses employ a clear structural bay scheme that consists of two types of modules, a wide room-type module (represented by "R") for habitable spaces and a narrow hall-type module (represented by "H") for circulation. For example, the north pavilion of the *Marie Short House* consists of a two-room type ($2R$) transit node and a four-room type ($4R$) common node. The hall is composed of five hall-type modules ($5H$). The south pavilion of the house has a four-room type ($4R$) private node and a two-room type ($2R$) second transit node (see Figure 6.7 (a) in the previous chapter). The length of the common and private sectors in the ten cases ranges from 1 to 4 modules, while the length of the hall sectors varies more, by between $1/2R$ and $6H$ modules. The length of the remaining transit and garage sectors range between 1 and 2 modules. The length is determined by the design requirements. For example, two cases (2 and 4) require more common spaces (including a second common sector), and because of this their lengths reach up to 5 modules. Three cases (7, 8 and 10) appear to have more private spaces (over 3.5 modules) than common spaces (under 2.5 modules). In the other three cases (1, 6 and 9) the length of their common sectors is similar to one of their private sectors. Even though the current grammar disregards the exact dimensions of each module to develop more simplified rules, they can still be used as a means to examine and generate various volumes of the modular blocks for the design. In future, they can also be augmented to consider detailed dimensions if needed.

The four wall-faces can either simply adopt the same type or be of different types. Figure 15 presents the 3D projection of the different wall-type blocks. Most of Murcutt's houses visually open to the north and the south is enclosed to protect the rear wall from severe winds. For example, the north façade of his buildings is often made up of glass and metal louvres, while the south has a solid wall. Hanson and Radford also consider adding glazing to the north with louvres and solid walls to the south in their Murcutt Shape Grammar (Hanson & Radford, 1986a). Acting as a partition between rooms, as well as a privacy enclosure, the east and west walls of a modular block are often solid. Thus, the north wall of a room-type block can be "transparent", "semi-transparent" and "solid", but the other walls are solid for the wall-type configuration. Conversely, the east and west walls of a hall-type block frequently adopt a "transparent" type because they often have sub-entrances. In this way, four

Table 14. Derivations of the grammar rules configuring block properties

Case	Shape rule
1	shape (T_{c0}, *2R.open*); shape (C, *4R.transparent*); shape (H, *5H.transparent*); shape (P, *4R.transparent*); shape (T^2, *2R.open*)
2	shape (T_{c0}, *2R.open*); shape (C, *2R.transparent*); shape (P, *1R.solid*); shape (H, *3H.transparent*); shape (C^2, *3R/2.solid*)
3	shape (H_{c0}, *3R/2.transparent*); shape (P, *3R/2.solid*); shape (C, *4R.transparent*)
4	shape (C_{c0}, *2R.transparent*); shape (P, *2R.transparent*); shape (C^2, *3R.transparent*); shape (P^2, *2R.transparent*); shape (H, *1H.transparent*); shape (G, *2R.solid*)
5	shape (H_{c0}, *3R2/3.solid*); shape (P, *1R.solid*); shape (C, *2R.solid*); shape (T, *1R.open*); shape (T^2, *2R/3.open*)
6	shape (T_{c0}, *1R.open*); shape (C, *1R.transparent*); shape (P, *1R.transparent*); shape (G, *1R.transparent*); shape (C^2, *1R.transparent*); shape (P^2, *1R.transparent*) ; shape (A, *6H.solid*); shape (A^2, *6H.solid*)
7	shape (H_{c0}, *4H.transparent*); shape (C, *3R.solid*); shape (P, *3/2R.solid*); shape (P^2, *3/2R.solid*); shape (G, *2R.solid*)
8	shape (H_{c0}, *1/2R.transparent*); shape (C, *2R.semi-transparent*); shape (P, *5/2R.semi-transparent*); shape (P^2, *2R.solid*); shape (G, *2R.solid*)
9	shape (C_{c0}, *10/3R.semi-transparent*); shape (C^2, *1R.transparent*); shape (P, *1R.solid*); shape (P^2, *2R. semi-transparent*); shape (G, *1R.solid*); shape (H, *5H.transparent*)
10	shape (H_{c0}, *1R.solid*); shape (C, *2R.transparent*); shape (P, *2R.semi-transparent*); shape (P^2, *3/2R.semi-transparent*); shape (G, *3/2R.solid*)

Ten cases: 1. *Marie Short House*, 2. *Nicholas House*, 3. *Carruthers House*, 4. *Fredericks House*, 5. *Ball-Eastaway House*, 6. *Magney House*, 7. *Simpson-Lee House*, 8. *Fletcher-Page House*, 9. *Southern Highlands House*, 10. *Walsh House*.

simplified types of blocks – "open", "transparent", "semi-transparent" and "solid" – are considered in the wall-type configuration in Murcutt's massing grammar. However, these wall types cannot include the angled bay windows found in two cases (8 and 10), because the grammar configures sectored blocks, not individual rooms. In addition, when overlapping two different wall types in the compositions, the face adopts the thicker and more opaque types from open to solid. For example, merging the "transparency" wall of the hall block with the "solid" southern wall of the common block results in a "solid" wall in the first case of Figure 16.

Figure 16 illustrates the configuration of block properties (size and wall type) of each case. The room-type module ("*R*") is naturally a dominant shape in the set of Murcutt's houses. Across all ten cases, 47 "*R*" and 7 "*H*" modular blocks are generated. In the four cases featuring a single pavilion (cases 3, 5, 8 and 10), their architectural forms adopt only "*R*" modular blocks. By adding a hall-type module (an internal corridor), the massing grammar can generate two pavilions in his domestic architecture. In cases 1, 2 and 4 the "*R*" modular blocks are connected by the "*H*" module, while the form of

Figure 15. Wall types in Murcutt's massing grammar

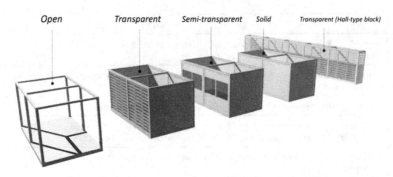

the *Simpson-Lee House* and the *Southern Highlands House* (cases 7 and 9) are expanded by adding a long "*H*" modular block. In an unusual case, the *Magney House*, the massing grammar needs to add two hall-type modules because the house has an asymmetrical, butterfly roof along its three-layered plan. Thus, two long "*H*" modular blocks are added for both corridor-type zones along the south façade. In this case, the added blocks are denoted as "A" and "A²", to be distinguished from the other functional sector blocks. To create this addition, the first shape rule set (SR_1) includes one more rule, $S \rightarrow$ shape (a), where S is a start symbol and a is a formal node that is not a functional node. This rule allows the massing grammar to directly develop the additional modular block.

Composition

The third shape rule set (SR_3) of the massing grammar composes the overall form of the design. A core block is the centre of the design planning and it is used as the starting point for formal composition as well. The massing grammar uses the links developed by the s-JPG grammar as a reference, providing links to adjacent blocks. This process also highlights *direction* and *alignment*. The third shape rule set considers eight cardinal and sub-cardinal directions: east, west, north, south, northeast, northwest, southeast, southwest. The grammar also uses five types of *alignment* relationships: equal, centre, left, right and interleaving.

For the *Marie Short House* in Figure 16, the transit block is denoted as "T_{c0}" by the s-JPG grammar, as it is a core block in this configuration, and the common sector node is to the east of the core block and equally shares the wall between two blocks. These compositions are configured by two shape

Figure 16a. Configuration of block properties (size, wall type)

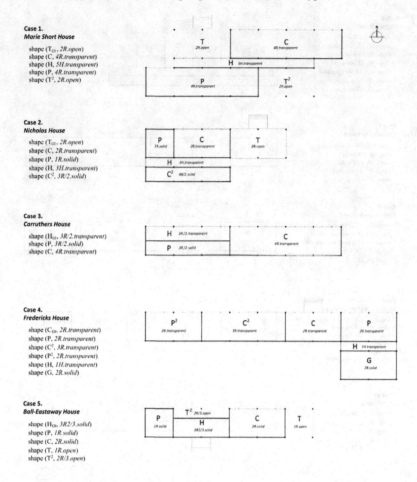

Case 1.
Marie Short House

shape (T_{c0}, *2R.open*)
shape (C, *4R.transparent*)
shape (H, *5H.transparent*)
shape (P, *4R.transparent*)
shape (T^2, *2R.open*)

Case 2.
Nicholas House

shape (T_{c0}, *2R.open*)
shape (C, *2R.transparent*)
shape (P, *1R.solid*)
shape (H, *3H.transparent*)
shape (C^2, *3R/2.solid*)

Case 3.
Carruthers House

shape (H_{c0}, *3R/2.transparent*)
shape (P, *3R/2.solid*)
shape (C, *4R.transparent*)

Case 4.
Fredericks House

shape (C_{c0}, *2R.transparent*)
shape (P, *2R.transparent*)
shape (C^2, *3R.transparent*)
shape (P^2, *2R.transparent*)
shape (H, *1H.transparent*)
shape (G, *2R.solid*)

Case 5.
Ball-Eastaway House

shape (H_{c0}, *3R2/3.solid*)
shape (P, *1R.solid*)
shape (C, *2R.solid*)
shape (T, *1R.open*)
shape (T^2, *2R/3.open*)

rules: shape (T_{c0}, *2R.open*) → shape (T_{c0}, *2R.open, coreblock*) and shape (C, *4H.transparent*) → shape (C, *4H.transparent, T.east.equal*). The hall block (H) is located at the south of the transit block (T_{c0}) and is right-aligned, which is configured by shape (H, *5H.transparent*) → shape (H, *5H.transparent, T.south.right*). In this way, the massing grammar can be used to compose all blocks for the ten cases as shown in Figure 16.

The links (semantics) specified between different nodes in the JPGs (see Figure 13) not only guide shape composition on a step by step basis, but they also allow unnecessary or unconventional form generation to be avoided. The process of shape composition is finalised by examining and selecting from the generated alternatives according to the syntactic structure of the architecture. For example, the shape composition for the *Marie Short House* follows the

Figure 16b.

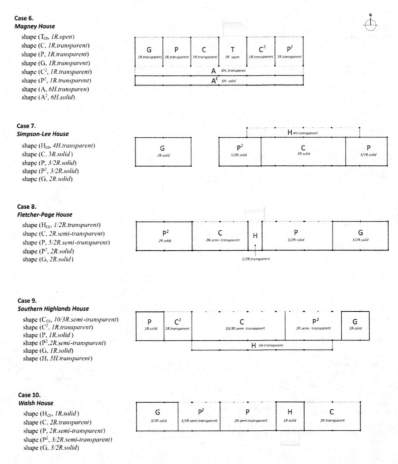

Case 6.
Magney House

shape (T_{co}, *1R.open*)
shape (C, *1R.transparent*)
shape (P, *1R.transparent*)
shape (G, *1R.transparent*)
shape (C^2, *1R.transparent*)
shape (P^2, *1R.transparent*)
shape (A, *6H.transparen*)
shape (A^2, *6H.solid*)

Case 7.
Simpson-Lee House

shape (H_{co}, *4H.transparent*)
shape (C, *3R.solid*)
shape (P, *3/2R.solid*)
shape (P^2, *3/2R.solid*)
shape (G, *2R.solid*)

Case 8.
Fletcher-Page House

shape (H_{co}, *1/2R.transparent*)
shape (C, *2R.semi-transparent*)
shape (P, *5/2R.semi-transparent*)
shape (P^2, *2R.solid*)
shape (G, *2R.solid*)

Case 9.
Southern Highlands House

shape (C_{co}, *10/3R.semi-transparent*)
shape (C^2, *1R.transparent*)
shape (P, *1R.solid*)
shape (P^2, *2R.semi-transparent*)
shape (G, *1R.solid*)
shape (H, *5H.transparent*)

Case 10.
Walsh House

shape (H_{co}, *1R.solid*)
shape (C, *2R.transparent*)
shape (P, *2R.semi-transparent*)
shape (P^2, *3/2R.semi-transparent*)
shape (G, *3/2R.solid*)

steps from the first depth to the third depth of the JPG and generates a corpus of design variations. Keeping the nodes and links specified in the JPG, the massing grammar can generate alternatives that have the same syntactical structures. In this way, for example, the massing grammar is not only able to generate the right forms for the *Marie Short House* but also alternatives that share the same spatial characteristics of the original design, by altering different growth directions in this shape composition. Figure 17 illustrates examples of design variations using different shape compositions from the JPG of the *Marie Short House.*

Figure 17. Examples of design alternatives for the Marie Short House by the third shape rule set

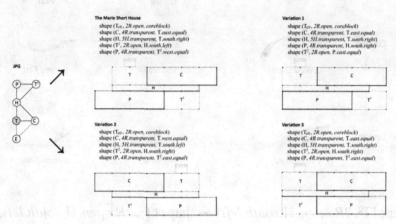

Roof Types

Roof types in Murcutt's architecture actually vary in response to climatic and contextual issues, including sunlight, winds and views (Hanson & Radford, 1986a). Furthermore, the corrugated metal sheets that Murcutt uses for roofs allow for a wide variety of shapes. The massing grammar focuses on the combination of the possible roof sub-shapes that make up the overall roof shape. Under this constraint, a pavilion employing only an *"R"* or *"H"* block shape has a roof sub-shape, while the buildings featuring two pavilions (cases 1, 2 and 4) that consist of three block shapes (*"R"*, *"H"* and *"R"*) also have three roof sub-shapes. In addition, the *Magney House* (case 6), which includes two additional modular blocks ("A" and "A²") has three different roof sub-shapes.

Figure 18 illustrates roof types used in the ten cases. Twin pavilion buildings (cases 1, 2 and 4) have three roof sub-shapes consisting of two pitched roofs, linear gable (LG) or curved gable (CG), for *"R"* block shapes and a flat roof, linear flat (LF), for *"H"* block shapes. For example, the roof of the first case consisting of CG, LF and CG sub-shapes is configured by five rules (due to its five blocks):

shape (T_{c0}, *2R.open, coreblock*) → shape (T_{c0}, *2R.open, coreblock, CG*);

shape (C, *4R.transparent,* T.*east.equal*) → shape (C, *4R.transparent,* T.*east.equal, CG*);

shape (H, *5H.transparent,* T.*south.right*) → shape (H, *5H.transparent,* T.*south.right, LF*);

Figure 18. Roof types

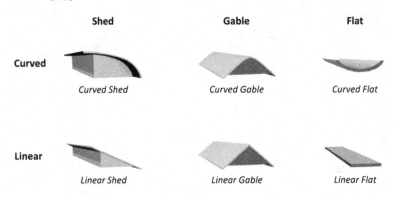

shape (T², *2R.open*, H.*south.left*) → shape (T², *2R.open*, H.*south.left*, *CG*);
shape (P, *4R.transparent*, T².*west.equal*) → shape (P, *4R.transparent*, T².*west.equal*, *CG*).

By following these configuration processes, the application of the massing grammar generates a simplified model of the 3D forms of the ten selected Murcutt domestic buildings (Figure 19). The more recent cases (7, 8 and 10) possess simple linear, mono-pitch roof pavilions and have a linear shed (LS) roof shape, while the large and complex houses, such as the *Southern Highlands House* (case 9) have two roof sub-shapes of "CG" for the main building and curved shed (CS) for the single-loaded hallway. The orientation of shed roofs in Murcutt's houses follows a common design strategy, with "open fronts" and "protective backs". Thus, the rooflines of the linear, mono-pitch forms (7, 8 and 10) are tilted up to the north. Since the modular blocks of a building are already joined in the previous process, roof shapes are also automatically merged into a roof over the long, narrow form unless a case consists of two or more roof types or two separate buildings. As a typical case, the roof of the *Magney House* (6) consists of "CS", "LF" sub-shapes and a mirrored "CS" roof to develop its butterfly roof, along with its three-layered plan. A mirrored "CS" sub-shape is identified as "mCS" in the grammar.

Figure 19a. The final productions of the massing grammar application and the final 3D forms for the ten cases.

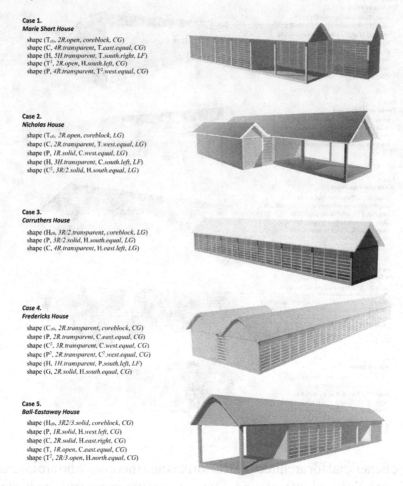

Case 1.
Marie Short House

shape (T$_{c0}$, 2R.open, coreblock, CG)
shape (C, 4R.transparent, T.east.equal, CG)
shape (H, 5H.transparent, T.south.right, LF)
shape (T^2, 2R.open, H.south.left, CG)
shape (P, 4R.transparent, T^2.west.equal, CG)

Case 2.
Nicholas House

shape (T$_{c0}$, 2R.open, coreblock, LG)
shape (C, 2R.transparent, T.west.equal, LG)
shape (P, 1R.solid, C.west.equal, LG)
shape (H, 3H.transparent, C.south.left, LF)
shape (C^2, 3R/2.solid, H.south.equal, LG)

Case 3.
Carruthers House

shape (H$_{c0}$, 3R/2.transparent, coreblock, LG)
shape (P, 3R/2.solid, H.south.equal, LG)
shape (C, 4R.transparent, H.east.left, LG)

Case 4.
Fredericks House

shape (C$_{c0}$, 2R.transparent, coreblock, CG)
shape (P, 2R.transparent, C.east.equal, CG)
shape (C^2, 3R.transparent, C.west.equal, CG)
shape (P^2, 2R.transparent, C^2.west.equal, CG)
shape (H, 1H.transparent, P.south.left, LF)
shape (G, 2R.solid, H.south.equal, CG)

Case 5.
Ball-Eastaway House

shape (H$_{c0}$, 3R2/3.solid, coreblock, CG)
shape (P, 1R.solid, H.west.left, CG)
shape (C, 2R.solid, H.east.right, CG)
shape (T, 1R.open, C.east.equal, CG)
shape (T^2, 2R/3.open, H.north.equal, CG)

CONCLUSION

This chapter describes and demonstrates the grammatical and syntactical method for recording and extrapolating design instances from a set of Glenn Murcutt's house designs. The generic method develops two specific grammars, s-JPG grammar and massing grammar, and captures both syntactic (function-based) and stylistic (form-based) characteristics of a design. The final forms (Figure 19) produced by the massing Shape Grammar follow the syntactic relationships of the JPGs generated by the s-JPG grammar. These outcomes

Figure 19b.

Case 6.
The Magney House

shape (T, *1R.open, coreblock, CS*)
shape (C, *1R.transparent, T.west.equal, CS*)
shape (P, *1R.transparent, C.west.equal, CS*)
shape (G, *1R.transparent, P.west.equal, CS*)
shape (C², *1R.transparent, T.east.equal, CS*)
shape (P², *1R.transparent, C².east.equal, CS*)
shape (A, *6H.transparen, P².south.left, LF*)
shape (A², *6H.solid, A.south.equal, mCS*)

Case 7.
The Simpson-Lee House

shape (H, *4H.transparent, coreblock, LS*)
shape (C, *3R.transparent, H.south.centre, LS*)
shape (P², *3/2R.solid, C.west.equal, LS*)
shape (G, *2R.solid, P².west.separated, LS*)

Case 8.
The Fletcher-Page House

shape (H, *1/2R.transparent, coreblock, LS*)
shape (C, *2R.semi-transparent, H.west.equal, LS*)
shape (P, *5/2R.solid, H.east.equal, LS*)
shape (P², *2R.solid, C.west.equal, LS*)
shape (G, *3/2R.solid, P.east.equal, LS*)

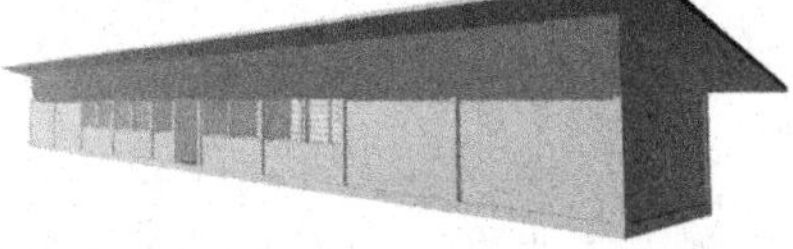

Case 9.
The Southern Highlands House

shape (C, *8/3R.semi-transparent, coreblock, CG*)
shape (C², *1R.transparent, C.west.equal, CG*)
shape (P, *1R.semi-transparent, C².west.equal, CG*)
shape (P², *8/3R.transparent, C.east.equal, CG*)
shape (G, *1R.solid, P².east.equal, CG*)
shape (H, *6H.solid, C.south.right, CS*)

Case 10.
The Walsh house

shape (H, *1R.transparent, coreblock, LS*)
shape (C, *2R.solid, H.east.equal, LS*)
shape (P, *2R.solid, H.west.equal, LS*)
shape (P², *3/2R.solid, P.west.equal, LS*)
shape (G, *3/2R.solid, P².west.equal, LS*)

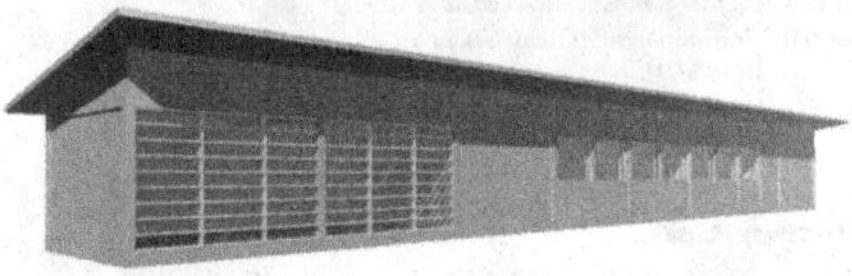

could be beneficial for architectural historians and theorists who are interested in understanding and interpreting different stylistic approaches to design.

The JPG grammar's unearthing of a hidden topological design structure enables the analysis of a possible (sequential) design process that has been used to construct the functional relationships in a work. The results of the syntactical analysis of the JPG grammar contribute to determining some of the characteristics of an architectural design and to supporting the evolution of designs by way of the topological relationships generated by the JPG rules. Importantly, the JPG grammar allows both rule-based and syntax-based analysis and facilitates the exploration of the design instances and inequality genotypes of the set of given cases. In contrast, the massing grammar's three major configurational processes enables the generation and semantic presentation of a conceptual 3D form that conforms to the syntactic and functional relations specified in the JPG, although the grammar disregards many subtle architectural details. Furthermore, both grammars contribute to the generation of new variations by altering rule applications.

Finally, since both grammars use simplified vocabularies, sector nodes and modular blocks, they have fundamental limitations. However, the use of functional sectors rather than convex spaces enables this method to address larger epistemological questions raised by design. To formally accommodate a much higher level of detailed mapping more closely aligned to the particular design styles being studied may also be too impractical to implement. Obviously, such factors are shaped by complex external issues and various contexts. Ultimately, this chapter describes and demonstrates the method, combining selected aspects of two accepted computational approaches to provide a new critical knowledge base about architecture in terms of forms, styles and spatial configurations.

REFERENCES

Baker, G. (1996). *Design strategies in architecture: An approach to the analysis of form*. New York, NY: Van Nostrand Reinhold.

Economou, A. (2000). *Shape grammars in architectural design studio*. Paper presented at the 2000 ACSA Technology Conference, Hong Kong.

Fromonot, F. (1995). *Glenn Murcutt buildings and projects*. London, UK: Thames and Hudson.

Gero, J. S., & Coyne, R. D. (1985). Logic programming as a means of representing semantics in design languages. *Environment and Planning. B, Planning & Design, 12*(3), 351–369. doi:10.1068/b120351

Hanson, N. L. R., & Radford, A. D. (1986a). Living on the edge: A grammar for some country houses by Glenn Murcutt. *Architecture Australia, 75*(5), 66–73.

Hanson, N. L. R., & Radford, A. D. (1986b). On modelling the work of the architect Glenn Murcutt. *Design Computing, 1*(3), 189–203.

Hillier, B. (1999). *Space is the machine: A configurational theory of architecture*. Cambridge, UK: Cambridge University Press.

Krstic, D. (1999). Constructing algebras of design. *Environment and Planning. B, Planning & Design, 26*(1), 45–57. doi:10.1068/b260045

Lee, J. H., Ostwald, M. J., & Gu, N. (2015). A syntactical and grammatical approach to architectural configuration, analysis and generation. *Architectural Science Review, 58*(3), 189–204. doi:10.1080/00038628.2015.1015948

Lee, J. H., Ostwald, M. J., & Gu, N. (2018). A justified plan graph (JPG) grammar approach to identifying spatial design patterns in an architectural style. *Environment and Planning B. Urban Analytics and City Science, 45*(1), 67–89. doi:10.1177/0265813516665618

Ostwald, M. J. (2011a). Examining the relationship between topology and geometry: A configurational analysis of the rural houses (1984-2005) of Glenn Murcutt. *Journal of Space Syntax, 2*(2), 223–246.

Ostwald, M. J. (2011b). A justified plan graph analysis of the early houses (1975-1982) of Glenn Murcutt. *Nexus Network Journal, 13*(3), 737–762. doi:10.100700004-011-0089-x

Ostwald, M. J. (2011c). The mathematics of spatial configuration: Revisiting, revising and critiquing justified plan graph theory. *Nexus Network Journal, 13*(2), 445–470. doi:10.100700004-011-0075-3

Spence, R. (1986). At Bingie Point house, Moruya, New South Wales. *The Architectural Review, 1068,* 70-75.

van der Voordt, T. J. M., Vrielink, D., & van Wegen, H. B. R. (1997). Comparative floorplan-analysis in programming and architectural design. *Design Studies, 18*(1), 67–88. doi:10.1016/S0142-694X(96)00016-6

Chapter 8
The Language of Frank Lloyd Wright's Prairie Houses

ABSTRACT

This chapter uses a combined syntactical and grammatic method to analyse 19 of Frank Lloyd Wright's Prairie houses. The purpose of this analysis is to illuminate the formal and social properties of Wright's early architecture. The data developed through this process is used to provide mathematical insights into the topological and geometric patterns that provide the foundation for Wright's Prairie style language. The data is then used to generate a new socially and formally derived and compliant instance of this style. Whereas past research has shown how Wright's architecture might be computationally generated solely on the basis of its formal composition, this chapter shows how its social and functional properties can also be replicated as part of such a process.

INTRODUCTION

This chapter uses the new combined grammatical and syntactical method to analyse Frank Lloyd Wright's early twentieth century "Prairie style" architecture. Wright's Prairie style has not only fascinated a large number of architects, but over time historians have also begun to document and debate its properties. In particular, historians have identified a high level of complexity in the spatial planning and formal modelling of Wright's architecture of the era. In order to better understand these properties, Koning and Eizenberg (1981)

DOI: 10.4018/978-1-7998-1698-0.ch008

developed one of the most well-known early Shape Grammar applications to investigate thirteen Prairie style houses built between 1900 and 1909. Koning and Eizenberg's additive Shape Grammar had its origins in Wright's admission that Froebel blocks had a profound influence on his early childhood experience of form-making (Alofsin, 1993). The Shape Grammar starts with the generation of a central fireplace as the core of the plan, and sequentially adds rectangular Froebel-esque blocks before configuring exterior details. This Shape Grammar not only successfully captures the major formal properties of Wright's Prairie houses, but Koning and Eizenberg showed how it could be used to convincingly generate a new Prairie-style form.

Despite its capacity to model the formal properties of the Prairie style, Koning and Eizenberg's grammar ignores its underlying socio-functional properties, which are arguably more significant for the architecture (Chan 1992; Pinnell 2005). Furthermore, historians describe the Prairie Style as featuring complex overlapping formal compositions in both massing *and* planning, and suggest that it is the combination of the two that is significant (Lind 1994). The combined spatial and formal properties of Wright's Prairie houses have repeatedly drawn architectural scholars to attempt to uncover their underlying rules and properties. For example, Laseau and Tice (1992) develop two-dimensional formal patterns, highlighting the connection between space, form and principle. Computational and mathematical studies have also examined the formal complexity of Wright's Prairie style designs using fractal dimension analysis (Ostwald & Vaughan, 2010, 2016), social properties using syntactical comparative analysis (Amini Behbahani, Ostwald, & Gu, 2016) and experiential characteristics using isovist fields (Ostwald & Dawes, 2013, 2018). All of these past studies have uncovered various parts of the larger formal, functional and spatio-visual patterns in Wright's architecture. However, as past research notes, it is the combination of space and form which makes the language both distinctive and difficult to analyse (Laseau & Tice, 1992).

In response to this issue, the present chapter uses a combined method to analyse the grammatical (rule or form-based) and syntactical (social or function-based) language of Wright's Prairie architecture. The method identifies dominant patterns in Wright's design strategies and a design permutation that most closely captures its linguistic characteristics. The method starts by developing the specific Justified Plan Graph (s-JPG) grammar that systematically captures aspects of the two-dimensional socio-functional structure of an architectural style (Lee, Ostwald, & Gu, 2015a, 2015b, 2017). It then employs the massing grammar to derive the three-dimensional formal expression of each sector node developed by the s-JPG grammar. The body of work which is analysed in the present chapter comprises nineteen of Wright's Prairie designs, spanning from the 1902 *Little House* to the 1912 *Harry S. Adams House*. Data developed using the two grammars is used to identify the dominant rules in the language and their sequential application, which in turn captures the underlying socio-functional and formal properties of the houses. The chapter concludes by identifying the most dominant or characteristic JPG of the Prairie houses and its formal massing.

The S-JPG Grammar of Wright's Prairie Houses

The nineteen Prairie houses analysed in this chapter are: 1. *F. W. Little House* (1902), 2. *Ross House* (1902), 3. *Robert Houses* (c 1903), 4. *Walser House* (1903), 5. *Barnes House* (1905), 6. *Mary W. Adams House* (1905), 7. *Sutton House* (1905), 8. *Brown House* (1906), 9. *DeRhodes House* (1906), 10. *Nichols House* (1906), 11. *Fuller House* (1906), 12. *Fireproof House* (1906), 13. *Stockman House* (1908), 14. *Baker House* (1909), 15. *Little House II* (1908), 16. *Larwill House* (1909), 17. *Waller House* (1909), 18. *Ziegler House* (1910), and 19. *Harry S. Adams House* (1912). Note that Francis and Mary Little commissioned two houses from Wright, in 1902 and 1908, with the latter normally differentiated by the addition of "II" to its name. Both of these houses are included in the set. Furthermore, some of these nineteen houses were constructed, whereas others, like the *Fireproof House*, were created as model designs and used as the basis for multiple works, including the *Nichols House* and the *Stockman House*. Two of the houses, the *Walser* and *Barnes* houses, are effectively the same in syntactical and grammatical terms, despite superficial differences in planning and formal modelling. This is not unexpected, given that Wright was developing a particular stylistic language and consistent approach to the problems of a then contemporary middle-American household. A few of the houses, like the *Brown House* and the *Little House II* were singular works that remained unbuilt despite being fully documented. In all cases, the plans analysed in this chapter are based on Wright's final construction drawings or the developed design drawings if they did not proceed to construction (Futagawa & Pfeiffer, 1987a, 1987b).

The nineteen cases are all single-family residences with relatively simple floor plans and functional sets of rooms that are typical of the majority of Wright's Prairie style works. Some of these cases possess multiple disconnected stand-alone structures – generally garages or coach houses – which are excluded from the analysis. In most of the cases, the ground floor plans include entry, living and dining rooms, halls and parlours, kitchens and occasionally a maid's room. This is significant because the four wings of the cruciform plan of the Prairie style typically serve four functional uses (entry, living, dining and kitchen) with a hall space and staircase at the centre. Several of the houses also include smaller service rooms on the ground floor (such as a pantry, laundry or bathrooms), while bedrooms and bathrooms dominate the upper level of these designs. Importantly, the selected cases exclude designs with extensive servants' wings, along with those that have multiple large alternative social zones (such as music rooms, galleries, libraries, games rooms and conservatories). Thus, while many of Wright's most well-known Prairie houses are included in the set, a few major works, like the *Robie House*, *Darwin D. Martin House* and the *Dana-Thomas House*, are not.

The first stage in the development of the Wright s-JPG grammar is the definition of a set of nodes in a design based on functional sectors and taking into account a consideration of connectivity, adjacency and modularity (see Chapters 6 and 7). In the s-JPG grammar for Wright's Prairie houses, nine functional sectors are required. The exterior (E) is simply the surrounding site or exterior environment. The entry (N) not only acts as the separator between interior and exterior, but is often associated with the space of the hall and the staircase. Thus, the hall (H) sector includes corridors, hallways, stairs and linking spaces that are locally grouped. If a hall includes an entry, the combination of an entry and a hall is regarded as a hall sector. Common and service spaces are categorised into three functional sectors, living (L), dining (D), and kitchen (K). The kitchen sector often includes multiple sub-spaces, such as pantries and sometimes even small servant rooms. The private (P) sector contains bedrooms and bathrooms. If bathrooms are formally separated from bedrooms, the independent space is regarded as a service sector (S). Transit (T) spaces are intermediate, roofed or semi-enclosed zones between interior and exterior, which include verandas and porches.

If there is a separate grouping in each sector, it is represented by a second or third sector node such as P^2, H^2 or P^3. For example, the second hall node (H^2) is frequently developed for the first floor, and some Prairie houses have four private sectors denoted by P, P^2, P^3 and P^4. In addition, the grammar denotes P^S as another private sector for servants' bedrooms. Some houses only have a single hall (H) as a circulation sector, while others have three circulation sectors consisting of N (the entry), H and H^2. A garage (G) primarily functions as storage for cars (or coaches), but may include adjacent workshops, laundries and service areas. However, in many of the Prairie designs the garage or coach house is not connected to the main residence and is therefore not considered in the s-JPG grammar. In summary, for Wright's Prairie houses, including any required second, third and fourth functional sector nodes, the node set, N, which is used to generate the nineteen cases, is represented by

$$N = \{E, H, H^2, N, L, L^2, D, D^2, K, S, P, P^2, P^3, P^4, P^5, T, T^2, T^3, T^4, T^5\}.$$

Applying the s-JPG grammar for Wright's Prairie houses to each floor of the nineteen designs identifies the specific rules for generating each case and these are grammatically segmented according to the syntactic process. These rules are an algorithmic or mathematical representation of the unique syntactic structure of Wright's Prairie architecture. By analysing the rule sets and their most frequent applications across the nineteen designs, multiple outcomes can be produced, of which the most significant is the identification of the dominant pattern of rules found in Wright's Prairie architecture. Before the chapter undertakes an integrated review of the set of Prairie houses, the following sections describe the grammatical and syntactical analysis of a JPG of each of Wright's nineteen designs. For each design, a figure illustrates the annotated plans, a sector diagram depicting sector nodes and links and JPG productions with the derivations of the grammar rules. The syntactic data for each JPG also includes Real Relative Asymmetry (*RRA*) to compare the results of the JPGs of the Prairie buildings.

F. W. Little House

The *Francis W. and Mary Little House* was constructed in 1902 in Peoria, Illinois. Its truncated cruciform plan (Figure 1) consists of four main functional spaces on the ground floor, with the more expansive living and dining room wings to the east and west, and the shortened kitchen and hall wings to the north and south. Notably, both the living and dining rooms have secondary spaces, with similar functions but different massing and modularity associated with them, triggering the need for additional nodes. Interestingly, the south porch has no connection to any interior space, while the kitchen is linked to the exterior as well as to a service room that is part of the dining sector node. Four bedrooms, including a servant bedroom, are located on the first floor. The JPG productions for the rule sets of the s-JPG grammar determine that the fifth rule set at the ground floor (L_0R_5) develops a "bush-like" structure and the seventh rule set (L_0R_7) makes a ring structure with the exterior. The hall nodes at both levels provide a constant point of connection and passage in the building. Developing two links at the fourth rule set for the first floor $(L_I R_4)$ results in the circulation loop between bedrooms and a service room, while the servant bedroom remains an "a-type" node, or a dead-end space.

The JPG of the *Little House* (Table 1) has a mean total depth (*TD*) of 40.20 and the mean depth (*MD*) of rooms in the house is 2.87. The most isolated node in the configuration is the transit (*MD* = 3.86). The second living and dining room nodes are also isolated, but these results can be disregarded for functional reasons as they are developed largely in response to formal configuration and massing needs. Thus, the second and third most isolated nodes are the third bedroom (*MD* = 3.57) and the servant bedroom (*MD* = 3.00). Conversely, the relatively accessible nodes are the hall (*MD* = 1.86) at the ground floor and the second hall (*MD* = 2.07) at the first floor. The integration values confirm that the hall (i_{RRA} = 1.96) is double the average value, while the transit has the least integration value (i_{RRA} = 0.59).

Table 1. F. W. Little House, syntactical data

Node	TD_n	MD_n	RA	i	RRA	i_{RRA}
E	41	2.93	0.30	3.37	1.15	0.87
H	26	1.86	0.13	7.58	0.51	1.96
N	34	2.43	0.22	4.55	0.85	1.18
L	37	2.64	0.25	3.96	0.98	1.02
D	33	2.36	0.21	4.79	0.81	1.24
K	41	2.93	0.30	3.37	1.15	0.87
L^2	50	3.57	0.40	2.53	1.53	0.65
D^2	47	3.36	0.36	2.76	1.40	0.71
T	54	3.86	0.44	2.28	1.70	0.59
H^2	29	2.07	0.16	6.07	0.64	1.57
P	39	2.79	0.27	3.64	1.06	0.94
P^2	40	2.86	0.29	3.50	1.10	0.91
P^3	50	3.57	0.40	2.53	1.53	0.65
P^s	42	3.00	0.31	3.25	1.19	0.84
S	40	2.86	0.29	3.50	1.10	0.91
Maximum	54.00	3.86	0.44	7.58	1.70	1.96
Mean	40.20	2.87	0.29	3.84	1.11	1.00
Minimum	26.00	1.86	0.13	2.28	0.51	0.59
H						0.9969
H*						0.7492

Figure 1. F. W. Little House, annotated plan, sector diagram and JPG production

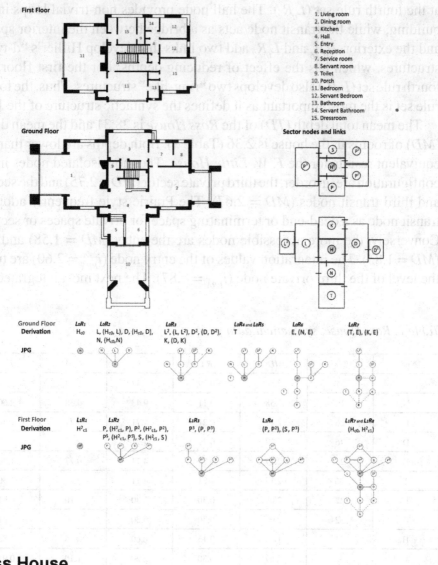

First Floor		1. Living room
		2. Dining room
		3. Kitchen
		4. Hall
		5. Entry
		6. Reception
		7. Service room
		8. Servant room
		9. Toilet
		10. Porch
		11. Bedroom
		12. Servant Bedroom
		13. Bathroom
		14. Servant Bathroom
		15. Dressroom

Ground Floor

Sector nodes and links

Ground Floor Derivation	LoR_1	LoR_2	LoR_3	LoR_4 and LoR_5	LoR_6	LoR_7
	H_{co}	L, (H_{co}, L), D, (H_{co}, D), N, (H_{co}, N)	L^2, (L, L^2), D^2, (D, D^2), K, (D, K)	T	E, (N, E)	(T, E), (K, E)
JPG						

First Floor Derivation	L_1R_1	L_1R_2	L_1R_3	L_1R_4	L_1R_7 and L_1R_8
	H^2_{c1}	P, (H^2_{c1}, P), P^2, (H^2_{c1}, P^2), P^5, (H^2_{c1}, P^5), S, (H^2_{c1}, S)	P^3, (P, P^3)	(P, P^2), (S, P^3)	(H_{co}, H^2_{c1})
JPG					

Ross House

The 1902 *Ross House* (also known as the *Forest House*) is located on the south shore of Lake Delavan in Wisconsin. The house has a partial cruciform floor plan, with a central fireplace underneath a hipped roof and overhanging eaves. The interior spaces are less physically defined or constrained than those in the *F. W. Little* House with, for example, a diagonally overlapping dining and living room and transit spaces that surround a minimalist hall (Figure 2). The grammatical analysis of the JPG of the *Ross House* reveals that a "bush-like" structure at the third rule set (L_0R_3) is developed into two "ring-like" structures at the fourth rule set (L_0R_4). The hall node provides non-trivial loops in the building, while the transit node acts as a bridge between the interior spaces and the exterior. L_0R_6 and L_0R_7 add two links that develop Hillier's "d-type" structures, which has the effect of reducing depths. For the first floor, the fourth rule set (L_1R_4) also develops two "ring-like" structures. Thus, the fourth rule set is the most important as it defines the syntactic structure of the JPG.

The mean total depth (*TD*) of the *Ross House* is 28.31 and the mean depth (*MD*) of rooms in the house is 2.36 (Table 2). Both depths are lower than the equivalent results for the *F. W. Little House*. The most isolated nodes in the configuration are, in order, the third private sector ($MD = 2.75$) and the second and third transit nodes ($MD = 2.67$). The Prairie style frequently adopts a transit node as a dead-end or terminating space for private spaces or sectors. Conversely, the more accessible nodes are the entry ($MD = 1.58$) and hall ($MD = 1.83$). The integration values of the entry node ($i_{RRA} = 2.60$) are triple the level of the third private node ($i_{RRA} = 0.87$). The next most integrated are

Table 2. Ross House, syntactical data

Node	TD_n	MD_n	RA	i	RRA	i_{RRA}
E	31	2.58	0.29	3.47	1.04	0.96
N	19	1.58	0.11	9.43	0.38	2.60
L	26	2.17	0.21	4.71	0.77	1.30
D	26	2.17	0.21	4.71	0.77	1.30
K	26	2.17	0.21	4.71	0.77	1.30
T	26	2.17	0.21	4.71	0.77	1.30
T^2	32	2.67	0.30	3.30	1.10	0.91
T^3	32	2.67	0.30	3.30	1.10	0.91
H	22	1.83	0.15	6.60	0.55	1.82
P	32	2.67	0.30	3.30	1.10	0.91
P^2	31	2.58	0.29	3.47	1.04	0.96
P^3	33	2.75	0.32	3.14	1.15	0.87
S	32	2.67	0.30	3.30	1.10	0.91
Maximum	33.00	2.75	0.32	9.43	1.15	2.60
Mean	28.31	2.36	0.25	4.48	0.90	1.24
Minimum	19.00	1.58	0.11	3.14	0.38	0.87
H						1.0133
H*						0.7895

Figure 2. Ross House, annotated plan, sector diagram and JPG production

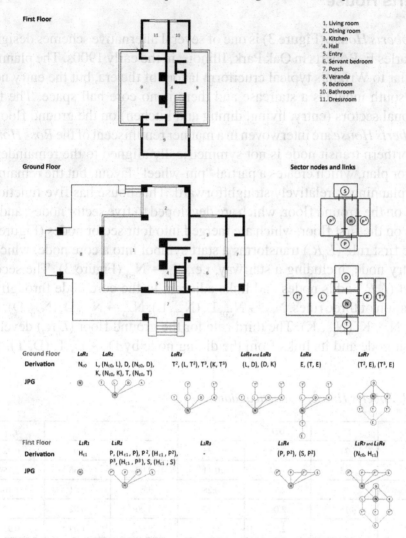

the main functional spaces, living, dining and kitchen nodes ($i_{RRA} = 1.30$). These values are higher than those of the *F. W. Little House*, which may imply that the modified cruciform plan consists of more integrated spaces than the traditional "pinwheel" structure. The H^* measure of 0.7895 suggests a low level of determination or deliberation, leaning towards the undifferentiated.

Roberts House

The *Roberts House* (Figure 3) is one of several alternative schemes designed for Charles E. Roberts in Oak Park, Illinois, in the early 1900s. The planning is similar to Wright's typical cruciform layout of the era, but the entry node to the south includes a staircase and there is no core hall space. The four functional sectors (entry, living, dining and kitchen) on the ground floor of the *Roberts House* are interwoven in a manner reminiscent of the *Ross House*. The northern transit node is not symmetrically aligned to the remainder of the floor plan, which creates a partial "pin-wheel" layout, but the remainder of the planning is relatively straightforward. This house has five functional spaces on the ground floor, which are developed to five sector nodes, and six spaces on the first floor, which are merged into four sector nodes (Figure 3).

The first rule (L_0R_1) transforms a start symbol into a core node, which is the entry node, including a stairway, i.e., $S_0 \rightarrow N_{c0}$ (Figure 3). The second rule set (L_0R_2) adds nodes and links adjacent to the core node through the application of three rules, $N_{C0} \rightarrow N_{C0}$, L, (N_{C0}, L); $N_{C0} \rightarrow N_{C0}$, D, (N_{C0}, D); and $N_{C0} \rightarrow N_{C0}$, K, (N_{C0}, K). The third rule for the ground floor (L_0R_3) develops a transit node and its links from the dining node by $D \rightarrow D$, T, (D, T). The

Table 3. Roberts House, syntactical data

Node	TD_n	MD_n	RA	i	RRA	i_{RRA}
E	21	2.33	0.33	3.00	1.09	0.92
N	13	1.44	0.11	9.00	0.36	2.75
L	19	2.11	0.28	3.60	0.91	1.10
D	18	2.00	0.25	4.00	0.82	1.22
K	21	2.33	0.33	3.00	1.09	0.92
T	30	3.33	0.58	1.71	1.91	0.52
H	15	1.67	0.17	6.00	0.54	1.84
P	23	2.56	0.39	2.57	1.27	0.79
P^2	23	2.56	0.39	2.57	1.27	0.79
P^3	23	2.56	0.39	2.57	1.27	0.79
Maximum	30.00	3.33	0.58	9.00	1.91	2.75
Mean	20.60	2.29	0.32	3.80	1.05	1.16
Minimum	13.00	1.44	0.11	1.71	0.36	0.52
H						0.9249
H*						0.5715

fourth rule set (L_0R_4) develops L, D → L, D, (L, D), being a ring-like structure that is the only loop in the final JPG of the *Roberts House*. The sixth rule set (L_0R_6) connects the core node to the exterior by $N_{C0} → N_{C0}$, E, (N_{C0}, E). For the first floor, the s-JPG grammar generates one simple tree structure at the syntax head stage (L_1R_2). L_1R_7 connects two different topological levels, ground floor (L_0) and first floor (L_1), linking N_{C0} to H_{C1}. Finally, the generating process is terminated by L_1R_8.

The syntactical structure of the *Roberts House* (Table 3) has a mean total depth (*TD*) of 20.60 and the mean depth (*MD*) of rooms is 2.29. The most accessible nodes are both core nodes (*MD* = 1.44 for entry and 1.67 for hall),

Figure 3. Roberts House, annotated plan, sector diagram and JPG production

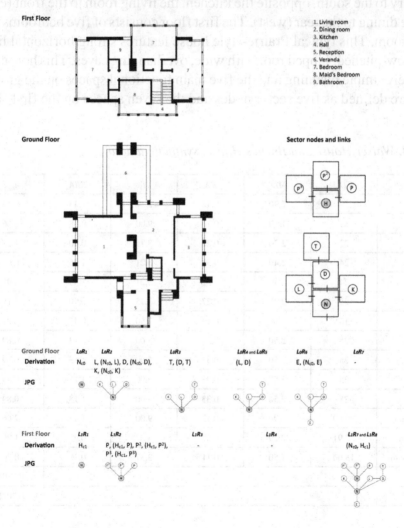

273

followed by the dining ($MD = 2.00$) and the living ($MD = 2.11$) nodes. The most accessible or integrated nodes are the entry ($i_{RRA} = 2.75$) and the hall ($i_{RRA} = 1.84$). In contrast, the transit node is the least integrated sector ($i_{RRA} = 0.52$), followed by the private nodes ($i_{RRA} = 0.79$). The H^* measure of 0.5715 is in the middle range and the most balanced result of the nineteen cases.

Walser House and Barnes House

The *Walser* and *Barnes* houses were designed by Wright for different clients and in different locations, but they had similar floor plans and identical s-JPG grammar productions and syntactical values. The 1903 *Walser House* is located on Central Avenue in Chicago, Illinois. It has a cruciform plan, with the entry to the south, opposite the kitchen, the living room to the front (east) and the dining to the rear (west). The first floor consists of five bedrooms and a bathroom. This typical Prairie-style house features strong horizontal lines and a low-pitched, hipped roof with wide, overhanging eaves. This house has relatively simple planning and the five main functional spaces on the ground floor are defined as five sector nodes and the seven spaces on the first floor

Table 4. Walser House and Barnes House, syntactical data

Node	TD_n	MD_n	RA	i	RRA	i_{RRA}
E	29	2.90	0.42	2.37	1.43	0.70
H	15	1.50	0.11	9.00	0.38	2.66
N	22	2.20	0.27	3.75	0.90	1.11
L	24	2.40	0.31	3.21	1.05	0.95
D	24	2.40	0.31	3.21	1.05	0.95
K	22	2.20	0.27	3.75	0.90	1.11
H^2	16	1.60	0.13	7.50	0.45	2.21
P	25	2.50	0.33	3.00	1.13	0.89
P^2	25	2.50	0.33	3.00	1.13	0.89
P^3	25	2.50	0.33	3.00	1.13	0.89
P^4	25	2.50	0.33	3.00	1.13	0.89
Maximum	29.00	2.90	0.42	9.00	1.43	2.66
Mean	22.91	2.29	0.29	4.07	0.97	1.20
Minimum	15.00	1.50	0.11	2.37	0.38	0.70
H						0.9801
H^*						0.7076

Figure 4. Walser House, annotated plan, sector diagram and JPG production

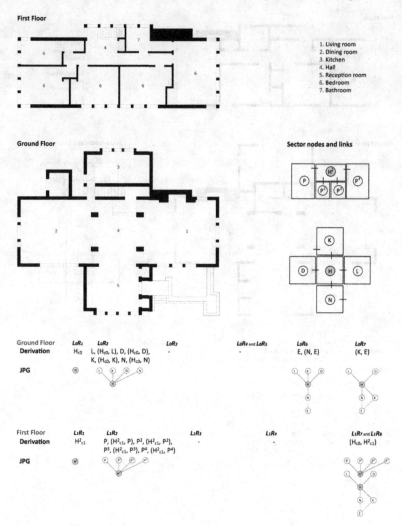

are merged into a hall and four private nodes in the sector diagram (Figure 4). The 1904 *Barnes House* in McCook, Nebraska, was designed for Charles Wood Barnes, who did not proceed with Wright's design (Figure 5). It was proposed to have slightly different window configurations and proportions to the *Walser House*, along with a brick entry arch and a coal cellar or store.

The s-JPG grammar for the two houses generates simple tree structures at the syntax head stages of both floors (L_0R_2 and L_1R_2), which are the major rule sets that shape the syntactical structure of the JPG. The seventh rule set (L_0R_7), connecting the kitchen node to the exterior by K, E → K, E, (K, E),

Figure 5. Barnes House, annotated plan, sector diagram and JPG production

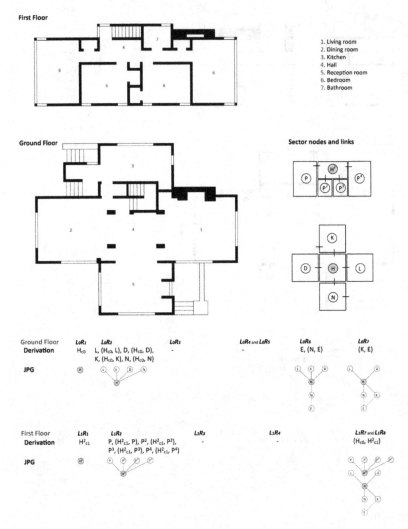

develops a ring-like structure that is the only non-trivial loop in the JPG. The *Walser House* and the *Barnes House* plans have a mean total depth (*TD*) of 22.91 with eleven sector nodes. The most integrated node is the hall (i_{RRA} = 2.66), followed by the second hall on the first floor (i_{RRA} = 2.21). The least integrated nodes are the exterior (i_{RRA} = 0.70) and the private nodes (i_{RRA} = 0.89). The two hall nodes (or the entry) with the stairway are naturally the most integrated, while the private nodes are often isolated in Wright's Prairie works. The *H** measure of 0.7076 suggests a low level of determination or deliberation towards the undifferentiated.

Mary W. Adams House

The *Mary W. Adams House* was constructed in 1905 in Highland Park, Illinois. With the exception of the addition of two verandas, its cruciform plan and central fireplace are reminiscent of the plan of Wright's design for *Fireproof House for $5000*, published in the *Ladies Home Journal* in 1907. This plan could be thought of as a transitional stage between the rectangular or square forms of the early Prairie style and the later T-shaped or truncated cruciform plans. In this particular case, to improve the view from the dining room, Wright interchanged the location of the kitchen with the dining room.

The first rule set (L_0R_1) of the s-JPG grammar transforms a start symbol into a core node (hall) by $S_0 \rightarrow H_{c0}$. The second rule set (L_0R_2) adds four major sector nodes (entry, living, dining and kitchen) that are typically in the four wings of the cruciform shape. This combination of four rules is a frequently used rule set; $H_{C0} \rightarrow H_{C0}$, L, (H_{C0}, L); $H_{C0} \rightarrow H_{C0}$, D, (H_{C0}, D); $H_{C0} \rightarrow H_{C0}$, K, (H_{C0}, K); and $H_{C0} \rightarrow H_{C0}$, N, (H_{C0}, N). L_0R_3 develops two transit

Table 5. Mary W. Adams House, syntactical data

Node	TD_n	MD_n	RA	i	RRA	i_{RRA}
E	32	2.67	0.30	3.30	1.10	0.91
H	19	1.58	0.11	9.43	0.38	2.60
N	27	2.25	0.23	4.40	0.82	1.21
L	27	2.25	0.23	4.40	0.82	1.21
D	26	2.17	0.21	4.71	0.77	1.30
K	27	2.25	0.23	4.40	0.82	1.21
T	34	2.83	0.33	3.00	1.21	0.83
T^2	38	3.17	0.39	2.54	1.43	0.70
H^2	22	1.83	0.15	6.60	0.55	1.82
P	32	2.67	0.30	3.30	1.10	0.91
P^2	32	2.67	0.30	3.30	1.10	0.91
P^3	33	2.75	0.32	3.14	1.15	0.87
P^S	33	2.75	0.32	3.14	1.15	0.87
Maximum	38.00	3.17	0.39	9.43	1.43	2.60
Mean	29.38	2.45	0.26	4.28	0.95	1.18
Minimum	19.00	1.58	0.11	2.54	0.38	0.70
H						0.9828
H*						0.7143

Figure 6. Mary W. Adams House, annotated plan, sector diagram and JPG production

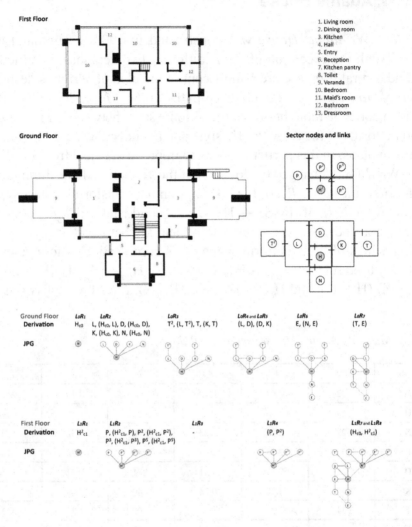

nodes extended from the living room and kitchen by L → L, T², (L, T²) and K → K, T, (K, T). The fourth rule set (L_0R_4) develops two links by L, D → L, D, (L, D) and D, K → D, K, (D, K), creating two ring-like structures. The sixth rule set (L_0R_6) connects the hall to the exterior by H_{C0} → H_{C0}, E, (H_{C0}, E). The final rule set for the ground floor develops a link between the transit and exterior nodes that also forms a circulation loop. For the first floor, the s-JPG grammar generates a tree structure at its second rule set (L_1R_2) and adds a link between the private and second private nodes by P, P² → P, P², (P, P²). The application of the second and the seventh rule sets results in the four non-trivial loops of the final JPG. The mean total depth (*TD*) of the house is

29.38, with thirteen sector nodes (Table 5). The most integrated node is the hall ($i_{RRA} = 2.60$), followed by the second hall ($i_{RRA} = 1.82$) and dining room ($i_{RRA} = 1.30$). The least integrated nodes are the transit nodes ($i_{RRA} = 0.70$ and 0.83). Interestingly, the transit nodes in the Prairie style tend to be segregated.

Sutton House

The *Sutton House* is in McCook, Nebraska, near the planned site of the *Barnes House*. Built in 1905, this classic Prairie Style design has the fireplace and living room in the centre of the cruciform plan, instead of a hall space. Thus, the four wings surrounding the living room are the dining, kitchen, entry and veranda (Figure 7). The northern wing of the cruciform plan has the kitchen with a sub-entrance, while the entry space with a stairway in the east wing provides both interior and exterior circulation. There are two unusual planning elements in this design, with a bedroom in the corner between the north and east wings and a balcony space in the northeast corner of the first floor.

Table 6. Sutton House, syntactical data

Node	TD_n	MD_n	RA	i	RRA	i_{RRA}
E	29	2.42	0.26	3.88	0.93	1.07
N	21	1.75	0.14	7.33	0.49	2.02
L	26	2.17	0.21	4.71	0.77	1.30
D	35	2.92	0.35	2.87	1.26	0.79
K	34	2.83	0.33	3.00	1.21	0.83
T	37	3.08	0.38	2.64	1.37	0.73
P	32	2.67	0.30	3.30	1.10	0.91
H	22	1.83	0.15	6.60	0.55	1.82
P^2	33	2.75	0.32	3.14	1.15	0.87
P^3	33	2.75	0.32	3.14	1.15	0.87
P^4	31	2.58	0.29	3.47	1.04	0.96
P^5	42	3.50	0.45	2.20	1.65	0.61
T^2	33	2.75	0.32	3.14	1.15	0.87
Maximum	42.00	3.50	0.45	7.33	1.65	2.02
Mean	31.38	2.62	0.29	3.80	1.06	1.05
Minimum	21.00	1.75	0.14	2.20	0.49	0.61
H						0.9964
H*						0.7480

Six sector nodes are defined for each floor by the s-JPG grammar. After the first rule set defines the entry and core (N), the second rule set (L_0R_2) adds two sector nodes (living and private) and their links, while L_0R_3 develops the other three sector nodes (dining, kitchen and transit) and links from the living room by L → L, D, (L, D); L → L, K, (L, K); and L → L, T, (L, T). Compared to the previous cases, the living room (L) provides more connections to the other nodes than the core node (N). L_0R_4 and L_0R_7 develop two "ring-like" structures that are only two non-trivial loops in the final JPG.

The syntactical properties of the *Sutton House* (Table 6) include a mean total depth (*TD*) of 31.38 and mean depth (*MD*) of rooms in the house of 2.62. The most isolated nodes in the configuration are, in order, the fifth

Figure 7. Sutton House, annotated plan, sector diagram and JPG production

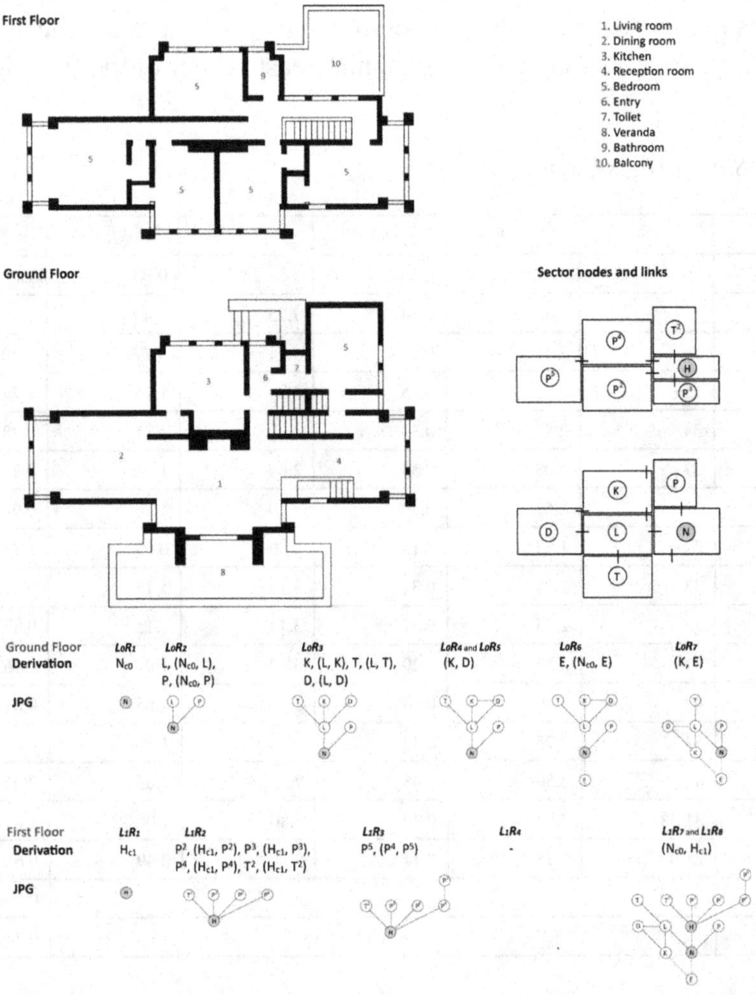

private node ($MD = 3.50$), the transit node ($MD = 3.08$) and the dining node ($MD = 2.92$). Interestingly, the dining and kitchen nodes are more segregated than most of the private nodes. This may be caused by the centralised living room. Conversely, the relatively accessible nodes are the entry ($MD = 1.75$), hall ($MD = 1.83$) and living ($MD = 2.17$) and the integration values confirm the entry ($i_{RRA} = 2.02$) and hall ($i_{RRA} = 1.82$) are the most integrated pair of nodes. The transit, dining and kitchen nodes are relatively isolated (ranging from 0.73 to 0.83). The $H*$ measure of 0.7480 is towards the undifferentiated spectrum of indicators.

Brown House

The *Brown House* was commissioned in 1906 by Harry E. Brown as his family residence in Genesco, Illinois. Although the house was not built, it is

Table 7. Brown House, syntactical data

Node	TD_n	MD_n	RA	i	RRA	i_{RRA}
E	41	2.93	0.30	3.37	1.15	0.87
H	44	3.14	0.33	3.03	1.27	0.79
N	26	1.86	0.13	7.58	0.51	1.96
L	35	2.50	0.23	4.33	0.89	1.12
D	40	2.86	0.29	3.50	1.10	0.91
K	35	2.50	0.23	4.33	0.89	1.12
T	34	2.43	0.22	4.55	0.85	1.18
T²	46	3.29	0.35	2.84	1.36	0.74
L²	40	2.86	0.29	3.50	1.10	0.91
H²	29	2.07	0.16	6.07	0.64	1.57
P	42	3.00	0.31	3.25	1.19	0.84
P²	42	3.00	0.31	3.25	1.19	0.84
P³	42	3.00	0.31	3.25	1.19	0.84
P⁴	42	3.00	0.31	3.25	1.19	0.84
S	42	3.00	0.31	3.25	1.19	0.84
Maximum	46.00	3.29	0.35	7.58	1.36	1.96
Mean	38.67	2.76	0.27	3.96	1.05	1.03
Minimum	26.00	1.86	0.13	2.84	0.51	0.74
H						1.0284
H*						0.8269

regarded as Wright's first attempt to use a concrete block construction system. The plan is also unusual because it has several of the properties of Wright's typical cruciform layouts, but the northeast and northwest corners, which are normally empty, are filled with functional spaces (Figure 8). That is, the four wings of the traditional "pinwheel" plan are expanded and the main spatial programs are distributed into the resulting rectangular-plan. This plan form has some similarities to that of Wright's compact, square-form version of the Prairie style (in, for example, the *Nichols House* or the *Fireproof House*). Only two transit nodes provide a formal clue to the vertical axis of the Prairie style that is embedded in the plan. The entry, including a stairway, is in the

Figure 8. Brown House, annotated plan, sector diagram and JPG production

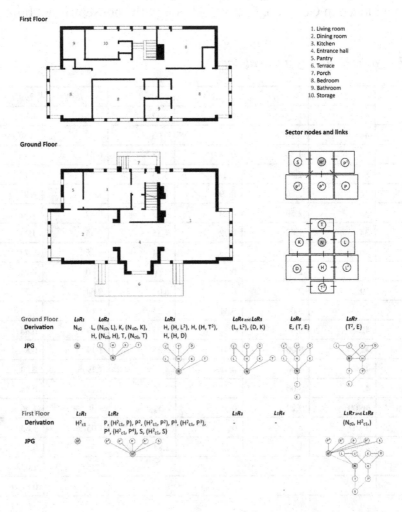

northern centre of the plan, while the living room is to the east. Following the standard approach of defining sector nodes to take into account functional and modular changes, the living room is developed into two nodes (see the sector diagram in Figure 8). In this way, the s-JPG grammar for the *Brown House* deals with 15 nodes (including the exterior).

The second and third rule sets (L_0R_2 and L_0R_3) of the s-JPG grammar develop a "bush-like" structure, while L_0R_4 and L_0R_7 formulate three non-trivial loops at the ground floor. The entry provides a constant point of connection between the two floors as well as indoor circulation loops through the hall node. The second hall node provides a basic connection to the other nodes at the first floor. The total depth of the deepest node in the *Brown House* is 46 (the second transit node) and, interestingly, the hall node is the second most isolated node ($MD = 3.14$) (Table 7) This occurs because the hall node (entrance hall) is related to the local syntax (configured by L_0R_3) so that it is far from the private nodes at the first floor. The more accessible nodes are the entry ($MD = 1.86$) and the second hall node ($MD = 2.07$). Similarly, the entry node is the most integrated space ($i_{RRA} = 1.96$), while the second transit node is the least integrated space ($i_{RRA} = 0.74$). The H^* measure of 0.8269 suggests a low level of determination or deliberation.

DeRhodes House

The 1906 *DeRhodes House* is located in South Bend, Indiana. This home has planning that is reminiscent of Wright's 1904 *Barton House* in Buffalo. The four functional sectors (entry, living, dining and kitchen) on the ground floor are separated into the wings of the plan, with the hall sector in the centre of the cruciform layout. Thus, the spatial configuration is similar to that of the *F. W. Little House*, but the horizontal axis is south to north. That is, the entry node is to the east (not south) and the kitchen to the west (not north). Whilst the *F. W. Little House* has expanded interior living and dining rooms, two terraces to the north and south ends of the *DeRhodes House* extend the living and dining spaces into the exterior (Figure 9).

The grammatical analysis of the *DeRhodes House* reveals that a "tree-like" structure at the head syntax (L_0R_2) becomes a deeper system at the third rule set (L_0R_3) by adding three nodes and links, T, (D, T), T^2, (L, T^2), and S, (K, S). However, the sixth rule set (L_0R_6) connects the entry node to the exterior by N → N, E, (N, E) and the seventh rule set (L_0R_7) links three nodes to the exterior by T → T, E, (T, E); T → T^2, E, (T^2, E); and K → K, E, (K, E). As

Table 8. DeRhodes House, syntactical data

Node	TD_n	MD_n	RA	i	RRA	i_{RRA}
E	27	2.25	0.23	4.40	0.82	1.21
H	19	1.58	0.11	9.43	0.38	2.60
N	26	2.17	0.21	4.71	0.77	1.30
L	27	2.25	0.23	4.40	0.82	1.21
D	27	2.25	0.23	4.40	0.82	1.21
K	24	2.00	0.18	5.50	0.66	1.52
T	31	2.58	0.29	3.47	1.04	0.96
T^2	31	2.58	0.29	3.47	1.04	0.96
S	35	2.92	0.35	2.87	1.26	0.79
H^2	24	2.00	0.18	5.50	0.66	1.52
P	35	2.92	0.35	2.87	1.26	0.79
P^2	35	2.92	0.35	2.87	1.26	0.79
P^3	35	2.92	0.35	2.87	1.26	0.79
Maximum	35.00	2.92	0.35	9.43	1.26	2.60
Mean	28.92	2.41	0.26	4.37	0.93	1.21
Minimum	19.00	1.58	0.11	2.87	0.38	0.79
H						1.0011
H*						0.7596

a result, the global syntax of the JPG at the ground floor becomes a shallow system with four ring-like structures. In contrast, the s-JPG grammar for the first floor develops a simple tree structure at the syntax head stage (L_1R_2). Table 8 provides the syntactical results of the grammatical productions. The most integrated space is the hall $(i_{RRA} = 2.60)$ and the least integrated space is the private node $(i_{RRA} = 0.79)$. Interestingly, the kitchen node and second hall node are the next most integrated $(i_{RRA} = 1.52)$. The living, kitchen and exterior integration measures are also the same $(i_{RRA} = 1.21)$. The H* measure of 0.7596 belongs toward the undifferentiated spectrum of indicators, like many other Prairie style designs, confirming a similar looseness or flexibility in the planning.

Nichols House

The *Nichols House* is located on the south side of Chicago, Illinois, and was constructed in 1906. This summer house has a square-shaped plan that is

Figure 9. DeRhodes House, annotated plan, sector diagram and JPG production

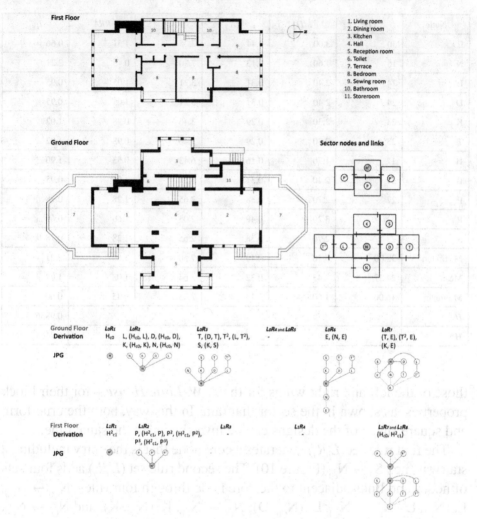

First Floor

1. Living room
2. Dining room
3. Kitchen
4. Hall
5. Reception room
6. Toilet
7. Terrace
8. Bedroom
9. Sewing room
10. Bathroom
11. Storeroom

Ground Floor

Sector nodes and links

Ground Floor Derivation	LoR₁	LoR₂	LoR₃	LoR₄ and LoR₅	LoR₆	LoR₇
	H_{co}	L, (H_{co}, L), D, (H_{co}, D), K, (H_{co}, K), N, (H_{co}, N)	T, (D, T), T², (L, T²), S, (K, S)	-	E, (N, E)	(T, E), (T², E), (K, E)
JPG						

First Floor Derivation	L₁R₁	L₁R₂	L₁R₃	L₁R₄	L₁R₇ and L₁R₈
	H^2_{c1}	P, (H^2_{c1}, P), P², (H^2_{c1}, P²), P³, (H^2_{c1}, P³)	-	-	(H_{co}, H^2_{c1})
JPG					

effectively a mirrored version of the 1907 *Fireproof House* plan. With its compact planning, the *Nichols House* shares many traits with the American "foursquare" home (also known as the "Prairie Box"). On the ground floor, the living room is to the front of the house and the dining room and kitchen are to the back (Figure 10). A stairwell and entrance space depart from the foursquare tradition and, as a result, the living room occupies half of the ground floor area. There is no clear wall or partition between the living and dining rooms, but a central fireplace effectively divides the spaces. The stairwell is defined as a core node for the s-JPG grammar and the porch space is a transit node. The living and dining room are defined as vertical modules – like

Table 9. Nichols House, syntactical data

Node	TD_n	MD_n	RA	i	RRA	i_{RRA}
E	30	3.00	0.44	2.25	1.51	0.66
N	16	1.60	0.13	7.50	0.45	2.21
L	24	2.40	0.31	3.21	1.05	0.95
D	24	2.40	0.31	3.21	1.05	0.95
K	23	2.30	0.29	3.46	0.98	1.02
T	23	2.30	0.29	3.46	0.98	1.02
H	17	1.70	0.16	6.43	0.53	1.90
P	24	2.40	0.31	3.21	1.05	0.95
P^2	27	2.70	0.38	2.65	1.28	0.78
P^3	32	3.20	0.49	2.05	1.66	0.60
S	27	2.70	0.38	2.65	1.28	0.78
Maximum	32.00	3.20	0.49	7.50	1.66	2.21
Mean	24.27	2.43	0.32	3.64	1.08	1.07
Minimum	16.00	1.60	0.13	2.05	0.45	0.60
H						0.9836
H*						0.7164

those of the left and right wings for the *F. W. Little House* – for their block properties, as shown in the sector diagram. In this way, both the cruciform and square shape of the designs can be investigated at the same time.

The first rule set $(L_0 R_1)$ generates a core node that is the entry including a stairway, i.e., $S_0 \rightarrow N_{c0}$ (Figure 10). The second rule set $(L_0 R_2)$ adds four sets of nodes and links adjacent to the core node through four rules, $N_{C0} \rightarrow N_{C0}$, L, (N_{C0}, L); $N_{C0} \rightarrow N_{C0}$, D, (N_{C0}, D); $N_{C0} \rightarrow N_{C0}$, K, (N_{C0}, K); and $N_{C0} \rightarrow N_{C0}$, T, (N_{C0}, T), producing the head syntax of the JPG. The fourth rule set $(L_0 R_4)$ develops L, D → L, D, (L, D), being a ring-like structure. The sixth rule set $(L_0 R_6)$ connects the core node to the exterior by $N_{C0} \rightarrow N_{C0}$, E, (N_{C0}, E). The seventh rule set $(L_0 R_7)$ develops another ring-like structure by K, E → K, E, (K, E). For the first floor, the s-JPG grammar generates a simple tree structure at the syntax head stage $(L_1 R_2)$ and the third private node (P^3) is then generated from the private node (P) by the third rule set $(L_1 R_3)$. $L_1 R_7$ connects N_{C0} with $H_{C1,}$ and $L_1 R_8$ terminates the generating process. Table 1 show that the mean total depth (*TD*) of the house is 24.27 and the mean depth (*MD*) of rooms in the house is 2.43. The two most isolated nodes in the configuration are the third private sector (*MD* = 3.20) and exterior (*MD* = 3.00). As in many of

Figure 10. Nichols House, annotated plan, sector diagram and JPG production

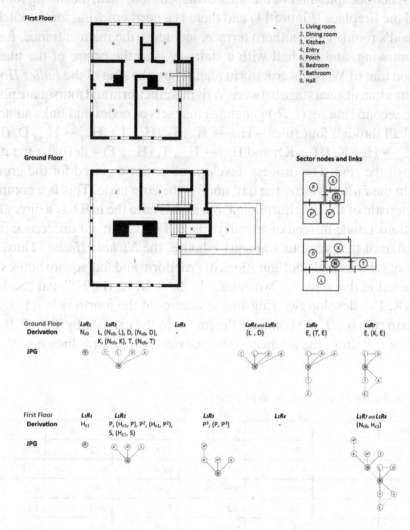

Wright's Prairie houses the exterior is often more segregated than the other nodes. The integration values indicate that the entry (i_{RRA} = 2.21) is double the average value for the house, while the private nodes ranges from 0.60 to 0.95. This order is common in Wright's square-plan houses.

Fuller House

The *Fuller House* is a suburban cottage designed for Miss Grace Fuller in Glencoe, Illinois, in 1906. As a variation of Wright's foursquare house, the living space occupies half of the square-shaped floor plan, the dining room is behind the fireplace (Figure 11) and there is a northern wing for the kitchen and maid's room. The southern terrace, including the main entrance, forms the front wing, and the hall with a stairway is in the centre of the plan, a common trait of Wright's cruciform plan. Thus, the plan of the *Fuller House* suggests a transitional stage between Wright's cruciform and foursquare plans.

The second rule set (L_0R_2) generates four sets of nodes and links adjacent to the hall through four rules – $H_{C0} \rightarrow H_{C0}$, L, (H_{C0}, L); $H_{C0} \rightarrow H_{C0}$, D, (H_{C0}, D); $H_{C0} \rightarrow H_{C0}$, K, (H_{C0}, K); and $H_{C0} \rightarrow H_{C0}$, T, (H_{C0}, T) – defining the head syntax of the JPG. The process develops all nodes required for the ground floor. In the *Fuller House,* the hall node is the core node. This is a common characteristic of the cruciform plan, but in this case the hall has a direct link to the transit node instead of an entry space. This is a major difference from the design of the previous foursquare house, the *Nichols House.* Thus, the functional and formal configurations of cruciform and foursquare houses are also mixed in this design. Two rules, "D, K $\rightarrow$ D, K, (D, K)" and "K, L $\rightarrow$ K, L, (K, L)', develop two ring-like structures at the fourth rule set (L_0R_4). The sixth rule set (L_0R_6) connects the transit to the exterior by T $\rightarrow$ T, E, (T, E), while L_0R_6 links the kitchen to the exterior. In this way, three non-trivial

Table 10. *Fuller House, syntactical data*

Node	TD_n	MD_n	RA	i	RRA	i_{RRA}
E	23	2.56	0.39	2.57	1.27	0.79
H	13	1.44	0.11	9.00	0.36	2.75
L	18	2.00	0.25	4.00	0.82	1.22
D	18	2.00	0.25	4.00	0.82	1.22
K	18	2.00	0.25	4.00	0.82	1.22
T	18	2.00	0.25	4.00	0.82	1.22
H^2	16	1.78	0.19	5.14	0.64	1.57
P	23	2.56	0.39	2.57	1.27	0.79
P^2	23	2.56	0.39	2.57	1.27	0.79
P^3	23	2.56	0.39	2.57	1.27	0.79
Maximum	23.00	2.56	0.39	9.00	1.27	2.75
Mean	19.30	2.14	0.29	4.04	0.94	1.24
Minimum	13.00	1.44	0.11	2.57	0.36	0.79
H						0.9926
H^*						0.7385

Figure 11. Fuller House, annotated plan, sector diagram and JPG production

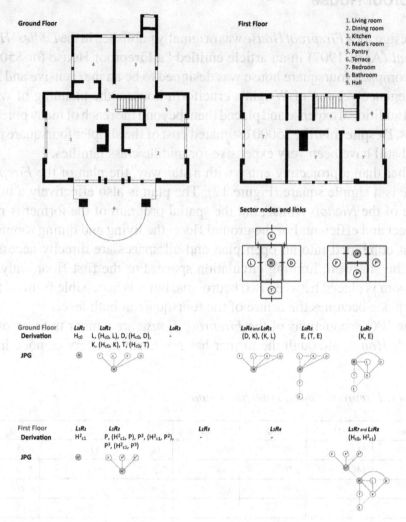

loops are developed from the kitchen. Four nodes (L, D, K, T) at the four wings, consequently, have the same syntactical properties (*MD* is 2.00 and $i_{RRA} = 1.22$) which are close to the average values in Table 10. For the first floor, the s-JPG grammar generates three private nodes at the second rule set (L_1R_2), leading to a simple tree structure. After skipping the other rule sets, L_1R_7 connects H_{C0} with H^2_{C1} and L_1R_8 terminates the process. As a result, the private nodes are the most isolated (*MD* = 2.56) and the least integrated (i_{RRA} = 0.79). The exterior is also the most isolated node, while the hall nodes are the most integrated. This result is similar to many of the Prairie houses.

Fireproof House

The design for a *Fireproof House* was originally published in the *Ladies' Home Journal* (April 1907) in an article entitled "a Fireproof House for $5000". This compact, foursquare house was designed to be an inexpensive and low-maintenance version of Wright's cruciform houses, the planning of which added additional expense and placed them beyond the reach of many potential clients. Despite this, the $5000 estimated cost of the simpler foursquare plan, would still have been very expensive for middle class families.

Other than a projecting entry with a stairway, the plan of the *Fireproof House* is a simple square (Figure 12). The plan is also effectively a mirror image of the *Nichols House*, but the spatial program of the former is more compact and efficient. For the ground floor, the living and dining rooms are almost combined into an open plan and all spaces are directly accessible from the stairwell, limiting circulation space. For the first floor, only one bathroom is placed between two bedrooms, but it is accessible from all four. A fireplace occupies the centre of the foursquare at both levels.

The JPG productions of the *Fireproof House* are similar to those of the *Nichols House*, although the former has no transit and service node in the

Table 11. Fireproof House, syntactical data

Node	TD_n	MD_n	RA	i	RRA	i_{RRA}
E	21	2.33	0.33	3.00	1.09	0.92
N	14	1.56	0.14	7.20	0.45	2.20
L	21	2.33	0.33	3.00	1.09	0.92
D	21	2.33	0.33	3.00	1.09	0.92
K	21	2.33	0.33	3.00	1.09	0.92
H	14	1.56	0.14	7.20	0.45	2.20
P	22	2.44	0.36	2.77	1.18	0.85
P^2	22	2.44	0.36	2.77	1.18	0.85
P^3	20	2.22	0.31	3.27	1.00	1.00
P^4	28	3.11	0.53	1.89	1.72	0.58
Maximum	28.00	3.11	0.53	7.20	1.72	2.20
Mean	20.40	2.27	0.32	3.71	1.03	1.14
Minimum	14.00	1.56	0.14	1.89	0.45	0.58
H						0.9753
H^*						0.6960

Figure 12. Fireproof House, annotated plan, sector diagram and JPG production

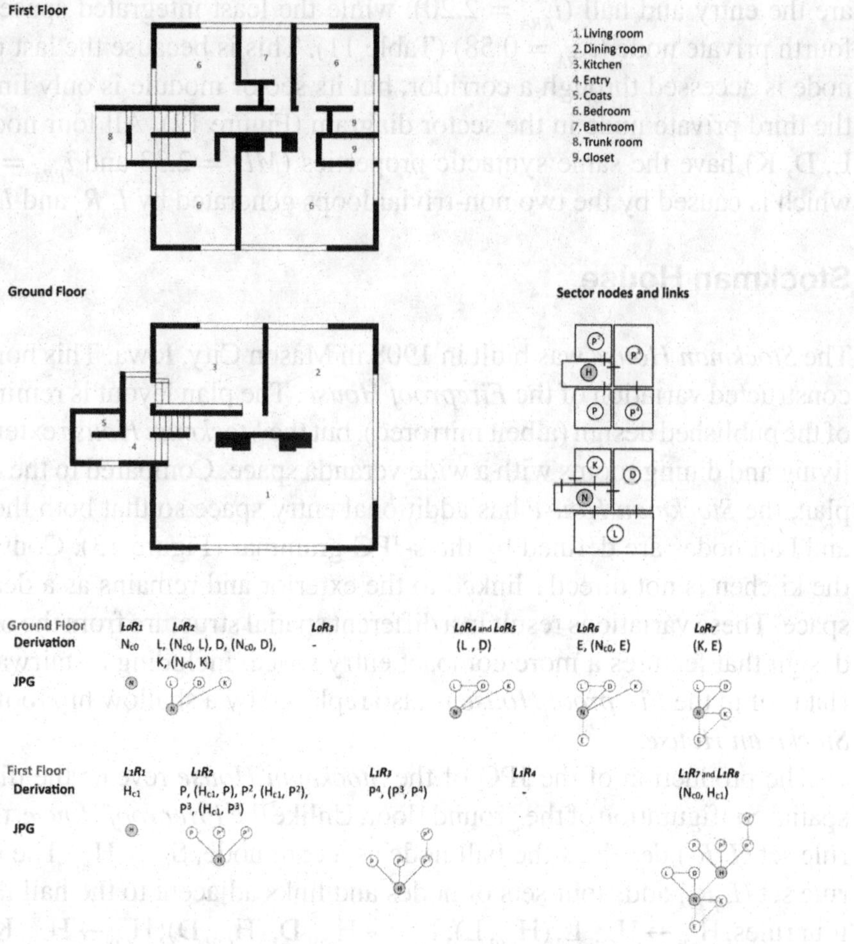

sector diagram (Figure 12). The bathroom of the earlier case was separately located at the northeast corner of the plan, while in the *Fireproof House* the bathroom space is merged into the third private node due to its formal sector module. In addition to this difference, the kitchen node is directly connected to the exterior in the *Fireproof House*. Nonetheless, the final JPGs of both cases, as well as their syntactical properties, are very similar. Like the *Nichols House*, the first rule set (L_0R_1) develops the entry node as a core node, $S_0 \rightarrow N_{c0}$. The second rule set (L_0R_2) adds three sets of nodes and links adjacent to the entry through three rules, $N_{CO} \rightarrow N_{CO}$, L, ($N_{CO}$, L); $N_{CO} \rightarrow N_{CO}$, D, ($N_{CO}$, D); and $N_{CO} \rightarrow N_{CO}$, K, ($N_{CO}$, K). The fourth rule set (L_0R_4), L, D → L, D, (L, D), and the seventh rule set (L_0R_7), K, E → K, E, (K, E), develop two non-trivial loops for the final JPG of the *Fireproof House*. The most integrated spaces are the entry and hall (i_{RRA} = 2.20), while the least integrated space is the fourth private node (i_{RRA} = 0.58) (Table 11). This is because the last private node is accessed through a corridor, but its sector module is only linked to the third private node in the sector diagram (Figure 12). All four nodes (E, L, D, K) have the same syntactic properties (*MD* = 2.33 and i_{RRA} = 0.92), which is caused by the two non-trivial loops generated by L_0R_4 and L_0R_7.

Stockman House

The *Stockman House* was built in 1908 in Mason City, Iowa. This home is a constructed variation of the *Fireproof House*. The plan layout is reminiscent of the published design (albeit mirrored), but the *Stockman House* extends the living and dining rooms with a wide veranda space. Compared to the former plan, the *Stockman House* has additional entry space so that both the entry and hall nodes are defined by the s-JPG grammar (Figure 13). Conversely, the kitchen is not directly linked to the exterior and remains as a dead-end space. These variations result in a different spatial structure from the original design that features a more compact entry space, including a stairway. The flat roof in the *Fireproof House* is also replaced by a shallow hip roof in the *Stockman House*.

The production of the JPG of the *Stockman House* reveals the different spatial configuration of the ground floor. Unlike the *Fireproof House*, the first rule set (L_0R_1) develops the hall node as a core node, $S_0 \rightarrow H_{c0}$. The second rule set (L_0R_2) adds four sets of nodes and links adjacent to the hall through four rules, $H_{C0} \rightarrow H_{C0}$, L, ($H_{C0}$, L); $H_{C0} \rightarrow H_{C0}$, D, ($H_{C0}$, D); $H_{C0} \rightarrow H_{C0}$, K, ($H_{C0}$, K); and $H_{C0} \rightarrow H_{C0}$, N, ($H_{C0}$, N). The set of four rules is a frequently-used rule set for the cruciform designs that is also found in the *Walser House* and the *Mary W. Adams House*. L_0R_3 develops a transit node extending the living and dining room by D $\rightarrow$ D, T, (D, T). The fourth rule set (L_0R_4) develops three non-trivial loops by L, N $\rightarrow$ L, N, (L, N); L, D $\rightarrow$ L, D, (L, D); and L, T $\rightarrow$ L, T, (L, T) and the seventh rule set (L_0R_7), T, E $\rightarrow$ T, E, (T, E), develops one more circulation loop for the final JPG (Figure 13). Thus, a shallow spatial system is constructed for the ground floor of the *Stockman House*.

The mean total depth (*TD*) of the *Stockman House* is 27.00 and the mean depth (*MD*) of rooms in the house is 2.45 (Table 12). The most isolated node in the configuration is the fourth private node (*MD* = 3.45) and the exterior is the next most isolated node (*MD* = 2.82). Conversely, the relatively accessible

Table 12. *Stockman House, syntactical data*

Node	TD_n	MD_n	RA	i	RRA	i_{RRA}
E	31	2.82	0.36	2.75	1.28	0.78
H	18	1.64	0.13	7.86	0.45	2.24
N	24	2.18	0.24	4.23	0.83	1.21
L	23	2.09	0.22	4.58	0.77	1.31
D	24	2.18	0.24	4.23	0.83	1.21
K	28	2.55	0.31	3.24	1.08	0.92
T	30	2.73	0.35	2.89	1.21	0.83
H^2	20	1.82	0.16	6.11	0.57	1.74
P	30	2.73	0.35	2.89	1.21	0.83
P^2	30	2.73	0.35	2.89	1.21	0.83
P^3	28	2.55	0.31	3.24	1.08	0.92
P^4	38	3.45	0.49	2.04	1.72	0.58
Maximum	38.00	3.45	0.49	7.86	1.72	2.24
Mean	27.00	2.45	0.29	3.91	1.02	1.12
Minimum	18.00	1.64	0.13	2.04	0.45	0.58
H						0.9726
H*						0.6893

nodes are the hall ($MD = 1.64$) on the ground floor and the second hall ($MD = 1.82$) on the first floor. The integration values confirm that the hall ($i_{RRA} = 2.24$) is double the average value for the house, while the fourth private node has the least integration value ($i_{RRA} = 0.58$). In the *Fireproof House* all four nodes (E, L, D, K) have the same syntactic properties ($i_{RRA} = 0.92$), whereas in the *Stockman House* the living and dining rooms are more accessible than the entry and kitchen.

Baker House

The 1908 *Baker House* is located in Wilmette, Illinois. This Prairie style house has a "T-shaped" plan where the vertical bar consists of living and dining rooms. The left wing of the building has a long porch, while the right is, consequently, occupied by an entry, kitchen and workroom (Figure 14). With a centred fireplace, this dwelling is a variation of Wright's cruciform layout. The size and location of the living room (south wing) and the long porch (west wing) results in the unusual spatial composition of the building.

Figure 13. Stockman House, annotated plan, sector diagram and JPG production

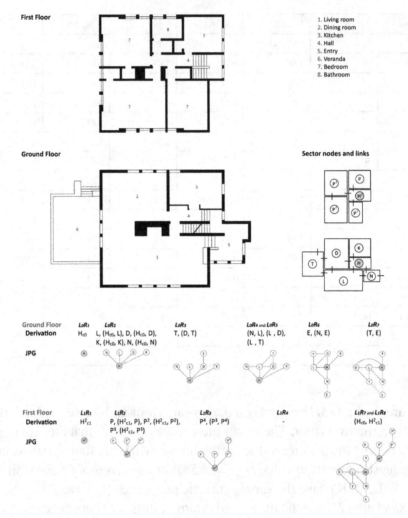

In particular, the first floor is largely sited on the vertical bar of the T-plan, while in most of the other T-shaped Prarie houses the horizontal bar is for the private zone.

Although the T-shaped plan of the *Baker House* is formally close to the cruciform, the spatial configuration is closest to that found in Wright's square-shaped houses (like the *Stockman House* and the *Fireproof House*). The first rule set (L_0R_1) for the *Baker House* develops the entry node, including a stairway, as a core (N_{c0}). The second rule set (L_0R_2) adds three sets of nodes and links adjacent to the entry through three rules, $N_{C0} \to N_{C0}, L, (N_{C0}, L); N_{C0} \to N_{C0}, D, (N_{C0}, D);$ and $N_{C0} \to N_{C0}, K, (N_{C0}, K)$. Like the *Stockman House*,

Table 13. Baker House, syntactical data

Node	TD_n	MD_n	RA	i	RRA	i_{RRA}
E	27	2.45	0.29	3.44	1.02	0.98
N	18	1.64	0.13	7.86	0.45	2.24
L	26	2.36	0.27	3.67	0.96	1.05
D	23	2.09	0.22	4.58	0.77	1.31
K	24	2.18	0.24	4.23	0.83	1.21
T	30	2.73	0.35	2.89	1.21	0.83
S	31	2.82	0.36	2.75	1.28	0.78
H	20	1.82	0.16	6.11	0.57	1.74
P	29	2.64	0.33	3.06	1.15	0.87
P^2	28	2.55	0.31	3.24	1.08	0.92
P^3	38	3.45	0.49	2.04	1.72	0.58
S^2	29	2.64	0.33	3.06	1.15	0.87
Maximum	38.00	3.45	0.49	7.86	1.72	2.24
Mean	26.92	2.45	0.29	3.91	1.02	1.11
Minimum	18.00	1.64	0.13	2.04	0.45	0.58
H						0.9723
H*						0.6886

the transit node (T) extends the dining room into a wide veranda space by D → D, T, (D, T). In addition, a workroom service node is added from the kitchen by K → K, S, (K, S). The fourth rule set $(L_0 R_4)$, L, D → L, D, (L, D) and K, D → K, D, (K, D), and the seventh rule set $(L_0 R_7)$, K, E → K, E, (K, E) and S, E → S, E, (S, E), develop four non-trivial loops for the final JPG. As a result, the dining node with four links is identified as a "d-type" node, minimising depths. The kitchen with three links is also a "d-type" node in the final JPG. Thus, the syntactical data confirms that the integration values of two nodes (D and K) are the third and fourth most integrated (i_{RRA} = 1.31 and 1.21, respectively) (Table 13). The two most integrated nodes are the entry (i_{RRA} = 2.24) and hall (i_{RRA} = 2.24), while the private nodes are the least integrated ones ranging from 0.58 to 0.92. The two service nodes (S and S^2) are also the least integrated (i_{RRA} = 0.78 and 0.87, respectively). The H* measure of 0.6886 implies a slightly more balanced approach to the plan than is seen in the previous cruciform houses (except for the *Roberts House*), although it is still suggestive of a lack of configurational determination.

Figure 14. Baker House, annotated plan, sector diagram and JPG production

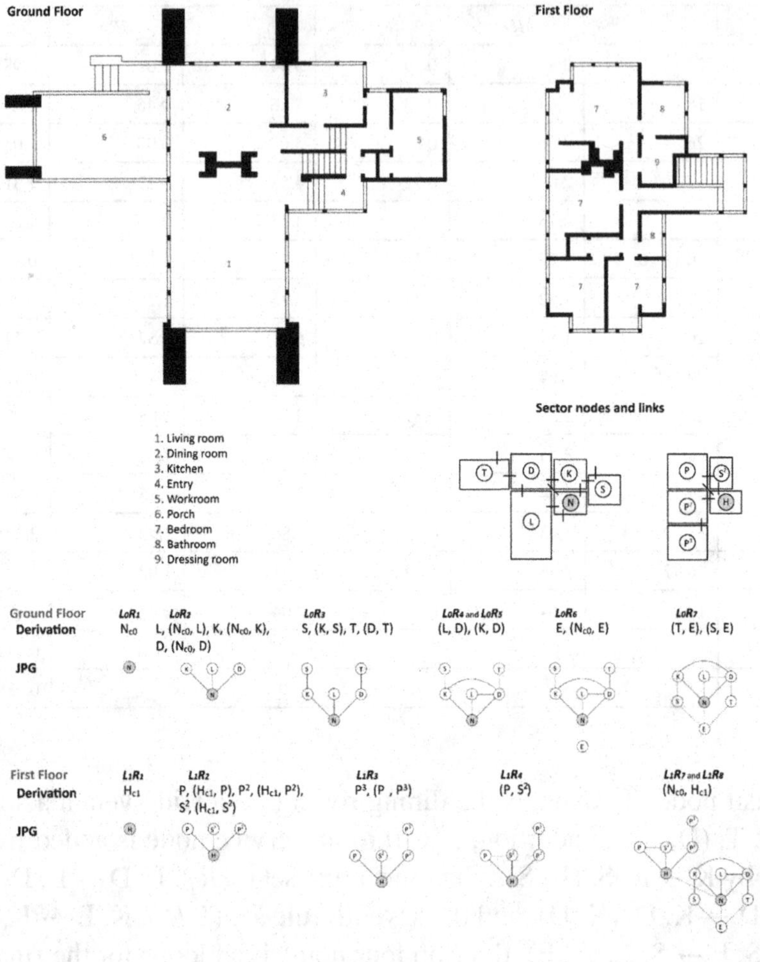

Ground Floor   First Floor

Sector nodes and links

1. Living room
2. Dining room
3. Kitchen
4. Entry
5. Workroom
6. Porch
7. Bedroom
8. Bathroom
9. Dressing room

Ground Floor	LoR_1	LoR_2	LoR_3	LoR_4 and LoR_5	LoR_6	LoR_7
Derivation	N_{co}	L, (N_{co}, L), K, (N_{co}, K), D, (N_{co}, D)	S, (K, S), T, (D, T)	(L, D), (K, D)	E, (N_{co}, E)	(T, E), (S, E)
JPG						

First Floor	L_1R_1	L_1R_2	L_1R_3	L_1R_4	L_1R_7 and L_1R_8
Derivation	H_{c1}	P, (H_{c1}, P), P^2, (H_{c1}, P^2), S^2, (H_{c1}, S^2)	P^3, (P, P^3)	(P, S^2)	(N_{co}, H_{c1})
JPG					

Little House II

The *Little House II* was the second of Wright's designs for Francis and Mary Little. In 1908 the couple commissioned Wright to design their summer home on the shore of Lake Minnetonka, Minnesota, but the design was never built. The plan features a strong cruciform layout of which four wings are extended into porches (Figure 15). Both floors have clearly defined hall spaces, while a stairway is in the right wing of the building. Thus, three hall nodes are identified and provide ring-like connections between spaces.

This design has a complex spatial program, with 18 nodes and 22 links in the sector diagram (Figure 15). The ground floor consists of two halls, four

Table 14. Little House II, syntactical data

Node	TD_n	MD_n	RA	i	RRA	i_{RRA}
E	62	3.65	0.33	3.02	1.40	0.72
H	39	2.29	0.16	6.18	0.68	1.47
H²	34	2.00	0.13	8.00	0.53	1.90
N	50	2.94	0.24	4.12	1.02	0.98
L	51	3.00	0.25	4.00	1.05	0.95
D	41	2.41	0.18	5.67	0.74	1.34
K	43	2.53	0.19	5.23	0.81	1.24
T	53	3.12	0.26	3.78	1.12	0.90
T²	57	3.35	0.29	3.40	1.24	0.81
T³	67	3.94	0.37	2.72	1.55	0.64
T⁴	59	3.47	0.31	3.24	1.30	0.77
Pˢ	56	3.29	0.29	3.49	1.21	0.83
H³	40	2.35	0.17	5.91	0.71	1.40
P	56	3.29	0.29	3.49	1.21	0.83
P²	54	3.18	0.27	3.68	1.15	0.87
P³	53	3.12	0.26	3.78	1.12	0.90
S	56	3.29	0.29	3.49	1.21	0.83
T⁵	69	4.06	0.38	2.62	1.61	0.62
Maximum	69.00	4.06	0.38	8.00	1.61	1.90
Mean	52.22	3.07	0.26	4.21	1.09	1.00
Minimum	34.00	2.00	0.13	2.62	0.53	0.62
H						1.0093
H*						0.7797

main functional nodes (L, D, K, N), a servant bedroom (Pˢ) and four transit nodes. The first floor includes three private nodes, a service node (S) and a transit node (T⁵). As a result, the mean total depth (*TD*) of the house is 52.22 and the mean depth (*MD*) of rooms in the house is 3.07 (Table 14). These are the deepest syntactical values in the nineteen cases. The most isolated node in the configuration is the fifth transit node (*MD* = 4.06) and the exterior is the next isolated node (*MD* = 3.65). The final JPG also confirms the fifth transit note (the private balcony to an upper level bedroom) is located at the sixth depth from the exterior. Conversely, the more accessible nodes are the second hall, including a stairway (*MD* = 2.00), the centred hall (*MD* = 2.29) and the third hall on the first floor (*MD* = 2.35). Like the *Baker House*, the

Figure 15. Little House II, annotated plan, sector diagram and JPG production

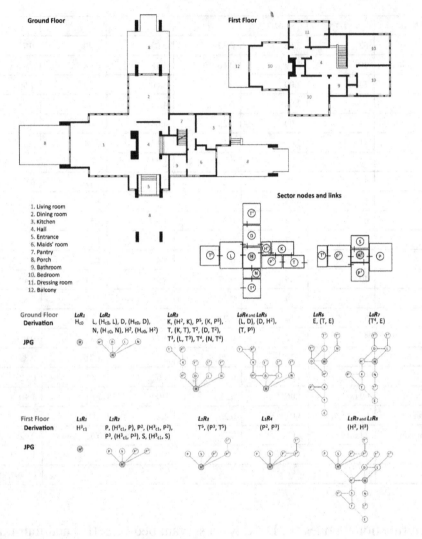

dining node, as a "d-type" node, is relatively integrated ($i_{RRA} = 1.34$) as too is the kitchen ($i_{RRA} = 1.24$). In contrast, the entry and living node are slightly isolated in the spatial structure of this house ($i_{RRA} = 0.98$ and 0.95, respectively).

Larwill House

The 1909 *Larwill House* was designed for Mary Todd Larwill in Muskegon, Michigan. The layout of the house has similarities to a mirrored version of the *Stockman House* or *Baker House* plan. That is, the *Larwill House* plan

Table 15. Larwill House, syntactical data

Node	TD_n	MD_n	RA	i	RRA	i_{RRA}
E	21	2.10	0.24	4.09	0.83	1.21
N	14	1.40	0.09	11.25	0.30	3.32
L	21	2.10	0.24	4.09	0.83	1.21
D	19	1.90	0.20	5.00	0.68	1.48
K	20	2.00	0.22	4.50	0.75	1.33
T	23	2.30	0.29	3.46	0.98	1.02
T^2	28	2.80	0.40	2.50	1.36	0.74
H	17	1.70	0.16	6.43	0.53	1.90
P	26	2.60	0.36	2.81	1.21	0.83
P^2	26	2.60	0.36	2.81	1.21	0.83
P^s	26	2.60	0.36	2.81	1.21	0.83
Maximum	28.00	2.80	0.40	11.25	1.36	3.32
Mean	21.91	2.19	0.26	4.52	0.90	1.33
Minimum	14.00	1.40	0.09	2.50	0.30	0.74
H						0.9558
H*						0.6478

can be interpreted as a transitional design between Wright's compact square-plan houses and the "T-shaped" ones. Like the *Baker House*, the living room occupies the southern wing of the house and a full-size veranda is to the west (Figure 16). In contrast, the entry, stairway, kitchen and dining spaces share the rear of the building, much like a foursquare dwelling. Although the plan layout of the ground floor looks compact, the first floor has three bedrooms, two bathrooms and a servant room. Like the *Stockman House*, the shape of the first floor, excluding the verandas, follows the ground floor.

The first rule set (L_0R_1) develops the entry node as a core node (N_{c0}) and the second rule set (L_0R_2) adds four sets of nodes and links adjacent to the entry: L, (N_{C0}, L); D, (N_{C0}, D); K, (N_{C0}, K); and T, (N_{C0}, T). Like the *Stockman* and *Baker* houses, a full-size veranda (T^2) extends from the dining room by D → D, T^2, (D, T^2). The fourth rule set (L_0R_4), L, D → L, D, (L, D) and K, D → K, D, (K, D), and the seventh rule set (L_0R_7), T, E → T, E, (T, E) and K, E → K, E, (K, E), develops four non-trivial loops. As a result, four nodes (E, N, D, K) are identified as "d-type" nodes, thereby minimising the depth of

Figure 16. Larwill House, annotated plan, sector diagram and JPG production

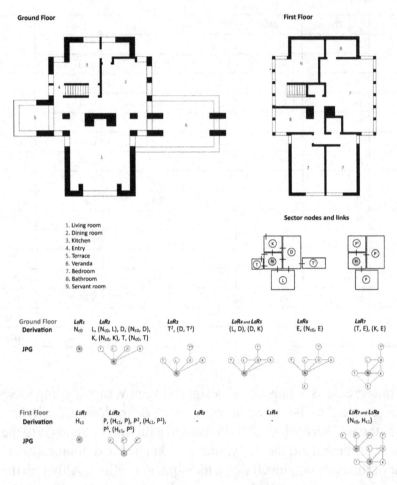

Ground Floor

First Floor

Sector nodes and links

1. Living room
2. Dining room
3. Kitchen
4. Entry
5. Terrace
6. Veranda
7. Bedroom
8. Bathroom
9. Servant room

Ground Floor Derivation	LoR₁	LoR₂	LoR₃	LoR₄ and LoR₅	LoR₆	LoR₇
	N_c0	L, (N_c0, L), D, (N_c0, D), K, (N_c0, K), T, (N_c0, T)	T², (D, T²)	(L, D), (D, K)	E, (N_c0, E)	(T, E), (K, E)

First Floor Derivation	L₁R₁	L₁R₂	L₁R₃	L₁R₄	L₁R₇ and L₁R₈
	H_c1	P, (H_c1, P), P², (H_c1, P²), P⁵, (H_c1, P⁵)	-	-	(N_c0, H_c1)

the plan. The farthest nodes from the exterior are the private nodes and the second transit node, which are only three depths from the carrier. Thus, the final JPG is the most integrated of the nineteen Prairie houses examined in this chapter. For example, the most integrated node is the entry ($i_{RRA} = 3.32$), which has the highest integration value in all cases (Table 15). The syntactical data confirms that the integration values of two "d-type" nodes (D and K) are the third and fourth most integrated ($i_{RRA} = 1.48$ and 1.33, respectively), while the second transit node is the least integrated ($i_{RRA} = 0.74$). The *H** measure of 0.6478 suggests a slightly more balanced approach to the plan than is seen in many previous cases.

Waller House

The 1909 *Waller House* was designed for Edward Waller in River Forest, Illinois, and its square-shaped plan is another variation of the *Fireproof House*. In the *Waller House,* the living room is extended by the inclusion of a full-size porch and a separate entry space from the hall (Figure 17). In addition, the living room faces west, while the dining and kitchen are oriented to the east. Interestingly, the entry node is only linked to the living room, of which the southern part can function as a reception space. The kitchen node is directly linked to the exterior as it is in the *Fireproof House.*

The production of the *Waller House* JPG commences with the first rule set (L_0R_1), which develops the hall node as a core node; $S_0 \rightarrow H_{c0}$ (Figure 17). The second rule set (L_0R_2) adds three sets of nodes and links to the hall through three rules, $H_{C0} \rightarrow H_{C0}$, L, ($H_{C0}$, L); $H_{C0} \rightarrow H_{C0}$, D, ($H_{C0}$, D); and $H_{C0} \rightarrow H_{C0}$, K, ($H_{C0}$, K). L_0R_3 develops a transit node, extending the living room by L $\rightarrow$ L, T, (L, T), in contrast to the previous two cases (*Stockman* and *Baker*), which generated transit nodes from their dining rooms. L_0R_3 also develops

Table 16. Waller House, syntactical data

Node	TD_n	MD_n	RA	i	RRA	i_{RRA}
E	32	2.91	0.38	2.62	1.34	0.75
H	19	1.73	0.15	6.88	0.51	1.96
N	30	2.73	0.35	2.89	1.21	0.83
L	23	2.09	0.22	4.58	0.77	1.31
D	26	2.36	0.27	3.67	0.96	1.05
K	26	2.36	0.27	3.67	0.96	1.05
T	34	3.09	0.42	2.39	1.47	0.68
H^2	21	1.91	0.18	5.50	0.64	1.57
P	29	2.64	0.33	3.06	1.15	0.87
P^2	31	2.82	0.36	2.75	1.28	0.78
P^3	31	2.82	0.36	2.75	1.28	0.78
T^2	39	3.55	0.51	1.96	1.79	0.56
Maximum	39.00	3.55	0.51	6.88	1.79	1.96
Mean	28.42	2.58	0.32	3.56	1.11	1.01
Minimum	19.00	1.73	0.15	1.96	0.51	0.56
H						0.9883
H*						0.7280

Figure 17. Waller House, annotated plan, sector diagram and JPG production

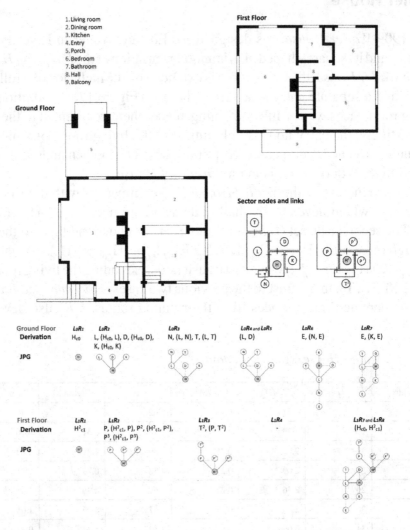

the entry node from the living room by L → L, E, (L, E). The fourth rule set (L_0R_4) generates a link between the living and dining nodes, which is "(L, D)". Thus, the living node is connected to four nodes and consequently is the third most integrated space (i_{RRA} = 1.31). The sixth rule set (L_0R_6), N, E → N, E, (N, E), and the seventh rule set (L_0R_7), K, E → K, E, (K, E), develop two links to the exterior. The syntactical data (Table 16) show that the mean total depth (*TD*) of the house is 28.42 and the mean depth (*MD*) of rooms is 2.58. The most isolated node in the configuration is the second transit node (*MD* = 3.55) and the exterior is the next most isolated node (*MD* = 2.91). The entry without a stairway is also marginally segregated ($MD = 2.73$). Conversely, more accessible nodes are the hall ($MD = 1.73$) at the ground floor and the second hall ($MD = 1.91$) at the first floor. The integration values confirm that the two hall nodes are the most integrated spaces ($i_{RRA} = 1.96$ and 1.57, respectively), while the transit nodes are the least integrated spaces ($i_{RRA} = 0.68$ and 0.56, respectively). The H^* measure of 0.7280 suggests a low level of determination and the value is close to the average (0.7231) of all cases.

Ziegler House

The *Ziegler House* sits on a narrow lot in Frankfort, Kentucky. This 1910 dwelling is another variation of the *Fireproof House*, although in this case the plan is extended through the addition of two porches. The entry hall is directly connected to three main functional areas: living, dining and kitchen (Figure 18). Using a rear stair, the kitchen is accessible from the exterior, as, too, is any room on the first floor, without interrupting the living and dining spaces. The earlier variations of this planning (the *Stockman House*

Table 17. Ziegler House, syntactical data

Node	TD_n	MD_n	RA	i	RRA	i_{RRA}
E	24	2.18	0.24	4.23	0.83	1.21
N	18	1.64	0.13	7.86	0.45	2.24
L	24	2.18	0.24	4.23	0.83	1.21
D	24	2.18	0.24	4.23	0.83	1.21
K	28	2.55	0.31	3.24	1.08	0.92
T	31	2.82	0.36	2.75	1.28	0.78
T^2	31	2.82	0.36	2.75	1.28	0.78
H	20	1.82	0.16	6.11	0.57	1.74
P	30	2.73	0.35	2.89	1.21	0.83
P^2	28	2.55	0.31	3.24	1.08	0.92
P^3	28	2.55	0.31	3.24	1.08	0.92
P^4	37	3.36	0.47	2.12	1.66	0.60
Maximum	37.00	3.36	0.47	7.86	1.66	2.24
Mean	26.92	2.45	0.29	3.91	1.02	1.11
Minimum	18.00	1.64	0.13	2.12	0.45	0.60
H						0.9795
H^*						0.7062

Figure 18. Ziegler House, annotated plan, sector diagram and JPG production

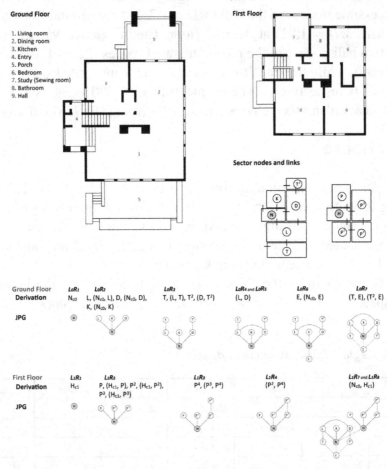

and the *Waller House*) each have one transit zone, whereas the *Ziegler House* extends its living and dining rooms with the southern and northern porches, respectively. As a result, the plan layout fits the narrow site, emphasising its vertical axis.

The first rule set (L_0R_1) develops the entry stairwell of the *Ziegler House* as a core node (N_{c0}) and the second rule set (L_0R_2) adds three sets of nodes and links adjacent to the entry; $N_{C0} \rightarrow N_{C0}$, L, $(N_{C0}$, L); $N_{C0} \rightarrow N_{C0}$, D, $(N_{C0}$, D); and $N_{C0} \rightarrow N_{C0}$, K, $(N_{C0}$, K). Two transit nodes are then developed at the third rule set (L_0R_3), from the living room by L $\rightarrow$ L, T, (L, T) and from the dining room by D $\rightarrow$ D, T^2, (D, T^2). The fourth rule set (L_0R_4), L, D $\rightarrow$ L, D, (L, D), and the seventh rule set (L_0R_7), T, E $\rightarrow$ T, E, (T, E) and T^2, E $\rightarrow$ T^2, E, (T^2, E), develop three non-trivial loops. As a result, three nodes (E, L,

D) are identified as "d-type" nodes, minimising overall structural depths. In addition, each transit node linking to the exterior minimises the depth levels from the carrier and thus, the exterior becomes a relatively accessible node ($MD = 2.18$) (Table 17). The mean total depth (TD) of the *Ziegler House* is 26.92, and the mean depth (MD) of rooms in the house is 2.45, which is slightly shallower than the previous case. The most isolated node in the configuration is the fourth private node ($MD = 3.36$), which is only accessed through the third private node. The transit nodes are the next most isolated ($MD = 2.82$). Conversely, the relatively accessible nodes are the entry ($MD = 1.64$) at the ground floor and the hall ($MD = 1.82$) at the first floor. The integration values confirm that the entry is the most integrated ($i_{RRA} = 2.24$), while the fourth private node has the least integration value ($i_{RRA} = 0.60$). The kitchen is also segregated ($i_{RRA} = 0.92$) in comparison to the living and dining nodes ($i_{RRA} = 1.21$). In part, it is the addition of the two porches to the *Ziegler House* that explains its formal and syntactical differences from its close relatives, the *Fireproof House* and the *Stockman House*.

H. S. Adams House

The 1912 *H. S. Adams House* was the first of Wright's schemes designed for Harry S. Adams in Oak Park, Illinois. Including a full-size veranda space in the southern wing, the spatial layout of the design resembles the standard cruciform plan, although there are several significant departures from it. For example, the living room occupies the centre and the left wing of the building, and the open porch is the only part of the plan to the south, meaning that, in practice, the *H. S. Adams House* is one of Wright's "T-shaped" designs (Figure 19). The kitchen also sits on the corner between the north and east wings, further undermining the clarity of the cruciform layout. The kitchen is accessible from the exterior through a small porch at the northeast corner, but internally is only linked to the dining room, which also has a connection to the living room. Thus, both the kitchen and dining rooms are relatively isolated in the plan. In addition, the entry and stairway are only connected to the living room. Viewed collectively, these differences suggest that the *H. S. Adams House* is not as typical for a Prairie style work as it might initially appear.

Six sector nodes are defined for each floor of the *H. S. Adams House* by the s-JPG grammar (Figure 19). The first rule set ($L_0 R_1$) develops the entry node, including a stairway, as a core node (N_{c0}), while the second rule set

Table 18. H. S. Adams House, syntactical data

Node	TD_n	MD_n	RA	i	RRA	i_{RRA}
E	30	2.50	0.27	3.67	0.99	1.01
N	22	1.83	0.15	6.60	0.55	1.82
L	26	2.17	0.21	4.71	0.77	1.30
D	34	2.83	0.33	3.00	1.21	0.83
K	36	3.00	0.36	2.75	1.32	0.76
T	37	3.08	0.38	2.64	1.37	0.73
L^2	37	3.08	0.38	2.64	1.37	0.73
H	23	1.92	0.17	6.00	0.60	1.66
P	32	2.67	0.30	3.30	1.10	0.91
P^2	34	2.83	0.33	3.00	1.21	0.83
P^3	43	3.58	0.47	2.13	1.70	0.59
P^S	34	2.83	0.33	3.00	1.21	0.83
S	34	2.83	0.33	3.00	1.21	0.83
Maximum	43.00	3.58	0.47	6.60	1.70	1.82
Mean	32.46	2.71	0.31	3.57	1.12	0.99
Minimum	22.00	1.83	0.15	2.13	0.55	0.59
H						1.0068
H*						0.7736

(L_0R_2), somewhat unusually, adds only one sector node (living) and a link by $N_{C0} \rightarrow N_{C0}$, L, (N_{C0}, L). L_0R_3 develops three sector nodes (D, L^2, T) and related links from the living node, and to the kitchen from the dining node. Compared to the previous cases, the living node (L) provides more connections to the other nodes than the core node (N). L_0R_7 then develops a "ring-like" structure that is the only non-trivial loop in the final JPG.

The mean total depth (*TD*) of the *H. S. Adams House* is 32.46 and the mean depth (*MD*) of rooms is 2.71 (Table 18). The most isolated nodes in the configuration are, in order, the third private node ($MD = 3.58$), the transit node ($MD = 3.08$) and the second living node ($MD = 3.08$). The dining ($MD = 2.83$) and kitchen ($MD = 3.00$) nodes are relatively segregated, while the living is the third most accessible node ($MD = 2.17$) after the entry and hall nodes. Like the *Sutton House*, the formally and functionally centred living room creates these unique spatial properties. The integration values confirm that the entry ($i_{RRA} = 1.82$) and hall ($i_{RRA} = 1.66$) are the most integrated

Figure 19. H. S. Adams House, annotated plan, sector diagram and JPG production

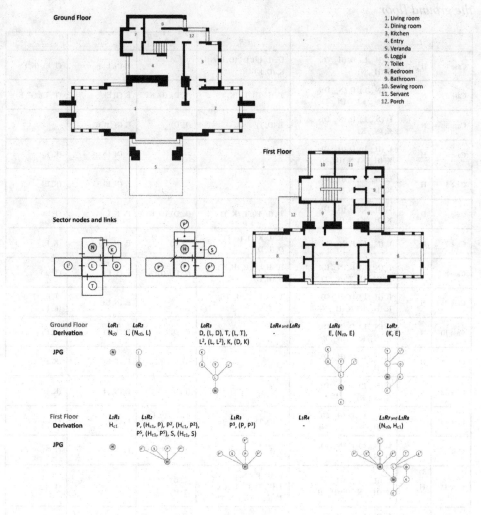

nodes, followed by the living ($i_{RRA} = 1.30$). In contrast, the transit, dining and kitchen nodes are less integrated ($i_{RRA} = 0.73, 0.83,$ and 0.76, respectively).

The Grammatical Analysis

Tables 19 and 20 describe derivations (on the right-hand side) of the applied rules used for generating each case. These rule combinations are specific to the syntactic structure of Wright's Prairie houses. As illustrated throughout the previous sections, the first rule set (L_0R_1) of the s-JPG grammar transforms a start symbol (S_0) into a core node at the ground level (L_0). For the set of

Table 19. Derivations of the specific rules for generating the JPG of each case for the ground floor

	L_0R_1	L_0R_2	L_0R_3	$L_0R_{4(5)}$	L_0R_6	L_0R_7
Case 1	H_{c0}	L, (H_{c0}, L), D, (H_{c0}, D), N, (H_{c0}, N)	L^2, (L, L^2), D^2, (D, D^2), K, (D, K)	T	E, (N, E)	(T, E), (K, E)
Case 2	N_{c0}	L, (N_{c0}, L), D, (N_{c0}, D), K, (N_{c0}, K), T, (N_{c0}, T)	T^2, (L, T^2), T^3, (K, T^3)	(L, D), (D, K)	E, (T, E)	(T^2, E), (T^3, E)
Case 3	N_{c0}	L, (N_{c0}, L), D, (N_{c0}, D), K, (N_{c0}, K)	T, (D, T)	(L, D)	E, (N_{c0}, E)	-
Case 4	H_{c0}	L, (H_{c0}, L), D, (H_{c0}, D), K, (H_{c0}, K), N, (H_{c0}, N)	-	-	E, (N, E)	(K, E)
Case 5	H_{c0}	L, (H_{c0}, L), D, (H_{c0}, D), K, (H_{c0}, K), N, (H_{c0}, N)	-	-	E, (N, E)	(K, E)
Case 6	H_{c0}	L, (H_{c0}, L), D, (H_{c0}, D), K, (H_{c0}, K), N, (H_{c0}, N)	T^2, (L, T^2), T, (K, T)	(L, D), (D, K)	E, (N, E)	(T, E)
Case 7	N_{c0}	L, (N_{c0}, L), P, (N_{c0}, P)	K, (L, K), T, (L, T), D, (L, D)	(D, K)	E, (N_{c0}, E)	(K, E)
Case 8	N_{c0}	L, (N_{c0}, L), K, (N_{c0}, K), H, (N_{c0}, H), T, (N_{c0}, T)	H, (H, L^2), H, (H, T^2), H, (H, D)	(L, L^2), (D, K)	E, (T, E)	(T^2, E)
Case 9	H_{c0}	L, (H_{c0}, L), D, (H_{c0}, D), K, (H_{c0}, K), N, (H_{c0}, N)	T, (D, T), T^2, (L, T^2), S, (K, S)	-	E, (N, E)	(T, E), (T^2, E), (K, E)
Case 10	N_{c0}	L, (N_{c0}, L), D, (N_{c0}, D), K, (N_{c0}, K), T, (N_{c0}, T)	-	(L, D)	E, (T, E)	(K, E)
Case 11	H_{c0}	L, (H_{c0}, L), D, (H_{c0}, D), K, (H_{c0}, K), T, (H_{c0}, T)	-	(D, K), (K, L)	E, (T, E)	(K, E)
Case 12	N_{c0}	L, (N_{c0}, L), D, (N_{c0}, D), K, (N_{c0}, K)	-	(L, D)	E, (N_{c0}, E)	(K, E)
Case 13	H_{c0}	L, (H_{c0}, L), D, (H_{c0}, D), K, (H_{c0}, K), N, (H_{c0}, N)	T, (D, T)	(N, L), (L, D), (L, T)	E, (N, E)	(T, E)
Case 14	N_{c0}	L, (N_{c0}, L), K, (N_{c0}, K), D, (N_{c0}, D)	S, (K, S), T, (D, T)	(L, D), (D, K)	E, (N_{c0}, E)	(T, E), (S, E)
Case 15	H_{c0}	L, (H_{c0}, L), D, (H_{c0}, D), N, (H_{c0}, N), H^2, (H_{c0}, H^2)	P^S, (K, P^S), K, (H^2, K), T, (K, T), T^2, (D, T^2), T^3, (L, T^3), T^4, (N, T^4)	(L, D), (D, H^2), (T, P^S)	E, (T, E)	(T^4, E)
Case 16	N_{c0}	L, (N_{c0}, L), D, (N_{c0}, D), K, (N_{c0}, K), T, (N_{c0}, T)	T^2, (D, T^2)	(L, D), (D, K)	E, (N_{c0}, E)	(T, E), (K, E)
Case 17	H_{c0}	L, (H_{c0}, L), D, (H_{c0}, D), K, (H_{c0}, K)	N, (L, N), T, (L, T)	(L, D)	E, (N, E)	(K, E)
Case 18	N_{c0}	L, (N_{c0}, L), D, (N_{c0}, D), K, (N_{c0}, K)	T, (L, T), T^2, (D, T^2)	(L, D)	E, (N_{c0}, E)	(T, E), (T^2, E)
Case 19	N_{c0}	L, (N_{c0}, L)	D, (L, D), T, (L, T), L^2, (L, L^2), K, (D, K)	-	E, (N_{c0}, E)	(K, E)

Wright's Prairie houses, a hall sector tends to be the core node because it is

Table 20. Derivations of the specific rules for generating the JPG of each case for the first floor

	L_iR_1	L_iR_2	L_iR_3	L_iR_4	L_iR_7
Case 1	H^2_{c1}	P, (H^2_{c1}, P), P^2, (H^2_{c1}, P^2), P^S, (H^2_{c1}, P^S), S, (H^2_{c1}, S)	P^3, (P, P^3)	(P, P^2), (S, P^3)	(H_{c0}, H^2_{c1})
Case 2	H_{c1}	P, (H_{c1}, P), P^2, (H_{c1}, P^2), P^3, (H_{c1}, P^3), S, (H_{c1}, S)	-	(P, P^2), (S, P^2)	(N_{c0}, H_{c1})
Case 3	H_{c1}	P, (H_{c1}, P), P^2, (H_{c1}, P^2), P^3, (H_{c1}, P^3)	-	-	(N_{c0}, H_{c1})
Case 4	H^2_{c1}	P, (H^2_{c1}, P), P^2, (H^2_{c1}, P^2), P^3, (H^2_{c1}, P^3), P^4, (H^2_{c1}, P^4)	-	-	(H_{c0}, H^2_{c1})
Case 5	H^2_{c1}	P, (H^2_{c1}, P), P^2, (H^2_{c1}, P^2), P^3, (H^2_{c1}, P^3), P^4, (H^2_{c1}, P^4)	-	-	(H_{c0}, H^2_{c1})
Case 6	H^2_{c1}	P, (H^2_{c1}, P), P^2, (H^2_{c1}, P^2), P^3, (H^2_{c1}, P^3), P^S, (H^2_{c1}, P^S)	-	(P, P^2)	(H_{c0}, H^2_{c1})
Case 7	H_{c1}	P^2, (H_{c1}, P^2), P^3, (H_{c1}, P^3), P^4, (H_{c1}, P^4), T^2, (H_{c1}, T^2)	P^5, (P^4, P^5)	-	(N_{c0}, H_{c1})
Case 8	H^2_{c1}	P, (H^2_{c1}, P), P^2, (H^2_{c1}, P^2), P^3, (H^2_{c1}, P^3), P^4, (H^2_{c1}, P^4), S, (H^2_{c1}, S)	-	-	(N_{c0}, H^2_{c1})
Case 9	H^2_{c1}	P, (H^2_{c1}, P), P^2, (H^2_{c1}, P^2), P^3, (H^2_{c1}, P^3)	-	-	(H_{c0}, H^2_{c1})
Case 10	H_{c1}	P, (H_{c1}, P), P^2, (H_{c1}, P^2), S, (H_{c1}, S)	P^3, (P, P^3)	-	(N_{c0}, H_{c1})
Case 11	H^2_{c1}	P, (H^2_{c1}, P), P^2, (H^2_{c1}, P^2), P^3, (H^2_{c1}, P^3)	-	-	(H_{c0}, H^2_{c1})
Case 12	H_{c1}	P, (H_{c1}, P), P^2, (H_{c1}, P^2), P^3, (H_{c1}, P^3)	P^4, (P^3, P^4)	-	(N_{c0}, H_{c1})
Case 13	H^2_{c1}	P, (H^2_{c1}, P), P^2, (H^2_{c1}, P^2), P^3, (H^2_{c1}, P^3)	P^4, (P^3, P^4)	-	(H_{c0}, H^2_{c1})
Case 14	H_{c1}	P, (H_{c1}, P), P^2, (H_{c1}, P^2), S, (H_{c1}, S)	P^3, (P^2, P^3)	(P, S)	(N_{c0}, H_{c1})
Case 15	H^3_{c1}	P, (H^3_{c1}, P), P^2, (H^3_{c1}, P^2), P^3, (H^3_{c1}, P^3), S, (H^3_{c1}, S)	T^5, (P^3, T^5)	(P^2, P^3)	(H^2, H^3)
Case 16	H_{c1}	P, (H_{c1}, P), P^2, (H_{c1}, P^2), P^S, (H_{c1}, P^S)	-	-	(N_{c0}, H_{c1})
Case 17	H_{c1}	P, (H_{c1}, P), P^2, (H_{c1}, P^2), P^3, (H_{c1}, P^3)	T^2, (P, T^2)	-	(N_{c0}, H_{c1})
Case 18	H_{c1}	P, (H_{c1}, P), P^2, (H_{c1}, P^2), P^3, (H_{c1}, P^3)	P^4, (P^3, P^4)	(P^2, P^4)	(N_{c0}, H_{c1})
Case 19	H_{c1}	P, (H_{c1}, P), P^2, (H_{c1}, P^2), P^S, (H_{c1}, P^S), S, (H_{c1}, S)	P^3, (P, P^3)	-	(N_{c0}, H_{c1})

commonly located in the middle of the cruciform plan of the Prairie style, and it often serves to link to at least three sectors. These links from a core node commence production of a syntactical head. However, in total, in ten cases an entry sector, N_{c0}, is the core node whereas in the other nine a hall sector functions as the core, H_{C0}. Thus, for L_0R_1 the dominant rule is: $S_0 \rightarrow N_{c0}$ (52.6%), and it is also notable this this rule is largely associated with the cruciform-planned dwellings.

The second rule set (L_0R_2) produces nodes and links adjacent to a core node. This is topologically significant in the grammar because it completes the syntactic head of a graph. In Wright's architecture, the syntactic head develops the basic cruciform of a truncated T-shaped plan that consists of four main functional sectors (L, D, K, N), with the hall (H_{c0}) in the centre. However, the components of each individual syntactic head vary slightly across the nineteen cases (LDKN: 26.3%, LDKT: 26.3%, LDK: 21.1%, etc.). Thus, for L_0R_2 the dominant rule set from the hall node is: $H_{c0} \rightarrow H_{c0}$, L, ($H_{c0}$, L); $H_{c0} \rightarrow H_{c0}$, D, ($H_{c0}$, D); $H_{c0} \rightarrow H_{c0}$, K, ($H_{c0}$, K); $H_{c0} \rightarrow H_{c0}$, N, ($H_{c0}$, N) (26.3%). However, if the core node is the entry, the dominant rule set is $N_{c0} \rightarrow N_{c0}$, L, ($N_{c0}$, L); $N_{c0} \rightarrow N_{c0}$, D, ($N_{c0}$, D); $N_{c0} \rightarrow N_{c0}$, K, ($N_{c0}$, K) or plus $N_{c0} \rightarrow N_{c0}$, T, ($N_{c0}$, T) (21.1%).

The third rule set (L_0R_3) for the ground floor generates nodes and a second set of links, starting from a node generated by the previous rule set to the adjacent nodes at the next depth. Node and link additions from non-core nodes through L_0R_3 usually relate to the expansion of wings, and the transit sector (i.e., T, T^2 and T^3) is the dominant node in the generation produced in L_0R_3. For example, the transit node is developed from the living node in eight houses (case 2, 6, 7, 9, 15, 17, 18, 19), while it also extends the dining by D $\rightarrow$ D, T, (D, T) or D $\rightarrow$ D, T^2, (D, T^2) in seven houses (case 3, 9, 13, 14, 15, 16, 18). The kitchen is developed from the dining node in two cases (1, 19) where the kitchen is relatively segregated.

The fourth rule set (L_0R_4) provides links between non-core nodes at the same depth. After the last two rule sets, the links are locally configured to generate a JPG to represent the interior topology of each house. While L_0R_4 is skipped in five cases (26.3%), the dominant links generated by L_0R_4 are (L, D) (57.9%) and (D, K) (36.8%), which happen eleven and seven times respectively. This result suggests that the living, dining and kitchen sectors are treated in a surprisingly similar manner. Before addressing the global connectedness in the s-JPG grammar, rule five (L_0R_5) accomodates nodes that are locally isolated but formally connected on a level. Only one rule (N $\rightarrow$ N, T) is developed for the first case. This is natural because most of the sector nodes are internally linked to at least one functional sector. The local configuration ends with the fifth rule set.

The sixth rule set (L_0R_6) adds the exterior node (E) and a link to a core node on the ground level. The dominant set of nodes and links generated by this rule are "E, (N, E)" and "E, (N_{c0}, E)', both of which occur seven times. The second dominant set is E, (T, E) (26.3%). This would also be a general consequence of the rules of the s-JPG grammar rather than of Wright's Prairie style. Rule seven (L_0R_7) generates links between the remaining non-core nodes on the ground level and the exterior node. For L_0R_7 the dominant rule is: K, E → K, E, (K, E) (57.9%). The next most common rules are: T, E → T, E, (T, E) (36.8%) and T^2, E → T^2, E, (T^2, E) (21.1%). Thus, considering both L_0R_6 and L_0R_7, the transit nodes are fundamentally linked to the exterior, but, if not, the transit node remains isolated. The same process is repeated for the upper level plan. Specifically, the first rule (L_1R_1) develops a second hall sector, including a staircase, into a core node on the upper level (L_1). The second rule L_1R_2 tends to generate three private sectors (P, P^2, P^3) from the core node and then L_1R_3 develops either another private sector or a transit sector. After L_1R_4 adds links between non-core nodes, the s-JPG grammar finalises the local syntax of the upper floor without the application of L_1R_5. For the upper floor, the grammar also skips the consideration of L_1R_6 and adds a global link between the two levels through L_1R_7 that is applied to the core node including a staircase on the first floor. For L_1R_1 the dominant rule set is: $S_1 → H_{c1}$ (52.6%). For L_1R_2 the dominant rule set is: $H_{c1} → H_{c1}$, P, (H_{c1}, P); $H_{c1} → H_{c1}, P^2, (H_{c1}, P^2)$; $H_{c1} → H_{c1}, P^3, (H_{c1}, P^3)$ (26.3%). The s-JPG grammar skips rules L_1R_3 to L_1R_6, and for L_1R_7 the dominant rule set is: $N_{c0}, H_{c1} → N_{c0}, H_{c1}, (N_{c0}, H_{c1})$ (52.6%). In each case, the dominant rule sets capture the grammar of the socio-functional properties of Wright's Prairie architecture and also identify a clear pattern in its linguistic structure. However, in order to determine the right rule sets, the s-JPG grammar should also consider the shape of the plan layout because the dominant rule sets vary if the plan is cruciform, T-shaped or foursquare.

The Syntactical Analysis

The analysis of the syntactical properties of each case is focused on the integration value of functional sector nodes. As described in Table 21, the integration value deals with Real Relative Asymmetry (*RRA*), which is useful for comparisons between cases with radically different *K* values. The mathematical data for Wright's Prairie architecture is calculated for all major functional programs: exterior (E), entry (N), hall (H), living (L), dining (D), kitchen (K), private (P), service (S) and transit (T). If there is a second node or more, the integration values in Table 21 describe the average value of all of the same functional nodes. Thus, inequality genotypes of Wright's nineteen houses can be generated by the integration value (i_{RRA}) of each sector node.

Table 21 reveals that the hall node, on average, has the highest integration value, while the private and transit nodes tend to be the least integrated. Interestingly, the exterior is less integrated in Wright's houses than Murcutt's, where it was the second most integrated node. In addition, many of Wright's transit nodes are segregated and inaccessible to the exterior in the Prairie style. In contrast, in Murcutt's rural houses they not only provide an important connection between indoor and outdoor spaces but also interior circulation. This is an interesting finding because both architects sought to create a harmonious relationship between the house and its surroundings. That is, the syntactical properties of two architects' dwellings reveals that their spatial configurations are different. This is also because, conceptually, Wright's designs grow out from a central space before they allow inhabitants to connect with the site, whereas Murcutt's allows direct access to their surroundings.

On average, the most integrated of Wright's Prairie houses is the *Ross House* (case 2), while the *Brown House* (case 8) is the least integrated. The JPG of the *Ross House* features four non-trivial loops at the ground floor and two circulation loops at the first floor. Consequently, the entry node ($i_{RRA} = 2.60$) is more than double the integration level of the private node ($i_{RRA} = 0.91$), whereas the major functional sectors (L, D, K) are all equally well integrated ($i_{RRA} = 0.87$). In contrast, the *Brown House* has five dead-end private nodes that increase the mean depths of their plans. For example, considering the mean value of all nodes of the nineteen cases ($i_{RRA} = 1.18$) and its standard deviation (SD = 0.13), all nodes of the *Brown House*, except for the hall, entry and dining, are relatively less integrated (under 1.05). The highest integration value for an exterior is 1.21 (cases 9, 16 and 18), while the lowest is 0.70 (cases 4 and 5). There are four links to the exterior in the ninth case, the *DeRhode House* (case 5), while the *Walser House* (case 4) has two exterior links and six dead-end nodes (living, dining and private nodes).

The integration values of the entry nodes in Table 20 are also revealing. For example, the *Larwill House* (case 16), has the highest integration value for the entry ($i_{RRA} = 3.32$), while the *Waller House* (case 17), has the lowest value ($i_{RRA} = 0.83$), with the former being four times the value of the latter. This occurs because the entry node with a stairway in the *Larwill House* has five links to the other nodes, while the entry node of the *Waller House* only bridges between the exterior and living nodes. Usually, Wright's foursquare houses (cases 10, 12, 18) configure the entry with a stairway that also provides indoor circulation, but in two foursquare houses (cases 13 and 17) the entry space is only an additional node for formal and functional needs. The living nodes of both the *Stockman House* (case 13) and the *Waller House* (case 17) have the highest integration values (i_{RRA} = 1.31) of their peers.

As observed in the grammatical analysis, the dining room frequently provides circulation loops and links to other nodes. For example, seven cases have a link between the dining and transit nodes, (D, T) or (D, T²), and eleven cases connect the dining with the living nodes. Importantly, nine cases have a connection between the dining and kitchen, (D, K). Thus, on average the dining is a more integrated node than the living and kitchen. The dining room is usually located near a hall or entry with a stairway, but in *Sutton House* (case 7) and the *H. S. Adams House* (case 19) it is two depths away from the circulation core. Those cases have the least integrated dining nodes (i_{RRA} = 0.79 and 0.83, respectively), while the dining node of the Larwill House (case 16) with four links has its highest integration value (i_{RRA} = 1.58). On average, the kitchen is not well integrated (i_{RRA} = 1.07), in part because it is sometimes a dead-end space and is only accessed through the dining room.

Table 21 reports the relative difference factor (H^*) of each case. There is no case below the 0.5 benchmark and the mean value of all cases is 0.7231, which confirms the JPGs generated by the s-JPG grammar do not provide any evidence of a deliberate or singular strategy producing a specific spatial configuration. The third case, the *Roberts House*, is the most balanced approach to the plan in all cases (H^* = 0.5715). This result simply means that, compared with an evenly distributed volume of nodes, Wright's Prairie architecture does not display a particularly different distribution. It may be because the general distribution of functional spaces in Wright's architecture is sufficiently equalised or homogenous that a more distinct structural form is not required.

Wright's Massing Grammar

Whilst the s-JPG grammar of Wright's Prairie Houses addresses the spatial and functional configurations of a plan, the massing grammar completes the formal configurations using a basic schema, "shape (*x*)". Like a massing study

Table 21. Integration values (i_{RRA}) of all sector nodes of each case and its relative difference factor (H*)

	E	H	N	L	D	K	P	S	T	Mean	H*
Case 1	0.87	1.77	1.18	1.02	1.24	0.87	0.84	0.91	0.59	1.03	0.7492
Case 2	0.96	1.82	2.60	1.30	1.30	1.30	0.91	0.91	1.04	1.35	0.7895
Case 3	0.92	1.84	2.75	1.10	1.22	0.92	0.79	-	0.52	1.26	0.5715
Case 4	0.70	2.44	1.11	0.95	0.95	1.11	0.89	-	-	1.16	0.7076
Case 5	0.70	2.44	1.11	0.95	0.95	1.11	0.89	-	-	1.16	0.7076
Case 6	0.91	2.21	1.21	1.21	1.30	1.21	0.89	-	0.77	1.21	0.7143
Case 7	1.07	1.82	2.02	1.30	0.79	0.83	0.84	-	0.80	1.18	0.7480
Case 8	0.87	1.18	1.96	0.91	1.12	0.91	0.84	0.84	0.96	1.07	0.8269
Case 9	1.21	2.06	1.30	1.21	1.21	1.52	0.79	0.79	0.96	1.23	0.7596
Case 10	0.66	1.90	2.21	0.95	0.95	1.02	0.78	0.78	1.02	1.14	0.7164
Case 11	0.79	2.16	-	1.22	1.22	1.22	0.79	-	1.22	1.23	0.7385
Case 12	0.92	2.20	2.20	0.92	0.92	0.92	0.82	-	-	1.27	0.6960
Case 13	0.78	1.99	1.21	1.31	1.21	0.92	0.79	-	0.83	1.13	0.6893
Case 14	0.98	1.74	2.24	1.05	1.31	1.21	0.79	0.83	0.83	1.22	0.6886
Case 15	0.72	1.59	0.98	0.95	1.34	1.24	0.86	0.83	0.75	1.03	0.7797
Case 16	1.21	1.90	3.32	1.21	1.48	1.33	0.83	-	0.88	1.52	0.6478
Case 17	0.75	1.77	0.83	1.31	1.05	1.05	0.81	-	0.62	1.02	0.7280
Case 18	1.21	1.74	2.24	1.21	1.21	0.92	0.82	-	0.78	1.27	0.7062
Case 19	1.01	1.66	1.82	1.30	0.83	0.76	0.79	0.83	0.73	1.08	0.7736
Mean	0.91	1.91	1.79	1.13	1.14	1.07	0.83	0.84	0.83	1.19	0.7231
SD	0.18	0.30	0.71	0.15	0.19	0.20	0.04	0.05	0.18	0.12	0.0560

at the conceptual design stage, the massing grammar deals with a simplified form that consists of three-dimensional modular blocks, much like Koning and Eizenberg's additive Shape Grammar (Koning & Eizenberg, 1981). As discussed in previous chapters, the first shape rule set (SR_1) transforms sector nodes – which are already identified by the s-JPG grammar – into three-dimensional modular blocks by a rule, $x \rightarrow shape\ (x)$, where x is a node. That is, all sector nodes of the JPG are transformed into three-dimensional blocks. After developing these blocks, the massing grammar configures block properties (SR_2), composition (SR_3) and roof types (SR_4). The final shape rule set (SR_5) terminates the configuration process.

Block Properties

The second shape rule set (SR_2) is the first configuration process of the massing grammar. Block size and wall type are defined in this process, along with orientation of the modules. In the case of the Prairie houses, there are both horizontal (*h*-type) and vertical (*v*-type) modules. The modules are based on the cruciform plan, but applicable to all its variations as well as his foursquare designs. Figure 20 displays the ground floors of the *Ross House* (1902) and the *Fireproof House* (1912), with sector nodes transformed into modular blocks and each annotated in accordance with the grammar. The remainder of the module orientations are documented in the sector nodes and links diagram of each case (in Figures 8.1 – 8.19). As shown in Figure 20 (a), the dining and kitchen nodes of the *Ross House*'s cruciform plan are horizontal modules, while the transit block (T) is half of the normal horizontal module, meaning its size is expressed as *1/2h*. The living (L), kitchen (K) and the second transit nodes (T^2) are vertical modules (*v*), while the third

Figure 20. Configuration of block properties for Wright's two different shapes

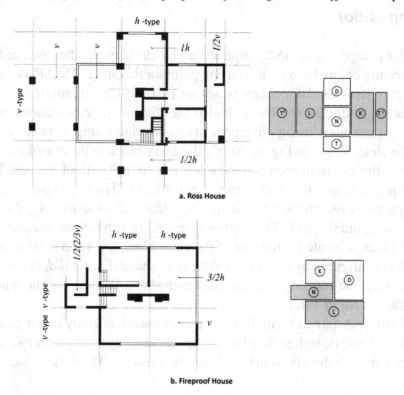

a. Ross House

b. Fireproof House

transit node (T^3) is a quarter of this, still vertically arrayed. In contrast, for the *Fireproof House*, the two rear modules (kitchen and dining) are horizontal modules, while the entry and living are interpreted as vertical modules that are rotated 90-degrees from their normal orientations, much like the use of a Froebel-block.

The massing grammar develops the overall three-dimensional properties of the modular blocks by configuring wall properties. Whereas Murcutt's architecture could be represented using four wall types, "open', "transparent', "semi-transparent" and "solid', Wright's dwellings tend to be either largely "open" (for porticos, porches and verandas) or largely "solid" (for most walls, including those with windows in them). Thus, only transit modules are identified as the "open" wall type, as they are roofed and visually defined by columns, but they open to the weather. In this way, the massing grammar configures the seven modular blocks of the *Ross House* in Figure 20 (a) using seven rules: shape (N) $\rightarrow$ shape (N, *1h.solid*); shape (D) $\rightarrow$ shape (D, *1h.solid*); shape (T) $\rightarrow$ shape (T, *1/2h.open*); shape (L) $\rightarrow$ shape (L, *1v.solid*); shape (K) $\rightarrow$ shape (K, *1v.solid*); shape (T^2) $\rightarrow$ shape (T^2, *1v.open*); shape (T^3) $\rightarrow$ shape (T^4, *1/2v.open*).

Composition

The third shape rule set (SR_3) connects all blocks to each other. A core block is the centre of any form as the starting point for this stage. The SR_3 considers eight compass-based directions, which are east, west, north, south, northeast, northwest, southeast, southwest. It also uses five alignments – equal, centre, left, right and interleaving – to represent formal relationships between blocks. For the *Ross House* in Figure 20 (a), the entry block is described as a core block in this configuration and the kitchen is to the north of the core block and equally shares the wall between two blocks. These compositions are configured by two shape rules: shape (N_{c0}, *1h.solid*) $\rightarrow$ shape (N_{c0}, *1h.solid*, *coreblock*); and shape (K, *1h.solid*) $\rightarrow$ shape (K, *1h.solid*, N.*north.equal*). The living block is located at the east of the entry block (N_{c0}) and is left-aligned, which is configured by shape (L, *1v.solid*) $\rightarrow$ shape (L, *1v.solid*, N.*east.left*). In this way, the massing grammar can compose all blocks for the nineteen cases as shown in Table 22.

The third shape rule set of the massing grammar is not only able to generate Wright's domestic architecture but also produces many alternatives by altering different growth directions in this shape composition. Those variations share

Table 22. Derivations of the composition rules for generating massing blocks on the ground levels

Case	Block composition
Case 1	shape (H$_{c0}$, *1h.solid, coreblock*); shape (D, *1v.solid, H.east.right*); shape (L, *1v.solid, H.west.left*); shape (N, *1h.solid, H.south.equal*); shape (K, *1h.solid, H.north.equal*); shape (L^2, *1/2(1/2v).solid, L.west.centre*); shape (D^2, *1/2(1/2v).solid, D.east.right*); shape (T, *2h.open, N.south.equal*)
Case 2	shape (N$_{c0}$, *1h.solid, coreblock*); shape (K, *1v.solid, N.east.right*); shape (L, *1v.solid, N.west.left*); shape (T, *1/2h.open, N.south.equal*); shape (D, *1h.solid, N.north.equal*); shape (T^2, *1v.open, L.east.centre*); shape (T^3, *(1/2v).open, K.west.centre*)
Case 3	shape (N$_{c0}$, *1h.solid, coreblock*); shape (D, *1h.solid, N.north.equal*); shape (K, *1/2v.solid, N.northeast.Interleaving*); shape (L, *1v.solid, N.northwest.Interleaving*); shape (T, *1h.open, D.northwest.Interleaving*)
Case 4	shape (H$_{c0}$, *1h.solid, coreblock*); shape (L, *1v.solid, H.east.equal*); shape (D, *1v.solid, H.west.equal*); shape (N, *1h.solid, H.south.equal*); shape (K, *1h.solid, H.north.equal*)
Case 5	shape (H$_{c0}$, *1h.solid, coreblock*); shape (L, *1v.solid, H.east.equal*); shape (D, *1v.solid, H.west.equal*); shape (N, *1h.solid, H.south.equal*); shape (K, *1h.solid, H.north.equal*)
Case 6	shape (H$_{c0}$, *1h.solid, coreblock*); shape (K, *3/4v.solid, H.east.right*); shape (L, *1v.solid, H.west.left*); shape (N, *1h.solid, H.south.equal*); shape (D, *1h.solid, H.north.equal*); shape (T, *(1/2v).open, K.east.centre*); shape (T^2, *(1/2v).open, L.west.centre*)
Case 7	shape (N$_{c0}$, *1v.solid, coreblock*); shape (L, *1h.solid, N.west.left*); shape (P, *(1/2h).solid, N.north.equal*); shape (K, *1h.solid, L.north.equal*); shape (D, *1v.solid, L.west.right*); shape (T, *1h.open, L.south.equal*)
Case 8	shape (N$_{c0}$, *1h.solid, coreblock*); shape (T, *(1/3v).open, N.east.equal*); shape (H, *1v.solid, N.west.equal*); shape (L, *4/3h.solid, N.south.equal*); shape (K, *4/3h.solid, N.north.equal*); shape (L^2, *2v.solid, H.south.equal*); shape (D, *2v.solid, H.north.equal*); shape (T^2, *(2/3v).open, H.west.equal*)
Case 9	shape (H$_{c0}$, *1h.solid, coreblock*); shape (D, *1v.solid, H.north.equal*); shape (L, *1v.solid, H.south.equal*); shape (N, *2/3h.solid, H.east.equal*); shape (K, *2/3h.solid, H.west.equal*); shape (T, *1v.open, D.north.equal*); shape (T^2, *1v.open, L.south.equal*);, shape (S, *(1/2h).solid, K.north.equal*)
Case 10	shape (N$_{c0}$, *1/2(2/3v).solid, coreblock*); shape (T, *1/2(2/3v).open, N.east.equal*); shape (D, *3/2h.solid, N.west.left*); shape (L, *1v.solid, D.south.right*); shape (K, *1h.solid, N.north.equal*)
Case 11	shape (H$_{c0}$, *1h.solid, coreblock*); shape (T, *1v.solid, H.east.centre*); shape (K, *1v.solid, H.west.centre*); shape (L, *1h.solid, H.south.equal*); shape (D, *1h.solid, H.north.equal*)
Case 12	shape (N$_{c0}$, *1/2(2/3v).solid, coreblock*); shape (K, *1h.solid, N.north.equal*); shape (D, *3/2h.solid, N.east.right*); shape (L, *1v.solid, D.south.left*).
Case 13	shape (N$_{c0}$, *1/2(2/3v).solid, coreblock*); shape (D, *3/2h.solid, N.west.left*); shape (L, *1v.solid, D.south.right*); shape (K, *1h.solid, N.north.equal*); shape (T, *5/2h.open, L.northwest.Interleaving*)
Case 14	shape (N$_{c0}$, *(1/2v).solid, coreblock*); shape (K, *(1/2v).solid, N.north.equal*); shape (D, *1h.solid, K.west.right*); shape (L, *2h.solid, D.south. equal*); shape (S, *1/2v.solid, K.southeast.Interleaving*); shape (T, *1v.open, D.west.right*)

continued on following page

Table 22. Continued

Case	Block composition
Case 15	shape (H$_{co}$, *1h.solid, coreblock*); shape (H^2, *1/2(1/2v).solid, H.northeast.Interleaving*); shape (L, *1v.solid, H.west.left*); shape (N, *1/3h.solid, H.south.equal*); shape (D, *1h.solid, H.north.equal*); shape (K, *(1/2v).solid, H^2.east.left*); shape (P^s, *(1/2v).solid, K.southwest.Interleaving*); shape (T, *(1/2v).open, P^s.east.equal*); shape (T^2, *1h).open, D.north.equal*); shape (T^3, *(3/4v).open, L.west.centre*); shape (T^4, *1h.open, N.south.equal*)
Case 16	shape (N$_{co}$, *1h.solid, coreblock*); shape (D, *2h.solid, N.east.right*); shape (T^2, *1/2v.open, D.southeast. Interleaving*); shape (T, *1/2(1/2v).open, N.west.left*); shape (L, *1v.solid, N.southwest.Interleaving*); shape (K, *1h.solid, N.noth.equal*)
Case 17	shape (H$_{co}$, *2/3(2/3v).solid, coreblock*); shape (D, *3/2h.solid, H.north.right*); shape (L, *1v.solid, D.west.right*); shape (K, *1h.solid, H.east.left*); shape (N, *1/2(1/3h).solid, L.south.left*); shape (T, *1h.open, L.north.left*)
Case 18	shape (N$_{co}$, *2/3(2/3v).solid, coreblock*); shape (D, *3/2h.solid, N.east.right*); shape (L, *1v.solid, D.south.left*); shape (K, *1h.solid, N.north.right*); shape (T, *(2/3v), L.south.equal*); shape (T^2, *1h.open, D.north.equal*)
Case 19	shape (N$_{co}$, *1h.solid, coreblock*); shape(L, *1h.solid, N.south.equal*); shape (D, *1v.solid, L.east.equal*); shape (L^2, *1v.solid, L.west.equal*); shape (T, *1h.open, L.south.equal*); shape (K, *2/3v.solid, D.north.left*)

the same syntactical characteristics as the original design. For example, the third shape rule set for the *Fireproof House* in Figure 20 (a) includes four rules:

shape (N$_{c0}$, *1/2(2/3v).solid*) → shape (N$_{c0}$, *1/2(2/3v).solid, coreblock*);

shape (K, *1h.solid*) → shape (K, *1h.solid, N.north. equal*);

shape (D, *3/2h.solid*) → shape (D, *3/2h.solid, N.east.right*);

shape (L, *1v.solid*) → shape (L, *1v.solid, D.south.left*).

Using the same nodes and links specified in the JPG of the *Fireproof House*, the massing grammar can generate an alternative using another four rules:

shape (N$_{c0}$, *1/2(2/3v).solid*) → shape (N$_{c0}$, *1/2(2/3v).solid, coreblock*);

shape (K, *1h.solid*) → shape (K, *1h.solid, N.north.equal*);

shape (D, *3/2h.solid*) → shape (D, *3/2h.solid, N.west.left*);

shape (L, *1v.solid*) → shape (L, *1v.solid, D.south.right*).

The alternative is a mirrored plan of the original design and its four rules are also used for the shape composition of both the *Nichols House* and the *Stockman House*, which are also examples of Wright's foursquare houses. That is, the composition rules are useful to capture variations and transformational forms of any design. That is why the spatial composition of Wright's Prairie Houses is often described in terms of the use of Froebel blocks.

Roof Types

The fourth shape rule set (SR_4) determines roof types. For the Prairie houses the massing grammar considers two roof types: hip and flat. Most blocks use a hip roof, while some blocks of Wright's foursquare houses have a flat-type roof. For the ground floor, a hipped roof is usually applied to transit blocks and the remaining roofs tend to be linked to the upper level blocks. Thus, most of the blocks at the ground floor have a flat roof, while blocks at the first floor are naturally covered by a hip roof. Figure 21 illustrates the generated massing of two Prairie house examples using this roof configuration. For example, the fourth shape rule set (SR_4) for the *Ross House* consists of 11 rules:

shape (N_{c0}, *1h.solid, coreblock*) → shape (N_{c0}, *1h.solid, coreblock, flat*);

shape (K, *1v.solid, N.east.right*) → shape (K, *1v.solid, N.east.right, hip*);

shape (L, *1v.solid, N.west.left*) → shape (L, *1v.solid, N.west.left, hip*);

shape (T, *1/2h.open, N.south.equal*) → shape (T, *1/2h.open, N.south. equal, hip*);

shape (D, *1h.solid, N.north.equal*) → shape (D, *1h.solid, N.north.equal, flat*);

shape (T^2, *1v.open, L.east.centre*) → shape (T^2, *1v.open, L.east.centre, hip*);

Figure 21. The final productions of the roof type configuration and the final forms for the F. W. Little House and the Ross House

Case 1. Little House (1902)

shape (H_{c0}, *1h.solid, coreblock, flat*)
shape (D, *1v.solid, H.east.right, flat*)
shape (L, *1v.solid, H.west.left, flat*)
shape (N, *1h.solid, H.south.equal, flat*)
shape (K, *1h.solid, H.north.equal, flat*)
shape (L^2, *1/2(1/2v).solid, L.west.centre, flat*)
shape (D^2, *1/2(1/2v).solid, D.east.right*)
shape (T, *2h.open, N.south.equal, hip*)
shape (H^2_{c1}, *1h.solid, coreblock, hip*)
shape (P, *1h.solid, H^2.south.equal, hip*)
shape (P^2, *1/2v.solid, H^2.southeast.interleaving, hip*)
shape (P^3, *1v.solid, H.west.centre, hip*)
shape (P^5, *1/2v.solid, P^2.north.equal, hip*)
shape (S, *1h.solid, H^2.north.equal, hip*)

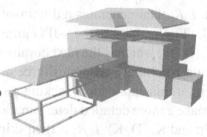

Case 2. Ross House (1902)

shape (N_{c0}, *1h.solid, coreblock, flat*)
shape (K, *1v.solid, N.east.right, hip*)
shape (L, *1v.solid, N.west.left, hip*)
shape (T, *1/2h.open, N.south.equal, hip*)
shape (D, *1h.solid, N.north.equal, flat*)
shape (T^2, *1v.open, L.east.centre, hip*)
shape (T^3, *(1/2v).open, K.west.centre, hip*)
shape (H_{c1}, *1/2v.solid, coreblock, hip*)
shape (P, *1/2h.solid, H.south.left, hip*)
shape (P^2, *1v.solid, H.west.equal, hip*)
shape (P^3, *1/2v.solid, H.east.equal, hip*)
shape (S, *1/2h.solid, H.north.right, hip*)

shape (T^3, *(1/2v).open*, K.*west.centre*) → shape (T^3, *(1/2v).open*, K.*west. centre, hip*);

shape (H_{c1}, *1/2v.solid, coreblock*) → shape (H_{c1}, *1/2v.solid, coreblock, hip*);

shape (P, *1/2h.solid*, H.*south.left*) → shape (P, *1/2h.solid*, H.*south.left, hip*);

shape (P^2, *1v.solid*, H.*west.equal*) → shape (P^2, *1v.solid*, H.*west.equal, hip*);

shape (P^3, *1/2v.solid*, H.*east.equal*) → shape (P^3, *1/2v.solid*, H.*east.equal, hip*);

shape (S, *1/2h.solid*, H.*north.right*) → shape (S, *1/2h.solid*, H.*north. right, hip*).

A Dominant Prairie House

Using the data developed from the s-JPG and massing grammars, it is possible to identify an architect's tendency to use a particular rule or pattern for creating socio-functional relationships and then expressing these formally. To do this, a dominant JPG, as a prevalent syntactic type, is determined and a dominant massing is then developed for the JPG. Larger sample sizes for this process will typically result in more robust outcomes, as they are used to identify the tendancy for a rule to be applied.

As discussed in the previous grammatical analysis to develop a cruciform design, the s-JPG grammar identifies $S_0 \to H_{c0}$ as a dominant rule for the first step (L_0R_1), and then develops a basic cruciform form that consists of four main functional sectors (L, D, K, N) in the wings, with the core nodes in the centre, through the dominant rule set of L_0R_2, which is $H_{c0} \to H_{c0}$, L, (H_{c0}, L); $H_{c0} \to H_{c0}$, D, (H_{c0}, D); $H_{c0} \to H_{c0}$, K, (H_{c0}, K); and $H_{c0} \to H_{c0}$, N, (H_{c0}, N). L_0R_3 then generates a dominant set of nodes and links, L^2, (L, L^2) and T, (L, T). In addition, the s-JPG grammar generates K, (D, K) or T^2, (L, T^2) or T, (D, T), which is the next dominant set. This is because the grammar application commonly generates three dominant sets in this rule. K, (D, K) is chosen for this application, lacking a sufficiently large enough volume of data to make a more detailed determination. Thus, L_0R_3 generates L^2, (L, L^2); T, (L, T); and K, (D, K). L_0R_4 is then skipped or generates one link between the two dominant links, (L, D) and (D, K). L_0R_4 and L_0R_5 are not applied to generate this syntactic type because the skipped links are the dominant condition. L_0R_6 adds the exterior node, E, and a link, (N, E). L_0R_7 can generate the most dominant link, (K, E), but if there is a transit node it develops a link between the transit node to the exterior, which is the second dominant link, (T, E). Finally, the s-JPG grammar identifies a prevalent syntactic type of JPG for the ground floor, which can be represented as follows.

Figure 22. The dominant Prairie house's socio-functional relationship (JPG) and formal expression (massing)

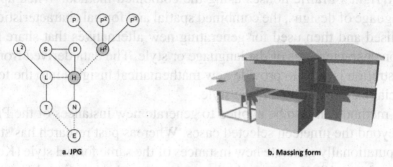

a. JPG   b. Massing form

$g_{\text{dominant JPG} - \text{L0}}$ = {H_{c0}, L, D, S, N, L^2, T, E, (H_{c0}, L), (H_{c0}, D), (H_{c0}, K), (H_{c0}, N), (L, L^2), (L, T), (D, K), (N, E), (T, E)}.

This is repeated for the upper floor, where the dominant first rule set (L_lR_l) develops a second hall node (H^2_{c1}) and L_lR_2 generates three private nodes (P, P^2, P^3). The s-JPG grammar skips the next rules until it adds a global link between the two levels through L_lR_7. By identifying the most common rule sets in the given cases, the s-JPG grammar identifies a prevalent JPG.

In the same way the massing grammar rules and data can be used to identify the most prevalent outcome. Based on this information, the grammar identifies three *v*-type blocks for L, D, L^2 and four *h*-type blocks for H_{c0}, K, N, T on the ground floor. All blocks conform to the simplified-modular size and only the transit block has open walls. The hall block lies in the centre and then the other blocks are located using the data from block compositions. For example, L is most commonly located to the west of the hall block and N to the south. Figure 22 illustrates the prevalent form generated by the combined plan graph and massing grammar approach.

CONCLUSION

This chapter describes and demonstrates the complete approach for recording and extrapolating design instances through the integrated JPG and massing grammars. The method captures both syntactic (space-based) and formal (three-dimensional shape-based or massing-based) characteristics of Wright's Prairie style. Through the grammatical and syntactical analysis of each case, this chapter uncovers the most frequently applied rules and sequences in the set of nineteen of Wright's houses. However, the most important contribution of this chaper is the in-depth review of the language of Frank Lloyd Wright's Prairie houses using the combined method. When applied to a language of designs, the combined spatial and formal characteristics are generalised and then used for generating new alternatives that share these common characteristics of the language or style. The data derived from the demonstration is used to provide new mathematical insights into the formal and social patterns of the Prairie style.

The method can also be applied to generate new instances of the Prairie style beyond the nineteen selected cases. Whereas past research has started to computationally generate new instances of the same formal style (Koning and Eizenberg, 1981), our method encompasses the social and functional properties of the style as well as their formal characteristics. What is signficant about this outcome is that it is the first time that both the spatial and formal properties of the Prairie houses have been simultaneously captured and then retained through the process of generating, or identifying, what is effectively a new design.

REFERENCES

Alofsin, A. (1993). *Frank Lloyd Wright—the lost years, 1910-1922: A study of influence*. Chicago, IL: University of Chicago Press.

Amini Behbahani, P., Ostwald, M. J., & Gu, N. (2016). A syntactical comparative analysis of the spatial properties of Prairie style and Victorian domestic architecture. *The Journal of Architecture*, *21*(3), 348–374. doi:10. 1080/13602365.2016.1179661

Chan, C.-S. (1992). Exploring individual style in design. *Environment and Planning. B, Planning & Design*, *19*(5), 503–523. doi:10.1068/b190503

Futagawa, Y., & Pfeiffer, B. B. (1987a). *Frank Lloyd Wright monograph 1901-1906* (Vol. 2). Tokyo, Japan: A.D.A. Edita.

Futagawa, Y., & Pfeiffer, B. B. (1987b). *Frank Lloyd Wright monograph 1907-1913* (Vol. 3). Tokyo, Japan: A.D.A. Edita.

Koning, H., & Eizenberg, J. (1981). The language of the prairie: Frank Lloyd Wright's Prairie houses. *Environment & Planning B*, *8*(3), 295–323. doi:10.1068/b080295

Laseau, P., & Tice, J. (1992). *Frank Lloyd Wright: Between principles and form*. New York, NY: Van Nostrand Reinhold.

Lee, J. H., Ostwald, M. J., & Gu, N. (2015a). A syntactical and grammatical approach to architectural configuration, analysis and generation. *Architectural Science Review*, *58*(3), 189–204. doi:10.1080/00038628.2015.1015948

Lee, J. H., Ostwald, M. J., & Gu, N. (2015b). Using a JPG grammar to explore the syntax of a style: An application to the architecture of Glenn Murcutt. In J. S. Gero & S. Hanna (Eds.), *Design computing and cognition "14* (pp. 589–604). Cham, Switzerland: Springer International Publishing. doi:10.1007/978-3-319-14956-1_33

Lee, J. H., Ostwald, M. J., & Gu, N. (2017). A combined plan graph and massing grammar approach to Frank Lloyd Wright's Prairie architecture. *Nexus Network Journal*, *19*(2), 279–299. doi:10.100700004-017-0333-0

Lind, C. (1994). *Frank Lloyd Wright's Prairie houses*. Archetype Press.

Ostwald, M. J., & Dawes, M. (2018). *The mathematics of the modern villa: An analysis using space syntax and isovists*. Basel, Switzerland: Birkhäuser.

Ostwald, M. J., & Dawes, M. J. (2013). Prospect-refuge patterns in Frank Lloyd Wright's Prairie houses: Using isovist fields to examine the evidence. *Journal of Space Syntax*, *4*(1), 136–159.

Ostwald, M. J., & Vaughan, J. L. (2010). The mathematics of style in the architecture of Frank Lloyd Wright: A computational, fractal analysis of formal complexity in fifteen domestic designs. In P. S. Geller (Ed.), *Built environment: Design, management and applications*. New York, NY: Nova Scientific.

Ostwald, M. J., & Vaughan, J. L. (2016). *The fractal dimension of architecture*. Cham, Switzerland: Birkhauser. doi:10.1007/978-3-319-32426-5

Pinnell, P. (2005). Academic tradition and the individual talent. In R. McCarter (Ed.), *On and By Frank Lloyd Wright* (pp. 22–55). New York, NY: Phaidon.

Chapter 9
Conclusion

ABSTRACT

The final chapter of the book revisits the emerging Shape Grammar research presented in Chapter 2 and the quantitative analysis and guided generation using a Palladian Grammar in Chapter 3. It then revisits the limitations of Space Syntax approaches and of the justified planning graph (JPG) method and its measures, described in Chapters 4 and 5. Finally, this chapter discusses the new combined grammatical and syntactical method presented in Chapters 6, 7, and 8. This concluding chapter emphasises the book's contribution to advances in Shape Grammar and Space Syntax research for architectural design analysis and generation. In addition to these theoretical contributions, the primary computational approaches in the book, which have been demonstrated using the domestic designs of Palladio, Wright, and Murcutt, are also valuable for architectural education and practice.

INTRODUCTION

The content of this book is concerned with two significant computational theories, Shape Grammar and Space Syntax, which have been separately developed but rarely combined in any significant way. The first of these is typically used to investigate or generate the formal or geometric properties of architecture, while the second is used to analyse the spatial, topological or social properties of architecture. Despite the reciprocal relationship between form and space in architecture – it is difficult to conceptualise a completed building without a sense of both of these properties – the two

DOI: 10.4018/978-1-7998-1698-0.ch009

major computational theories have been largely developed and applied in isolation from each another.

This book is the first to take a consistent approach to explaining the application and limits of *both* theories and trace emerging research in each. However, the book's purpose is not just to explain these theories or propose methodological advances in each. Instead, this book demonstrates the first detailed, combined grammatical and syntactical computational method. This new combined method can be used to analyse an architectural language or style in terms of its combined formal and spatial properties. It can also be used to support the generation of new instances of a style that are compliant with both the formal and spatial properties of the original language. In essence, this new combined method reconnects form and space, or *firmness* and *commodity* in a Vitruvian sense, in architectural computational analysis. This concluding chapter briefly revisits the content of the book, including both grammatical and syntactical approaches and emerging trends and developments. Thereafter, it reiterates the primary frameworks and limitations of the new combined method.

Shape Grammar

The design process is conventionally conceptualised and explained as a progressive or staged sequence of actions with only a limited number of recursive steps (Lawson, 2006). The recursive stages are typically regarded as either corrective, being used to return a design process to its ideal path or to assess the degree to which a design fulfils its functional or aesthetic goals (Anderson, 2011). Furthermore, when the building that results from the design process is analysed, it is usually understood as exhibiting the architect's true and unexpurgated design intention, regardless of how it was actually produced (Pressman, 2012). Thus, even if the process was intuitive or non-linear, the resultant building is taken to represent a reasoned, consistent or optimal set of design decisions by an architect. This assumption is at the core of many computational models of design analysis and generation. Such approaches accept that design is not necessarily a straightforward process, but argue that architecture can, nevertheless, be usefully examined on this basis. With this in mind, a Shape Grammar is a production system for an architectural language, which comprises a set of rules and a behavioural engine that determines the sequence in which the rules are applied. In effect, this production system is an analogue of the conventional design process used by an architect. The grammar serves as a record of the sequence of design decisions, and their formal impacts, from the first shape drawn by an architect to the design of the completed plan. Thus, while grammatical research is often celebrated for its capacity to model or generate forms, one of its greatest values is found in the idealised design process its constructs.

The introduction to Shape Grammars and emerging research in the field is contained in Section 2 of the present book. Chapter 2 presents a literature review of Shape Grammar research published between 2008 and 2018; it has an emphasis on uncovering new or emerging trends in grammatical research in architecture, art, design and engineering. While acknowledging some methodological limitations associated with the use of the three major research databases, one of the important findings of Chapter 2 is that the advances in automated design and generative algorithms have been adopted by researchers to enhance or improve practical and theoretical grammatical applications. Furthermore, although many previous Shape Grammars have been only manually or graphically presented, recent algorithmic advances in grammatical applications have enabled researchers to effectively generate, optimise and evaluate design variations. Advances in procedural modelling and genetic algorithms have also been combined with grammatical methods to develop new techniques to support architectural practitioners. In addition, progress in algebraic research has led to the development of *generic* Shape Grammars and contributed to design automation and optimisation systems. These advances have kept grammatical research relevant in architecture and design, and revitalised its potential as both an analytical and generative approach.

Chapter 3 demonstrates a simple Shape Grammar for an architectural language and introduces a new mathematical approach to measuring and guiding the grammatical application of a set of rules. While past research has suggested the use of parametric algorithms to support design analysis and generation (Eilouti & Hamamieh Al Shaar, 2012; Hyun, Lee, Kim, & Cho, 2015; Tepavčević & Stojaković, 2013), the use of rule application frequencies for generating a set of designs is a unique approach to understanding the possible design process employed by the architect. Both the Shape Grammar method, and the rule frequency approach are demonstrated using a Palladian language, based on ten architectural plans in *I Quattro Libri dell'Architettura*. The Palladian language is associated with Palladio's eight, 5×3-grid villas and two, 5×4-grid villas. The grammar consists of four stages using eleven rule sets, which commence with the generation of initial modules and then end with a termination rule. The grammar is then used to analyse the design process for these works and generate a new instance that encapsulates the dominant design process.

It is important to remember that in all Shape Grammar research, the reliability of the rules and veracity of any newly generated instances are both relative to the body of works that make up the language (Seebohm & Chan, 2001). For example, with a starting point of ten similarly designed Palladian floor plans, each with a rigorous geometric basis, it is possible to develop detailed and consistent rules and then generate new instances of these. But with a less well-defined set of works, the resultant language may be so lacking in structure that the grammatical productions are not useful. Nevertheless, the Palladian grammar is sufficiently consistent as to offer several new insights, including, for example, that the *Villa Cornaro*, which was previously grammatically generated using a 3×4 gridded plan (Benrós, Duarte & Hanna 2012), has a proportional ratio that is better suited to a 5×4 grid. Despite such observations, the grammar is necessarily simplified for the present purposes, and it does not consider wall inflections, door and window openings or entrance details. Nonetheless, this fundamental approach to an architectural grammar could be extended to other design grammars for addressing more complex or detailed factors.

Space Syntax

The origins of Space Syntax are often traced to the 1970s, and the first attempts to use computational techniques to investigate the properties of architectural plans. Since then it has become an important method for exploring the relations between spatial organisation and social, behavioural and cognitive effects. Despite criticisms of Space Syntax (Netto, 2016; Ratti, 2004a, 2004b), and some practical limitations (Pafka, Dovey, & Aschwanden, 2018), it remains one of the most influential methods for analysing urban and architectural spatial configurations. Importantly, Space Syntax has continued to evolve over the last four decades, with increasingly sophisticated applications in urban analysis and architectural optimisation. Chapter 4 categorises the emerging themes in Space Syntax research in terms of connections to axial line, convex space and visibility analysis.

Each of these three Space Syntax techniques – axial line, convex space and visibility analysis – are presented in this book using case studies. Chapter 4 uses two case studies to demonstrate the axial line and visibility graph techniques, while Chapter 5 demonstrates convex space analysis, focusing on the justified plan graph (JPG) and its mathematical measures. The first of these case studies is an application of axial line analysis to four street-networks in Seoul. The case study derives measures for connectivity and global and local integration values to develop a quantitative understanding of the difference between planned and evolving street patterns and neighbourhoods. The second case study in Chapter 4 employs visibility graph analysis (VGA) and isovist techniques to reveal different spatial characteristics of the experience of user groups in residential aged-care facilities in Australia and Korea. The joint VGA-Isovist technique captures syntactical and visibility characteristics of the architectural plans, both of which may be examined quantitatively and qualitatively. Acknowledging the small sample size, the data derived from the case study can be used to provide an insight into the spatial and social properties of each case. These properties may be related to the particular design typologies that their architects adopted, either from policy guides or from *a priori* knowledge or reasoning. Some classic aged-care planning types are also questioned in this analysis, wherein, for example, the "double loaded corridor" evolves into a "racetrack" or "mall" planning configuration (Brawley, 2006). For this reason, the comparative case study needs to be able to measure and differentiate the properties of building configurational typologies. The results of the isovist analysis from four locations also imply that there might be social and cultural differences in the visibility configurations of the different facilities. The syntactical measures provide a number of different ways of analysing and interpreting the plans used for residential aged care. The third case study, in Chapter 5, examines three Palladian villas (two by Palladio, and one grammatically generated by Stiny) using convex space analysis and Justified Plan Graphs (JPGs) This detailed demonstration is, in part, a response to the common criticism of syntactical methods, that they are not always transparent in their explanations of key processes (Dovey 1999). A further source of criticism is the interpretation of mathematical results (Dovey, 2010; Osman & Suliman, 1994). As such, in Chapter 5 the primary derived measures (TD, MD, RA and i) are introduced and discussed along with an interpretation of the results for the three Palladian plans in the case study.

As alluded to in the previous paragraph, there are several known limitations to the primary Space Syntax techniques, and Chapter 5 proposes an alternative way of measuring spatial properties, using centrality indices, to overcome some of these. In Chapter 5, three centrality indices – degree centrality (C_D), closeness centrality (C_C) and betweenness centrality (C_B) – and their use in a weighted, directed JPG are illustrated with a worked example. In axial line analysis, C_C and C_B tend to be used almost interchangeably with "integration" and "choice" values. However, despite obvious similarities, they are not the same. The alternative approach described in Chapter 5 can be used to accommodate multiple links, directed links and "distance" between spaces, factors that are disregarded in the conventional JPG method. Thus, the alternative method is useful for investigating the spatial configurations of urban-scale architecture and urban planning, rather than domestic buildings. However, the weighted and directed JPG method is more complicated than the classic method. In practice, multiple and directed links are unusual in a building program, and different distances between spaces are only rarely significant in domestic architecture. Furthermore, centrality measures of the type introduced here are not yet fully understood or used in architectural design. Thus, the remainder of the examples in this book employ conventional syntactical measures for JPGs.

The JPG Grammar and The Massing Grammar

Section 3 in this book describes two applications of generic grammars and a new computational method for a syntactically derived massing grammar. The new approach is demonstrated in two detailed case studies of the domestic architecture of Frank Lloyd Wright and Glenn Murcutt. The concept of a generic Shape Grammar is not a new one, but, to date, researchers have not successfully demonstrated its use for architectural design, partially because of the complexity inherent in most architectural languages (Benrós et al., 2012; Costa & Duarte, 2015). Section 3 of this book demonstrates the development and application of two generic shape grammars: a massing grammar and a JPG grammar. These generic grammars are converted into specific grammars in Chapters 7 and 8, being a grammar for Murcutt's domestic rural architecture and Wright's Prairie Style architecture, respectively. The use of algebraic expression and simplified components (including sectored spatial modules and massing blocks) supports the success of both grammars. However, ultimately, the JPG grammar is not strictly a grammar in the conventional design sense, but rather it is a tool that captures information about the functional and spatial properties of a design, and then allows for the development of a generalised set of rule conditions that reflect aspects of an architectural style. It is effectively a syntactical grammar, and it is the other major contribution of the present book to the development of new knowledge in computational design.

The benefits of the combined JPG Grammar and Massing Grammar are that they capture both the topological and geometric structures of an architectural language, while recording the sequence of spatial and formal rules required to produce an existing example of the language or generate a new one. Murcutt and Wright are ideal cases to demonstrate these combined benefits. Both architects' works are regarded as representing a coherent and consistent architectural language, yet important properties of Murcutt's and Wright's works are often overlooked in computational analysis. For example, Hanson and Radford (1986a, 1986b) claim that Murcutt's architectural formal language is structured around rules for environmental adaptation. Their grammatical analysis provides an evaluation of the rules that most clearly account for the shape of Murcutt's architecture, but without much consideration of the programmatic or social function of the design. Ostwald echoes their proposition that formal or environmental priorities could be more important in Murcutt's architecture than socio-spatial factors (Ostwald, 2011a, 2011b). His syntactical analysis of a larger set of Murcutt's houses identifies a range of mathematical evidence for this proposition, but it is limited by the fact that most Space Syntax methods only consider form as an indirect reflection of spatial results. Wright's Prairie style domestic architecture has also previously been subjected to both grammatical (Koning & Eizenberg, 1981) and syntactical analysis (Amini Behbahani, Ostwald, & Gu, 2016), with the former case arguing that the complex formal modelling of this particular language is its unique characteristic, while the latter notes that its planning, while highly consistent, is not necessarily so ground-breaking as historians often observe. These views, while seemingly contradictory, are both products of their methodologies. The former grammatical method uncovered a consistent, if complex, set of rules for generating Prairie houses, but without a consideration of their planning. The second, syntactical, approach measured, for the first time, the social structure of the planning. As such, these designs are founded in a strong architectural language that has both formal and spatial rules that must be followed. Thus, both Murcutt's and Wright's works are ideal cases for the application of a combined syntactical and grammatical method.

The grammatical and syntactically-derived method demonstrated in Chapter 7 provides both statistical and graphical support for defining and exploring spatial and formal design patterns in a family of works. The method focuses on Space Syntax as an analytic-generative theory for design and the possibilities that arise for design analysis and generation when combining

Space Syntax and Shape Grammar approaches. Despite this strength, the JPG grammar approach has some disadvantages over the two traditional, separate methods. Its primary disadvantage is that, in the variation presented in this book, it only examines larger spatial groupings, limiting its effectiveness for detailed social analysis. That is, the particular JPG-grammar-based framework relies on programmatic adjacencies as much as it does direct connectivity, and so may not provide the same level of insight into syntactical relations as it does for spatial topologies. Furthermore, even though the modular plan facilitates the generation of the block-shape forms, the outcome is necessarily simplified, and it only allows for a basic massing to be developed. Thus, it should be obvious for anyone who knows Murcutt's or Wright's architecture that the building forms produced in Chapters 7 (Figure 19) or 8 (Figure 21) lack the finesse and lightness of Murcutt's or Wright's detailing, as each architect modifies individual surfaces and joints to improve their environment performance. Furthermore, while an architect like Glenn Murcutt, Frank Lloyd Wright or Alvaro Siza might employ a consistent approach to spatial and formal structures, the vagaries of individual clients' needs and resources, and local site conditions, will often work to undermine the consistency that would otherwise be apparent. This is one of the advantages of adopting sector nodes for spatial analysis and simplified massing for formal derivation. By keeping the analysis to a higher level, the larger patterns and trends should be more apparent, and the localised differences may play a reduced role.

CONCLUSION

The results developed in Chapters 7 and 8 using the new combined grammatical and syntactical method confirm that it is capable of identifying patterns in social and functional planning, as expressed in design decisions that have their own innate grammar. They confirm that a closely related set of works could be analysed in this way to reveal a spatial and social structure that is reiterated and reinterpreted across multiple design, and which is emphasised in the formal language used in the set of cases. The presence of this particular syntactic or formal pattern across multiple works by an architect seems to suggest that the architect's syntactic and formal style at the very least embraces this pattern. In the case studies in Chapter 7 and 8, although such characteristics are captured in a relatively small body of work (ten design instances for Glenn Murcutt and 19 for Frank Lloyd Wright), the effectiveness of the combined grammatical and syntactic approach to architectural analysis is demonstrated, capturing the language of the domestic architecture of two modernists, Murcutt and Wright.

The s-JPG grammars in Chapters 7 and 8 not only provide a capacity to identify spatial and formal design patterns in a body of work, they can also suggest a new way of generating variations of these, as well as capturing a dominant JPG in a syntactic style. Such an approach provides quantitative and graphical aids to generate design variations. When applied to a set of designs, both spatial and formal characteristics can be generalised and then used for generating new variations that represent these characteristics. Such knowledge enables an appropriate abstraction for understanding a design language and for the search for an optimal design and its variations (Gero & Coyne, 1985). For example, the frequencies of the rules being applied in the configuration process can serve as a potential guide for identifying the dominant design characteristics of the set and generating these characteristics. Augmented with other computational design and knowledge-based systems, it can be expanded to accommodate more complex or detailed issues that are pertinent to design practice or historiography. In addition, the new method can be used as a notation system to explore both analytical and generative issues at the conceptual design stage.

REFERENCES

Amini Behbahani, P., Ostwald, M. J., & Gu, N. (2016). A syntactical comparative analysis of the spatial properties of Prairie style and Victorian domestic architecture. *The Journal of Architecture*, *21*(3), 348–374. doi:10.1080/13602365.2016.1179661

Anderson, J. (2011). *Basics architecture 03: Architectural design*. Lausanne, Switzerland: AVA.

Benrós, D., Duarte, J. P., & Hanna, S. (2012). A new Palladian shape grammar: A Subdivision Grammar as alternative to the Palladian Grammar. *International Journal of Architectural Computing*, *10*(4), 521–540. doi:10.1260/1478-0771.10.4.521

Brawley, E. C. (2006). *Design innovations for aging and Alzheimer's: Creating caring environments*. Hoboken, NJ: John Wiley & Sons.

Costa, E. C., & Duarte, J. P. (2015). Generic shape grammars for mass customization of ceramic tableware. In J. S. Gero & S. Hanna (Eds.), *Design computing and cognition "14* (pp. 437–454). London, UK: Springer International Publishing. doi:10.1007/978-3-319-14956-1_25

Dovey, K. (1999). *Framing places: Mediating power in built form*. London, UK: Routledge. doi:10.4324/9780203267639

Dovey, K. (2010). *Becoming places: Urbanism / architecture / identity / power*. London, UK: Routledge.

Eilouti, B. H., & Hamamieh Al Shaar, M. J. (2012). Shape grammars of traditional Damascene houses. *International Journal of Architectural Heritage*, *6*(4), 415–435. doi:10.1080/15583058.2011.575530

Gero, J. S., & Coyne, R. D. (1985). Logic programming as a means of representing semantics in design languages. *Environment and Planning. B, Planning & Design*, *12*(3), 351–369. doi:10.1068/b120351

Hanson, N. L. R., & Radford, A. D. (1986a). Living on the edge: A grammar for some country houses by Glenn Murcutt. *Architecture Australia*, *75*(5), 66–73.

Hanson, N. L. R., & Radford, A. D. (1986b). On modelling the work of the architect Glenn Murcutt. *Design Computing*, *1*(3), 189–203.

Hyun, K. H., Lee, J.-H., Kim, M., & Cho, S. (2015). Style synthesis and analysis of car designs for style quantification based on product appearance similarities. *Advanced Engineering Informatics*, *29*(3), 483–494. doi:10.1016/j.aei.2015.04.001

Koning, H., & Eizenberg, J. (1981). The language of the prairie: Frank Lloyd Wright's prairie houses. *Environment & Planning B*, *8*(3), 295–323. doi:10.1068/b080295

Lawson, B. (2006). *How designers think: The design process demystified*. Burlington, MA: Elsevier. doi:10.4324/9780080454979

Netto, V. M. (2016). "What is space syntax not?" Reflections on space syntax as sociospatial theory. *URBAN DESIGN International*, *21*(1), 25–40. doi:10.1057/udi.2015.21

Osman, K. M., & Suliman, M. (1994). The space syntax methodology: Fits and misfit. *Architecture & Comportement/Architecture & Behaviour, 10*(2), 189-204.

Ostwald, M. J. (2011a). Examining the relationship between topology and geometry: A configurational analysis of the rural houses (1984-2005) of Glenn Murcutt. *Journal of Space Syntax, 2*(2), 223–246.

Ostwald, M. J. (2011b). A justified plan graph analysis of the early houses (1975-1982) of Glenn Murcutt. *Nexus Network Journal, 13*(3), 737–762. doi:10.100700004-011-0089-x

Pafka, E., Dovey, K., & Aschwanden, G. D. P. A. (2018). Limits of space syntax for urban design: Axiality, scale and sinuosity. *Environment and Planning B. Urban Analytics and City Science*. doi:10.1177/2399808318786512

Pressman, A. (2012). *Designing architecture: The elements of process*. London, UK: Routledge. doi:10.4324/9780203122174

Ratti, C. (2004a). Rejoinder to Hillier and Penn. *Environment and Planning. B, Planning & Design, 31*(4), 513–516. doi:10.1068/b3019b

Ratti, C. (2004b). Space syntax: Some inconsistencies. *Environment and Planning. B, Planning & Design, 31*(4), 487–499. doi:10.1068/b3019

Seebohm, T., & Chan, D. (2001). The design space of schematic palladian plans for two villa topologies. In *Reinventing the Discourse - How Digital Tools Help Bridge and Transform Research, Education and Practice in Architecture: Proceedings of the Twenty First Annual Conference of the Association for Computer-Aided Design in Architecture* (pp. 156-165). Buffalo, NY: SUNY Buffalo.

Tepavčević, B., & Stojaković, V. (2013). Procedural modeling in architecture based on statistical and fuzzy inference. *Automation in Construction, 35*, 329–337. doi:10.1016/j.autcon.2013.05.015

Related Readings

To continue IGI Global's long-standing tradition of advancing innovation through emerging research, please find below a compiled list of recommended IGI Global book chapters and journal articles in the areas of urban planning, architecture, and sustainable urban development. These related readings will provide additional information and guidance to further enrich your knowledge and assist you with your own research.

Ahuja, K., & Khosla, A. (2019). A Framework to Develop a Zero-Carbon Emission Sustainable Cognitive City. In K. Ahuja & A. Khosla (Eds.), *Driving the Development, Management, and Sustainability of Cognitive Cities* (pp. 1–26). Hershey, PA: IGI Global. doi:10.4018/978-1-5225-8085-0.ch001

Akkucuk, U. (2016). SCOR Model and the Green Supply Chain. In U. Akkucuk (Ed.), *Handbook of Research on Waste Management Techniques for Sustainability* (pp. 108–124). Hershey, PA: IGI Global. doi:10.4018/978-1-4666-9723-2.ch006

Albuquerque, C. M. (2017). Cities Really Smart and Inclusive: Possibilities and Limits for Social Inclusion and Participation. In L. Carvalho (Ed.), *Handbook of Research on Entrepreneurial Development and Innovation Within Smart Cities* (pp. 229–247). Hershey, PA: IGI Global. doi:10.4018/978-1-5225-1978-2.ch011

Angelucci, F., Di Girolamo, C., & Zazzero, E. (2018). New Designing Codes for Urban Infrastructures: A Hypothesis of a Transdisciplinary Approach. In G. Carlone, N. Martinelli, & F. Rotondo (Eds.), *Designing Grid Cities for Optimized Urban Development and Planning* (pp. 209–237). Hershey, PA: IGI Global. doi:10.4018/978-1-5225-3613-0.ch012

Avdimiotis, S., & Tilikidou, I. (2017). Smart Tourism Development: The Case of Halkidiki. In L. Carvalho (Ed.), *Handbook of Research on Entrepreneurial Development and Innovation Within Smart Cities* (pp. 491–513). Hershey, PA: IGI Global. doi:10.4018/978-1-5225-1978-2.ch021

Ayvaz, B., & Görener, A. (2016). Reverse Logistics in the Electronics Waste Industry. In U. Akkucuk (Ed.), *Handbook of Research on Waste Management Techniques for Sustainability* (pp. 155–171). Hershey, PA: IGI Global. doi:10.4018/978-1-4666-9723-2.ch008

Bagnato, V. P. (2018). Technology and Urban Structure: The Grid City Between Technological Innovation and New Public Space System. In G. Carlone, N. Martinelli, & F. Rotondo (Eds.), *Designing Grid Cities for Optimized Urban Development and Planning* (pp. 238–253). Hershey, PA: IGI Global. doi:10.4018/978-1-5225-3613-0.ch013

Bala, I., & Singh, G. (2019). Green Communication for Cognitive Cities. In K. Ahuja & A. Khosla (Eds.), *Driving the Development, Management, and Sustainability of Cognitive Cities* (pp. 87–110). Hershey, PA: IGI Global. doi:10.4018/978-1-5225-8085-0.ch004

Bernardino, S., & Santos, J. F. (2017). Building Smarter Cities through Social Entrepreneurship. In L. Carvalho (Ed.), *Handbook of Research on Entrepreneurial Development and Innovation Within Smart Cities* (pp. 327–362). Hershey, PA: IGI Global. doi:10.4018/978-1-5225-1978-2.ch015

Bernardo, M. D. (2017). Smart City Governance: From E-Government to Smart Governance. In L. Carvalho (Ed.), *Handbook of Research on Entrepreneurial Development and Innovation Within Smart Cities* (pp. 290–326). Hershey, PA: IGI Global. doi:10.4018/978-1-5225-1978-2.ch014

Bhatia, P., & Singh, P. (2019). Technological and Gamified Solutions for Pollution Control in Cognitive Cities. In K. Ahuja & A. Khosla (Eds.), *Driving the Development, Management, and Sustainability of Cognitive Cities* (pp. 234–249). Hershey, PA: IGI Global. doi:10.4018/978-1-5225-8085-0.ch010

Bhatt, R. (2017). Zero Tillage for Mitigating Global Warming Consequences and Improving Livelihoods in South Asia. In W. Ganpat & W. Isaac (Eds.), *Environmental Sustainability and Climate Change Adaptation Strategies* (pp. 126–161). Hershey, PA: IGI Global. doi:10.4018/978-1-5225-1607-1.ch005

Bolívar, M. P. (2018). Governance in Smart Cities: A Comparison of Practitioners' Perceptions and Prior Research. *International Journal of E-Planning Research*, 7(2), 1–19. doi:10.4018/IJEPR.2018040101

Bostanci, S. H., & Albayrak, A. N. (2017). The Role of Eco-Municipalities in Climate Change for a Sustainable Future. In W. Ganpat & W. Isaac (Eds.), *Environmental Sustainability and Climate Change Adaptation Strategies* (pp. 213–231). Hershey, PA: IGI Global. doi:10.4018/978-1-5225-1607-1.ch008

Brkljačić, T., Majetić, F., & Tarabić, B. N. (2017). Smart Environment: Cyber Parks (Connecting Nature and Technology). In L. Carvalho (Ed.), *Handbook of Research on Entrepreneurial Development and Innovation Within Smart Cities* (pp. 150–172). Hershey, PA: IGI Global. doi:10.4018/978-1-5225-1978-2.ch008

Cai, Y. Z., Wu, F., Li, J., Wang, J., & Huang, M. (2019). Application of UAV Technology to Planning Study on Chinese Villages in Guanzhong. In J. Vargas-Hernández & J. Zdunek-Wielgołaska (Eds.), *Bioeconomical Solutions and Investments in Sustainable City Development* (pp. 180–195). Hershey, PA: IGI Global. doi:10.4018/978-1-5225-7958-8.ch008

Calisto, M. D., & Gonçalves, A. (2017). Smart Citizens, Wise Decisions: Sustainability-Driven Tourism Entrepreneurs. In L. Carvalho (Ed.), *Handbook of Research on Entrepreneurial Development and Innovation Within Smart Cities* (pp. 20–43). Hershey, PA: IGI Global. doi:10.4018/978-1-5225-1978-2.ch002

Capelo, C. (2017). Exploring the Dynamics of an Energy Service Venture. In L. Carvalho (Ed.), *Handbook of Research on Entrepreneurial Development and Innovation Within Smart Cities* (pp. 269–289). Hershey, PA: IGI Global. doi:10.4018/978-1-5225-1978-2.ch013

Caridi, G. (2018). Calabria 1783: The Orthogonal Grid as a Physical and Ideological Device of Reconstruction. In G. Carlone, N. Martinelli, & F. Rotondo (Eds.), *Designing Grid Cities for Optimized Urban Development and Planning* (pp. 176–187). Hershey, PA: IGI Global. doi:10.4018/978-1-5225-3613-0.ch010

Carlone, G. (2018). Cities and Extension Plans in the Kingdom of the Two Sicilies: Borgo Murattiano of Bari (1812-1859). In G. Carlone, N. Martinelli, & F. Rotondo (Eds.), *Designing Grid Cities for Optimized Urban Development and Planning* (pp. 1–18). Hershey, PA: IGI Global. doi:10.4018/978-1-5225-3613-0.ch001

Carvalho, L. C. (2017). Entrepreneurial Ecosystems: Lisbon as a Smart Start-Up City. In L. Carvalho (Ed.), *Handbook of Research on Entrepreneurial Development and Innovation Within Smart Cities* (pp. 1–19). Hershey, PA: IGI Global. doi:10.4018/978-1-5225-1978-2.ch001

Castagnolo, V. (2018). Analyzing, Classifying, Safeguarding: Drawing for the Borgo Murattiano Neighbourhood of Bari. In G. Carlone, N. Martinelli, & F. Rotondo (Eds.), *Designing Grid Cities for Optimized Urban Development and Planning* (pp. 93–108). Hershey, PA: IGI Global. doi:10.4018/978-1-5225-3613-0.ch006

Castilla-Polo, F., Gallardo-Vázquez, D., Sánchez-Hernández, M. I., & Ruiz-Rodríguez, M. D. (2017). Cooperatives as Responsible and Innovative Entrepreneurial Ecosystems in Smart Territories: The Olive Oil Industry in the South of Spain. In L. Carvalho (Ed.), *Handbook of Research on Entrepreneurial Development and Innovation Within Smart Cities* (pp. 459–490). Hershey, PA: IGI Global. doi:10.4018/978-1-5225-1978-2.ch020

Charalabidis, Y., & Theocharopoulou, C. (2019). A Participative Method for Prioritizing Smart City Interventions in Medium-Sized Municipalities. *International Journal of Public Administration in the Digital Age, 6*(1), 41–63. doi:10.4018/IJPADA.2019010103

Chatsiwa, J., Mujere, N., & Maiyana, A. B. (2016). Municipal Solid Waste Management. In U. Akkucuk (Ed.), *Handbook of Research on Waste Management Techniques for Sustainability* (pp. 19–43). Hershey, PA: IGI Global. doi:10.4018/978-1-4666-9723-2.ch002

Chawla, R., Singhal, P., & Garg, A. K. (2019). Impact of Dust for Solar PV in Indian Scenario: Experimental Analysis. In K. Ahuja & A. Khosla (Eds.), *Driving the Development, Management, and Sustainability of Cognitive Cities* (pp. 111–138). Hershey, PA: IGI Global. doi:10.4018/978-1-5225-8085-0.ch005

Cılız, N., Yıldırım, H., & Temizel, Ş. (2016). Structure Development for Effective Medical Waste and Hazardous Waste Management System. In U. Akkucuk (Ed.), *Handbook of Research on Waste Management Techniques for Sustainability* (pp. 303–327). Hershey, PA: IGI Global. doi:10.4018/978-1-4666-9723-2.ch016

Collignon de Alba, C., Haberleithner, J., & López, M. M. (2017). Creative Industries in the Smart City: Overview of a Liability in Emerging Economies. In L. Carvalho (Ed.), *Handbook of Research on Entrepreneurial Development and Innovation Within Smart Cities* (pp. 107–126). Hershey, PA: IGI Global. doi:10.4018/978-1-5225-1978-2.ch006

Corum, A. (2016). Remanufacturing, an Added Value Product Recovery Strategy. In U. Akkucuk (Ed.), *Handbook of Research on Waste Management Techniques for Sustainability* (pp. 347–367). Hershey, PA: IGI Global. doi:10.4018/978-1-4666-9723-2.ch018

Crosas, C. (2018). Latin American Cities: Modern Grids From 1850s. In G. Carlone, N. Martinelli, & F. Rotondo (Eds.), *Designing Grid Cities for Optimized Urban Development and Planning* (pp. 39–51). Hershey, PA: IGI Global. doi:10.4018/978-1-5225-3613-0.ch003

D'Onofrio, S., Habenstein, A., & Portmann, E. (2019). Ontological Design for Cognitive Cities: The New Principle for Future Urban Management. In K. Ahuja & A. Khosla (Eds.), *Driving the Development, Management, and Sustainability of Cognitive Cities* (pp. 183–211). Hershey, PA: IGI Global. doi:10.4018/978-1-5225-8085-0.ch008

Dalzero, S. (2018). The Time of the Finished World Has Begun: A New Map of the World – National Borders Partially or Fully Fenced-Off. In G. Carlone, N. Martinelli, & F. Rotondo (Eds.), *Designing Grid Cities for Optimized Urban Development and Planning* (pp. 254–275). Hershey, PA: IGI Global. doi:10.4018/978-1-5225-3613-0.ch014

Damurski, L. (2016). Recent Progress in Online Communication Tools for Urban Planning: A Comparative Study of Polish and German Municipalities. *International Journal of E-Planning Research*, 5(1), 39–54. doi:10.4018/IJEPR.2016010103

Damurski, L. (2016). Smart City, Integrated Planning, and Multilevel Governance: A Conceptual Framework for e-Planning in Europe. *International Journal of E-Planning Research*, 5(4), 41–53. doi:10.4018/IJEPR.2016100103

Das, K. K., & Sharma, N. K. (2016). Post Disaster Housing Management for Sustainable Urban Development: A Review. *International Journal of Geotechnical Earthquake Engineering*, 7(1), 1–18. doi:10.4018/IJGEE.2016010101

Das, S., & Nayyar, A. (2019). Innovative Ideas to Manage Urban Traffic Congestion in Cognitive Cities. In K. Ahuja & A. Khosla (Eds.), *Driving the Development, Management, and Sustainability of Cognitive Cities* (pp. 139–162). Hershey, PA: IGI Global. doi:10.4018/978-1-5225-8085-0.ch006

Deakin, M., & Reid, A. (2017). The Embedded Intelligence of Smart Cities: Urban Life, Citizenship, and Community. *International Journal of Public Administration in the Digital Age*, 4(4), 62–74. doi:10.4018/IJPADA.2017100105

Djukic, A., Stupar, A., & Antonic, B. M. (2018). The Orthogonal Urban Matrix of the Towns in Vojvodina, Northern Serbia: Genesis and Transformation. In G. Carlone, N. Martinelli, & F. Rotondo (Eds.), *Designing Grid Cities for Optimized Urban Development and Planning* (pp. 128–156). Hershey, PA: IGI Global. doi:10.4018/978-1-5225-3613-0.ch008

Dolunay, O. (2016). A Paradigm Shift: Empowering Farmers to Eliminate the Waste in the Form of Fresh Water and Energy through the Implementation of 4R+T. In U. Akkucuk (Ed.), *Handbook of Research on Waste Management Techniques for Sustainability* (pp. 368–379). Hershey, PA: IGI Global. doi:10.4018/978-1-4666-9723-2.ch019

Dowling, C. M., Walsh, S. D., Purcell, S. M., Hynes, W. M., & Rhodes, M. L. (2017). Operationalising Sustainability within Smart Cities: Towards an Online Sustainability Indicator Tool. *International Journal of E-Planning Research*, 6(4), 1–17. doi:10.4018/IJEPR.2017100101

Ekman, U. (2018). Smart City Planning: Complexity. *International Journal of E-Planning Research*, 7(3), 1–21. doi:10.4018/IJEPR.2018070101

Erdogan, S. (2016). The Effect of Working Capital Management on Firm's Profitability: Evidence from Istanbul Stock Exchange. In U. Akkucuk (Ed.), *Handbook of Research on Waste Management Techniques for Sustainability* (pp. 244–261). Hershey, PA: IGI Global. doi:10.4018/978-1-4666-9723-2.ch013

Related Readings

Eudoxie, G., & Roopnarine, R. (2017). Climate Change Adaptation and Disaster Risk Management in the Caribbean. In W. Ganpat & W. Isaac (Eds.), *Environmental Sustainability and Climate Change Adaptation Strategies* (pp. 97–125). Hershey, PA: IGI Global. doi:10.4018/978-1-5225-1607-1.ch004

Fasolino, I. (2018). Rules for a New Town After a Disaster: The Gridded Schemes in the Plans. In G. Carlone, N. Martinelli, & F. Rotondo (Eds.), *Designing Grid Cities for Optimized Urban Development and Planning* (pp. 157–175). Hershey, PA: IGI Global. doi:10.4018/978-1-5225-3613-0.ch009

Fernandes, C. M., & Dias de Sousa, I. (2017). Digital Swarms: Social Interaction and Emergent Phenomena in Personal Communications Networks. In L. Carvalho (Ed.), *Handbook of Research on Entrepreneurial Development and Innovation Within Smart Cities* (pp. 44–59). Hershey, PA: IGI Global. doi:10.4018/978-1-5225-1978-2.ch003

Fernandes, V., Moreira, A., & Daniel, A. I. (2017). A Qualitative Analysis of Social Entrepreneurship Involving Social Innovation and Intervention. In L. Carvalho (Ed.), *Handbook of Research on Entrepreneurial Development and Innovation Within Smart Cities* (pp. 417–438). Hershey, PA: IGI Global. doi:10.4018/978-1-5225-1978-2.ch018

Gabriel, B. F., Valente, R. A., Dias-de-Oliveira, J., Neto, V. F., & Andrade-Campos, A. (2017). Methodologies for Engineering Learning and Teaching (MELT): An Overview of Engineering Education in Europe and a Novel Concept for Young Students. In L. Carvalho (Ed.), *Handbook of Research on Entrepreneurial Development and Innovation Within Smart Cities* (pp. 363–391). Hershey, PA: IGI Global. doi:10.4018/978-1-5225-1978-2.ch016

Garrick, T. A., & Liburd, O. E. (2017). Impact of Climate Change on a Key Agricultural Pest: Thrips. In W. Ganpat & W. Isaac (Eds.), *Environmental Sustainability and Climate Change Adaptation Strategies* (pp. 232–254). Hershey, PA: IGI Global. doi:10.4018/978-1-5225-1607-1.ch009

Gencer, Y. G. (2016). Mystery of Recycling: Glass and Aluminum Examples. In U. Akkucuk (Ed.), *Handbook of Research on Waste Management Techniques for Sustainability* (pp. 172–191). Hershey, PA: IGI Global. doi:10.4018/978-1-4666-9723-2.ch009

Gencer, Y. G., & Akkucuk, U. (2016). Reverse Logistics: Automobile Recalls and Other Conditions. In U. Akkucuk (Ed.), *Handbook of Research on Waste Management Techniques for Sustainability* (pp. 125–154). Hershey, PA: IGI Global. doi:10.4018/978-1-4666-9723-2.ch007

Gonçalves, J. M., Martins, T. G., & Vilhena da Cunha, I. B. (2017). Local Creative Ecosystems as a Strategy for the Development of Low-Density Urban Spaces. In L. Carvalho (Ed.), *Handbook of Research on Entrepreneurial Development and Innovation Within Smart Cities* (pp. 127–149). Hershey, PA: IGI Global. doi:10.4018/978-1-5225-1978-2.ch007

Goundar, S., & Appana, S. (2017). Mainstreaming Development Policies for Climate Change in Fiji: A Policy Gap Analysis and the Role of ICTs. In W. Ganpat & W. Isaac (Eds.), *Environmental Sustainability and Climate Change Adaptation Strategies* (pp. 1–31). Hershey, PA: IGI Global. doi:10.4018/978-1-5225-1607-1.ch001

Grochulska-Salak, M. (2019). Urban Farming in Sustainable City Development. In J. Vargas-Hernández & J. Zdunek-Wielgołaska (Eds.), *Bioeconomical Solutions and Investments in Sustainable City Development* (pp. 43–64). Hershey, PA: IGI Global. doi:10.4018/978-1-5225-7958-8.ch003

Gruszecka, K. (2019). Ecological Centre of Warsaw as a Development Path. In J. Vargas-Hernández & J. Zdunek-Wielgołaska (Eds.), *Bioeconomical Solutions and Investments in Sustainable City Development* (pp. 117–150). Hershey, PA: IGI Global. doi:10.4018/978-1-5225-7958-8.ch006

Hesapci-Sanaktekin, O., & Aslanbay, Y. (2016). The Networked Self: Collectivism Redefined in Civic Engagements through Social Media Causes. In U. Akkucuk (Ed.), *Handbook of Research on Waste Management Techniques for Sustainability* (pp. 262–276). Hershey, PA: IGI Global. doi:10.4018/978-1-4666-9723-2.ch014

Ikeda, M. (2019). Developing a Sustainable Eco-City in Pre-Olympic Tokyo: Potential of New Methods and Their Limits in an Urban Era. In J. Vargas-Hernández & J. Zdunek-Wielgołaska (Eds.), *Bioeconomical Solutions and Investments in Sustainable City Development* (pp. 196–223). Hershey, PA: IGI Global. doi:10.4018/978-1-5225-7958-8.ch009

İşcan, E. (2019). Strategies of Sustainable Bioeconomy in the Industry 4.0 Framework for Inclusive and Social Prosperity. In J. Vargas-Hernández & J. Zdunek-Wielgołaska (Eds.), *Bioeconomical Solutions and Investments in Sustainable City Development* (pp. 21–42). Hershey, PA: IGI Global. doi:10.4018/978-1-5225-7958-8.ch002

J., J., Samui, P., & Dixon, B. (2016). Determination of Rate of Medical Waste Generation Using RVM, MARS and MPMR. In U. Akkucuk (Ed.), *Handbook of Research on Waste Management Techniques for Sustainability* (pp. 1-18). Hershey, PA: IGI Global. doi:10.4018/978-1-4666-9723-2.ch001

Jiménez, R., Rodríguez, P. L., & Fernández, R. R. (2019). Green Spaces of the Metropolitan Area of Guadalajara. In J. Vargas-Hernández & J. Zdunek-Wielgołaska (Eds.), *Bioeconomical Solutions and Investments in Sustainable City Development* (pp. 151–179). Hershey, PA: IGI Global. doi:10.4018/978-1-5225-7958-8.ch007

Kais, S. M. (2017). Climate Change: Vulnerability and Resilience in Commercial Shrimp Aquaculture in Bangladesh. In W. Ganpat & W. Isaac (Eds.), *Environmental Sustainability and Climate Change Adaptation Strategies* (pp. 162–187). Hershey, PA: IGI Global. doi:10.4018/978-1-5225-1607-1.ch006

Khan, B. (2019). Bio-Economy: Visions, Strategies, and Policies. In J. Vargas-Hernández & J. Zdunek-Wielgołaska (Eds.), *Bioeconomical Solutions and Investments in Sustainable City Development* (pp. 1–20). Hershey, PA: IGI Global. doi:10.4018/978-1-5225-7958-8.ch001

Khanna, B. K. (2017). Indian National Strategy for Climate Change Adaptation and Mitigation. In W. Ganpat & W. Isaac (Eds.), *Environmental Sustainability and Climate Change Adaptation Strategies* (pp. 32–63). Hershey, PA: IGI Global. doi:10.4018/978-1-5225-1607-1.ch002

Khanna, B. K. (2017). Vulnerability of the Lakshadweep Coral Islands in India and Strategies for Mitigating Climate Change Impacts. In W. Ganpat & W. Isaac (Eds.), *Environmental Sustainability and Climate Change Adaptation Strategies* (pp. 64–96). Hershey, PA: IGI Global. doi:10.4018/978-1-5225-1607-1.ch003

Kocasoy, G. (2016). Economic Instruments for Sustainable Environmental Management. In U. Akkucuk (Ed.), *Handbook of Research on Waste Management Techniques for Sustainability* (pp. 192–211). Hershey, PA: IGI Global. doi:10.4018/978-1-4666-9723-2.ch010

Lallo, C. H., Smalling, S., Facey, A., & Hughes, M. (2017). The Impact of Climate Change on Small Ruminant Performance in Caribbean Communities. In W. Ganpat & W. Isaac (Eds.), *Environmental Sustainability and Climate Change Adaptation Strategies* (pp. 296–321). Hershey, PA: IGI Global. doi:10.4018/978-1-5225-1607-1.ch011

Li, Z., Wang, Y., & Chen, Q. (2017). Real-Time Monitoring of Intercity Passenger Flows Based on Big Data: A Decision Support Tool for Urban Sustainability. *International Journal of Strategic Decision Sciences*, 8(4), 120–128. doi:10.4018/IJSDS.2017100106

Loi, N. K., Huyen, N. T., Tu, L. H., Tram, V. N., Liem, N. D., Dat, N. L., ... Minh, D. N. (2017). Sustainable Land Use and Watershed Management in Response to Climate Change Impacts: Case Study in Srepok Watershed, Central Highland of Vietnam. In W. Ganpat & W. Isaac (Eds.), *Environmental Sustainability and Climate Change Adaptation Strategies* (pp. 255–295). Hershey, PA: IGI Global. doi:10.4018/978-1-5225-1607-1.ch010

López-Arranz, M. A. (2017). The Role Corporate Social Responsibility Has in the Smart City Project in Spain. In L. Carvalho (Ed.), *Handbook of Research on Entrepreneurial Development and Innovation Within Smart Cities* (pp. 439–458). Hershey, PA: IGI Global. doi:10.4018/978-1-5225-1978-2.ch019

Lucas, M. R., Rego, C., Vieira, C., & Vieira, I. (2017). Proximity and Cooperation for Innovative Regional Development: The Case of the Science and Technology Park of Alentejo. In L. Carvalho (Ed.), *Handbook of Research on Entrepreneurial Development and Innovation Within Smart Cities* (pp. 199–228). Hershey, PA: IGI Global. doi:10.4018/978-1-5225-1978-2.ch010

Magrinho, A., Neves, J., & Silva, J. R. (2017). The Triple Helix Model: Evidence in the Internationalization of the Health Industry. In L. Carvalho (Ed.), *Handbook of Research on Entrepreneurial Development and Innovation Within Smart Cities* (pp. 60–79). Hershey, PA: IGI Global. doi:10.4018/978-1-5225-1978-2.ch004

Maiorano, A. C. (2018). Urban Fronts in Murattiano Neighbourhood of Bari: A Selective Survey of the Built Environment. In G. Carlone, N. Martinelli, & F. Rotondo (Eds.), *Designing Grid Cities for Optimized Urban Development and Planning* (pp. 78–92). Hershey, PA: IGI Global. doi:10.4018/978-1-5225-3613-0.ch005

Martinelli, N., & Mangialardi, G. (2018). Cities With Grid Layout: Ubiquitousness and Flexibility of an Urban Model. In G. Carlone, N. Martinelli, & F. Rotondo (Eds.), *Designing Grid Cities for Optimized Urban Development and Planning* (pp. 188–208). Hershey, PA: IGI Global. doi:10.4018/978-1-5225-3613-0.ch011

Mizutani, S., Liao, K., & Sasaki, T. G. (2019). Forest-River-Ocean Nexus-Based Education for Community Development: Aiming at Resilient Sustainable Society. In J. Vargas-Hernández & J. Zdunek-Wielgołaska (Eds.), *Bioeconomical Solutions and Investments in Sustainable City Development* (pp. 224–248). Hershey, PA: IGI Global. doi:10.4018/978-1-5225-7958-8.ch010

Moreira, A., & Ferreira, M. A. (2017). Strategic Challenges of the Portuguese Molds Industry: A Sectoral Innovation Perspective. In L. Carvalho (Ed.), *Handbook of Research on Entrepreneurial Development and Innovation Within Smart Cities* (pp. 534–560). Hershey, PA: IGI Global. doi:10.4018/978-1-5225-1978-2.ch023

Mujere, N., & Moyce, W. (2017). Climate Change Impacts on Surface Water Quality. In W. Ganpat & W. Isaac (Eds.), *Environmental Sustainability and Climate Change Adaptation Strategies* (pp. 322–340). Hershey, PA: IGI Global. doi:10.4018/978-1-5225-1607-1.ch012

Mundula, L., & Auci, S. (2017). Smartness, City Efficiency, and Entrepreneurship Milieu. In L. Carvalho (Ed.), *Handbook of Research on Entrepreneurial Development and Innovation Within Smart Cities* (pp. 173–198). Hershey, PA: IGI Global. doi:10.4018/978-1-5225-1978-2.ch009

Nath, R. (2019). Parametric Evaluation of Beam Deflection on Piezoelectric Material Using Implicit and Explicit Method Simulations: A Study in Energy Engineering. In J. Vargas-Hernández & J. Zdunek-Wielgołaska (Eds.), *Bioeconomical Solutions and Investments in Sustainable City Development* (pp. 65–87). Hershey, PA: IGI Global. doi:10.4018/978-1-5225-7958-8.ch004

Nayyar, A., Jain, R., Mahapatra, B., & Singh, A. (2019). Cyber Security Challenges for Smart Cities. In K. Ahuja & A. Khosla (Eds.), *Driving the Development, Management, and Sustainability of Cognitive Cities* (pp. 27–54). Hershey, PA: IGI Global. doi:10.4018/978-1-5225-8085-0.ch002

Odabasi, A., & Tiryaki, C. S. (2016). An Empirical Review of Long Term Electricity Demand Forecasts for Turkey. In U. Akkucuk (Ed.), *Handbook of Research on Waste Management Techniques for Sustainability* (pp. 227–243). Hershey, PA: IGI Global. doi:10.4018/978-1-4666-9723-2.ch012

Okay, E. (2016). Towards Smart Cities in Turkey?: Transitioning from Waste to Creative, Clean and Cheap Eco-Energy. In U. Akkucuk (Ed.), *Handbook of Research on Waste Management Techniques for Sustainability* (pp. 277–302). Hershey, PA: IGI Global. doi:10.4018/978-1-4666-9723-2.ch015

Pawlikowska-Piechotka, A., Łukasik, N., Ostrowska-Tryzno, A., & Sawicka, K. (2017). A Smart City Initiative: Urban Greens and Evaluation Method of the Sport and Recreation Potentials (SEM). In L. Carvalho (Ed.), *Handbook of Research on Entrepreneurial Development and Innovation Within Smart Cities* (pp. 561–583). Hershey, PA: IGI Global. doi:10.4018/978-1-5225-1978-2.ch024

Raisinghani, M. S., & Idemudia, E. C. (2016). Green Information Systems for Sustainability. In U. Akkucuk (Ed.), *Handbook of Research on Waste Management Techniques for Sustainability* (pp. 212–226). Hershey, PA: IGI Global. doi:10.4018/978-1-4666-9723-2.ch011

Rathee, D. S., Ahuja, K., & Hailu, T. (2019). Role of Electronics Devices for E-Health in Smart Cities. In K. Ahuja & A. Khosla (Eds.), *Driving the Development, Management, and Sustainability of Cognitive Cities* (pp. 212–233). Hershey, PA: IGI Global. doi:10.4018/978-1-5225-8085-0.ch009

Rotondo, F. (2018). The Grid Cities: Between Tradition and Innovation. In G. Carlone, N. Martinelli, & F. Rotondo (Eds.), *Designing Grid Cities for Optimized Urban Development and Planning* (pp. 109–127). Hershey, PA: IGI Global. doi:10.4018/978-1-5225-3613-0.ch007

Sánchez-Fernández, M. D., & Cardona, J. R. (2017). The Perception of the Effect of Tourism on the Local Community before the Ibiza Smart Island Project. In L. Carvalho (Ed.), *Handbook of Research on Entrepreneurial Development and Innovation Within Smart Cities* (pp. 392–416). Hershey, PA: IGI Global. doi:10.4018/978-1-5225-1978-2.ch017

Santos, B. (2017). Improving Urban Planning Information, Transparency and Participation in Public Administrations. *International Journal of E-Planning Research*, 6(4), 58–75. doi:10.4018/IJEPR.2017100104

Sardà, J. F. (2018). Cerdà/Barcelona/Eixample: 1855-2017 … A Work in Progress. In G. Carlone, N. Martinelli, & F. Rotondo (Eds.), *Designing Grid Cities for Optimized Urban Development and Planning* (pp. 19–38). Hershey, PA: IGI Global. doi:10.4018/978-1-5225-3613-0.ch002

Selvi, M. S. (2016). Physical Distribution Problems of Textile Companies in Turkey. In U. Akkucuk (Ed.), *Handbook of Research on Waste Management Techniques for Sustainability* (pp. 328–346). Hershey, PA: IGI Global. doi:10.4018/978-1-4666-9723-2.ch017

Signorile, N. (2018). Pride and Prejudice: The Murattiano-Modernism. In G. Carlone, N. Martinelli, & F. Rotondo (Eds.), *Designing Grid Cities for Optimized Urban Development and Planning* (pp. 52–77). Hershey, PA: IGI Global. doi:10.4018/978-1-5225-3613-0.ch004

Singh, G., Kapoor, R., & Khosla, A. K. (2019). Intelligent Anomaly Detection Video Surveillance Systems for Smart Cities. In K. Ahuja & A. Khosla (Eds.), *Driving the Development, Management, and Sustainability of Cognitive Cities* (pp. 163–182). Hershey, PA: IGI Global. doi:10.4018/978-1-5225-8085-0.ch007

Singh-Ackbarali, D., & Maharaj, R. (2017). Mini Livestock Ranching: Solution to Reducing the Carbon Footprint and Negative Environmental Impacts of Agriculture. In W. Ganpat & W. Isaac (Eds.), *Environmental Sustainability and Climate Change Adaptation Strategies* (pp. 188–212). Hershey, PA: IGI Global. doi:10.4018/978-1-5225-1607-1.ch007

Sood, N., Saini, I., Awasthi, T., Saini, M. K., Bhoriwal, P., & Kaur, T. (2019). Fog Removal Algorithms for Real-Time Video Footage in Smart Cities for Safe Driving. In K. Ahuja & A. Khosla (Eds.), *Driving the Development, Management, and Sustainability of Cognitive Cities* (pp. 55–86). Hershey, PA: IGI Global. doi:10.4018/978-1-5225-8085-0.ch003

Stone, R. J. (2017). Modelling the Frequency of Tropical Cyclones in the Lower Caribbean Region. In W. Ganpat & W. Isaac (Eds.), *Environmental Sustainability and Climate Change Adaptation Strategies* (pp. 341–349). Hershey, PA: IGI Global. doi:10.4018/978-1-5225-1607-1.ch013

Stratigea, A., Leka, A., & Panagiotopoulou, M. (2017). In Search of Indicators for Assessing Smart and Sustainable Cities and Communities' Performance. *International Journal of E-Planning Research*, 6(1), 43–73. doi:10.4018/IJEPR.2017010103

Touq, A. B., & Ijeh, A. (2018). Information Security and Ecosystems in Smart Cities: The Case of Dubai. *International Journal of Information Systems and Social Change*, 9(2), 28–43. doi:10.4018/IJISSC.2018040103

Üç, M., & Elitaş, C. (2016). Life Cycle Costing for Sustainability. In U. Akkucuk (Ed.), *Handbook of Research on Waste Management Techniques for Sustainability* (pp. 96–107). Hershey, PA: IGI Global. doi:10.4018/978-1-4666-9723-2.ch005

Ulker-Demirel, E., & Demirel, E. (2016). Green Marketing and Stakeholder Perceptions. In U. Akkucuk (Ed.), *Handbook of Research on Waste Management Techniques for Sustainability* (pp. 75–95). Hershey, PA: IGI Global. doi:10.4018/978-1-4666-9723-2.ch004

Vargas-Hernández, J. G., López, J. J., & Zdunek-Wielgołaska, J. A. (2019). Entrepreneurial and Institutional Analysis of Biodiesel Companies in Mexico. In J. Vargas-Hernández & J. Zdunek-Wielgołaska (Eds.), *Bioeconomical Solutions and Investments in Sustainable City Development* (pp. 89–115). Hershey, PA: IGI Global. doi:10.4018/978-1-5225-7958-8.ch005

Vázquez, D. G., & Gil, M. T. (2017). Sustainability in Smart Cities: The Case of Vitoria-Gasteiz (Spain) – A Commitment to a New Urban Paradigm. In L. Carvalho (Ed.), *Handbook of Research on Entrepreneurial Development and Innovation Within Smart Cities* (pp. 248–268). Hershey, PA: IGI Global. doi:10.4018/978-1-5225-1978-2.ch012

Velozo, R. A., & Montanha, G. K. (2017). Evaluation of a Mobile Software Development Company. In L. Carvalho (Ed.), *Handbook of Research on Entrepreneurial Development and Innovation Within Smart Cities* (pp. 514–533). Hershey, PA: IGI Global. doi:10.4018/978-1-5225-1978-2.ch022

About the Authors

Ju Hyun Lee is a Scientia Fellow and Senior Lecturer in the Faculty of the Built Environment, University of New South Wales, Sydney. He has published 70+ research publications and made significant contributions towards research in design computing and cognition. His international reputation has been recognised by being invited to be a reviewer/editorial board/committee member for international journals and conferences; international reviewer for grants. Ju Hyun was invited to become a visiting academic at the University of Newcastle in 2011, where he as a senior lecturer completed five-year post-doctoral studies in Architecture. He was Senior Research Fellow at the University of South Australia in 2018.

Michael J. Ostwald is Associate Dean of Research and Professor of Architecture at UNSW, Sydney. He has a PhD in architectural history and theory and a DSc in design mathematics and computing. Michael is Co-Editor-in-Chief of the *Nexus Network Journal: Architecture and Mathematics* (Springer) and on the editorial boards of *ARQ* (Cambridge) and *Architectural Theory Review* (Taylor and Francis). He is co-editor with Kim Williams of *Architecture and Mathematics from Antiquity to the Future* (Springer 2015), co-author with Josephine Vaughan of *The Fractal Dimension of Architecture* (Birkhäuser 2016) and co-author with Michael J. Dawes of *The Mathematics of the Modernist Villa* (Birkhäuser 2018).

Index

Ensure Quality Research is Introduced to the Academic Community

Become an IGI Global Reviewer for Authored Book Projects

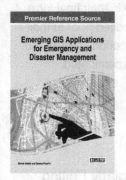

Premier Reference Source

Emerging GIS Applications for Emergency and Disaster Management

Premier Reference Source

Managerial Strategies and Green Solutions for Project Sustainability

Premier Reference Source

Comparative Approaches to Using R and Python for Statistical Data Analysis

Premier Reference Source

Solutions for High-Touch Communications in a High-Tech World

The overall success of an authored book project is dependent on quality and timely reviews.

In this competitive age of scholarly publishing, constructive and timely feedback significantly expedites the turnaround time of manuscripts from submission to acceptance, allowing the publication and discovery of forward-thinking research at a much more expeditious rate. Several IGI Global authored book projects are currently seeking highly-qualified experts in the field to fill vacancies on their respective editorial review boards:

Applications and Inquiries may be sent to:
development@igi-global.com

Applicants must have a doctorate (or an equivalent degree) as well as publishing and reviewing experience. Reviewers are asked to complete the open-ended evaluation questions with as much detail as possible in a timely, collegial, and constructive manner. All reviewers' tenures run for one-year terms on the editorial review boards and are expected to complete at least three reviews per term. Upon successful completion of this term, reviewers can be considered for an additional term.

If you have a colleague that may be interested in this opportunity, we encourage you to share this information with them.

Printed in the United States
By Bookmasters